508 TWO-STORY HOME PLANS

W9-AMB-078

TABLE OF CONTENTS

CREATIVE HOMEOWNER®

COPYRIGHT © 2002
CREATIVE HOMEOWNER®
A Division of Federal Marketing Corp.
Upper Saddle River, NJ

Library of Congress
Catalogue Card No.: 99-068502   ISBN: 1-58011-036-3

Creative Homeowner A Division of Federal Marketing Corp.
24 Park Way, Upper Saddle River, NJ 07458

Manufactured in the United States of America

Current Printing (last digit) 10 9 8 7 6 5 4

Cover Photography by Ron Starr

Windows and Decks

Located off the side deck is a play-house for the kids, which may also be used as a storage or gardening shed. The generous public spaces of this home are designed for comfortable, casual living. The kitchen has a serv-ing bar for extra dining room. This serving bar also defines the spaces in this open floor plan. Conveniently located behind the kitchen is the utility room. The master bedroom features a large private bath, which accesses an eight-by-ten greenhouse. Two addition-al bedrooms, a full bath, and a loft that is both dramatic and functional, com-prise the second floor. Place a futon or a sleep sofa in the upstairs loft for overnight guests.

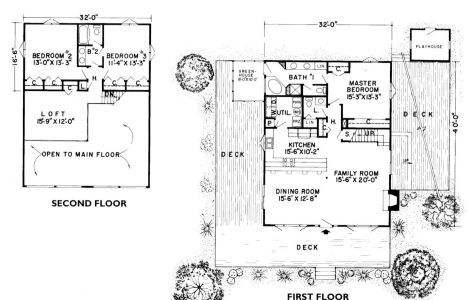

SECOND FLOOR

FIRST FLOOR

The family room provides a cozy atomosphere to the home, with a warm stone fireplace. Furniture arranged around the hearth provides a more intimate sitting area.

Plan info

First Floor	1,280 sq. ft.
Second Floor	735 sq. ft.
Bedrooms	Three
Baths	2 1/2
Foundation	Crawlspace

The openness of this floor plan allows for conversation to flow freely throughout the kitchen, family room and dining area without leaving out the chef.

3

Delightful Decks

This craftsman-inspired design opens itself to the great outdoors with gracious porches and a multitude of decking. The soaring ceiling in the living room lets in the light and takes advantage of the views, providing a bright and serene setting. The well-thought-out master bedroom makes good use of space, incorporating a bath and a generous closet. Two additional bedrooms on the second floor – each with its own ample closet – share a full bath.

WIDTH = 46'4"
DEPTH = 37'8"

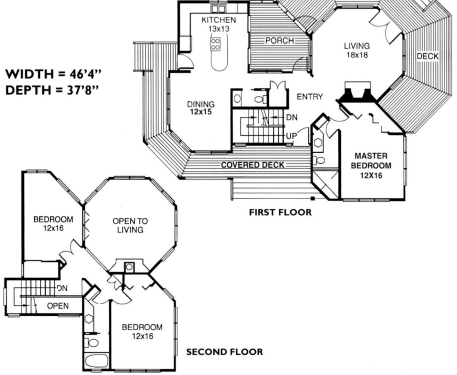

Photography supplied by The Meredith Corporation

An island in the kitchen doubles as an additional setting for meals on the go.

A sunny bright day or a dreary rainy day, drama surrounds the room with outdoor views.

Plan info

First Floor	1,213 sq. ft.
Second Floor	825 sq. ft.
Basement	1,213 sq. ft.
Bedrooms	Three
Baths	2 1/2
Foundation	Basement

Outstanding Design

From the grand foyer with its gently curving staircase and sweeping view through the dining room to the patio beyond, this house makes a statement. The sunken Great room is high impact with a beamed ceiling and built-ins beside the fireplace. The gourmet kitchen flows into a separate breakfast area filled with windows and topped with an octagonal ceiling. The master bedroom wing includes a sitting room and generous his and hers walk-in closets. Each bedroom in this impressive home has its own bath and a walk-in closet. The second floor also provides a cedar closet for seasonal clothes storage.

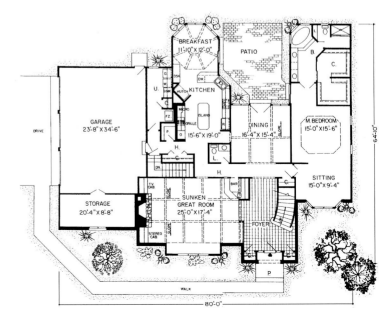

FIRST FLOOR

Cathedral ceilings and a balcony overlooking the formal dining room lend drama to this stately home.

Photography by John Ehrenclou

SECOND FLOOR

Plan info

First Floor	**2,579 sq. ft.**
Second Floor	**997 sq. ft.**
Garage	**1,001 sq. ft.**
Bedrooms	**Three**
Baths	**3 1/2**
Foundation	**Basement**

An island and a peninsula counter add to the efficiency of this gourmet's kitchen.

Old-Fashioned Look

This two-story brick home features an old-fashioned look while incorporating modern features inside. Large open spaces combine with multiple windows to create spectacular results. From the sunroom to the charming sitting area in the master bedroom, this house is ready to cater to your every need for space, light and amenities.

Note: This home cannot be built in a 75-mile radius of Cedar Rapids, IA.

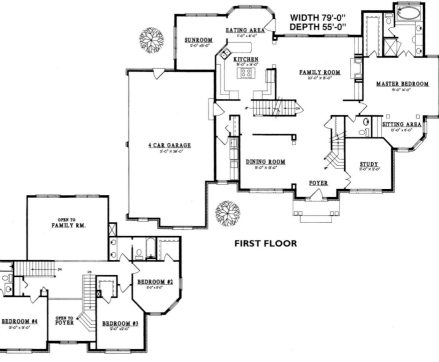

WIDTH 79'-0"
DEPTH 55'-0"

FIRST FLOOR

SECOND FLOOR

Photography supplied by Ahmann Design

The sumptuous master suite offers a cozy sitting area with a built-in entertainment center.

Informal meals are a pleasure in the eating area off the kitchen. The sunny bay includes a large decorative window for a sunny vantage point.

Plan info

First Floor	2,385 sq. ft.
Second Floor	1,012 sq. ft.
Basement	2,385 sq. ft.
Garage	846 sq. ft.
Bedrooms	Four
Baths	3 1/2
Foundation	Basement

Picture Perfect

Pretty as a picture, this is a design to make a homeowner proud, adding charm to any neighborhood. A nice deep wrap-around porch adds to the living space of this home, allowing you to create outdoor rooms. The floor plan is well-thought out and efficient, making the most of the space inside. The designer of this home has paid tremendous attention to fine details, among which are the built-in window seat and bookshelves on the second floor.

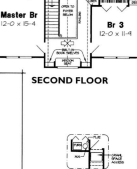

SECOND FLOOR

Master Br
12-0 x 15-4

Br 2
12-0 x 12-5

Br 3
12-0 x 11-9

CRAWLSPACE/SLAB FOUNDATION

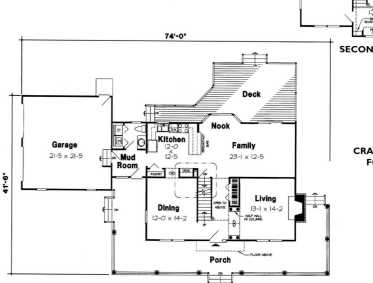

74'-0"

41'-6"

Garage
21-5 x 21-5

Mud Room

Kitchen
12-0 x 12-5

Deck

Nook

Family
23-1 x 12-5

Dining
12-0 x 14-2

Living
13-1 x 14-2

Porch

FIRST FLOOR

Photography by John Ehrenclou

A cozy window seat provides the perfect place to curl up with a book on a rainy day.

The sunny kitchen sports an efficient breakfast bar for meals on the run and additional workspace.

Plan info

First Floor	1,113 sq. ft.
Second Floor	970 sq. ft.
Basement	1,113 sq. ft.
Garage	480 sq. ft.
Bedrooms	Three
Baths	2 1/2
Foundation	Basement, Slab or Crawlspace

Wrap-Around Porch

The classic porch on the front of this stylish home wraps around the side to join the sundeck and screened porch at the rear of the house. This is a charming, traditional design with plenty of spaces for outdoor entertaining. The floor plan of this home clearly sets the formal spaces at the front and the generously proportioned casual spaces to the rear. Columns accentuate the Great room, while the fireplace and built-ins add attractive functionality. A well-appointed kitchen is conveniently placed between the formal dining room and the informal breakfast room.

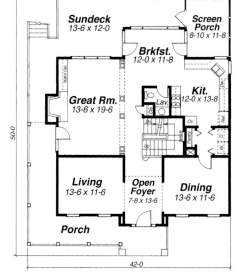

FIRST FLOOR

SECOND FLOOR

Photography by John Ehrenclou

The stairway dominates the foyer area while giving the home-owner opportunities for creative decorating.

The dining room is an open layout with the kitchen for an open and airy atmosphere. A wall of windows brings the outdoors in and provides natural illumination.

Plan info

First Floor	1,250 sq. ft.
Second Floor	1,166 sq. ft.
Staircase	48 sq. ft.
Basement	448 sq. ft.
Garage	706 sq. ft.
Bedrooms	Four
Baths	2 1/2
Foundation	Basement

Photography supplied by Larry E. Belk

For A Corner Lot

Suitable for any property and perfect for the corner or pie-shaped lot, this home features mirror elevations on the right and left that make it a winner from any direction. Entering the foyer, a lovely split stair leads to the second floor. The dining room opens to the right and features an elegant entrance flanked by square columns. The kitchen, with a cooktop work island, leads to the pleasant breakfast room with bay window and cathedral ceiling. A private study opens to the left of the foyer and can be used as bedroom five if needed. Along with the usual features – large bathroom, separate water closet, his and hers walk-in closets – the master suite also offers access to a private covered porch, making it a real retreat.

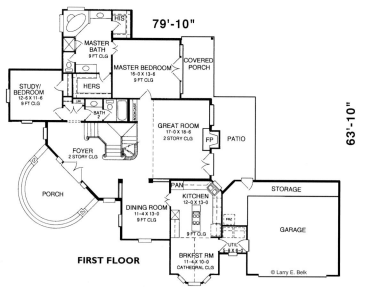

FIRST FLOOR

SECOND FLOOR

Plan info

First Floor	**1,966 sq. ft.**
Second Floor	**872 sq. ft.**
Garage	**569 sq. ft.**
Bedrooms	**Four**
Baths	**3(full)**
Foundation	**Basement, Slab or Crawlspace**

Photography by Fred Mudge

Stone & Stucco

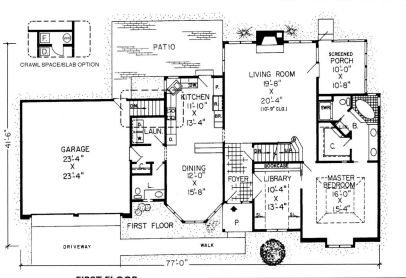

FIRST FLOOR

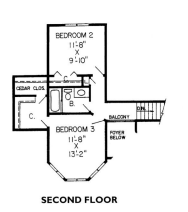

SECOND FLOOR

A unique custom look is achieved through the use of stone and stucco material on the exterior of the home. However you choose to side this plan, it is the inside that captures the imagination. This home combines style with practicality in a most elegant manner. Just inside the foyer, double doors lead to a slope-ceilinged library. The foyer itself ends at the oversized living room featuring a ten-foot ceiling and large fireplace. Tucked off to the side of the living room is a screened porch. The first floor master bedrooom has a private bath, large walk-in closet and private access to the library. Two additional bedrooms, a full bath, and a cedar closet for storing winter clothing comprise the second floor of this truly distinctive home.

Plan info

First Floor	1,671 sq. ft.
Second Floor	505 sq. ft.
Basement	1,661 sq. ft.
Garage	604 sq. ft.
Bedrooms	Three
Baths	2 1/2
Foundation	Basement, Slab or Crawlspace

Photography supplied by Studer Residential Design, Inc.

A Rich, Solid Look

The rich, solid look of this spacious two-story home introduces you to an interior that defines high style while offering family comfort and convenience. The first thing you see upon entering this home is the clever staircase which provides convenient access from the second floor to either the formal areas at the front of the house or the informal at the rear. Family activities will almost certainly center around the sunken Great room with fireplace, built-in entertainment center, and expansive rear door and window treatments. Surrounded by windows, the breakfast room with its sloped ceiling provides a bright and cheery spot to share family meals. Four bedrooms and three full baths in combination with ample closet space make up the second floor.

FIRST FLOOR

SECOND FLOOR

Plan info

First Floor	1,678 sq. ft.
Second Floor	1,766 sq. ft.
Basement	1,639 sq. ft.
Garage	761 sq. ft.
Bedrooms	Four
Baths	3 1/2
Foundation	Basement

Photography by John Ehrenclou

Elegant Bay

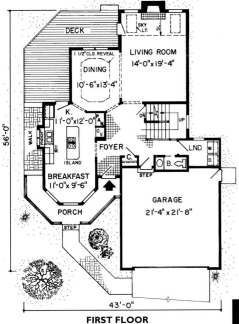

FIRST FLOOR

SECOND FLOOR

Here's a compact Victorian charmer that unites tradition with today in a perfect combination. Imagine waking up in the roomy master suite with its romantic bay window, plus full bath with double sinks. Two additional bedrooms, which feature generous closet space, share the second full bath. The romance of the home continues in the sunny breakfast room off the island kitchen, in the recessed ceilings of the formal dining room, and in the living room's cozy fireplace. Sun lovers will appreciate the sloping, skylit ceilings in the living room, and the rear deck that is accessible from both the kitchen and living room.

Plan info

First Floor	**1,027 sq. ft.**
Second Floor	**974 sq. ft.**
Basement	**978 sq. ft.**
Garage	**476 sq. ft.**
Bedrooms	**Three**
Baths	**2 1/2**
Foundation	**Basement**

Photography by John Ehrenclou

Bright and Spacious

Spectacular is one word you could use to describe the remarkable quality of light and space in this four-bedroom family home. Well-placed skylights and abundant windows bathe every room in sunlight. The huge, two-story foyer features an angular, open staircase that leads to the bedrooms, and divides the space between the vaulted living and dining rooms. At the rear of the house, the wide-open family area includes the kitchen, dinette, and fireplaced family room complete with built-in bar and bookcases. Vaulted ceilings in the screened porch are mirrored upstairs in the master suite, which features two walk-in closets, a double vanity and a luxurious jacuzzi.

Plan info

First Floor	**1,786 sq. ft.**
Second Floor	**1,490 sq. ft.**
Basement	**1,773 sq. ft.**
Garage	**579 sq. ft.**
Bedrooms	**Four**
Baths	**2 1/2**
Foundation	**Basement**

Photography by John Ehrenclou

Space for Everything

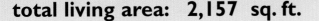

FIRST FLOOR

54'-0"

46'-0"

Deck

Kit 10 x 13-10

Brkfst 9 x 11-8

MBr 1 13 x 15-4

decor. ceiling

Dining Rm 12 x 12-10

pan.

DN

11'-0" height

Ldry W D

Living Rm 12 x 19-4

UP Foyer

Family/ Hearth Rm 12-10 x 15-4

Garage 20-4 x 21-8

slope

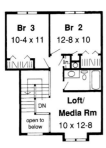

Br 3 10-4 x 11

Br 2 12-8 x 10

lin.

DN

open to below

Loft/ Media Rm 10 x 12-8

SECOND FLOOR

Plan info

First Floor	**1,590 sq. ft.**
Second Floor	**567 sq. ft.**
Basement	**1,576 sq. ft.**
Garage	**456 sq. ft.**
Bedrooms	**Three**
Baths	**2 1/2**
Foundation	**Basement, Slab or Crawlspace**

This magnificent plan offers space for every purpose. Once inside the two-story foyer, to the left are the formal areas; to the right, the informal. The large living room and dining room feature a dramatic sloped ceiling with elegant columns to separate the two spaces. The family or hearth room flows past a two-sided fireplace into the breakfast room with sliders to a rear deck. A kitchen with pantry at the rear of the house offers convenient access to both formal and informal spaces. There is a first floor master with tray ceiling, private bath and large closet, as well as two additonal bedrooms on the second floor. Rounding out the spaces on the second floor is a loft or media room, which could serve as an ideal spot to set up the kids' computer.

Photography by John Ehrenclou

Country Personified

One look at this home and it becomes clear why the versatile Cape has remained one of America's favorite styles for centuries. From the gabled dormers to the quaint front porch, this plan offers a welcoming face to the neighborhood. Once inside, the efficient floor plan makes the most of the space provided. The generous living room opens into a pleasantly proportioned dining room. The well-planned U-shaped kitchen opens to a sunny breakfast area with access to a rear deck. The first floor master includes a full private bath – with room for a garden tub – and a large walk-in closet. The second floor provides two additonal bedrooms, a full bath, and plenty of under-the-eaves storage. This great home offers a lot of carefully planned space for the growing family in a compact floor plan.

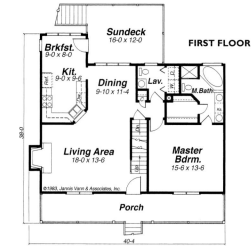

Plan info

First Floor	1,057 sq. ft.
Second Floor	611 sq. ft.
Basement	511 sq. ft.
Garage	546 sq. ft.
Bedrooms	Three
Baths	2 1/2
Foundation	Basement

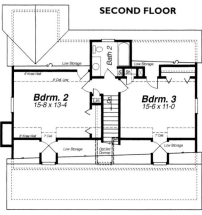

20

Photography supplied by Studer Residential Design, Inc.

A Touch of Drama

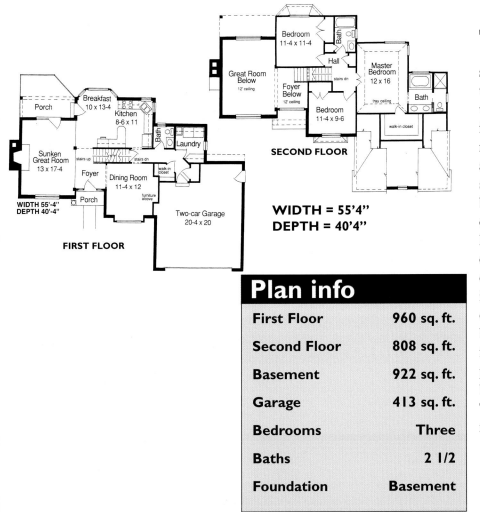

Breakfast 10 x 13-4

Porch

Kitchen 8-6 x 11

Bath

Laundry

Sunken Great Room 13 x 17-4

stairs up   stairs dn

walk-in closet

Foyer

Dining Room 11-4 x 12

furniture alcove

Porch

WIDTH 55'-4"
DEPTH 40'-4"

Two-car Garage 20-4 x 20

FIRST FLOOR

Bedroom 11-4 x 11-4

Bath

Great Room Below 12' ceiling

Hall

Master Bedroom 12 x 16

stairs dn

Foyer Below 12' ceiling

tray ceiling

Bath

Bedroom 11-4 x 9-6

walk-in closet

SECOND FLOOR

WIDTH = 55'4"
DEPTH = 40'4"

Plan info

First Floor	960 sq. ft.
Second Floor	808 sq. ft.
Basement	922 sq. ft.
Garage	413 sq. ft.
Bedrooms	**Three**
Baths	**2 1/2**
Foundation	**Basement**

This home's dramatic exterior features an entry with transom and sidelights, multiple gables and a box window. Inside, the drama continues with twelve-foot-high ceilings in the foyer and the large sunken Great room. The box window and furniture alcove make the dining room equally special. A tray ceiling tops the master bedroom, which is entered through double doors at the head of the stairs. However, rest assured that all that drama does not come at the expense of practicality. A large walk-in closet is conveniently located in the hall just outside the laundry room and half bath. The Great room and the breakfast room open onto a covered rear porch. Two additional second floor bedrooms each offer deep closets. This is a classic home with large rooms in a compact package.

21

Plan no. 64145

price code **I**

total living area: **2,847** sq. ft.

Beauty in the Details

From the two-story cove-lit foyer to the arches, niches and specialty windows throughout, this classic home aims to please. The volume ceilings and large windows make this home appear larger than it is, both inside and out. The double-height parlor with its box beam ceiling opens through a series of arches into the coffered-ceilinged leisure room. Details such as the fireplace surrounded by built-in bookshelves and the triple set of French doors leading out onto a covered porch make this room exceptional. All the bedrooms are on the second floor and each one has its own walk-in closet – the master bedroom has two. Hers is larger, of course. French doors open up from the master onto a private, rear-facing deck. This charming home is ideal for a traditional neighborhood setting.

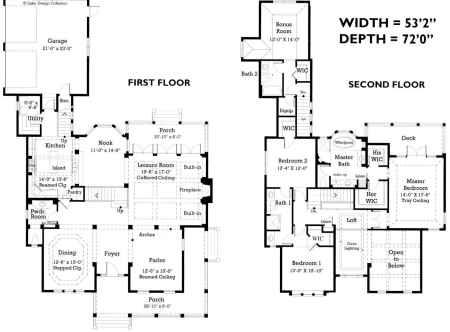

WIDTH = 53'2"
DEPTH = 72'0"

FIRST FLOOR

SECOND FLOOR

Plan info

First Floor	1,642 sq. ft.	**Bedrooms**	**Three**
Second Floor	1,205 sq. ft.	**Baths**	2 1/2
Bonus	340 sq. ft.	**Foundation**	Crawlspace
Garage	541 sq. ft.		

Alternate foundation options available at an additional charge.
Please call 1-800-235-5700 for more information.

Photography by Donna & Ron Kolb Exposures Unlimited

Luxury in a Moderate Size

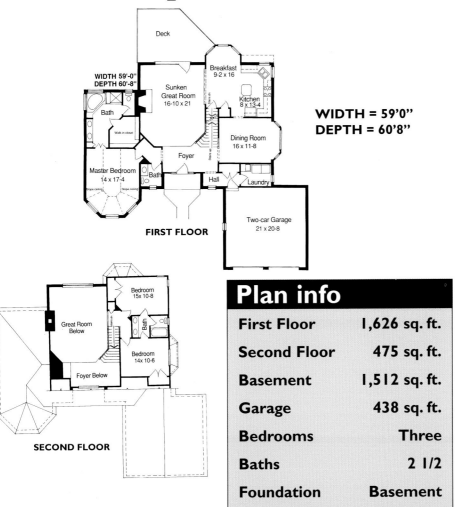

WIDTH 59'-0"
DEPTH 60'-8"

Deck

Breakfast
9-2 x 16

Sunken
Great Room
16-10 x 21

Kitchen
8 x 13-4

Bath

Walk-in closet

Dining Room
16 x 11-8

Foyer

Master Bedroom
14 x 17-4

Bath

Hall

Laundry

Two-car Garage
21 x 20-8

FIRST FLOOR

WIDTH = 59'0"
DEPTH = 60'8"

Bedroom
15x 10-8

Great Room
Below

Bath

Bedroom
14x 10-6

Foyer Below

SECOND FLOOR

An octagonal master bedroom with a vaulted ceiling, a sunken Great room with a balcony above, a bay-windowed dining room – these are just a few of the luxurious details that give form to this moderately sized home. The kitchen features a center island and a sunny breakfast nook ending in yet another bay window. The sunken Great room has a cozy fireplace and offers access to a rear deck. The master bath is large enough to accommodate a garden tub, separate shower, water closet, and a large walk-in closet. Elegant and luxurious in a moderate size with the practical features the discriminating home buyer looks for, this home offers the best of everything.

Plan info

First Floor	1,626 sq. ft.
Second Floor	475 sq. ft.
Basement	1,512 sq. ft.
Garage	438 sq. ft.
Bedrooms	Three
Baths	2 1/2
Foundation	Basement

Plan no. 24262

price code E

total living area: 2,411 sq. ft.

Hip and Valley Style Roof

This warm and inviting home features a see-through fireplace between the living room and family room. The gourmet kitchen gives the cook in your family the added workspace of an island, plus all the amenities you've come to expect. Efficiently designed, the kitchen easily serves both the formal dining room and the nook. Upstairs, four bedrooms accommodate your sleeping needs. The master bedroom adds interest with a vaulted ceiling. The master bath has a large double vanity, linen closet, corner tub, separate shower, compartmented toilet, and huge walk-in closet. The three additional bedrooms, one with a walk-in closet, share a full bath.

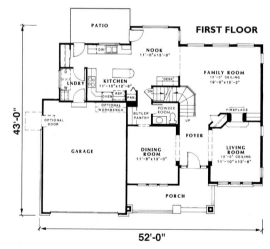

FIRST FLOOR

SECOND FLOOR

ALTERNATE KITCHEN

OPTIONAL RETREAT

Plan info

First Floor	1,241 sq. ft.
Second Floor	1,170 sq. ft.
Garage	500 sq. ft.
Bedrooms	Four
Baths	2 1/2
Foundation	Basement, Slab or Crawlspace

Victorian Farmhouse

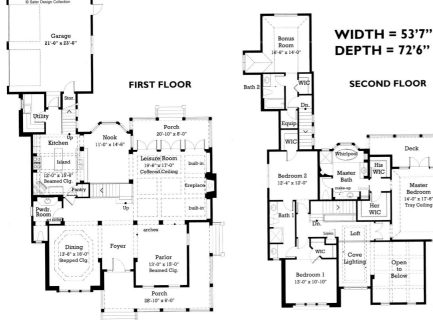

© Sater Design Collection

FIRST FLOOR

Garage 21'-0" x 23'-0"

Stor.

Utility

Up

Kitchen

Nook 11'-0" x 14'-6"

Island 12'-0" x 15'-6" Beamed Clg.

Pantry

Porch 20'-10" x 8'-0"

Leisure Room 19'-6" x 17'-0" Coffered Ceiling

built-in

fireplace

built-in

Pwdr. Room

Up

arches

Dining 13'-6" x 16'-0" Stepped Clg.

Foyer

Parlor 13'-0" x 15'-0" Beamed Clg.

Porch 28'-10" x 6'-0"

SECOND FLOOR

WIDTH = 53'7"
DEPTH = 72'6"

Bonus Room 18'-6" x 14'-0"

Bath 2

WIC

Dn.

Equip.

WIC

Whirlpool

His WIC

Deck

Bedroom 2 12'-4" x 12'-0"

Master Bath

make-up

Linen

Her WIC

Master Bedroom 14'-0" x 17'-6" Tray Ceiling

Bath 1

Dn.

Linen

Loft

WIC

Cove Lighting

Open to Below

Bedroom 1 13'-0" x 10'-10"

Bay windows, French doors and lovely covered porches combine to create an unforgettable exterior of timeless elegance in this fine home. And the interior spaces are just as remarkable, with a variety of window and ceiling treatments. Beamed ceilings highlight the parlor and kitchen. A coffered ceiling tops the magnificently detailed leisure room. The dining room walls rise to meet a gracious stepped ceiling. An elegant tray ceiling crowns the master bedroom. And underneath all of these beautiful ceiling treatments are well-proportioned rooms, seamlessly fitted together in an effortlessly convenient floor plan.

Plan info

First Floor	1,642 sq. ft.	**Bedrooms**	**Three**
Second Floor	1,205 sq. ft.	**Baths**	**2 1/2**
Bonus	340 sq. ft.	**Foundation**	**Crawlspace**
Garage	541 sq. ft.		

Alternate foundation options available at an additional charge.
Please call 1-800-235-5700 for more information.

Photography by Design Basics, Inc.

Sensible Style

The charming covered porch and interesting roof lines of this thoughtfully styled home belie the practicality and efficiency of its compact floor plan. This home packs a lot of living and generously proportioned spaces into its square footage. The entry leads past an open staircase to a large, fireplaced Great room with ten-foot ceilings and transom windows. The adjoining breakfast room offers equal access to the formal dining room at the front of the house and the efficient U-shaped kitchen with serving bar at the rear. The first floor master bedroom suite has a private hall that serves as a buffer from the public rooms of the house. The master bath includes space for all the amenities found in larger homes such as a separate shower, double-vanity sinks and large walk-in closet. On the second floor, two bedrooms with ample closet space and a full bath round out this home's full complement of rooms.

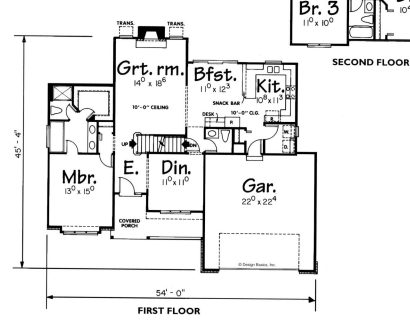

Plan info

First Floor	1,298 sq. ft.	Bedrooms	Three
Second Floor	396 sq. ft.	Baths	2 1/2
Basement	1,298 sq. ft.	Foundation	Basement
Garage	513 sq. ft.		

Alternate foundation options available at an additional charge.
Please call 1-800-235-5700 for more information.

Wide Open Spaces

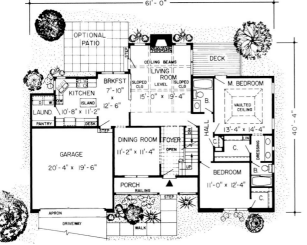

FIRST FLOOR

SECOND FLOOR

S loping ceilings and open spaces characterize this well-designed four-bedroom home. The dining room just off the two-story foyer adjoins the sunny breakfast room and the convenient U-shaped kitchen with island work area. The beamed living room – with its elegant fireplace flanked by tall windows – is crowned by a balcony overlook that links the two second floor bedrooms. We would certainly recommend making plans to include the optional patio just off the living room for seasonal outdoor living and entertaining. The vaulted first floor master suite features a private deck, a walk-in closet and a full bath with a double vanity.

Plan info

First Floor	**1,496 sq. ft.**
Second Floor	**520 sq. ft.**
Basement	**1,487 sq. ft.**
Garage	**424 sq. ft.**
Bedrooms	**Four**
Baths	**3(full)**
Foundation	**Basement, Slab or Crawl space**

27

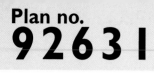

Two-Story with Character

Multiple gables and brick trim give character to this traditional two-story home. Interesting angles and varied ceiling treatments set the stage for pride of ownership, while an easy-flow traffic pattern, a kitchen pantry and large closet in the back hall provide convenience. A high window above the door in the Great room and the breakfast bay surrounded by windows provide a bright and cheery place for the family to gather. Preparing meals is a pleasure in the spacious kitchen with peninsula. A tray ceiling in the dining room, columns at the corner and a box window provide an elegant setting for entertaining. Rounding out the first floor is the master bedroom suite with an ultra bath featuring a dual bowl vanity and a whirlpool tub. An elegantly styled staircase leads to the three-bedroom second floor, where an expansive balcony overlooks the Great room and foyer.

FIRST FLOOR

Plan info	
First Floor	1,511 sq. ft.
Second Floor	646 sq. ft.
Basement	1,479 sq. ft.
Garage	475 sq. ft.
Bedrooms	Four
Baths	2 1/2
Foundation	Basement

SECOND FLOOR

28

price code **E**

Plan no.
10690

Gingerbread Charm

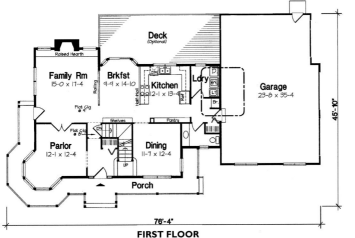

FIRST FLOOR

SECOND FLOOR

CRAWLSPACE / SLAB OPTION

Plan info

First Floor	**1,260 sq. ft.**
Second Floor	**1,021 sq. ft.**
Basement	**1,186 sq. ft.**
Garage	**851 sq. ft.**
Bedrooms	**Three**
Baths	**2 1/2**
Foundation	**Basement, Slab or Crawlspace**

Victorian elegance combines with a modern floor plan to make this a dream house without equal. A wraparound porch and rear deck add extra living space to the roomy first floor, which features a formal parlor and dining room just off the central entry. Informal areas at the rear of the house are wide open for family interaction. Gather the crew around the fireplace in the family room, or make supper in the kitchen while you supervise the kids' homework in the sunwashed breakfast room. Three bedrooms, tucked upstairs for a quiet atmosphere, feature skylit baths. And you'll love the five-sided sitting nook in your master suite, a perfect spot to relax after a luxurious bath in the sunken tub.

Designed to Impress

From the very curb, this outstanding traditional home is truly designed to impress. The varied window treatments and rooflines of the façade offer a gracious and stately face to the neighborhood. Inside the front door, the grand foyer offers up a striking view of the large living room with its multiple sets of French doors, large fireplace and the sweeping curved balcony above. Arch-topped corridors lead from the grand foyer to the other living spaces; the grand dining room just off the gallery, the large well-designed kitchen, the leisure room with its fireplace surrounded by built-ins and twelve-foot-high beamed ceiling. French doors are a theme of this home, opening out of the first floor from the leisure room, living room, study and master bedroom. On the second floor, two of the three bedrooms have French doors opening out onto private decks.

WIDTH = 87'4"
DEPTH = 80'4"

Plan info

First Floor	3,027 sq. ft.	Bedrooms	Four
Second Floor	1,079 sq. ft.	Baths	3 1/2
Basement	3,027 sq. ft.	Foundation	Basement / Slab Combo
Garage	802 sq. ft.		

Alternate foundation options available at an additional charge.
Please call 1-800-235-5700 for more information.

total living area: 1,249 sq. ft.

price code **A**

Plan no. 91033

A perfect second home, this plan features an expansive view through large windows that are shielded from the sun's heat by the gable brow. Or, build this plan as your main residence to enjoy that "vacation" feeling all year round. This efficient plan is lifted from the ordinary by its sweeping roof line and main living spaces defined by a massive fireplace centered on a cathedral ceiling. And that sloping roof provides ample under-the-eaves storage on the second floor.

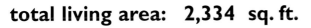

34'-0"

28'-0"

GARDEN WINDOW

DINING 10/0x11/0   KIT.   UT.

LIVING 13/6x16/0   BD 2 12/0x14/0

FIRST FLOOR

OPEN TO DINING   LOFT   STORAGE

MSTR. BD 16/0x18/0

OPEN TO LIVING   STORAGE

SECOND FLOOR

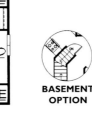

BASEMENT OPTION

Plan info

Main Floor	952 sq. ft.
Upper Floor	297 sq. ft.
Bedrooms	Two
Baths	2(full)
Foundation	Basement or Crawlspace

---

total living area: 2,334 sq. ft.

price code **H**

Plan no. 64128

This beautiful design, accented by arches and a wrap-around front porch, is the essence of country living. In the heart of the home, elegant columns define the main living spaces. Each space is made unique by the varied ceiling and window treatments found throughout. And everywhere you look, you find ample closet and storage space.

WIDTH = 47'0"
DEPTH = 50'0"

Master Suite 15'-0" x 13'-8" Stepped Clg.

Porch 16'-0" x 8'-0" Vaulted Clg.

Breakfast 12'-0" x 9'-10" 9'-4" Flat Clg.

WIC   WIC

built-ins

Great Room 15'-10" x 15'-4" Vaulted Clg.

Kitchen 12'-6" x 11'-8"

M. Bath   fireplace   Utility 8'-6"x9'-4"

CL.

Foyer   Dining 11'-8" x 13'-10" Tray Clg.

Bath 2   bench

Study/Office 13'-0" x 11'-6" Coffered Clg.

Porch 31'-0" x 6'-0" 9'-4" Flat Clg.

© Sater Design Collection

FIRST FLOOR

Bedroom 1 11'-0" x 13'-0" 8'-0" Flat Clg.

Bath 3

open to below   WIC desk

desk

Dn.   Dn.

WIC   L.   open to below   Bedroom 2 11'-0" x 13'-6" 8'-0" Flat Clg.

Equip.

plant shelf   plant shelf

SECOND FLOOR

Plan info

Main Floor	1,716 sq. ft.
Upper Floor	618 sq. ft.
Bedrooms	Three
Baths	2 3/4
Foundation	Slab

Alternate foundation options available at an additional charge. Please call 1-800-235-5700 for more information.

Gracious Country Estate

L ike the great country estates of the past, this home offers plenty of opportunity for gracious living inside and out. From the French doors on the front porch, flanked by tall multi-paned windows, the foyer opens up into the large, fireplaced Great room with its stepped ceiling and one wall composed entirely of three sets of French doors, which lead out onto the deep rear porch. Off the stair hall is the dining room, entered through a sweeping archway, that features a cof-fered ceiling and impressive bay win-dow. The master's wing includes a tray-ceilinged bedroom with French doors opening to the rear porch, his and her walk-in closets, a large bath, and a private study with beamed ceil-ing. On the second floor, two addi-tional bedroooms, a full bath and attic storage make this fine home complete.

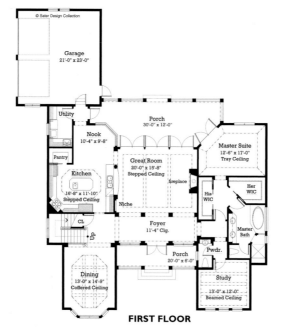

FIRST FLOOR

SECOND FLOOR

WIDTH = 64'0"
DEPTH = 76'2"

Plan info

First Floor	2,073 sq. ft.	Bedrooms	Three
Second Floor	869 sq. ft.	Baths	2 1/2
Garage	528 sq. ft.	Foundation	Crawlspace

Alternate foundation options available at an additional charge.
Please call 1-800-235-5700 for more information.

■ *Total living area 897 sq. ft.* ■ *Price Code A* ■

No. 24309

■ **This plan features:**

— Two bedrooms

— One full bath

■ The wrap-around Deck is equipped with a built-in barbeque for easy outdoor living

■ The Entry, in a wall of glass, opens the Living Area to the outdoors

■ A large fireplace highlights the Living Area, which opens into an efficient Kitchen with a built-in Pantry that serves the Nook Area

■ The two Bedrooms share a centrally located, full Bath with a window tub

■ The Loft Area is ready for multiple uses

■ This home is designed with a crawlspace foundation

Main floor — 789 sq. ft.
Loft — 108 sq. ft.

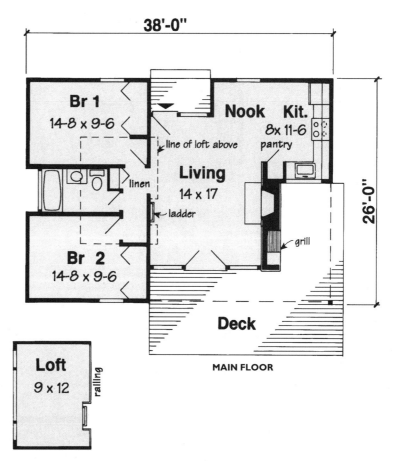

Cottage Charm

■ *Total living area 976 sq. ft.* ■ *Price Code A* ■

FIRST FLOOR

2,80 X 3,10
9'-4" X 10'-4"

2,40 X 4,30
8'-0" X 14'-4"

3,90 X 3,60
13'-0" X 12'-0"

3,00 X 7,20
10'-0" X 24'-0"

3,30 X 3,10
11'-0" X 10'-4"

3,50 X 3,50
11'-8" X 11'-8"

SECOND FLOOR

No. 65003

■ **This plan features:**

— Two bedrooms

— One full and one three-quarter baths

■ Thoughtful use of space packs a lot of living into this cozy design

■ The efficient Kitchen is open to the Dining Area and Living Room

■ The Living Room features a volume ceiling, which helps to define the space

■ The second floor Master Bedroom has a large walk-in closet

■ An upper-level Loft with open-rail balcony creates a private Sitting Area

■ This home is designed with a crawlspace foundation

First floor — 763 sq. ft.
Second floor — 240 sq. ft.

Simple and Practical

■ *Total living area 1,003 sq. ft.* ■ *Price Code A* ■

No. 35009

■ **This plan features:**

— One bedroom

— One full bath

■ The U-shaped Kitchen features an efficient layout, a double sink, and ample work and storage space

■ The Dining Area views the front Deck and yard

■ The Living Room has a built-in entertainment center and a view of the front Deck and yard

■ The large Bedroom includes a double closet

■ The Loft overlooks the Living Room, and can be used in many ways

■ This home is designed with basement, crawlspace, and slab foundation options.

First floor — 763 sq. ft.
Second floor — 240 sq. ft.

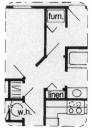

SLAB/CRAWLSPACE OPTION

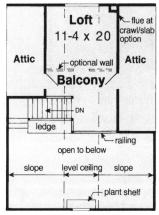

SECOND FLOOR

Loft
11-4 x 20

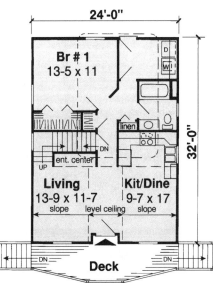

FIRST FLOOR

Br # 1
13-5 x 11

Living
13-9 x 11-7

Kit/Dine
9-7 x 17

Deck

35

Three Bedroom A-Frame

■ *Total living area 1,011 sq. ft.* ■ *Price Code A* ■

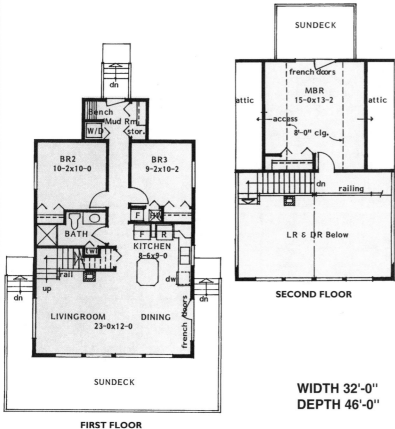

FIRST FLOOR

SECOND FLOOR

WIDTH 32'-0"
DEPTH 46'-0"

No. 90995

■ **This plan features:**

— Three bedrooms

— One full bath

■ The wrap-around Deck provides panoramic views and access to the Living Room and Dining Area through French doors

■ The spacious Living/Dining Area with a glass wall and a vaulted ceiling opens to the Kitchen

■ The well-equipped Kitchen with a serving island, opens to the Dining and Living Rooms

■ The Mud Room entrance has a large closet, a Laundry Area and a built-in bench

■ The large Master Bedroom has French doors to a private Deck

■ This home is designed with a crawlspace foundation

First floor — 768 sq. ft.
Second floor — 243 sq. ft.

Ideal for a Woodland Setting

■ *Total living area 1,027 sq. ft.* ■ *Price Code A* ■

No. 35007

■ This plan features:

— Two bedrooms

— One full bath

■ The Living Room and the Dining Room/Kitchen are located in the front of the house

■ A sloped ceiling adds a spacious feeling to the home

■ The L-shaped Kitchen includes a double sink and the Dining Area

■ The Loft and Balcony overlook the Living Room and the Dining Area

■ Storage space available on both sides of the Loft

■ This home is designed with basement, crawlspace, and slab foundation options.

First floor — 763 sq. ft.
Second floor — 264 sq. ft.

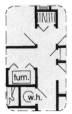

SLAB/CRAWLSPACE OPTION

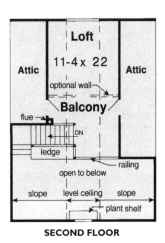

SECOND FLOOR

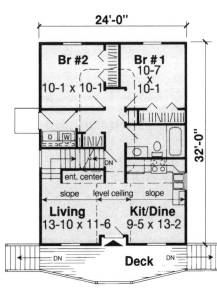

FIRST FLOOR

Contemporary Simplicity

■ *Total living area 1,038 sq. ft.* ■ *Price Code A* ■

No. 24307

■ **This plan features:**

— Two bedrooms

— One full and one three-quarter baths

■ The tiled Entrance leads into the two-story, beamed Living Room with a circular, center fireplace

■ The efficient U-shaped Kitchen, with plenty of counter and storage space, opens to the Dining Area, which has sliding glass doors to an optional Deck

■ The two Bedrooms, one with a private Bath, have ample closet space

■ The second floor Loft overlooks the living area

■ This home is designed with a crawlspace foundation

First floor — 866 sq. ft.
Second floor — 172 sq. ft.

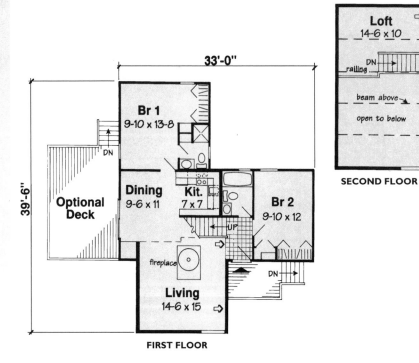

Loft
14-6 x 10

DN
railing

beam above →

open to below

SECOND FLOOR

33'-0"

Br 1
9-10 x 13-8

DN

Optional Deck

39'-6"

Dining
9-6 x 11

Kit.
7 x 7

Br 2
9-10 x 12

UP

fireplace

DN

Living
14-6 x 15

FIRST FLOOR

Lovely Second Home

■ *Total living area 1,096 sq. ft.* ■ *Price Code A* ■

No. 91002

■ **This plan features:**

— Two bedrooms

— One full and one three-quarter baths

■ A firedrum fireplace warms the whole house from its central location

■ The Dining and Living Rooms, with loads of windows, open onto the Deck, which surrounds the home on three sides

■ Vaulted ceilings and clerestory windows add natural light and volume to this home

■ The convenient Kitchen opens to both the Dining and Living Rooms

■ This home is designed with a crawlspace foundation

Main floor — 808 sq. ft.
Upper floor — 288 sq. ft.

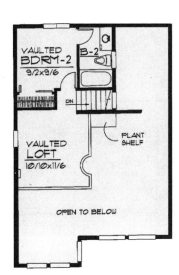

SECOND FLOOR

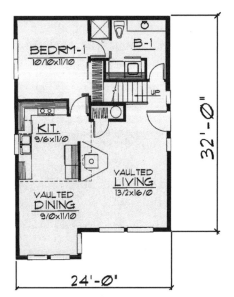

FIRST FLOOR

For a Small Lot

■ *Total living area 1,189 sq. ft.* ■ *Price Code A* ■

No. 92052

■ **This plan features:**

— Three bedrooms

— Two full and one half baths

■ Only 36 feet wide, this home has a double garage, a Great Room and a large Dining Area

■ The Great Room is topped by a cathedral ceiling, and opens to the Dining Area

■ The Dining Area has direct access to the Kitchen and Patio

■ The Master Bedroom is highlighted by a cathedral ceiling and a lovely arched window

■ The two secondary Bedrooms share a full Bath

■ This home is designed with a basement foundation

Main floor — 615 sq. ft.
Upper floor — 574 sq. ft.
Basement — 615 sq. ft.

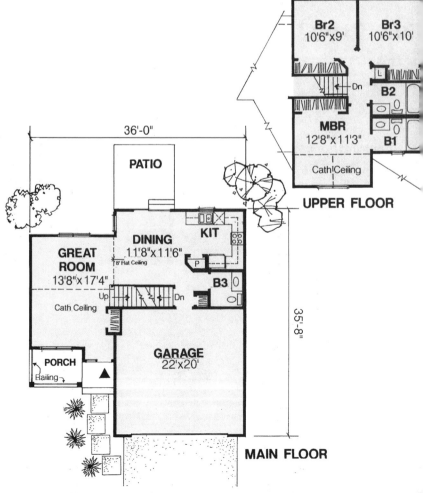

─■ *Total living area 1,206 sq. ft.* ■ *Price Code A* ■─

No. 90951

■ **This plan features:**

— Three bedrooms

— One full and two half baths

■ The covered Porch shelters the entrance into the central Foyer

■ The spacious Living Room has a cozy fireplace and an elegant bay window

■ The formal Dining Room has a view of the rear yard, and adjoins the Living Room

■ The efficient U-shaped Kitchen is highlighted by a bright eating Nook

■ Handy first floor Laundry Room, half Bath and Garage entrance

■ This home is designed with a basement slab foundation

Main floor — 670 sq. ft.
Second floor — 536 sq. ft.

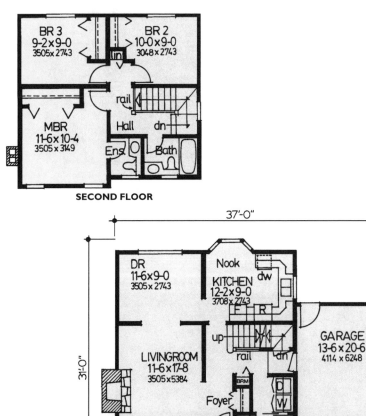

SECOND FLOOR

FIRST FLOOR

Cozy Rustic Exterior

■ *Total living area 1,210 sq. ft.* ■ *Price Code A* ■

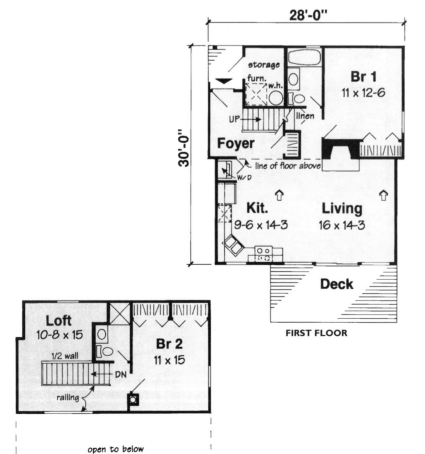

28'-0"

30'-0"

storage
furn.
w.h.
Br 1
11 x 12-6
UP
linen
Foyer
line of floor above
W/D
Kit.
9-6 x 14-3
Living
16 x 14-3

Deck

FIRST FLOOR

Loft
10-8 x 15
1/2 wall
Br 2
11 x 15
DN
railing

open to below

SECOND FLOOR

No. 24313

■ **This plan features:**

— Two bedrooms

— One full and one three-quarter baths

■ The front Deck has a double glass door entrance with large windows on each side

■ The open layout creates space and efficiency between the Kitchen and the Living Room

■ The first floor Bedroom has a large closet and a full Bath

■ The second floor Bedroom, with double closets, has a Loft area and a three-quarter Bath

■ This home is designed with a crawlspace foundation

First floor — 781 sq. ft.
Second floor — 429 sq. ft.

■ *Total living area 1,246 sq. ft.* ■ *Price Code A* ■

No. 90353

■ **This plan features:**

— Three bedrooms

— Two full baths

■ A vaulted ceiling in the Living Room and the Dining Room, with a clerestory window above

■ The Master Bedroom has a walk-in closet and a private Bath

■ The efficient Kitchen has a corner double sink and a peninsula counter

■ The Dining Room has sliding glass doors to the Deck

■ The Living Room has a fireplace and a great corner window

■ The two upstairs Bedrooms share a full Bath

■ This home is designed with a basement foundation

Main floor — 846 sq. ft.
Upper floor — 400 sq. ft.

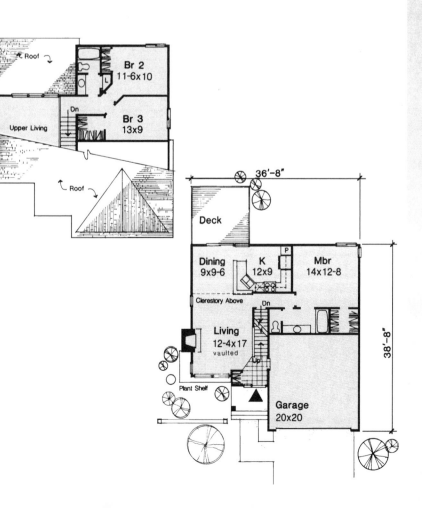

Compact Colonial

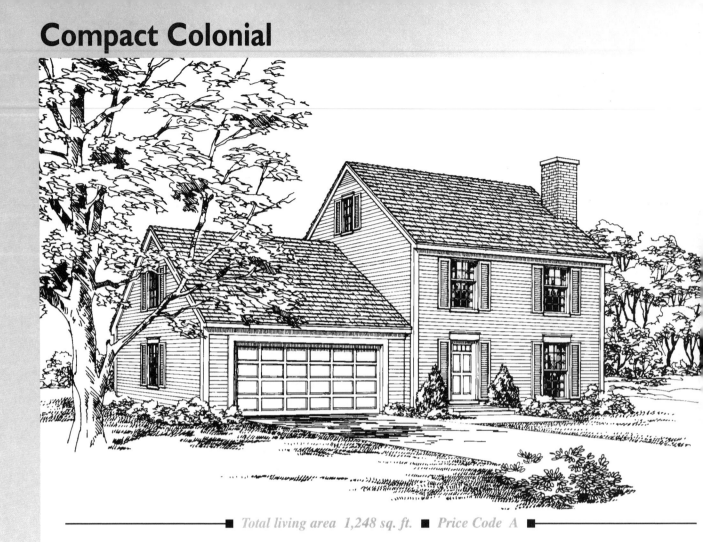

■ *Total living area 1,248 sq. ft.* ■ *Price Code A* ■

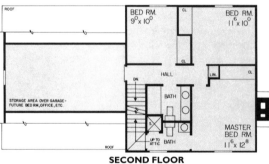

SECOND FLOOR

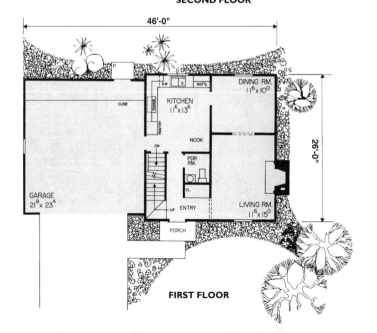

FIRST FLOOR

No. 99255

■ **This plan features:**

— Three bedrooms

— Two full and one half baths

■ The traditional Entry has a landing staircase, a closet and a Powder Room

■ The Living Room, with a focal point fireplace, opens to the formal Dining Room for ease in entertaining

■ The efficient L-shaped Kitchen has a built-in Pantry, an eating Nook and a Garage entry

■ The corner Master Bedroom has a private Bath

■ This home is designed with a basement foundation

First floor — 624 sq. ft.
Second floor — 624 sq. ft.
Garage — 510 sq. ft.

■ *Total living area 1,250 sq. ft.* ■ *Price Code A* ■

No. 91091

■ This plan features:

— Three bedrooms

— Two full baths

■ This home will easily accommodate a narrow lot

■ The covered Porch and a trellis highlight the front elevation

■ A vaulted ceiling and a wood stove complement the Living Room

■ The Kitchen, with a cooktop and work island, opens to the Dining and Living Rooms

■ The Garage is in the rear and has an optional door location

■ The Master Bedroom has a private Bath

■ This home is designed with a basement foundation

First floor — 842 sq. ft.
Second floor — 408 sq. ft.

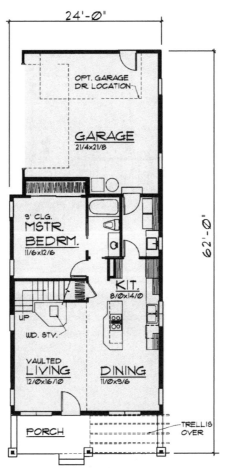

FIRST FLOOR

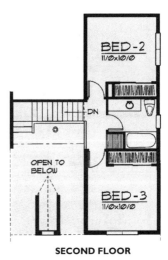

SECOND FLOOR

Suited for a Hill

■ *Total living area 1,263 sq. ft.* ■ *Price Code A* ■

No. 90822

■ **This plan features:**

— Three bedrooms

— One full and one half baths

■ Vaulted ceilings and a fieldstone fireplace enhance the Living Room and Dining Area

■ The two first floor Bedrooms have ample closet space and share a full Bath

■ The Master Bedroom on the Loft level includes a private Bath

■ The wrap-around Deck offers an abundance of outdoor living space

■ This home is designed with a basement foundation

Main floor — 925 sq. ft.
Loft — 338 sq. ft.
Basement — 864 sq. ft.

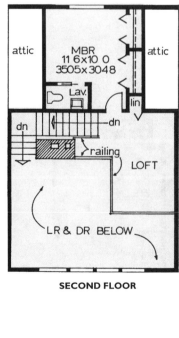

SECOND FLOOR

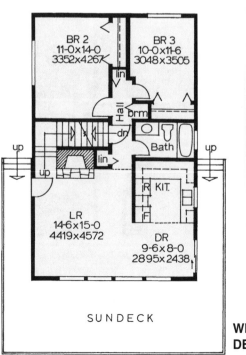

WIDTH 33'-0''
DEPTH 47'-0''

FIRST FLOOR

■ *Total living area 1,274 sq. ft.* ■ *Price Code A* ■

No. 90048

■ **This plan features:**

— Three bedrooms

— Two full baths

■ An oversized, log burning fireplace warms the spacious Living/Dining Area which is two stories high and has sliding glass doors to the Deck

■ Three Porches offer the maximum in outdoor living space

■ The private Bedroom/Den is located on the second floor

■ The efficient Kitchen includes an eating bar, and access to the covered Dining Porch

■ This home is designed with basement, crawlspace, and slab foundation

First floor — 974 sq. ft.
Second floor — 300 sq. ft.

SECOND FLOOR

FIRST FLOOR

Dynamic Angles

■ *Total living area 1,283 sq. ft.* ■ *Price Code A* ■

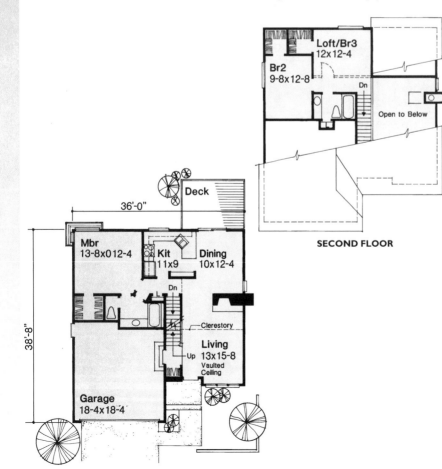

SECOND FLOOR

FIRST FLOOR

No. 90378

■ This plan features:

— Two bedrooms with possible third bedroom or loft

— Two full baths

■ The Living Room has dynamic, soaring angles, a clerestory window and a fireplace

■ The compact Kitchen has a corner sink and a peninsula counter to serve the Dining Area

■ The first floor Master Suite has a full Bath and walk in-closet

■ Walk-in closets are featured in all the Bedrooms

■ This home is designed with a basement foundation

Main floor — 878 sq. ft.
Upper floor — 405 sq. ft.

■ *Total living area 1,288 sq. ft.* ■ *Price Code A* ■

No. 98444

■ This plan features:

— Three bedrooms

— Two full and one half baths

■ A warm and cozy fireplace highlights the Great Room

■ The Dining Room and the Kitchen are adjoined, creating a comfortable living area

■ The Master Bedroom has a tray ceiling, and a vaulted ceiling tops the Master Bath

■ Two additional Bedrooms with ample closet space complete the second floor

■ This home is designed with basement, crawlspace, and slab foundation options.

First floor — 628 sq. ft.
Second floor — 660 sq. ft.
Basement — 628 sq. ft.
Garage — 424 sq. ft.

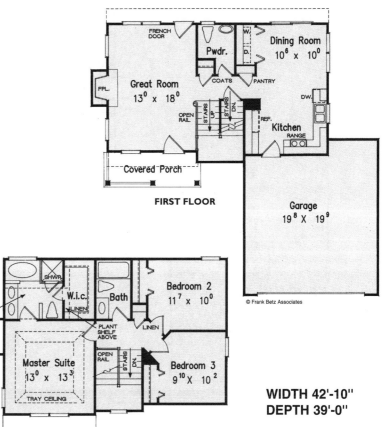

FIRST FLOOR

© Frank Betz Associates

SECOND FLOOR

WIDTH 42'-10"
DEPTH 39'-0"

Economical Vacation Home

■ *Total living area 1,288 sq. ft.* ■ *Price Code A* ■

SECOND FLOOR

DORMITORY
17⁴ x 9⁴

STOR.

STOR.

STOR.

ROOF

STORAGE

CL.

DN.

BATH

CL.

CL.

MASTER
BED RM.
15⁰ x 12⁰

ROOF

BALCONY

FIRST FLOOR

28'-0"

40'-0"

28'-0"

BED RM.
10⁰ x 11⁶

CL.

LIN.

BATH

SINK

KIT.
9⁴ x 15⁴

REF.

CL.

RANGE

UP

OPT.
BSMT.
STAIR

AIR
COND.

DINING

FIREPLACE

LIVING
27⁴ x 12⁰

DECK

R

No. 99238

■ **This plan features:**

— Three bedrooms

— Two full baths

■ The large, bright Living Room has a fireplace at one end and plenty of room for separate activities

■ The galley-style Kitchen adjoins the Dining area

■ The second-floor Master Bedroom has a children's Dormitory across the hall

■ The balcony is located outside the Master Bedroom

■ This home is designed with a basement foundation

First floor — 784 sq. ft.
Second floor — 504 sq. ft.

■ Total living area 1,289 sq. ft. ■ Price Code A ■

No. 99327

■ This plan features:

— Three bedrooms

— Two full baths

■ The Entry has a vaulted ceiling

■ The formal Living Room has a fireplace and a half-round transom window

■ The Dining Room has sliders to the deck, and easy access to the Kitchen

■ The main floor Master Suite has corner windows, a walk-in closet and private access to a full Bath

■ The two additional Bedrooms share a full Bath

■ This home is designed with a basement foundation

Main floor — 858 sq. ft.
Upper floor — 431 sq. ft.
Basement — 858 sq. ft.
Garage — 400 sq. ft.

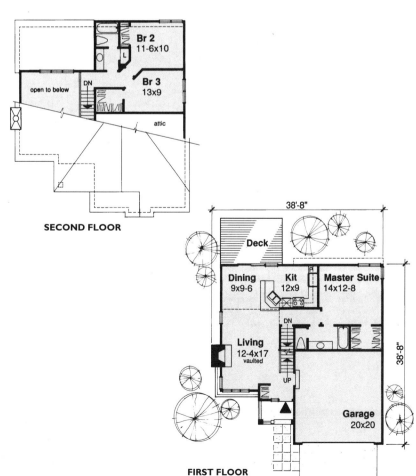

SECOND FLOOR

FIRST FLOOR

Contemporary Traditions

■ *Total living area 1,303 sq. ft.* ■ *Price Code A* ■

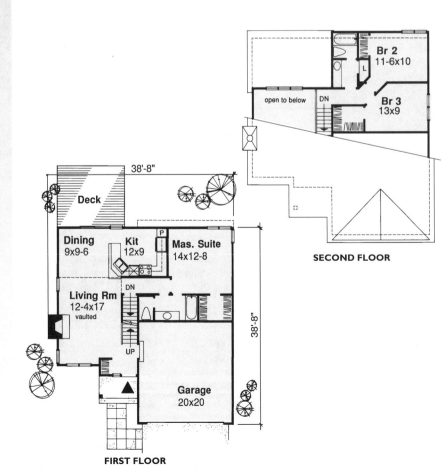

SECOND FLOOR

- Br 2 11-6x10
- open to below
- DN
- Br 3 13x9

FIRST FLOOR

- 38'-8"
- Deck
- Dining 9x9-6
- Kit 12x9
- P
- Mas. Suite 14x12-8
- Living Rm 12-4x17 vaulted
- DN
- UP
- 38'-8"
- Garage 20x20

No. 99339

■ **This plan features:**

— Three bedrooms

— Two full baths

■ The Living Room has a vaulted ceiling above a half-round transom window and a fireplace

■ The Dining Area is open to the Kitchen and the Living Room and has a sliding glass door to the Deck

■ The main floor Master Suite features corner windows, a walk-in closet, and private access to a full Bath

■ The two additional Bedrooms on the second floor, one with a walk-in closet, share a full Bath

■ This home is designed with a basement foundation

Main floor — 857 sq. ft.
Upper floor — 446 sq. ft.
Garage — 400 sq. ft.

■ *Total living area 1,309 sq. ft.* ■ *Price Code A* ■

No. 90025

■ This plan features:

— Three bedrooms

— Two full baths

■ The exterior of this home is highlighted by a fieldstone chimney, a red cedar roof, vertical siding and a redwood Deck

■ The open Living Room, Dinette and Kitchen layout provides convenience and comfort

■ The efficient U-shaped Kitchen has a built-in Pantry and serving bar

■ The spacious first floor Bedroom is convenient to a full Bath, a Dressing Room, and Laundry

■ The two second floor Bedrooms share a full Bath

■ This home is designed with a crawlspace foundation

First floor — 867 sq. ft.
Second floor — 442 sq. ft.

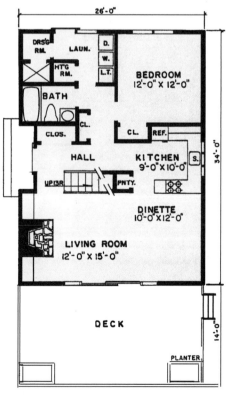

FIRST FLOOR

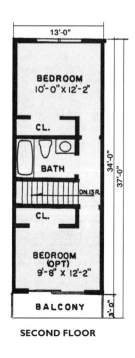

SECOND FLOOR

Simple and Practical

■ *Total living area 1.324 sq. ft.* ■ *Price Code A* ■

3,30 X 5,70
11'-0" X 19'-0"

4,20 X 4,80
14'-0" X 16'-0"

2,40 X 2,70
8'-0" X 9'-0"

FIRST FLOOR

WIDTH 26'-0"
DEPTH 33'-0"

8,40 X 5,70
28'-0" X 19'-0"

SECOND FLOOR
1 BEDROOM OPTION

3,60 X 3,60
12'-0" X 12'-0"

3,60 X 4,20
12'-0" X 14'-0"

SECOND FLOOR
2 BEDROOM OPTION

No. 65284

■ **This plan features:**

— One or two bedrooms

— One full and one half baths

■ The first floor Great Room combines Kitchen, Dining and Living Areas in one interesting space

■ The Laundry Room is conveniently located within the first floor half Bath

■ The Foyer contains a large closet

■ The Great Room opens out onto the large Deck

■ For the second floor, choose the one or the two Bedroom option

■ This home is designed with a basement foundation

First floor — 737 sq. ft.
Second floor — 587 sq. ft.

■ *Total living area 1,328 sq. ft.* ■ *Price Code A* ■

No. 34600

■ **This plan features:**

— Three bedrooms

— Two full baths

■ The stone fireplace and exposed beams add rustic charm to the two-story Living Room

■ The efficient, modern Kitchen provides ample work and storage space

■ The two first floor Bedrooms share a full Bath

■ The Master Bedroom, secluded on the second floor, has its own full bath

■ This home is designed with basement, crawlspace, and slab foundation options

Main floor — 1,013 sq. ft.
Upper floor — 315 sq. ft.
Basement — 1,013 sq. ft.

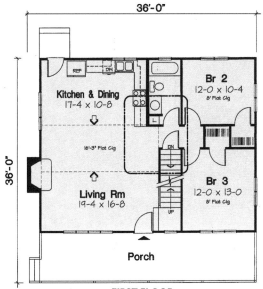

36'-0"

36'-0"

Kitchen & Dining
17-4 x 10-8

Br 2
12-0 x 10-4
8' Flat Clg

16'-3" Flat Clg

Living Rm
19-4 x 16-8

Br 3
12-0 x 13-0
8' Flat Clg

DN

UP

Porch

FIRST FLOOR

FURN   WH

Crawl
Space
Access

CRAWLSPACE / SLAB OPTION

Open to Living
Room Below

Flat Clg @ 7'-6"

Master Br
12-0 x 13-4

DN

SECOND FLOOR

Balcony Overlook

■ *Total living area 1,351 sq. ft.* ■ *Price Code A* ■

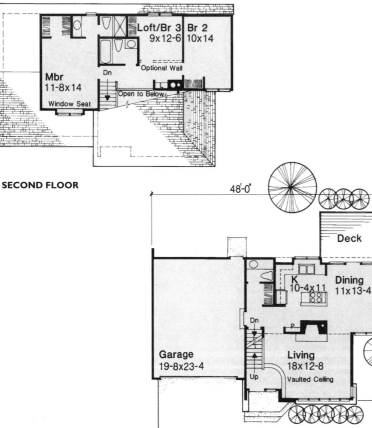

SECOND FLOOR

FIRST FLOOR

No. 90356

■ **This plan features:**

— Three bedrooms

— Two full and one half baths

■ The Living Room has a vaulted ceiling, a balcony, and a fireplace

■ This design has an efficient, well-equipped Kitchen with a cooktop work island

■ The Deck is accessible from the Living Room

■ The luxurious Master Suite has a bay window seat, a walk-in closet, a dressing area, and a private shower

■ The two additional Bedrooms share a full Bath

■ This home is designed with basement foundation

Main floor — 674 sq. ft.
Upper floor — 677 sq. ft.
Basement — 674 sq. ft.

■ *Total living area 1,354 sq. ft.* ■ *Price Code A* ■

No. 91026

■ **This plan features:**

— Three bedrooms

— One full and one three-quarter baths

■ Sweeping panels of glass and a wood stove create atmosphere in the Great Room

■ The Kitchen opens to the warmth of the Great Room

■ The two main floor Bedrooms share a full Bath

■ The huge Sleeping Loft has a three-quarter Bath

■ This home is designed with a basement foundation

Main floor — 988 sq. ft.
Upper floor — 366 sq. ft.
Basement — 742 sq. ft.
Garage — 283 sq. ft.

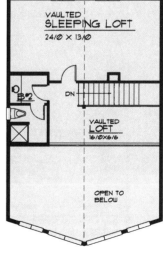

SECOND FLOOR

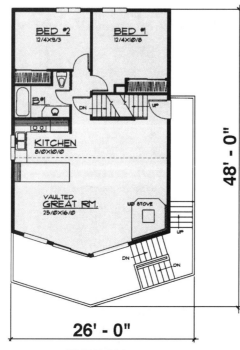

FIRST FLOOR

Versatile Chalet

■ *Total living area 1,360 sq. ft.* ■ *Price Code A* ■

No. 90847

■ **This plan features:**

— Two bedrooms

— Two full baths

■ There is a Deck Entry into a spacious Living Room/Dining Room which has a fieldstone fireplace, a large window and a sliding glass door

■ The well-appointed Kitchen has extended counter space and easy access to the Dining Room and the Utility Area

■ The first floor Bedroom adjoins a full Bath

■ The spacious Master Bedroom has a private Deck, a Bath, and plenty of storage

■ This home is designed with a basement foundation

Main floor — 864 sq. ft.
Second floor — 496 sq. ft.
Basement — 864 sq. ft.

WIDTH 27'-0''
DEPTH 32'-0''

A Modified "A" Frame

■ *Total living area 1,360 sq. ft.* ■ ● *Price Code A* ■

No. 99032

■ **This plan features:**

— Three bedrooms

— Two full baths

■ The Foyer opens to the large Living/Dining Area highlighted by a raised hearth fireplace and two sliding glass doors to the Terrace

■ The small, yet efficient Kitchen has an eating bar and Laundry Area

■ The two first floor Bedrooms share a full Bath

■ A spiral staircase leads to a third Bedroom or Studio Area

■ The balcony has a wood railing and overlooks the Living Room/Dining Room

■ This home is designed with basement and slab foundation options.

First floor — 994 sq. ft.
Second floor — 366 sq. ft.

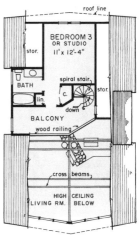

SECOND FLOOR

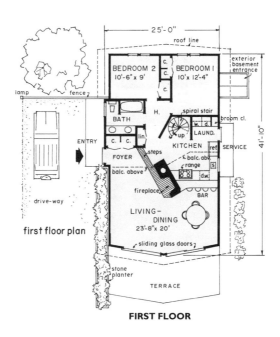

FIRST FLOOR

Contemporary Styling

Total living area 1,370 sq. ft. ■ Price Code A

FIRST FLOOR

30'

DECK LINE ABOVE
WD. DECK

BEDROOM
9'3"X10'6"

B.

KIT.
8'X17'

BEDROOM
11'X10'

LOFT LINE ABOVE

CL.

LIVING
17'6"X18'

F.P.

UP

40'

WD. DECK
18'X14'

12'

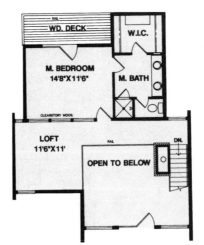

SECOND FLOOR

RAIL
WD. DECK

W.I.C.

M. BEDROOM
14'8"X11'6"

M. BATH

CLEARSTORY WDOS.

LOFT
11'6"X11'

RAIL

DN.

OPEN TO BELOW

No. 94311

■ **This plan features:**

— Three bedrooms

— Two full baths

■ This is the perfect plan for a mountainside or lot with a view

■ The large front Deck has a far-reaching view of surrounding vistas

■ The Living Room has a cozy corner fireplace and a wall of windows, plus access to the Deck

■ This plan has two first floor Bedrooms and a Loft overlooking the Living Room

■ The Master Bedroom has a private Deck, a Master Bath and a walk-in closet

■ This home is designed with a crawlspace foundation

First floor — 810 sq. ft.
Second floor — 560 sq. ft.

■ *Total living area 1,395 sq. ft.* ■ *Price Code A* ■

No. 97204

SECOND FLOOR

■ **This plan features:**

— Three bedrooms

— Two full and one half baths

■ From the covered Porch, the entry leads to the massive Family Room with a fireplace

■ The open Kitchen design includes a spacious Breakfast Area

■ The Master Suite, with a vaulted ceiling, enjoys a plush Bath leading to a generous walk-in closet

■ The Laundry Area is conveniently located near the Bedrooms on teh second floor

■ This home is designed with basement, crawlspace, and slab foundation options.

First floor — 708 sq. ft.
Second floor — 687 sq. ft.
Basement — 708 sq. ft.
Garage — 399 sq. ft.

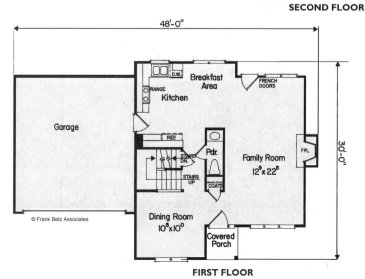

FIRST FLOOR

Family Faire

■ *Total living area 1,399 sq. ft.* ■ *Price Code A* ■

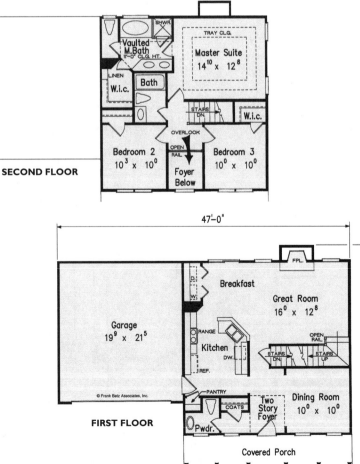

SECOND FLOOR

Vaulted M.Bath 11'-0" CLG. HT.
SHWR.
LINEN
W.i.c.
Bath
TRAY CLG.
Master Suite 14¹⁰ x 12⁸
STAIRS DN.
W.i.c.
OVERLOOK
OPEN RAIL
Bedroom 2 10³ x 10⁰
Bedroom 3 10⁰ x 10⁰
Foyer Below

FIRST FLOOR

47'-0"
34'-4"
Garage 19⁹ x 21⁵
Breakfast
RANGE
Kitchen
DW.
REF.
Great Room 16⁰ x 12⁸
OPEN RAIL
STAIRS DN
STAIRS UP
FPL.
PANTRY
COATS
Pwdr.
Two Story Foyer
Dining Room 10⁰ x 10⁰
© Frank Betz Associates, Inc.
Covered Porch

No. 98481

■ **This plan features:**

— Three bedrooms

— Two full and one half baths

■ The covered Porch leads into a two-story Foyer

■ The Great Room has a fireplace

■ The convenient Kitchen is partially open to the Breakfast Nook and Great Room

■ The large Master Suite with tray ceiling has a double-vanity Bath that leads to a walk-in closet

■ Two additional Bedrooms with ample closets share a full Bath

■ This home is designed with basement, crawlspace, and slab foundation options.

First floor — 729 sq. ft.
Second floor — 670 sq. ft.
Basement — 676 sq. ft.
Garage — 440 sq. ft.

Total living area 1,399 sq. ft. ■ *Price Code A* ■

No. 96803

■ **This plan features:**

— Three bedrooms

— One full and one half baths

■ This plan is designed with an eight foot-deep Porch that wraps around three sides of the house, perfect for outdoor living

■ The large Living Room has a cozy fireplace

■ The convenient first floor combination Laundry Room and half Bath makes efficient use of space

■ The Master Bedroom has a Sitting Area and access to a shared Bath

■ This home is designed with basement, crawlspace, and slab foundation options.

First floor — 732 sq. ft.
Second floor — 667 sq. ft.
Basement — 732 sq. ft.
Garage — 406 sq. ft.

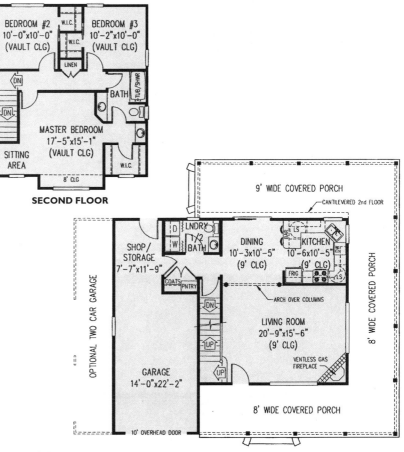

SECOND FLOOR

FIRST FLOOR

Easy Family Living

Design by Alan Mascord Design Associates

■ *Total living area 1,403 sq. ft.* ■ *Price Code A* ■

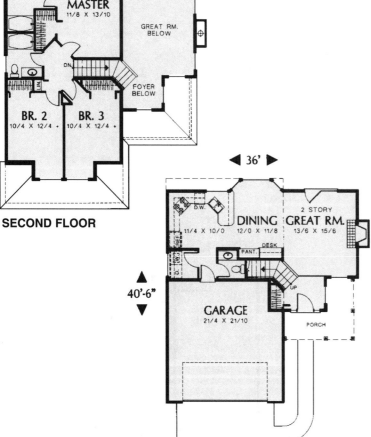

SECOND FLOOR

FIRST FLOOR

No. 91549

■ **This plan features:**

— Three bedrooms

— Two full and one half baths

■ The sheltered Porch leads into a bright Foyer with a lovely, angled staircase

■ The two-story Great Room has a hearth fireplace and an atrium door to the backyard

■ The convenient Kitchen has a serving counter/snack bar, a bright Dining Area, a built-in Pantry, and a nearby Laundry and Garage entry

■ The quiet Master Suite has a walk-in closet and double-vanity Bath

■ Two additional Bedrooms with ample closets share a full Bath

■ This home is designed with a crawlspace foundation

First floor — 663 sq. ft.
Second floor — 740 sq. ft.

Country Touch

■ *Total living area 1,415 sq. ft.* ■ *Price Code A* ■

No. 34601

■ **This plan features:**

— Three bedrooms

— Two full baths

■ This plan is designed with a Country-style front Porch

■ The Living Room has a vaulted ceiling and a cozy fireplace

■ The efficient Kitchen has a peninsula counter that may be used as an eating bar

■ The two first floor Bedrooms have a nearby Bath with a laundry closet

■ The second floor Master Suite has a sloped ceiling, a walk-in closet, and a private Master Bath

■ This home is designed with basement, crawlspace, and slab foundation options.

First floor — 1,007 sq. ft.
Second floor — 408 sq. ft.
Basement — 1,007 sq. ft.

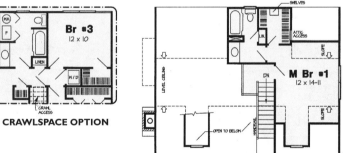

CRAWLSPACE OPTION

SECOND FLOOR

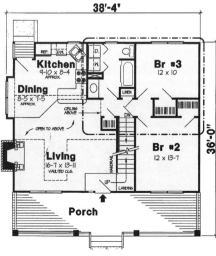

FIRST FLOOR

Charming Country Home

■ *Total living area 1,434 sq. ft.* ■ *Price Code A* ■

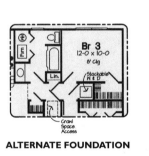

ALTERNATE FOUNDATION

Br 3
12-0 x 10-0
8' Clg

Lin.

Stackable
W & D

Crawl
Space
Access

SECOND FLOOR

Shelves

Attic
Access

Open To
Below

Railing Balcony

Master Br
12-2 x 15-0
8' clg

Flat Clg at 11'

Railing

attic
access

roof
below

No. 24711

■ **This plan features:**

— Three bedrooms

— Two full baths

■ The covered front Porch shelters the entrance

■ The Living Room has a dormer, vaulted ceiling and a fireplace

■ The Kitchen has a built-in Pantry and access to the Laundry, the Screened Area-way and Garage

■ The two first floor Bedrooms share a full Bath

■ The private second floor Master Suite features a dormer window, a walk-in closet and a private Bath

■ This home is designed with basement, crawlspace, and slab foundation options.

First floor — 1,018 sq. ft.
Second floor — 416 sq. ft.
Garage — 624 sq. ft.

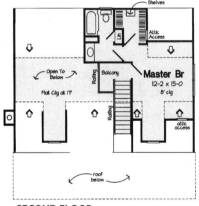

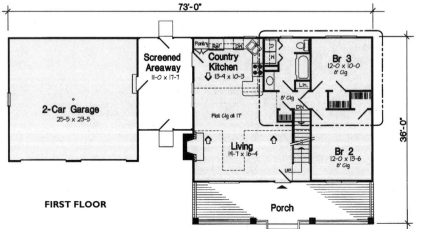

73'-0"

Screened
Areaway
11-0 x 17-7

2-Car Garage
25-5 x 23-5

Pantry Ref

Country
Kitchen
13-4 x 10-3

Br 3
12-0 x 10-0
8' Clg

Lin.

8' Clg

DN

Flat Clg at 11'

Living
14-7 x 16-4

Br 2
12-0 x 13-6
8' Clg

UP

36'-0"

FIRST FLOOR

Porch

■ *Total living area 1,436 sq. ft.* ■ *Price Code A* ■

No. 98422

■ **This plan features:**

— Three bedrooms

— Two full and one half baths

■ A convenient pass-through from the Kitchen into the Family Room

■ A fireplace highlights the spacious Family Room

■ A decorative ceiling treatment highlights the Master Bedroom while a vaulted ceiling tops the Master Bath

■ Two additional Bedrooms share the full Bath

■ This home is designed with basement and crawlspace foundation options.

First floor — 719 sq. ft.
Second floor — 717 sq. ft.
Bonus — 290 sq. ft.
Basement — 719 sq. ft.
Garage — 480 sq. ft.

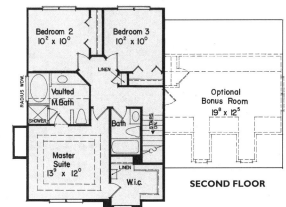

SECOND FLOOR

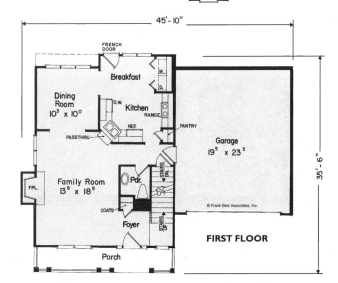

FIRST FLOOR

Country Contemporary

■ Total living area *1,443 sq. ft.* ■ Price Code A ■

No. 90372

■ **This plan features:**

— Three bedrooms

— Two full baths

■ The front Porch is a welcoming introduction for guests

■ The first floor Master Bedroom a walk-in closet and private access to a hall Bath

■ The efficient U-shaped Kitchen adjoins the Dining Room, which has a sliding glass door to the Deck

■ A vaulted, sunken Living Room is accentuated by a massive fireplace

■ The two second story Bedrooms share a full Bath

■ This home is designed with a basement foundation

Main floor — 1,006 sq. ft.
Upper floor — 437 sq. ft.

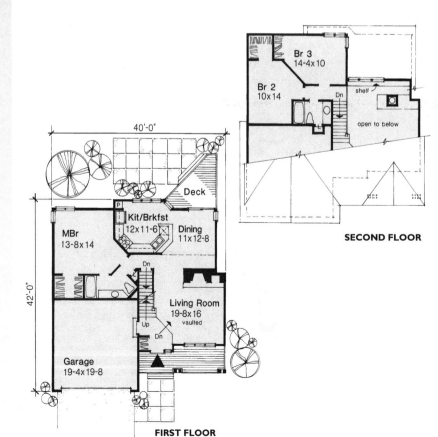

Stylish Smaller Home

■ *Total living area 1,448 sq. ft.* ■ *Price Code A* ■

No. 97201

■ **This plan features:**

— Three bedrooms

— Two full and one half baths

■ The impressive two-story Foyer leads into the Family Room which has a vaulted ceiling and fireplace

■ An extended counter adds to the work area of the centrally located Kitchen

■ A tray ceiling and a private Master Bath are featured in the Master Suite

■ Two second-floor Bedrooms with ample closet space share a Bath

■ This home is designed with basement, crawlspace, and slab foundation options.

First floor — 1,049 sq. ft.
Second floor — 399 sq. ft.
Basement — 1,051 sq. ft.
Garage — 400 sq. ft.

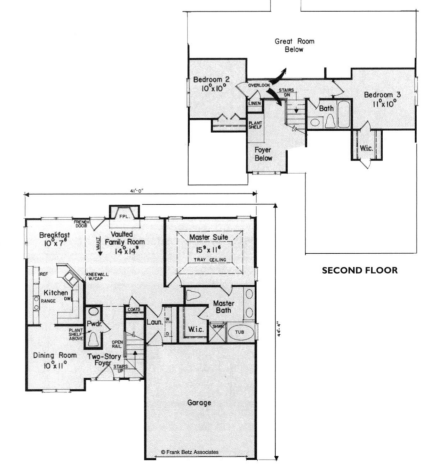

Relaxed Environment

■ *Total living area 1,453 sq. ft.* ■ *Price Code A* ■

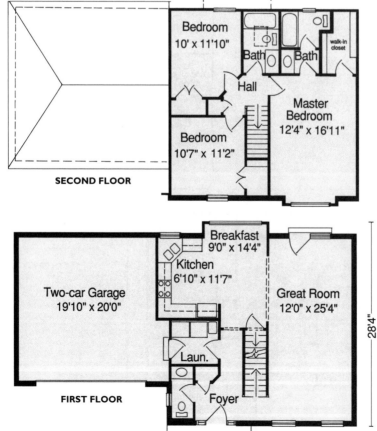

SECOND FLOOR

- Bedroom 10' x 11'10"
- Bath
- Bath
- walk-in closet
- Hall
- Master Bedroom 12'4" x 16'11"
- Bedroom 10'7" x 11'2"

FIRST FLOOR

- Breakfast 9'0" x 14'4"
- Kitchen 6'10" x 11'7"
- Two-car Garage 19'10" x 20'0"
- Great Room 12'0" x 25'4"
- Laun.
- Foyer

28'4"

49'8"

No. 92639

■ This plan features:

— Three bedrooms

— Two full and one half baths

■ The covered Porch and a boxed window enhance the exterior

■ The spacious Great Room and Breakfast Area form an area large enough for real family enjoyment

■ The U-shaped Kitchen is highlighted by a corner sink, and easily serves the Breakfast Area

■ The large Master Bedroom has a walk-in closet and a full Bath

■ The two additional Bedrooms share a full Bath with a skylight

■ This house is designed with a basement foundation

First floor — 748 sq. ft.
Second floor — 705 sq. ft.
Basement — 744 sq. ft.

Country Porch With Dormer

■ *Total living area 1,470 sq. ft.* ■ *Price Code A* ■

No. 24706

■ This plan features:

— Three bedrooms

— Two full baths

■ The front Porch offers outdoor living space and leads into a tiled Entry

■ The Country-size Kitchen has a cooktop island, a bright Breakfast Area and access to the Deck

■ The Master Bedroom offers a dormer window, a vaulted ceiling, a walk-in closet, and a double-vanity Bath

■ This home is designed with basement, crawlspace, and slab foundation options.

First floor — 1,035 sq. ft.
Second floor — 435 sq. ft.
Basement — 1,018 sq. ft.

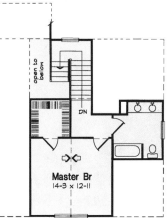

SECOND FLOOR

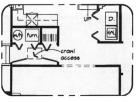

ALTERNATE FOUNDATION

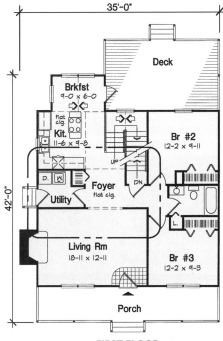

FIRST FLOOR

Contemporary Design

■ *Total living area 1,487 sq. ft.* ■ *Price Code A* ■

SECOND FLOOR

FIRST FLOOR

No. 26112

■ **This plan features:**

— Two bedrooms, with possible third bedroom/den

— One full and one half baths

■ This plan features a solar design with Southern glass doors, windows, and an air-lock Entry

■ R-26 insulation is used for floors and sloping ceilings

■ The Deck rims the front of the home

■ The Dining Room is separated from the Living Room by a half wall

■ The efficient Kitchen has an eating bar

■ This home is designed with basement foundation

First floor — 911 sq. ft.
Second floor — 576 sq. ft.
Basement — 911 sq. ft.

■ *Total living area 1,492 sq. ft.* ■ *Price Code A* ■

No. 97250

■ **This plan features:**

— Three bedrooms

— Two full and one half baths

■ This modern floor plan has a spacious, airy atmosphere

■ Decorative columns define the Great Room, which is enhanced by a fireplace

■ The U-shaped Kitchen includes a built-in Pantry

■ The grand Master Suite is topped by a vaulted ceiling

■ Two additonal Bedrooms contain generous closets

■ This home is designed with basement, crawlspace, and slab foundation options.

First floor — 757 sq. ft.
Second floor — 735 sq. ft.
Basement — 757 sq. ft.
Garage — 447 sq. ft.

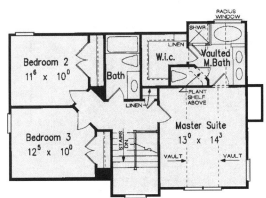

SECOND FLOOR

FIRST FLOOR

Secluded Suite

■ *Total living area 1,493 sq. ft.* ■ *Price Code A* ■

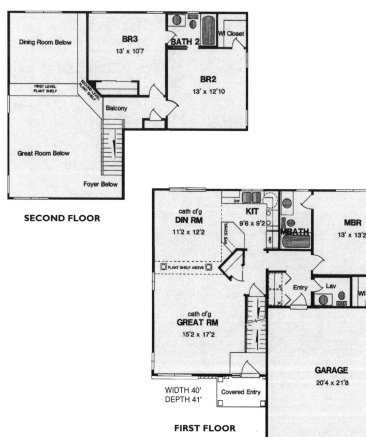

SECOND FLOOR

Second floor labels: Dining Room Below · BR3 13' x 10'7 · BATH 2 · WI Closet · FIRST LEVEL PLANT SHELF · SECOND LEVEL PLANT SHELF · Balcony · BR2 13' x 12'10 · Great Room Below · Foyer Below

First floor labels: DW · KIT 9'6 x 9'2 · cath cl'g DIN RM 11'2 x 12'2 · SNACK BAR · MBR 13' x 13'2 · BATH · REF · PLANT SHELF ABOVE · cath cl'g GREAT RM 15'2 x 17'2 · Entry · Lav · WI Closet · GARAGE 20'4 x 21'8 · WIDTH 40' DEPTH 41' · Covered Entry

FIRST FLOOR

No. 94135

■ **This plan features:**

— Three bedrooms

— Two full and one half baths

■ There are high ceilings in both the Great and Dining Rooms

■ Columns support a plant shelf at the entry to the Dining Room

■ The L-shaped Kitchen has an adjacent snack bar

■ The Master Bedroom is located on the first floor for privacy

■ A balcony and plant shelf overlook the first floor

■ The secondary Bedrooms upstairs share a full Bath

■ This home is designed with a basement foundation

First floor — 973 sq. ft.
Second floor — 520 sq. ft.
Basement — 973 sq. ft.
Garage — 462 sq. ft.

■ *Total living area 1,494 sq. ft.* ■ *Price Code A* ■

No. 99022

■ **This plan features:**

— Three bedrooms

— Two full and one half baths

■ The Vestibule has a coat closet

■ The ample Living Room has an inviting fireplace

■ The Dining Room has a triple window

■ The U-shaped Kitchen has a double sink, ample cabinet and counter space, and a side door

■ The first floor Master Suite has a private Master Bath

■ The two second floor Bedrooms share a full, double vanity Bath with a separate shower

■ This home is designed with a basement foundation

First floor — 913 sq. ft.
Second floor — 581 sq. ft.

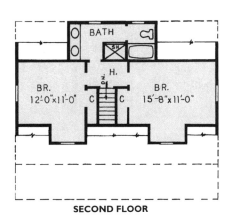

SECOND FLOOR

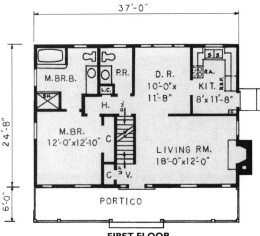

FIRST FLOOR

Contemporary Classic

■ *Total living area 1,498 sq. ft.* ■ *Price Code A* ■

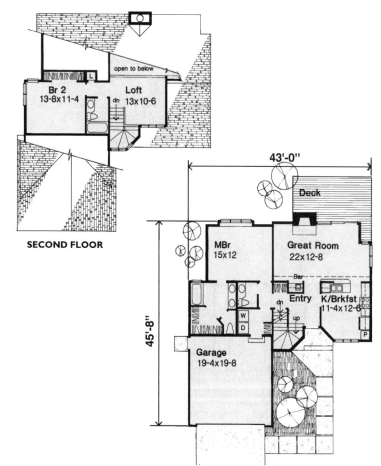

SECOND FLOOR

FIRST FLOOR

No. 99314

■ **This plan features:**

— Two bedrooms

— Two and a half baths

■ The well-appointed Kitchen has a serving bar

■ The two-story Great Room is accentuated by a large fireplace and glass sliders to the Deck

■ A bump-out window seat and a private Bath with a double vanity are featured in the Master Suite

■ The second floor Loft can serve as a third Bedroom

■ This home is designed with a basement foundation

First floor — 1,044 sq. ft.
Second floor — 454 sq. ft.
Basement — 1,044 sq. ft.
Garage — 380 sq. ft.

Fireplaced Family Room

1,500-2,000 sq.ft. HOME PLANS

■ *Total living area 1,505 sq. ft.* ■ *Price Code B* ■

No. 24326

■ **This plan features:**

– Four bedrooms

– One full, one three-quarter, and one half baths

■ The spacious Living Room opens to the Dining Area and efficient Kitchen

■ The Family Room is equipped with a cozy fireplace and sliding glass doors to the Patio

■ The Master Suite has a large walk-in closet and a private Bath with a step-in shower

■ Three additional second floor Bedrooms share a full Bath

■ This home is designed with basement, crawlspace, and slab foundation options.

First floor — 692 sq. ft.
Second floor — 813 sq. ft.
Basement — 699 sq. ft.
Garage — 484 sq. ft.

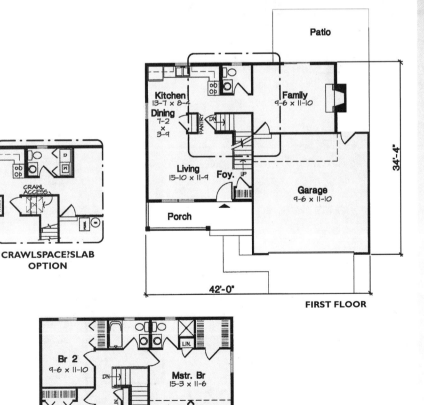

CRAWLSPACE?SLAB OPTION

FIRST FLOOR

SECOND FLOOR

Open Plan

■ Total living area 1,505 sq. ft. ■ Price Code B ■

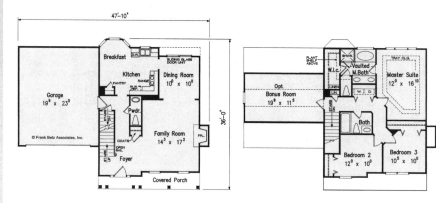

FIRST FLOOR   SECOND FLOOR

No. 98463

■ This plan features:

— Three bedrooms

— Two full and one half baths

■ The Foyer opens to the Family Room which is highlighted by a fireplace

■ The Dining Room has a sliding glass door to rear yard and adjoins the Family Room

■ The Kitchen and Breakfast Area offer an efficient, open layout

■ The second floor Master Suite is topped by a tray ceiling over the Bedroom and a vaulted ceiling over the lavish Bath

■ Two additional Bedrooms share a full Bath in the hall

■ This home is designed with basement and crawlspace foundation options

First floor — 767 sq. ft.
Second floor — 738 sq. ft.
Bonus room — 240 sq. ft.
Basement — 767 sq. ft.
Garage — 480 sq. ft.

Home Sweet Home

■ Total living area 1,508 sq. ft. ■ Price Code B ■

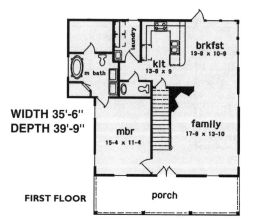

WIDTH 35'-6"
DEPTH 39'-9"

FIRST FLOOR   porch   SECOND FLOOR

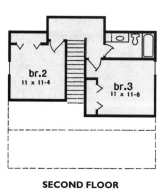

No. 97500

■ This plan features:

— Three bedrooms

— Two full and one half baths

■ The covered front Porch adds charm to this home

■ The Master Bedroom includes a private Bath and a walk-in closet

■ The secondary Bedrooms upstairs share a full Bath

■ The U-shaped Kitchen has a convenient serving bar

■ Two window walls brighten the Breakfast Area

■ The Family Room has a cozy corner fireplace

■ This home is designed with a pier/post foundation

First floor — 1,050 sq. ft.
Second floor — 458 sq. ft.

No. 99079

■ This plan features:

— Three bedrooms

— Two full and one half baths

■ Columns with stone pedestals support the covered front Porch

■ The Living Room overlooks the front Porch and has an impressive stone fireplace

■ The Dining Room has a sliding glass door to the rear yard

■ The Kitchen has a convenient arrangement, including a door to the Garage

■ The Master Bedroom is located on the first floor and has its own Bath

■ Upstairs are two more Bedrooms that share a full Bath

■ This home is designed with a basement foundation

First Floor — 934 sq. ft.

Second Floor — 581 sq. ft.

Basement — 928 sq. ft.

Garage — 509 sq. ft.

■ Total living area 1,515 sq. ft. ■ Price Code B ■

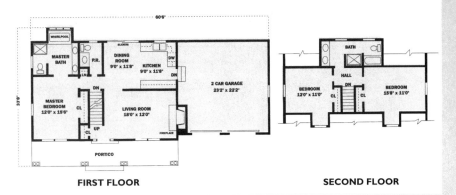

FIRST FLOOR

SECOND FLOOR

Popular Floor Plan

No. 94316

■ This plan features:

— Four bedrooms

— Two full and one half baths

■ This plan is designed with an open layout between the Kitchen and Living Room creating comfort and convenience

■ All bedrooms are on one floor, which is perfect for families with small children

■ The private Master Bath and walk-in closet are featured in the Master Bedroom Suite

■ The convenient utility closet is located in the hall outside Kitchen

■ The expansive Family Room has a cozy fireplace and access to the rear patio

■ This home is designed with a basement foundation

First floor — 736 sq. ft.

Second floor — 788 sq. ft.

Basement — 746 sq. ft.

Garage — 400 sq. ft.

■ Total living area 1,524 sq. ft. ■ Price Code B ■

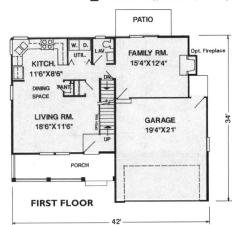

FIRST FLOOR

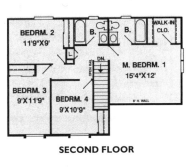

SECOND FLOOR

Four Bedroom Design

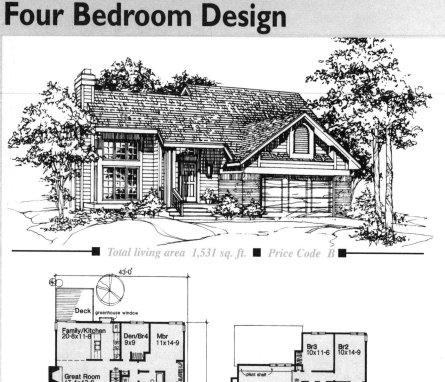

■ Total living area 1,531 sq. ft. ■ Price Code B ■

No. 90358

■ **This plan features:**

— Three bedrooms

— Two full baths

■ A vaulted ceiling and a fireplace are featured in the Great Room

■ The efficient Kitchen has a peninsula counter and a double sink

■ The Family Room has easy access to the Deck

■ The Master Bedroom has a private entrance to the Bath

■ Laundry facilities are conveniently located near the Master Bedroom

■ Two additional Bedrooms are upstairs with walk-in closets, and share a full Bath

■ This home is designed with a basement foundation

Main floor — 1,062 sq. ft.
Upper floor — 469 sq. ft.

FIRST FLOOR

SECOND FLOOR

Those Special Touches

■ Total living area 1,531 sq. ft. ■ Price Code B ■

No. 97612

■ **This plan features:**

— Three bedrooms

— Two full and one half baths

■ The two-story Foyer creates a great first impression

■ The Dining Room and the Family Room are crowned with vaulted ceilings

■ The Master Suite has a tray ceiling and a deluxe Master Bath

■ An optional Bonus Room over the Garage is available for future expansion

■ This home is designed with basement and crawlspace foundation option

First floor — 1,067 sq. ft.
Second floor — 464 sq. ft.
Bonus room — 207 sq. ft.
Basement — 1,067 sq. ft.
Garage — 398 sq. ft.

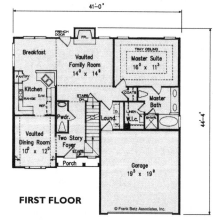

FIRST FLOOR

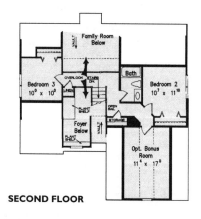

SECOND FLOOR

Stately Three Bedroom Home

No. 93175

This plan features:

- Three bedrooms

- Two full and one half baths

- Columns frame the front door, and window boxes create a charming exterior

- The extensive use of windows flood this home with natural light

- The Great Room has a cathedral ceiling over a corner fireplace and a decorative corner window

- The efficient U-shaped Kitchen features a breakfast counter and opens to the formal Dining Room

- The first floor Laundry Area has storage and a half Bath

- The Master Bedroom boasts a cathedral ceiling and a private Bath with a double vanity

- Two additional Bedrooms share a full Bath

- This home is designed with a basement foundation.

Main floor — 804 sq. ft.
Second floor — 746 sq. ft.
Basement — 804 sq. ft.

■ *Total living area 1,550 sq. ft.* ■ *Price Code B* ■

FIRST FLOOR

SECOND FLOOR

Compact Four Bedroom

No. 94315

This plan features:

- Four Bedrooms

- Two full and one half baths

- The open living space is between the Living Room and the Kitchen

- The convenient Pantry and the Utility Room are easily accessible from the Kitchen

- The Family Room is enhanced by a fireplace and has direct access to the Patio

- The Master Bedroom includes a full Bath and a walk-in closet

- The welcoming front Porch achieves curb appeal

- This home is designed with a basement foundation.

First floor — 736 sq. ft.
Second floor — 814 sq. ft.
Basement — 746 sq. ft.
Garage — 400 sq. ft.

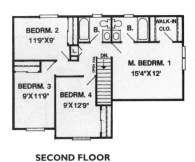

■ *Total living area 1,550 sq. ft.* ■ *Price Code B* ■

FIRST FLOOR

SECOND FLOOR

Charming Two-Story

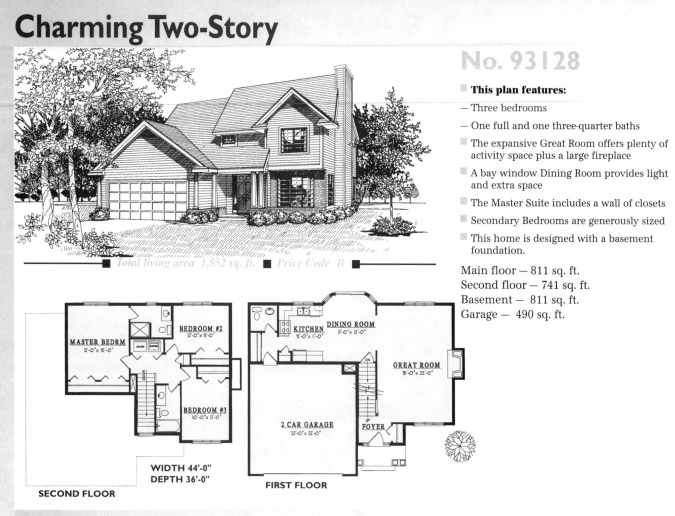

Total living area 1,552 sq. ft. ■ Price Code B

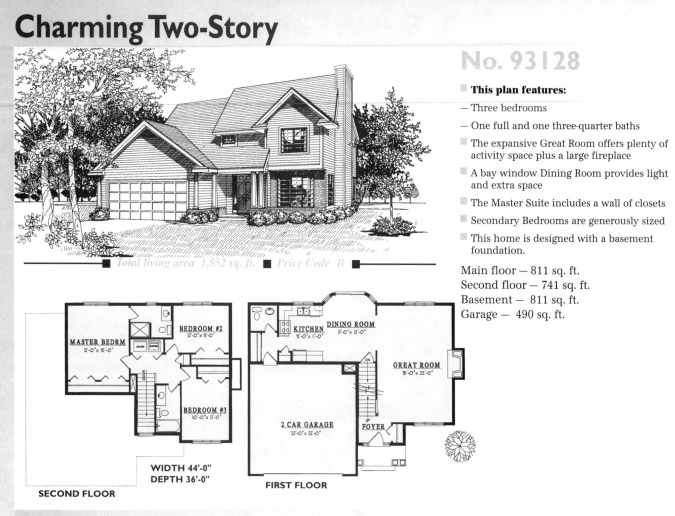

MASTER BEDRM
12'-0"x 15'-0"

BEDROOM #2
12'-0"x 9'-0"

BEDROOM #3
10'-0"x 12'-0"

SECOND FLOOR

WIDTH 44'-0"
DEPTH 36'-0"

KITCHEN
9'-0"x 11'-0"

DINING ROOM
11'-0"x 13'-0"

GREAT ROOM
15'-0"x 23'-0"

2 CAR GARAGE
22'-0"x 22'-0"

FOYER

FIRST FLOOR

No. 93128

■ **This plan features:**

— Three bedrooms

— One full and one three-quarter baths

■ The expansive Great Room offers plenty of activity space plus a large fireplace

■ A bay window Dining Room provides light and extra space

■ The Master Suite includes a wall of closets

■ Secondary Bedrooms are generously sized

■ This home is designed with a basement foundation.

Main floor — 811 sq. ft.
Second floor — 741 sq. ft.
Basement — 811 sq. ft.
Garage — 490 sq. ft.

Country Influence

Total living area 1,552 sq. ft. ■ Price Code B

36'-0"

MBR
12-0 X 12-0

BR
10-0 X 13-0

FOYER

LR
15-6 X 17-0

DINE
9-6 X 9-0

KIT
9-0 X 10-0

DECK

FIRST FLOOR

DECK

BR/STUDIO
12-0 X 15-0

ATTIC

ATTIC

LOFT

LR & DR Below

SECOND FLOOR

No. 90844

■ **This plan features:**

— Three bedrooms

— Two full and one half baths

■ The wrap-around Deck provides outdoor living space, ideal for a sloping lot

■ The two and a half-story glass wall and two separate atrium doors provide natural light for the Living/Dining Room area

■ The efficient galley Kitchen has easy access to the Dining Area

■ The Master Bedroom has a half Bath and ample closet space

■ Another Bedroom on the first floor adjoins a full Bath

■ The second floor Bedroom/Studio, with a private Deck, has a nearby full, Bath and a Loft Area

■ This home is designed with a basement foundation.

First floor — 1,086 sq. ft.
Second floor — 466 sq. ft.
Basement— 1,080 sq. ft.

Country Influence

No. 24654

This plan features:

— Three bedrooms

— Two full and one half baths

■ The Front Porch leads into a unique Sunroom with a half bath and a coat closet

■ The open Living Room is enhanced by a palladian window, a focal point fireplace and atrium doors to the Deck

■ A bay window brightens the formal Dining Room which is conveniently located between the Living Room and the Kitchen

■ The efficient L-shaped Kitchen has a bay window eating area, a Laundry closet and a handy Garage entrance

■ The plush Master Bedroom offers another bay window crowned by tray ceiling and a private Bath with double vanity

■ Two additional Bedrooms, with arched windows and ample closets, share a full Bath

■ This home is designed with basement, slab and crawlspace foundation options.

First floor — 806 sq. ft.
Second floor — 748 sq. ft.
Garage — 467 sq. ft.

Total living area 1,554 sq. ft. ■ *Price Code B* ■

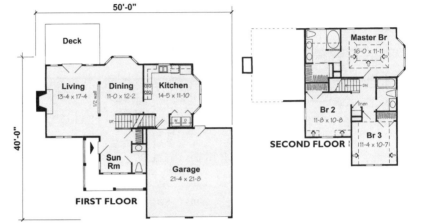

Beckoning Country Porch

No. 34603

This plan features:

— Three bedrooms

— Two full and one half baths

■ The Country-style exterior with dormer windows above friendly front Porch

■ A vaulted ceiling and a central fireplace accent the spacious Great Room

■ The L-shaped Kitchen/Dining Room has a work island and an atrium door to backyard

■ The first floor Master Suite features a vaulted ceiling, a walk-in closet, a private Bath, and an optional private Deck with a hot tub

■ Two additional Bedrooms on the second floor have easy access to full Bath

■ This home is designed with basement, slab and crawlspace foundation options.

First floor — 1,061 sq. ft.
Second floor — 499 sq. ft.
Basement — 1,061 sq. ft.

Total living area 1,560 sq. ft. ■ *Price Code B* ■

83

Family Get-Away

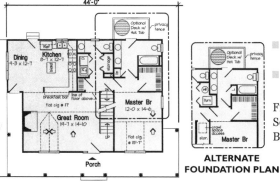

■ Total living area 1,560 sq. ft. ■ Price Code B ■

SECOND FLOOR

FIRST FLOOR

ALTERNATE FOUNDATION PLAN

This plan features:

— Three bedrooms

— Two full and one half baths

■ The wrap-around Porch, for views and visiting, provides access to the Great Room and the Dining Area

■ The spacious Great Room with a two-story ceiling and a dormer window above a massive fireplace

■ The combination Dining/Kitchen has an island work area and Breakfast Bar, and is adjacent to the Laundry/Storage and half Bath Area

■ The private two-story Master Bedroom with a dormer window, a walk-in closet, a double vanity Bath and an optional deck with a hot tub

■ Two additional Bedrooms on the second floor sharing a full Bath

■ This home is designed with basement, slab and crawlspace foundation options.

First floor — 1,061 sq. ft.
Second floor — 499 sq. ft.
Basement — 1,061 sq. ft.

Loads of Natural Light

■ Total living area 1,562 sq. ft. ■ Price Code B ■

FIRST FLOOR

SECOND FLOOR

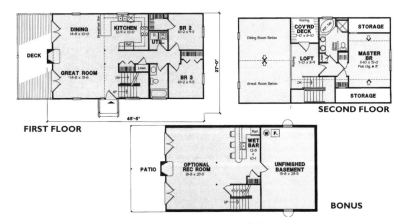

BONUS

This plan features:

— Three bedrooms

— Two full baths

■ Double French doors with arched transom windows access an elevated Deck

■ A spacious feeling created by the open Great Room, the Dining Area and the Kitchen

■ The two first floor Bedrooms have ample closets and share a full Bath

■ The secluded Master Bedroom has a covered Deck, a plush Bath, loads of storage and a Loft

■ The lower level offers an optional Recreation Room with a Patio, a fireplace and a wetbar

■ This home is designed with a basement foundation.

First floor — 1,062 sq. ft.
Second floor — 500 sq. ft.
Bonus — 678 sq. ft.
Basement — 384 sq. ft.

Comfort and Convenience

No. 98414

This plan features:

— Three bedrooms

— Two full baths

■ From the Foyer, the Great Room beckons with its focal point fireplace and high ceiling

■ The Master Suite features a tray ceiling, adjoining Sitting Room and luxurious Bath

■ The Sitting Room and Master Bath are topped with vaulted ceilings.

■ The angled Kitchen offers convenient access to the sun-filled Breakfast Area, plus the Great Room, Dining Room, Laundry, and Storage Area

■ Two secondary Bedrooms have access to a full Bath

■ This home is designed with basement and crawlspace foundation options.

First floor — 1,575 sq. ft.
Basement — 1,658 sq. ft.
Garage — 459 sq. ft.

Total living area 1,575 sq. ft. ■ Price Code B

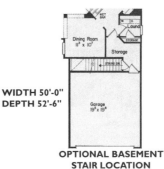

MAIN FLOOR

WIDTH 50'-0"
DEPTH 52'-6"

OPTIONAL BASEMENT STAIR LOCATION

Friendly Front Porch

No. 94138

This plan features:

— Three bedrooms

— One full and one half baths

■ Country, homey feeling with wrap-around Porch

■ The adjoining Living Room and Dining Room creates a spacious feeling

■ The efficient Kitchen easily serves the Dining Area with an extended counter and a built-in Pantry

■ The spacious Family Room has an optional fireplace and access to the Laundry/Garage entry

■ The large Master Bedroom features a walk-in closet and access to a full Bath

■ The two additional Bedrooms have ample closets and full Bath access

■ This home is designed with a basement foundation.

First floor — 900 sq. ft.
Second floor — 676 sq. ft.
Basement — 900 sq. ft.
Garage — 448 sq. ft.

Total living area 1,576 sq. ft. ■ Price Code B

FIRST FLOOR

SECOND FLOOR

WIDTH 58'-0"
DEPTH 34'-0"

Grand Front Window

■ *Total living area 1,583 sq. ft.* ■ *Price Code B* ■

FIRST FLOOR

SECOND FLOOR

No. 98552

■ **This plan features:**

— Three bedrooms

— Two full and one half baths

■ The high, arched front window gives this home curb appeal and natural illumination for the Living Room

■ The Living Room is topped by a cathedral ceiling and enhanced by a fireplace

■ The Master Suite has its own private corner and includes a double vanity Bath and a walk-in closet

■ The second floor Bedrooms share a full Bath

■ This home is designed with a slab foundation.

Main floor — 1, 777 sq. ft.
Second floor — 406 sq. ft.
Garage — 440 sq. ft.

Adaptable to Any Lifestyle

■ *Total living area 1,587 sq. ft.* ■ *Price Code B* ■

FIRST FLOOR

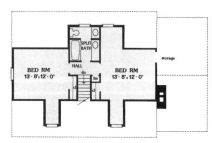

SECOND FLOOR

No. 90671

■ **This plan features:**

— Four bedrooms

— Two full baths

■ The Living Room has a beamed ceiling and an inviting fireplace

■ The eat-in Kitchen is efficient and easily serves the formal Dining Room

■ The Master Bedroom has two closets

■ The two upstairs Bedrooms share a split Bath

■ This home is designed with a basement foundation.

First floor — 1,056 sq. ft.
Second floor — 531 sq. ft.

Comfortable Contemporary

No. 99652

■ This plan features:

– Three bedrooms

– Two full and one half baths

■ A convenient Foyer with a closet and a Powder Room is entered from a covered Porch

■ A high ceiling accents an arched window in the Living Room, which opens to the Dining Room and Patio

■ The efficient U-shaped Kitchen has a serving counter, a Dinette Area and the indispensable Mud Room

■ The private, corner Master Bedroom features two closets and a plush Bath with a whirlpool tub

■ Two additional Bedrooms with ample closets share a full Bath

■ This home is designed with basement and slab foundation options.

First floor — 810 sq. ft.
Second floor — 781 sq. ft.
Basement — 746 sq. ft.
Garage/Storage — 513 sq. ft.

■ Total living area 1.591 sq. ft. ■ Price Code B ■

FIRST FLOOR

SECOND FLOOR

Visual Appeal

No. 94903

■ This plan features:

– Three bedrooms

– Two full and one half baths

■ Step down from the entry into the Living Room distinguished by a raised hearth fireplace under a cathedral ceiling

■ French doors seclude the formal Dining Room from Kitchen

■ The open Kitchen and Dinette provide a built-in Pantry, center island/snack bar and a sliding glass door to rear yard

■ The private Den with French doors is located in a quiet corner

■ The grand Master Bedroom offers a decorative ceiling, a large walk-in closet and a lavish Bath with a whirlpool tub

■ Two additional Bedrooms share a full Bath

■ This home is designed with a basement foundation.

■ Alternate foundation options available at an additional charge. Please call 1-800-235-5700 for more information.

First floor — 869 sq. ft.
Second floor — 725 sq. ft.
Basement — 869 sq. ft.
Garage — 430 sq. ft.

■ Total living area 1,594 sq. ft. ■ Price Code B ■

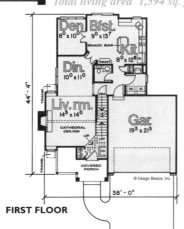

FIRST FLOOR

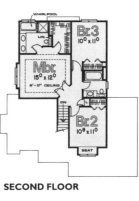

SECOND FLOOR

Charming Country Style

No. 99404

This plan features:

— Three bedrooms

— Two full and one half baths

■ The spacious Great Room enhanced by a fireplace and transom windows

■ The Breakfast Room with a bay window and direct access to the Kitchen

■ A Snack bar extending work space in the Kitchen

■ The Master Suite enhanced by a crowning in a boxed nine-foot ceiling, a whirlpool bath and a large walk-in closet

■ Two second floor bedrooms share a full bath

■ This home is designed with a basement foundation.

■ Alternate foundation options available at an additional charge. Please call 1-800-235-5700 for more information.

First floor — 1,191 sq. ft.
Second floor — 405 sq. ft.
Basement — 1,191 sq. ft.
Garage — 454 sq. ft.

Total living area 1,596 sq. ft. ■ Price Code B

SECOND FLOOR

FIRST FLOOR

Easy Living Plan

Total living area 1,600 sq. ft. ■ Price Code B

No. 98406

This plan features:

— Three bedrooms

— Two full and one half baths

■ The Kitchen, the Breakfast Bay, and the Family Room blend into a spacious comfortable living area

■ A convenient Laundry closet is tucked into a corner of the Kitchen

■ The luxurious Master Suite is topped by a tray ceiling and a vaulted ceiling is in the Master Bath

■ Two roomy, secondary Bedrooms share the full bath in the hall

■ This home is designed with basement, slab or crawlspace foundation options.

First floor — 828 sq. ft.
Second floor — 772 sq. ft.
Basement — 828 sq. ft.
Garage — 473 sq. ft.

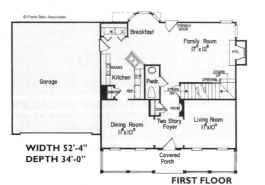

WIDTH 52'-4"
DEPTH 34'-0"

FIRST FLOOR

SECOND FLOOR

Family Living Made Easy

No. 35001

This plan features:

— Three bedrooms

— Two full and one half baths

■ The welcoming Country Porch shelters the entrance

■ The Living Room flows into the Dining Room, creating a great area for entertaining

■ The efficient, U-shaped Kitchen includes an informal Breakfast Area and a Laundry center

■ This design has a convenient entrance from the Garage into the Kitchen

■ The private Master Suite has a full Bath and two closets

■ The Den/Office, with ample closet space, enables it to double as a Guest Room

■ Two additional Bedrooms on the second floor share a full Bath

■ An optional Deck/Patio increases the living space in pleasant weather

■ This home is designed with basement, slab and crawlspace foundation options.

First floor — 1,081 sq. ft.
Second floor — 528 sq. ft.
Garage — 528 sq. ft.

■ Total living area 1,609 sq. ft. ■ Price Code B ■

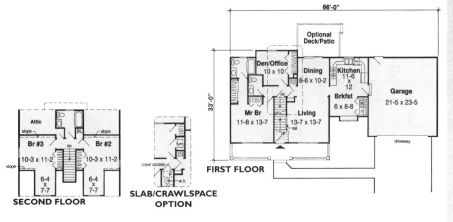

Bathed in Natural Light

No. 98416

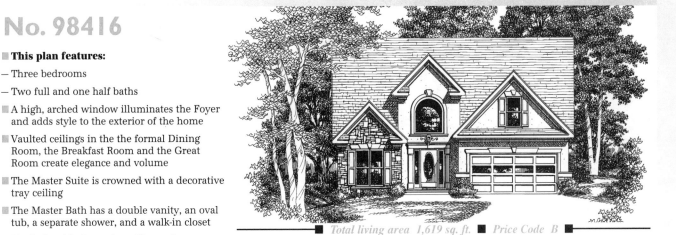

This plan features:

— Three bedrooms

— Two full and one half baths

■ A high, arched window illuminates the Foyer and adds style to the exterior of the home

■ Vaulted ceilings in the the formal Dining Room, the Breakfast Room and the Great Room create elegance and volume

■ The Master Suite is crowned with a decorative tray ceiling

■ The Master Bath has a double vanity, an oval tub, a separate shower, and a walk-in closet

■ The Loft, with the option of becoming a fourth bedroom, highlights the second floor

■ This home is designed with basement and crawlspace foundation options.

First floor — 1,133 sq. ft.
Second floor — 486 sq. ft.
Basement — 1,133 sq. ft.
Bonus — 134 sq. ft.
Garage — 406 sq. ft.

■ Total living area 1,619 sq. ft. ■ Price Code B ■

WIDTH 41'-0"
DEPTH 46'-4"

89

Charming Gabled Porch

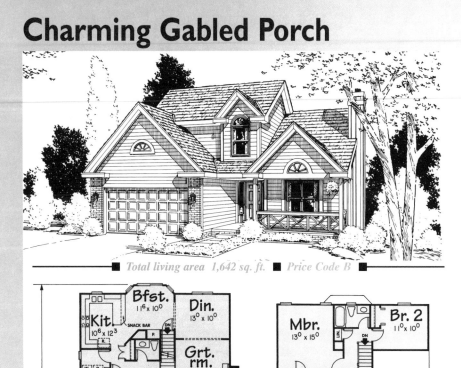

■ *Total living area 1,642 sq. ft.* ■ *Price Code B* ■

No. 94908

■ **This plan features:**

— Three bedrooms

— Two full and one half baths

■ The Formal Dining Room expands into the Great Room for easy entertaining

■ The Kitchen snack bar and Breakfast alcove provide two informal eating options

■ The corner Master Bedroom has a double vanity Bath, a large walk-in closet and an Unfinished Storage area beyond

■ Two additional Bedrooms share a full hall Bath and linen closet

■ This home is designed with a basement foundation.

■ Alternate foundation options available at an additional charge. Please call 1-800-235-5700 for more information.

First floor — 862 sq. ft.
Second floor — 780 sq. ft.
Bonus — 132 sq. ft.
Basement — 862 sq. ft.
Garage — 454 sq. ft.

FIRST FLOOR

SECOND FLOOR

© Design Basics, Inc.

Bright and Beautiful

■ *Total living area 1,646 sq. ft.* ■ *Price Code B* ■

No. 91008

■ **This plan features:**

— Three bedrooms

— Two full and one half baths

■ The Living Room flows into the Dining Room for easy entertaining

■ The Master Suite has a private Master Bath and a walk-in closet

■ A Kitchen with a bay window has an informal Eating Nook

■ Two second floor Bedrooms, one with a bay window, share a full Bath

■ This home is designed with crawlspace and slab foundation options.

First floor — 1,153 sq. ft.
Second floor — 493 sq. ft.

FIRST FLOOR

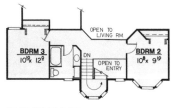

SECOND FLOOR

A Beautiful Setting

No. 90208

■ **This plan features:**

— Three bedrooms

— Two full baths

■ Rustic and modern elements combine to create a home worthy of a beautiful setting

■ A covered front Porch leads into an Entry hall with a lovely staircase

■ The Gathering Room features a sloped ceiling and a towering wall of windows

■ Located off the Dining Room is a deck, perfect for outdoor entertaining

■ The convenient U-shaped Kitchen offers a Pantry and a snack bar

■ The Master Bedroom on the first floor offers privacy with its own Bath and Dressing Room

■ Upstairs, two secondary Bedrooms share a full Bath, and a Lounge that overlooks the Gathering Room

■ This home is designed with a basement foundation.

First floor — 1,113 sq. ft.
Second floor — 543 sq. ft.
Basement — 1,113 sq. ft.

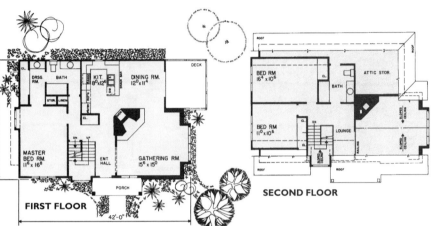

■ *Total living area 1,656 sq. ft.* ■ *Price Code B* ■

FIRST FLOOR

SECOND FLOOR

Towering Windows

No. 91071

■ **This plan features:**

— Three bedrooms

— Two full baths

■ The wrap-around Deck is found above the three-car Garage

■ Both the Dining and Living Areas feature vaulted ceilings

■ The octagonal Kitchen has a cooktop peninsula

■ The Master Bedroom on the upper level has an over-sized closet

■ This home is designed with basement, slab and crawlspace foundation options.

First floor — 1,329 sq. ft.
Second floor — 342 sq. ft.
Garage — 885 sq. ft.
Deck — 461 sq. ft.

■ *Total living area 1,671 sq. ft.* ■ *Price Code B* ■

FIRST FLOOR

SECOND FLOOR

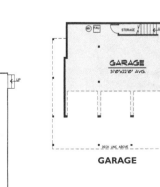

GARAGE

Cozy and Comfortable

■ Total living area 1,672 sq. ft. ■ Price Code B ■

No. 93306

■ **This plan features:**

— Three bedrooms

— Two full and one half baths

■ The center Foyer leads into formal Living and Dining Rooms

■ The open Family Room is accented by a hearth fireplace

■ The efficient Kitchen has a peninsula counter, nearby Laundry and Garage entry, and Dinette with access to rear yard

■ The corner Master Bedroom offers a plush Bath with a double vanity and whirlpool tub

■ Two additional Bedrooms with ample closets share a full Bath

■ This home is designed with a basement foundation.

First floor — 884 sq. ft.
Second floor — 788 sq. ft.
Garage — 450 sq. ft.
Basement — 884 sq. ft.

SECOND FLOOR

FIRST FLOOR

With Room to Expand

■ Total living area 1,675 sq. ft. ■ Price Code B ■

No. 98431

■ **This plan features:**

— Three bedrooms

— Two full and one half baths

■ This plan is designed with an impressive two-story Foyer

■ The Kitchen is equipped with ample cabinet and counter space

■ The spacious Family Room flows from the Breakfast Bay and is highlighted by a fireplace and a French door to the rear yard

■ The Master Suite is topped by a tray ceiling and is enhanced by a vaulted, five-piece Master Bath

■ Two additional Bedrooms share a full Bath

■ This home is designed with basement, slab and crawlspace foundation options.

First floor — 882 sq. ft.
Second floor — 793 sq. ft.
Bonus — 416 sq. ft.
Basement — 882 sq. ft.
Garage — 510 sq. ft.

WIDTH 49'-6"
DEPTH 35'-4"

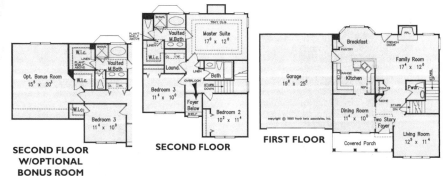

SECOND FLOOR W/OPTIONAL BONUS ROOM

SECOND FLOOR

FIRST FLOOR

No. 99914

This plan features:

– Two bedrooms

– Two full baths

■ The large Deck spans around the front and side of this rustic home

■ The Living Room and Dining Room are combined

■ The Living Room has a gas fireplace and sliders to the Deck

■ The large Kitchen features an angled counter

■ There is a Bedroom, Bath and an ample Utility Room on the first floor

■ Upstairs, the Master Bedroom has two closets and a private Deck

■ Relax in the whirlpool tub in the Master Bathroom

■ This home is designed with basement and crawlspace foundation options.

First floor — 1,064 sq. ft.
Second floor — 613 sq. ft.

■ Total living area 1,677 sq. ft. ■ Price Code B ■

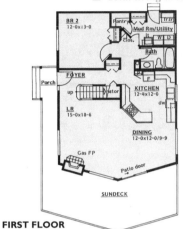

FIRST FLOOR

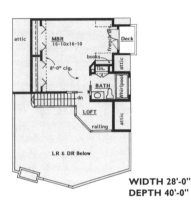

WIDTH 28'-0"
DEPTH 40'-0"

SECOND FLOOR

Country Style Charmer

No. 91903

This plan features:

– Three bedrooms

– Two full and one half baths

■ This design features a classical symmetry and gracious front Porch

■ Formal areas are zoned toward the front of the house

■ The large Family Room has a fireplace

■ A staircase is located off the Family Room

■ The Master Bedroom has a double vanity, separate glass shower and tub, and a built-in entertainment center

■ This home is designed with a basement foundation.

First floor — 910 sq. ft.
Second floor — 769 sq. ft.
Basement — 890 sq. ft.

■ Total living area 1,679 sq. ft. ■ Price Code B ■

FIRST FLOOR

SECOND FLOOR

Inviting Front Porch

■ Total living area 1,683 sq. ft. ■ Price Code B ■

FIRST FLOOR

- Sundeck 16-0 x 12-0
- Brkfst. 8-0 x 9-6
- Kitchen 9-4 x 11-8
- Living Area 18-0 x 11-8
- Stor. 5-6 x 12-0
- Dining 11-0 x 13-4
- Open Foyer 8-4 x 11-10
- Double Garage 19-8 x 21-4
- Porch

© 1996, Jannis Vann & Associates, Inc.

12'-0" 34'-5" 44'-0"

SECOND FLOOR

- M.Bath
- Bdrm. 3 13-0 x 9-6
- Master Bdrm. 15-6 x 11-0
- Bdrm. 2 13-0 x 9-6
- Open Foyer

No. 93298

This plan features:

– Three bedrooms

– Two full and one half baths

■ The detailed gables and inviting front Porch create a warm, welcoming facade

■ The open Foyer features an angled staircase, a half Bath and a coat closet

■ The expansive, informal Living Area at the rear of the home features a fireplace and opens onto the Deck

■ The efficient Kitchen has easy access to both the formal and informal Dining Areas

■ The Master Bedroom includes a walk-in closet and compartmented private Bath

■ This home is designed with basement, slab and crawlspace foundation options.

First floor — 797 sq. ft.
Second floor — 886 sq. ft.
Basement — 797 sq. ft.
Garage — 414 sq. ft.

Country Elegance

■ Total living area 1,684 sq. ft. ■ Price Code B ■

WIDTH 40'-0"
DEPTH 44'-0"

FIRST FLOOR

- Fam.Rm.
- Kit.
- Din.
- Liv.Rm.
- Garage
- E.
- Porch

SECOND FLOOR

- Br.
- Br.
- Mb.
- Mbr.
- B.
- Bonus

No. 93905

This plan features:

– Three bedrooms

– Two full and one half baths

■ The welcoming front Porch leads into an open Entry with landing staircase and convenient closet

■ The expansive Living Room/Dining Area is highlighted by multiple windows front and back

■ The comfortable Family Room has a gas fireplace, sliding glass door to Patio and adjoins the Kitchen, Laundry and Garage

■ The efficient U-shaped Kitchen has a built-in desk and eating bar

■ The private Master Bedroom has an arched window, plush Bath and walk-in closet

■ Two additional Bedrooms have large closets and share a full Bath

■ Bonus Room has another arched window and the storage space offers many options

■ This home is designed with a basement foundation.

Main area — 913 sq. ft.
Second floor — 771 sq. ft.
Garage — 483 sq. ft.

Attractive Roof Lines

No. 97207

■ This plan features:

— Three bedrooms

— Two full and one half baths

■ The Kitchen, with an open, angled countertop, enjoys views to the covered Porch and the rear yard beyond

■ The Master Bedroom includes a tray ceiling and an enormous walk-in closet

■ The upper level offers privacy for the secondary Bedrooms and includes a balcony overlook to the vaulted Great Room

■ This home is designed with basement, slab and crawlspace foundation options.

First floor — 1,236 sq. ft.
Second floor — 454 sq. ft.
Basement — 1,236 sq. ft.
Garage — 462 sq. ft.

■ *Total living area 1,690 sq. ft.* ■ *Price Code B* ■

FIRST FLOOR

SECOND FLOOR

Master Retreat Crowns Home

No. 19422

■ This plan features:

— Two bedrooms

— Two full baths

■ A unique four-sided fireplace separates the Living Room, Dining Area and Kitchen

■ The well-equipped Kitchen features a cooktop island, a walk-in Pantry and easy access to the Dining Area and Laundry Room

■ The three-season Screened Porch and Deck beyond adjoin the Dining Room, Living Room, and second Bedroom

■ The private Master Suite on the second floor offers a cozy dormer window seat, private Balcony, and window tub in the spacious Bath

■ This home is designed with basement and crawlspace foundation options.

First floor — 1,290 sq. ft.
Second floor — 405 sq. ft.
Screened porch — 152 sq. ft.
Garage — 513 sq. ft.

■ *Total living area 1,695 sq. ft.* ■ *Price Code B* ■

WIDTH 50'-8"
DEPTH 61'-8"

FIRST FLOOR

SECOND FLOOR

Arches Grace Facade

■ *Total living area   1,696 sq. ft.*   ■   *Price Code B*   ■

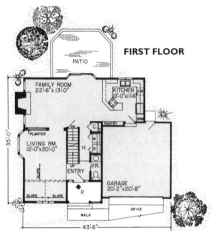

FIRST FLOOR

SECOND FLOOR

■ **This plan features:**

— Three bedrooms

— Two full and one half baths

■ Built-in planters and half walls are used to define rooms

■ The balcony connects the three upstairs Bedrooms

■ Double sinks and a built-in vanity are located in the Master Bath

■ Ample closet space is found throughout this plan

■ This home is designed with a basement foundation.

First floor — 932 sq. ft.
Second floor — 764 sq. ft.
Basement — 920 sq. ft.
Garage — 430 sq. ft.

Elegantly Styled

■ *Total living area   1,700 sq. ft.*   ■   *Price Code B*   ■

FIRST FLOOR

SECOND FLOOR

© Frank Betz Associates

OPTIONAL SECOND FLOOR

No. 98449

■ **This plan features:**

— Three bedrooms

— Two full and one half baths

■ Architectural details create eye-catching appeal to this home's facade

■ The convenient Kitchen with angled snack bar has easy access to the Dining Room, Breakfast Area, backyard and the Laundry/Garage

■ The second floor offers an optional Bonus Room for future expansion

■ This home is designed with basement and crawlspace foundation options.

First floor — 922 sq. ft.
Second floor — 778 sq. ft.
Bonus — 369 sq. ft.
Garage & storage — 530 sq. ft.
Basement — 922 sq. ft.

Simplicity and Efficiency

No. 93404

This plan features:

— Three bedrooms

— Two full and one half baths

▪ The well-appointed Kitchen is near both the formal Dining Room and the informal Breakfast Area

▪ The wood Deck, accessed from the Breakfast Area, increases the living space in the warmer months

▪ The Garage entrance, flanked by the Laundry Center and a half Bath, helps to keep the house cleaner

▪ The wood stove in the Family Room adds a cozy feeling

▪ The Master Suite has a walk-in closet and private Bath

▪ Two additional Bedrooms share a full Bath

▪ The Bonus Room is located above the Garage for future expansion

▪ This home is designed with a basement foundation.

First floor — 878 sq. ft.
Second floor — 823 sq. ft.
Bonus room — 257 sq. ft.
Basement — 878 sq. ft.
Garage — 427 sq. ft.

Total living area 1,701 sq. ft. ▪ Price Code B

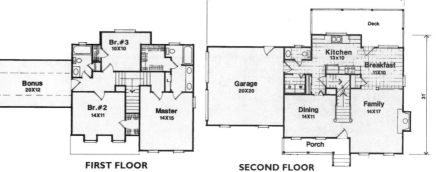

FIRST FLOOR

SECOND FLOOR

Year-Round A-Frame Living

No. 90930

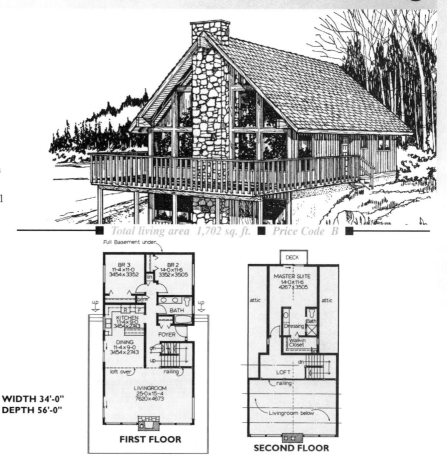

This plan features:

— Three bedrooms

— Two full and one three-quarter baths

▪ A vaulted ceiling is featured in the Living Room with a massive fireplace

▪ The wrap-around Deck gives you a lot of outdoor living space

▪ The luxurious Master Suite features a walk-in closet, a full Bath and private Deck

▪ The two additional Bedrooms share a full hall Bathroom

▪ This home is designed with a basement foundation.

First floor — 1,238 sq. ft.
Second floor — 464 sq. ft.
Basement — 1,175 sq. ft.

Total living area 1,702 sq. ft. ▪ Price Code B

WIDTH 34'-0"
DEPTH 56'-0"

FIRST FLOOR

SECOND FLOOR

Soaring Living Room

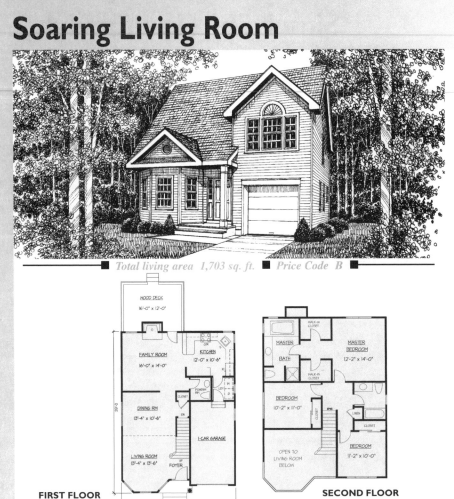

■ *Total living area 1,703 sq. ft.* ■ *Price Code B* ■

No. 99066

■ **This plan features:**

— Three bedrooms

— Two full and one half baths

■ The soaring, two-story Living Room is a dramatic first impression

■ The family Room with fireplace has access to the large, rear Deck

■ The Master Bedroom on the second floor features two large walk-in closets and the plush Bath

■ The secondary Bedrooms are generously sized and share a full Bath

■ This home is designed with a basement foundation.

First floor — 848 sq. ft.
Second floor — 855 sq. ft.
Basement — 848 sq. ft.
Garage — 220 sq. ft.

FIRST FLOOR **SECOND FLOOR**

Enchanting Elevation

■ *Total living area 1,704 sq. ft.* ■ *Price Code B* ■

No. 92695

■ **This plan features:**

— Three bedrooms

— One full, one three quarter, and one half baths

■ The large Foyer showcases interesting angled entries to the rooms beyond

■ The Dining Room has a tray ceiling and is directly connected to the Kitchen

■ The Great Room has a corner fireplace

■ The Breakfast Nook has an access door to the rear yard and stairs to the second floor

■ Upstairs are three Bedrooms, all with ample closet space, and two Baths

■ This home is designed with a basement foundation.

First floor — 906 sq. ft.
Second floor — 798 sq. ft.
Basement— 906 sq. ft.
Garage — 437 sq. ft.

FIRST FLOOR

SECOND FLOOR

Streaming Natural Light

No. 91514

This plan features:

- Three bedrooms

- Two full and one half baths

- The outstanding, two story Great Room has an unusual floor-to-ceiling corner front window and cozy, hearth fireplace

- The formal Dining Room opens from the Great Room to make entertaining easy

- The efficient Kitchen has a work island, a Pantry, a corner double sink and opens to the Great Room and Eating Nook with bay window

- The quiet Master Suite has a vaulted ceiling and a plush Bath with a double vanity, Spa tub and walk-in closet

- On the second floor, two additional Bedrooms share a full Bath

- There is a Bonus Area for multiple uses

- This home is designed with a crawlspace foundation.

First floor — 1,230 sq. ft.
Second floor — 477 sq. ft.
Bonus — 195 sq. ft.

Total living area 1,707 sq. ft. ■ *Price Code B*

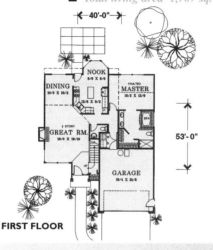

FIRST FLOOR

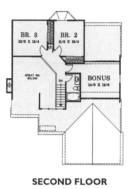

SECOND FLOOR

Home With Many Views

No. 24319

This plan features:

- Three bedrooms

- Two full baths

- Large Decks and windows take full advantage of the view

- The fireplace divides the Living Room and the Dining Room

- The Kitchen flows into the Dining Room

- The Master Bedroom features a full Master Bath

- The Recreation Room sports a whirlpool tub and a bar

- This home is designed with a basement foundation.

Main floor — 728 sq. ft.
Upper floor — 573 sq. ft.
Lower floor — 409 sq. ft.
Garage — 244 sq. ft.

Total living area 1,710 sq. ft. ■ *Price Code B*

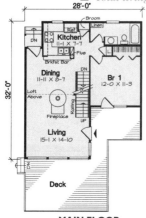

MAIN FLOOR

UPPER LEVEL

LOWER LEVEL

Three Bedroom Cape

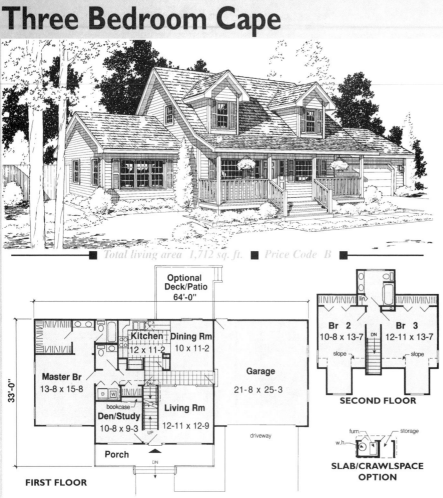

No. 35002

■ **This plan features:**

— Three Bedrooms

— Two full and one half baths

■ The wonderful big front Porch creates a homey welcome

■ The formal Living Room has a picture window that views the Porch and front yard

■ The formal Dining Room is directly across from the Living Room, allowing for a smooth transition from room to room when entertaining

■ The well-appointed Kitchen has ample storage and counter space and a double sink

■ The first floor private Master Suite has a double vanity, plush Bath and a large walk-in closet

■ Two secondary Bedrooms share a full Bath with double vanity

■ This home is designed with basement, slab and crawlspace foundation options.

First floor — 1,120 sq. ft.
Second floor — 592 sq. ft.
Garage — 528 sq. ft.

Angled Staircase Adds Style

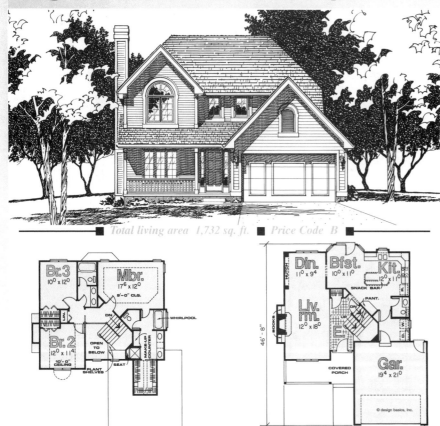

No. 94905

■ **This plan features:**

— Three bedrooms

— Two full and one half baths

■ The two-story Entry has sidelights

■ Built-ins and decorative windows highlight the Living and Dining Rooms

■ The Breakfast Area adds space to the open Kitchen with a large Pantry, island counter/snack bar and convenient access to Laundry Room

■ The Master Bedroom has a whirlpool Bath with double vanity and a generous walk-in closet

■ One of the other two Bedrooms contains a beautiful arched window below a volume ceiling

■ This home is designed with a basement foundation.

■ Alternate foundation options available at an additional charge. Please call 1-800-235-5700 for more information.

First floor — 884 sq. ft.
Second floor — 848 sq. ft.
Basement — 884 sq. ft.
Garage — 428 sq. ft.

Cozy Front Porch

No. 93269

This plan features:

— Three bedrooms

— Two full and one half baths

■ The Living Room is enhanced by a large fireplace

■ The formal Dining Room is open to the Living Room, giving a more spacious feel to the rooms

■ The efficient Kitchen includes ample counter and cabinet space as well as a double sink and pass-through window to Living Area

■ The sunny Breakfast Area has a vaulted ceiling and a door to the Deck

■ The first floor Master Suite has a separate tub, shower stall and walk-in closet

■ The first floor Powder Room has a hide-away Laundry Center

■ Two additional Bedrooms share a full Bath on the second floor

■ This home is designed with a basement foundation.

First floor — 1,045 sq. ft.

Second floor — 690 sq. ft.

Basement — 465 sq. ft.

Garage — 580 sq. ft.

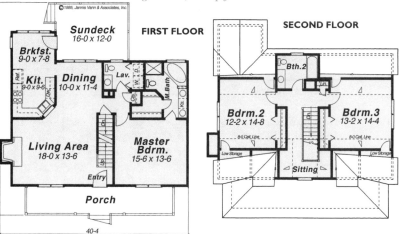

■ *Total living area 1,735 sq. ft.* ■ *Price Code B* ■

© 1985, Jannis Vann & Associates, Inc.

FIRST FLOOR

SECOND FLOOR

Sundeck 16-0 x 12-0
Brkfst. 9-0 x 7-8
Kit. 9-0 x 9-6
Dining 10-0 x 11-4
Lav.
M.Bath
Living Area 18-0 x 13-6
Master Bdrm. 15-6 x 13-6
Entry
Porch
44-0
40-4

Bth.2
Bdrm.2 12-2 x 14-8
Bdrm.3 13-2 x 14-4
Low Storage
Sitting

Compact Victorian

No. 90406

This plan features:

— Three bedrooms

— Three full baths

■ The large front Parlor has a raised hearth fireplace

■ The Dining Room has a sunny bay window

■ The efficient galley Kitchen easily serves the formal Dining Room and informal Breakfast Room

■ The beautiful Master Suite has two closets, an oversized tub and double vanity, plus a private Sitting Room with a bay window and vaulted ceiling

■ This home is designed with basement, slab and crawlspace foundation options.

First floor — 954 sq. ft.

Second floor — 783 sq. ft.

■ *Total living area 1,737 sq. ft.* ■ *Price Code B* ■

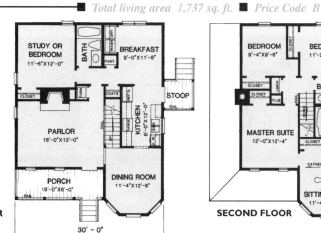

STUDY OR BEDROOM 11'-6"X12'-0"
BATH
BREAKFAST 9'-0"X11'-8"
STOOP
PARLOR 18'-0"X13'-0"
KITCHEN 8'-0"X12'-0"
PORCH 18'-0"X6'-0"
DINING ROOM 11'-4"X12'-8"
FIRST FLOOR
30'-0"

BEDROOM 9'-4"X9'-6"
BEDROOM 11'-2"X9'-6"
BATH
MASTER SUITE 12'-0"X12'-4"
BATH
CATHEDRAL CEILING CEILING FAN
SITTING ROOM 11'-4"X12'-4"
SECOND FLOOR
37'-6"

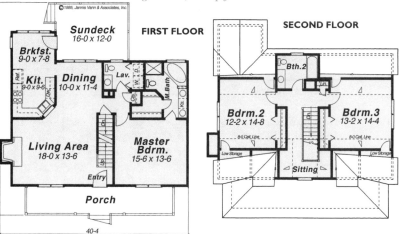

Secluded Master Suite

This plan features:

— Three bedrooms

— Two full and one half baths

■ An arched Porch shelters the Entry into an open Foyer with a cascading staircase

■ The Great Room is highlighted by a vaulted ceiling, sunburst window and hearth fireplace

■ Columns frame the entrance to the formal Dining Room with decorative ceiling

■ The efficient Kitchen has a Breakfast bar, and Screened Porch access and nearby Utility/Garage entry

■ The Master Bedroom offers an angled ceiling, private Deck, a large walk-in closet and plush Bath

■ Two additional Bedrooms have ample closets and share a full Bath

■ This home is designed with basement, slab and crawlspace foundation options.

First floor —900 sq. ft.
Second floor — 841 sq. ft.
Basement— 891 sq. ft.
Garage — 609 sq. ft.

Total living area 1,741 sq. ft. ■ **Price Code B**

SLAB/CRAWLSPACE OPTION

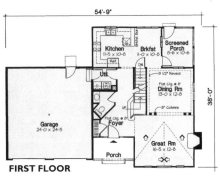

FIRST FLOOR

SECOND FLOOR

Triple Arched Porch

This plan features:

— Four bedrooms

— Three full baths

■ This home features a triple arched front Porch, segmented arched window keystones and shutters

■ The impressive two-story Foyer adjoins the elegant Dining Room

■ The Family Room, Breakfast Room and Kitchen have an open layout

■ The Study/Bedroom has a vaulted ceiling and is located close to a full Bath

■ The Master Suite is topped by a tray ceiling, while there is a vaulted ceiling over the luxurious Bath

■ This home is designed with basement and crawlspace foundation options.

First floor — 972 sq. ft.
Second floor — 772 sq. ft.
Bonus — 358 sq. ft.
Basement — 972 sq. ft.
Garage — 520 sq. ft.

Total living area 1,744 sq. ft. ■ **Price Code B**

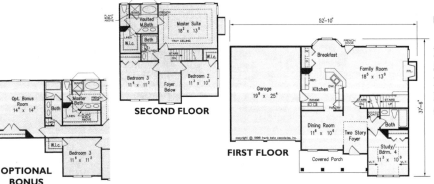

SECOND FLOOR

FIRST FLOOR

OPTIONAL BONUS ROOM

Elegant Front Porch

No. 98462

■ This plan features:

— Three bedrooms

— Two full and one half baths

■ The two-story Foyer opens to the Dining Room, Living Room and Family Room

■ The Kitchen opens to the Breakfast Area and the Breakfast Area is open to the Family Room

■ The Family Room is enhanced by a fireplace

■ The work island adds counter space to the Kitchen

■ The Master Suite with a private Bath is topped by a vaulted ceiling

■ The front secondary Bedroom is highlighted by a window seat

■ This home is designed with basement, slab and crawlspace foundation options.

First floor — 926 sq. ft.
Second floor — 824 sq. ft.
Bonus — 282 sq. ft.
Basement — 926 sq. ft.
Garage — 440 sq. ft.

■ Total living area 1,750 sq. ft. ■ Price Code B ■

FIRST FLOOR

SECOND FLOOR

OPTIONAL BONUS ROOM

Charming, Compact

No. 94803

■ This plan features:

— Three bedrooms

— Two full and one half baths

■ Double dormers, an arched window and the covered Porch add light and space

■ The open Foyer is graced by a banister staircase and balcony

■ The spacious Activity Room with a pre-fab fireplace opens to formal Dining Room

■ The Country-size Kitchen/Breakfast Area has an island counter and access to the Deck and Laundry/Garage entry

■ The first floor Bedroom is highlighted by a lovely arched window below a tray ceiling and includes a plush Bath

■ Two upstairs Bedrooms share a twin vanity Bath

■ This home is designed with basement and crawlspace foundation options.

First floor — 1,165 sq. ft.
Second floor — 587 sq. ft.
Basement — 1,165 sq. ft.
Garage — 455 sq. ft.

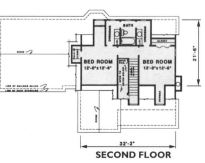

■ Total living area 1,752 sq. ft. ■ Price Code C ■

FIRST FLOOR

SECOND FLOOR

Attractive Styling

■ Total living area 1,753 sq. ft. ■ Price Code C ■

No. 98338

■ **This plan features:**

— Three bedrooms

— Two full and one half baths

■ Columns highlight the sheltered entrance

■ The Living Room is crowned in a vaulted ceiling and flows effortlessly into the Dining Room

■ The Kitchen/Breakfast Room is highlighted by a work island, large bay window and has access to the rear Deck

■ A fireplace accents the Family Room with a cozy atmosphere

■ The Master Suite is topped by a vaulted ceiling and enhanced by a bay window, a private Bath and a walk-in closet

■ Two secondary Bedrooms share a full Bath

■ This home is designed with a basement foundation.

Main floor — 945 sq. ft.
Upper floor — 808 sq. ft.
Basement — 945 sq. ft.

UPPER FLOOR

Expandable Home

■ Total living area 1,757 sq. ft. ■ Price Code C ■

No. 34077

■ **This plan features:**

— Four bedrooms

— Three full baths

■ The front Entry is open to the Living Room which is highlighted by a double window

■ The bright Dining Area opens to the optional Patio with a sliding glass door

■ The compact, efficient Kitchen has a peninsula serving/snack bar, Laundry closet and outdoor access

■ Two first floor Bedrooms have ample closet space and share a full Bath

■ The second floor Master Bedroom and an additional Bedroom feature dormer windows, private Baths and walk-in closets

■ This home is designed with basement, slab and crawlspace foundation options.

First floor — 957 sq. ft.
Second floor — 800 sq. ft.

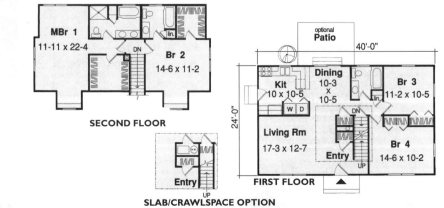

Farm Style Traditional

No. 34901

This plan features:

- Three bedrooms
- Two full and one half baths
- The Dining Room has a bay window and elevated ceiling
- The Living Room is complete with a gas fireplace
- The two-car Garage is also featured
- Ample storage space is found throughout the home
- This home is designed with basement, slab and crawlspace foundation options.

First floor — 909 sq. ft
Second floor — 854 sq. ft.
Basement — 899 sq. ft.
Garage — 491 sq. ft.

■ *Total living area 1,763 sq. ft.* ■ *Price Code C* ■

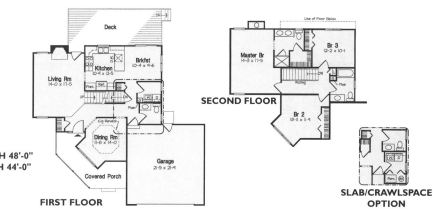

WIDTH 48'-0"
DEPTH 44'-0"

FIRST FLOOR

SECOND FLOOR

SLAB/CRAWLSPACE OPTION

Year-Round Living

No. 94204

This plan features:

- Three bedrooms
- Two full baths
- The "piling" design features the Garage and Storage/Bonus Area below the Living Area for coastal, waterfront or low-lying terrain
- The Entry Porch opens into the expansive Great Room with a hearth fireplace, a vaulted ceiling and double doors to the Deck
- The inviting Dining Area has a vaulted ceiling and double doors leading to the screened Veranda and Deck
- The efficient Kitchen has a peninsula counter and adjacent Laundry closet
- The airy Master Suite has a walk-in closet, double vanity and direct access to the outdoors
- Another Bedroom and the Bedroom/Loft Area on the second floor share a full Bath
- This home is designed with a pier/post foundation.

First floor — 1,189 sq. ft.
Second floor — 575 sq. ft.
Bonus — 581 Sq. ft.
Garage — 658 sq. ft.

■ *Total living area 1,764 sq. ft.* ■ *Price Code C* ■

FIRST FLOOR

SECOND FLOOR

GARAGE

Touch of Victorian Styling

Total living area 1,764 sq. ft. ■ Price Code C

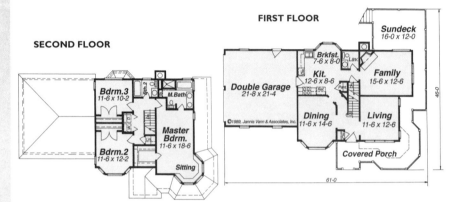

SECOND FLOOR

Bdrm.3
11-6 x 10-2

M.Bath

Master
Bdrm.
11-6 x 18-6

Bdrm.2
11-6 x 12-2

Sitting

FIRST FLOOR

Sundeck
16-0 x 12-0

Brkfst.
7-6 x 8-0

Lav.

Kit.
12-6 x 8-6

Family
15-6 x 12-6

Double Garage
21-8 x 21-4

©1989, Jannis Vann & Associates, Inc.

Dining
11-6 x 14-6

Living
11-6 x 12-6

Covered Porch

46-0

61-0

No. 93230

■ This plan features:

— Three bedrooms

— Two full and one half baths

■ The covered Porch and a pointed roof on the Sitting Alcove of the Master Suite give this home a Victorian look

■ The formal Living Room is directly across from the Dining Room for ease in entertaining

■ The efficient Kitchen has a bright bay window in the Breakfast Area

■ The Family Room has a cozy fireplace nestled in a corner

■ The large Master Suite has a Sitting Alcove and double vanity Bath

■ Two additional Bedrooms are serviced by a full Bath

■ This home is designed with a basement foundation.

First floor — 887 sq. ft.
Second floor — 877 sq. ft.
Basement — 859 sq. ft.
Garage — 484 sq. ft.

Convenient Country

Total living area 1,767 sq. ft. ■ Price Code C

WIDTH 67'-0"
DEPTH 30'-0"

2 CAR GARAGE
21'2" x 22'2"

PANTRY

PR

REF

DW

DINING
ROOM
8'1" x 11'4"

WIC
6'2" x 7'2"

MASTER
BATH
9'10" x 10'4"

KITCHEN
8'11" x 11'4"

HALL

RANGE

CL

CL

LAUNDRY
7'6" x 7'6"

DN

UP

MASTER
BEDROOM
13'2" x 13'8"

LIVING ROOM
13'2" x 20'2"

FIREPLACE

PORCH

FIRST FLOOR

BATH
7'4" x 8'2"

HALL

DN

BEDROOM 2
12'0" x 18'6"

BEDROOM 1
11'2" x 18'6"

KNEEWALL

KNEEWALL

SECOND FLOOR

No. 99045

■ This plan features:

— Three bedrooms

— Two full and one half baths

■ The full front Porch provides comfortable visiting and a sheltered entrance

■ The expansive Living Room with an inviting fireplace opens to the bright Dining Room and Kitchen

■ The U-shaped Kitchen has a peninsula serving counter to the Dining Room and nearby Pantry, Laundry and Garage entry

■ The secluded Master Bedroom has two closets and a double vanity Bath

■ This home is designed with a basement foundation.

First floor — 1,108 sq. ft.
Second floor — 659 sq. ft.
Basement — 875 sq. ft.

Farmhouse Flavor

■ *Total living area 1,770 sq. ft.* ■ *Price Code C* ■

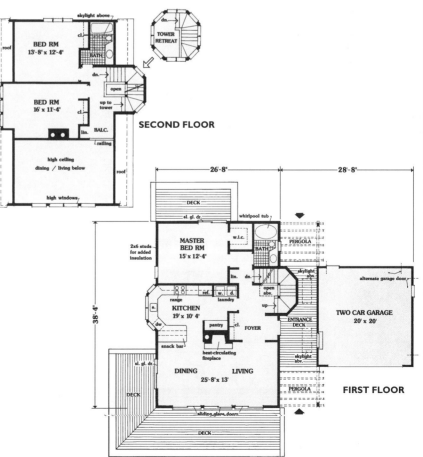

No. 90685

■ This plan features:

— Three bedrooms

— Two full baths

■ An unusual octagonal stair tower is featured

■ The Foyer opens to the Living and Dining Room combination, enhanced by a striking glass wall

■ A heat-circulating fireplace adds welcome warmth

■ The galley-style Kitchen includes a large Pantry, snack bar and Laundry Area

■ The Master Suite has a private Deck overlooking the backyard

■ This home is designed with basement and slab foundation options.

First floor — 1,073 sq. ft.
Second floor — 604 sq. ft.
Retreat tower — 93 sq. ft.
Garage — 428 sq. ft.

Southern Hospitality

■ *Total living area 1,771 sq. ft.* ■ *Price Code C* ■

FIRST FLOOR

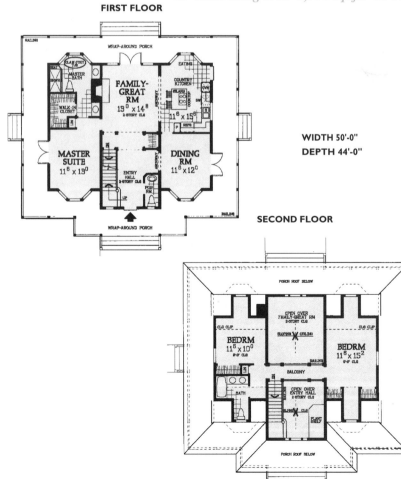

WIDTH 50'-0"
DEPTH 44'-0"

SECOND FLOOR

No. 99285

■ This plan features:

— Three bedrooms

— Two full and one half baths

■ The inviting atmosphere is enhanced by the Porch surrounding and shading the home

■ The two-story Entry Hall is graced by a landing staircase and arched window

■ The Country Kitchen has a cooktop island/snack bar, Eating Alcove and archway to the Family Room with cozy fireplace

■ The first floor Master Suite has a bay window, walk-in closet and plush Bath

■ This home is designed with a basement foundation.

First floor — 1171 sq. ft.
Second floor — 600 sq. ft.
Foundation — Basement only

■ *Total living area 1,785 sq. ft.* ■ *Price Code C* ■

No. 24610

■ **This plan features:**

— Three bedrooms

— Two full and one three-quarter and one half baths

■ The Great Room has a focal point fireplace and a two-story ceiling

■ The efficient Kitchen has an island, double sink, built-in Pantry and ample storage and counter space

■ The Laundry Room is located conveniently on the first floor

■ The Master Suite has a private Master Bath and a walk-in closet

■ This home is designed with basement, slab and crawlspace foundation options.

First floor — 891 sq. ft.
Second floor — 894 sq. ft.
Basement — 891 sq. ft.
Garage — 534 sq. ft.

WIDTH 46'-8"
DEPTH 35'-8"

Dining 12-1 x 11-4

Kitchen 13 x 11-4

pantry

Great Rm 14 x 21-8

open to above

Garage 22 x 23-4

DN

UP

FIRST FLOOR

Br 2 11-6 x 11-4

linen

Br 3 11 x 11-4

DN

railing

open to below

1/2 wall

Mstr Br 13-4 x 15

SECOND FLOOR

Classic Style and Comfort

Total living area 1,792 sq. ft. ■ **Price Code** C ■

No. 94105

This plan features:

— Three bedrooms

— Two full and one half baths

■ The covered Entry into the two-story Foyer has a dramatic landing staircase brightened by a decorative window

■ The spacious Living/Dining Room combination has a hearth fireplace and decorative windows

■ The hub Kitchen has a built-in Pantry and informal Dining Area with sliding glass door to rear yard

■ The first floor Master Bedroom offers a walk-in closet, Dressing Area and full Bath

■ Two additional Bedrooms on second floor share a full Bath

■ This home is designed with a basement foundation.

First floor — 1,281 sq. ft.
Second floor — 511 sq. ft.
Garage — 481 sq. ft.

FIRST FLOOR

SECOND FLOOR

WIDTH 58'-0"
DEPTH 44'-0"

Compact Dream House

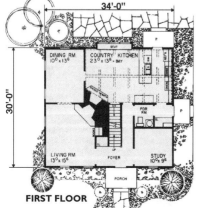

Total living area 1,797 sq. ft. ■ **Price Code** C ■

No. 90245

This plan features:

— Three bedrooms

— Two full and one half baths

■ The central Entry is flanked by a cozy Study and sunny formal Living Room

■ Two fireplaces help with heating bills

■ The Kitchen features a triple window with built-in seating and a beamed ceiling

■ This home is designed with a basement foundation.

First floor — 1,020 sq. ft.
Second floor — 777 sq. ft.

FIRST FLOOR

SECOND FLOOR

■ *Total living area 1,808 sq. ft.* ■ *Price Code C* ■

No. 93413

■ **This plan features:**

— Three bedrooms

— Two full and one half baths

■ The Family Room is highlighted by two front windows and a fireplace

■ The Kitchen includes an angled extended counter/snack bar and an abundance of counter/cabinet space

■ The roomy Master Suite is located on the first floor and has a private five-piece Bath plus a walk-in closet

■ The Laundry Room doubles as a Mud Room from the side entrance

■ This home is designed with a basement foundation.

First floor — 1,271 sq. ft.
Second floor — 537 sq. ft.
Basement — 1,271 sq. ft.
Garage — 555 sq. ft.

FIRST FLOOR

SECOND FLOOR

Plenty of Leisure Living Space

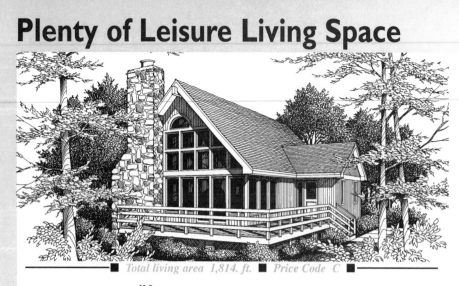

■ *Total living area 1,814. ft.* ■ *Price Code C* ■

FIRST FLOOR

- 41-5
- 42-3

B. R. 11 x 12
M. B. R. 12-2 x 12
GEAR EQUIP'T
LAUN.
K. 12-7 x 7-6
counter table
cathedral ceiling
L. R. 25-6 x 16
D. R.
DECK

B. R./STUDIO 14-10 x 12
skylight
railing
BALC.
upper part of dining/living room

SECOND FLOOR

No. 99645

■ **This plan features:**

— Three bedrooms

— Three full baths

■ The wrap-around Deck expands outdoor living space and provides multiple access to Living/Dining Room

■ The impressive fieldstone fireplace with log holder warms the Living/Dining Room below cathedral ceiling

■ The efficient L-shaped Kitchen has a built-in counter table and the Laundry Area with built-in Pantry

■ The Master Bedroom has double windows and a plush, double vanity Bath

■ The second Bedroom on the first floor and another Bedroom on the second floor each have access to full Baths

■ This plan features a side entrance into a Vestibule with Gear Equipment Area and a Foyer with two closets

■ This home is designed with basement and slab foundation options.

First floor — 1,361 sq. ft.
Loft floor — 453 sq. ft.
Basement — 694 sq. ft.

Easy Street

■ *Total living area 1,815 sq. ft.* ■ *Price Code C* ■

BOOKCASE W/ PLANT SHELF ABOVE
Vaulted Family Room 17' x 12⁹
Breakfast
FRENCH DOOR
RANGE
Kitchen
REF
DW
PANTRY
BOOKCASE W/ PLANT SHELF ABOVE
FPL.
Pwdr.
Laundry
COATS
Storage
Dining Room 12³ x 10⁰
ARCHED OPENING
Garage 19⁵ x 20²
Two Story Foyer
Living Room 12⁵ x 10⁴
45' - 0"
40' - 0"

FIRST FLOOR

Vaulted Family Room Below
VAULT
Vaulted M. Bath
TRAY CLG
Master Suite 15⁰ x 12⁰
FRENCH DOOR
PLANT SHELF ABOVE
W.I.C.
LINEN
OVERLOOK
Opt. Bonus/ Bedroom 4 14¹ x 26⁵
STAIRS
OPEN RAIL
OVERLOOK
Bedroom 3 10³ x 10⁰
Bath
Foyer Below
OPEN RAIL
LINEN
Bedroom 2 10³ x 10⁴

SECOND FLOOR

No. 97280

■ **This plan features:**

— Three bedrooms

— Two full and one half baths

■ The two-story Foyer is a grand introduction to this home

■ The Living Room and the Dining Room connect through an arched opening

■ The Kitchen opens to the Breakfast Room and accesses the Dining Room

■ The Family Room offers a vaulted ceiling, a fireplace with built-in bookcases and a plant shelf

■ The Master Suite includes a tray ceiling and a French door into the Master Bathroom

■ This home is designed with basement and crawlspace foundation options.

First floor — 1,073 sq. ft.
Second floor — 742 sq. ft.
Bonus — 336 sq. ft.
Basement — 1,073 sq. ft.
Garage — 495 sq. ft.

copyright © 1994 frank betz associates, inc.

Plenty of Special Touches

■ *Total living area 1,829 sq. ft.* ■ *Price Code C* ■

No. 93423

■ This plan features:

— Three bedrooms

— Two full and one half baths

■ The Breakfast Area, Kitchen and Laundry Room are tiled

■ The Family Room enjoys a fireplace and a view of the split staircase

■ The spacious rear Deck enhances time spent outdoors

■ The first floor Master Suite offers a large walk-in closet and a plush Bathroom

■ This home is designed with a basement foundation.

First floor — 1,339 sq. ft.
Second floor — 490 sq. ft.
Bonus — 145 sq. ft.
Garage — 491 sq. ft.

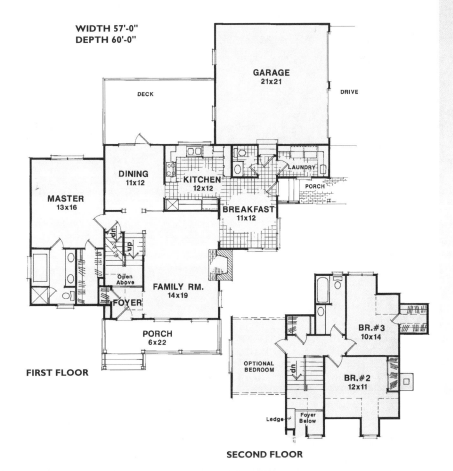

WIDTH 57'-0"
DEPTH 60'-0"

GARAGE 21x21

DECK

DRIVE

DINING 11x12

KITCHEN 12x12

LAUNDRY

PORCH

MASTER 13x16

BREAKFAST 11x12

Open Above

Up

FAMILY RM. 14x19

FOYER

PORCH 6x22

FIRST FLOOR

OPTIONAL BEDROOM

BR.#3 10x14

BR.#2 12x11

Ledge

Foyer Below

SECOND FLOOR

Porch Awaits a Comfy Chair

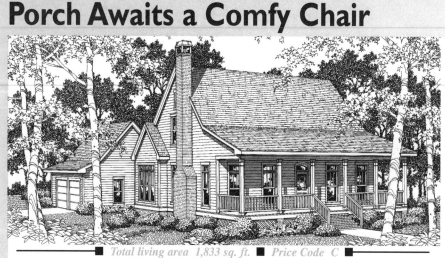

Total living area 1,833 sq. ft. ■ *Price Code C*

WIDTH 50'-8"
DEPTH 74'-0"

FIRST FLOOR

SECOND FLOOR

No. 93432

■ **This plan features:**

— Three bedrooms

— Two full and one half baths

■ The Country-style front Porch provides a warm welcome

■ The Family Room is highlighted by a fireplace and front windows

■ The Dining Room is separated from the U-shaped Kitchen by an extended counter

■ The first floor Master Suite has a walk-in closet and a five-piece Bath

■ There are two additional Bedrooms with a convenient Bath in the hall

■ This home is designed with slab and crawl-space foundation options.

First floor — 1,288 sq. ft.
Second floor — 545 sq. ft.
Garage — 540 sq. ft.

Dramatic Roof Lines

Total living area 1,834 sq. ft. ■ *Price Code C*

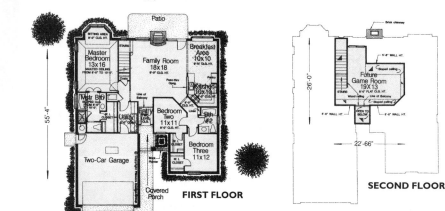

FIRST FLOOR

SECOND FLOOR

No. 98564

■ **This plan features:**

— Three bedrooms

— Two full baths

■ Privacy is key in the Master Bedroom, which boasts a decorative tray ceiling and a bay Sitting Area overlooking the rear yard

■ The Family Room is expansive and includes a fireplace and Patio access

■ The upstairs Game Room is ideal for setting up computer games, and spacious enough for a pool table

■ The Kitchen with ample counter space opens to the Breakfast Nook, where a tile floor makes upkeep easy

■ This home is designed with slab and crawl-space foundation options.

Lower floor — 1,552 sq. ft.
Upper floor — 282 sq. ft.
Garage — 422 sq. ft.

Secluded Vacation Retreat

No. 91704

■ **This plan features:**

— Two bedrooms

— One full and two three-quarter baths

■ The high vaulted ceiling in the Living Area has a large masonry fireplace and circular stairway, and high vaulted ceiling

■ A wall of windows is located along the full cathedral height of the Living Area

■ The Kitchen has ample storage and counter space, and includes a sink, a chopping block, and a work island

■ Each of the Bedrooms have a private full Bath and large closets

■ The Loft has French doors opening to a Deck

■ This home is designed with a crawlspace foundation.

First floor — 1,448 sq. ft.
Second floor — 389 sq. ft.
Carport — 312 sq. ft.

■ *Total living area 1,837 sq. ft.* ■ *Price Code C* ■

FIRST FLOOR

SECOND FLOOR

Stylish Stucco

No. 93218

■ **This plan features:**

— Three bedrooms

— Two full and one half baths

■ The expansive Living Area, which dominates the first floor, includes a massive fireplace surrounded by built-in shelving

■ The Dining Room is bathed in light from a bump-out window, and has access to the Deck

■ The angled countertop in the Kitchen includes a handy pass-through to the Living Area

■ Privacy is assured in the large Master Bedroom, which includes a full wall of windows and an opulent Bath

■ This home is designed with a basement foundation.

First floor — 850 sq. ft.
Second floor— 901 sq. ft.
Staircase — 88 sq. ft.
Basement — 740 sq. ft.

■ *Total living area 1,839 sq. ft.* ■ *Price Code C* ■

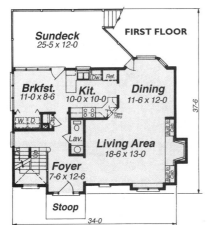

FIRST FLOOR

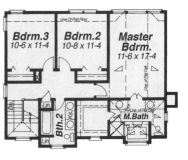

SECOND FLOOR

Appealing Front Porch

■ *Total living area 1,842 sq. ft.* ■ *Price Code C* ■

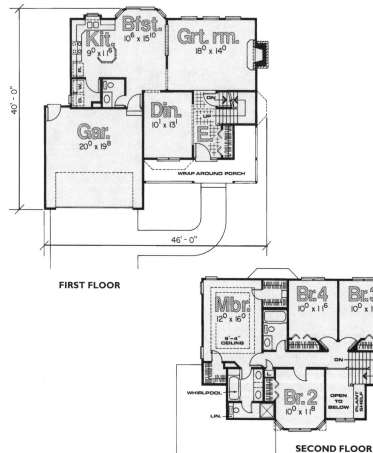

FIRST FLOOR

SECOND FLOOR

© Design Basics, inc.

No. 94935

■ **This plan features:**

— Four bedrooms

— Two full and one half baths

■ The appealing wrap-around Porch graces this home

■ The light and airy two-story Entry is equipped with a side-light, plant shelf and closet

■ The open Kitchen has easy access to the Breakfast Area, the Dining Room and the Garage

■ This home is designed with a basement foundation.

■ Alternate foundation options available at an additional charge. Please call 1-800-235-5700 for more information.

First floor — 919 sq. ft.
Second floor — 923 sq. ft.
Basement — 919 sq. ft.
Garage — 414 sq. ft.

Wrap-Around Porch

■ *Total living area 1,846 sq. ft.* ■ *Price Code C* ■

No. 99491

■ **This plan features:**

— Four bedrooms

— Two full and one half baths

■ The two-story Entry of this home includes a large coat closet and a plant shelf

■ Many windows and a fireplace highlight the Great Room

■ The bright Kitchen features a boxed window over the sink and an adjacent Breakfast Area

■ The volume ceiling and arched window in the front Bedroom add a touch of elegance

■ The large Master Suite has two walk-in closets

■ This home is designed with basement and slab foundation options.

First floor — 919 sq. ft.
Second floor — 927 sq. ft.
Garage — 414 sq. ft.

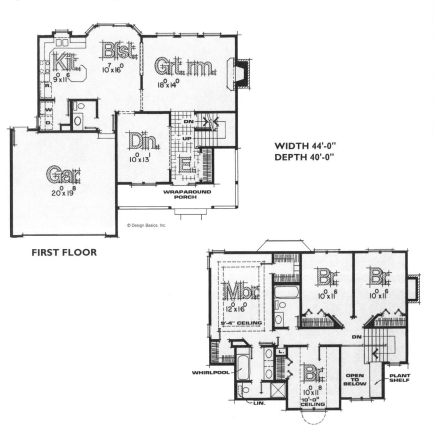

WIDTH 44'-0"
DEPTH 40'-0"

FIRST FLOOR

SECOND FLOOR

Delightful Home

■ *Total living area 1,853 sq. ft.* ■ *Price Code D* ■

FIRST FLOOR

SECOND FLOOR

No. 94248

■ **This plan features:**

— Three bedrooms

— Two full baths

■ The Grand Room has a fireplace, a vaulted ceiling and double French doors to the rear Deck

■ The Kitchen and Dining Room are open to continue the overall feel of spaciousness

■ The Kitchen has a large walk-in Pantry and an island with a sink and dishwasher, creating a perfect triangular workspace

■ The Dining Room with access to both Decks- creates a bright, airy eating experience

■ The Master Bedroom features a double-door entry, a private Bath, and an AM Kitchen

■ This home is designed with a pier/post foundation.

First floor — 1,342 sq. ft.
Second floor — 511 sq. ft.
Garage — 1,740 sq. ft.

Demonstrative Detail

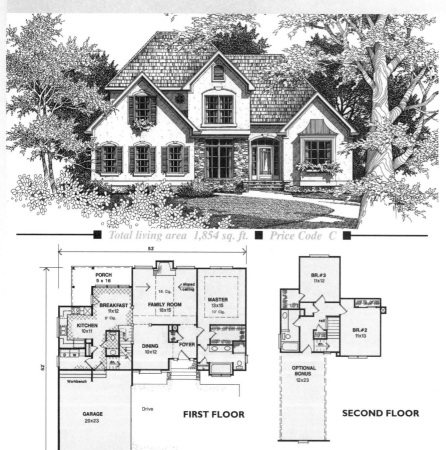

■ *Total living area 1,854 sq. ft.* ■ *Price Code C* ■

FIRST FLOOR

SECOND FLOOR

No. 93410

■ **This plan features:**

— Three bedrooms

— Two full and one half baths

■ Keystone arched windows, stone and stucco combine with shutters and a flower box to create an eye-catching elevation

■ The Foyer accesses the Dining Room, the Family Room and the Master Suite

■ The Family Room has a sloped ceiling and is accented by a fireplace with windows to either side

■ The Kitchen/Breakfast Area has easy access to the rear Porch

■ Two roomy Bedrooms on the second floor share the full Bath

■ An optional Bonus Area over the Garage offers possibilities for future expansion

■ This home is designed with a basement foundation.

First floor — 1,317 sq. ft.
Second floor — 537 sq. ft.
Bonus — 312 sq. ft.
Basement — 1,317 sq. ft.
Garage — 504 sq. ft.

Brick Beauty

No. 97707

This plan features:

– Three bedrooms

– Two full and one half baths

■ The stylish Foyer is complimented by a well-positioned, turned staircase

■ The full-sized Great Room is enhanced by a large fireplace and oversized windows

■ The Laundry Room is conveniently located just steps off the Kitchen and Garage

■ The Formal Dining Room has a stepped ceiling

■ This home is designed with a slab foundation.

First floor — 980 sq. ft.
Second floor — 876 sq. ft.
Bonus — 325 sq. ft.
Basement — 980 sq. ft.
Garage — 577 sq. ft.

WIDTH 50'-6"
DEPTH 38'-0"

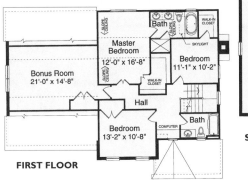

FIRST FLOOR

SECOND FLOOR

■ Total living area 1,856 sq. ft. ■ Price Code C ■

Fieldstone Facade

No. 94911

This plan features:

– Three bedrooms

– Two full and one half baths

■ The inviting covered Porch shelters the entrance

■ The expansive Great Room is enhanced by a warm fireplace and three transom windows

■ The Breakfast Area adjoins the Great Room giving a feeling of more space

■ The efficient Kitchen has a counter snack bar, and nearby is the Laundry and Garage Entry

■ The first floor Master Bedroom has an arched window below a sloped ceiling and a double vanity Bath

■ Two additional Bedrooms share the Bonus Area and the full Bath on the second floor

■ This home is designed with a basement foundation.

■ Alternate foundation options available at an additional charge. Please call 1-800-235-5700 for more information.

First floor — 1,405 sq. ft.
Second floor — 453 sq. ft.
Bonus — 300 sq. ft.
Basement — 1,405 sq. ft.
Garage — 490 sq. ft.

■ Total living area 1,858 sq. ft. ■ Price Code C ■

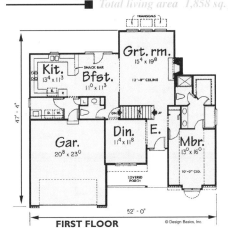

FIRST FLOOR

© Design Basics, Inc.

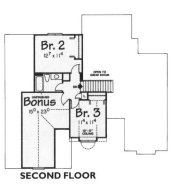

SECOND FLOOR

For the Growing Family

■ *Total living area 1,862 sq. ft.* ■ *Price Code C* ■

No. 98473

■ This plan features:

— Four bedrooms

— Three full baths

■ The formal areas are located to either side of the two-story Foyer

■ There is an open rail staircase in the Living Room, and the Dining Room features easy access to the Kitchen

■ The Kitchen is equipped with a corner double sink, a servicing bar and adjoins the Breakfest Area

■ The Master Suite is enhanced by a tray ceiling and a plush Bath

■ This home is designed with basement and crawlspace foundation options.

First floor — 1,103 sq. ft.
Second floor — 759 sq. ft.
Bonus — 342 sq. ft.
Basement — 1,103 sq. ft.
Garage — 420 sq. ft.

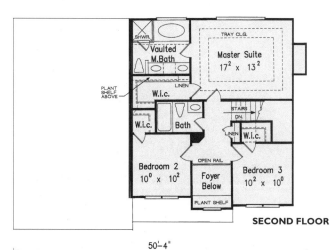

SECOND FLOOR

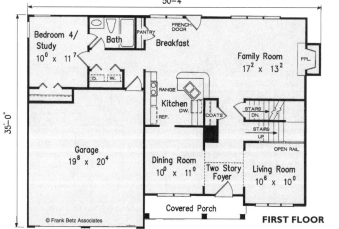

FIRST FLOOR

Family-Sized Accommodations

No. 98454

This plan features:

— Four bedrooms

— Two full and one half baths

■ A spacious feeling is provided by a vaulted ceiling in Foyer and Family Room

■ A fireplace is nestled in an alcove of windows in the Family Room which invites cozy gatherings

■ The Master Bedroom is accented by a tray ceiling, a lavish Bath and a walk-in closet

■ On second floor, three additional Bedrooms share a double vanity Bath and an optional Bonus Room

■ This home is designed with basement and crawlspace foundation options.

First floor — 1,320 sq. ft.
Second floor — 554 sq. ft.
Bonus — 155 sq. ft.
Basement — 1,320 sq. ft.
Garage — 406 sq. ft.

Total living area 1,874 sq. ft. ■ *Price Code C* ■

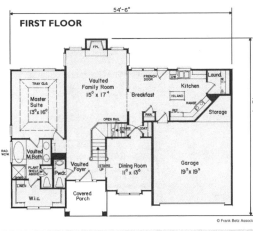

© Frank Betz Associates

Classic Exterior

No. 92674

This plan features:

— Three or four bedrooms

— Two full and one half baths

■ The front Porch leads into the open Foyer and Great Room that is accented by a sloped ceiling, a corner fireplace and multiple windows

■ The efficient Kitchen has a cooktop island, a walk-in Pantry, a bright Dining Area and nearby, a screened Porch, a Laundry and a Garage Entry

■ The deluxe Master Bedroom wing has a decorative ceiling, a large walk-in closet and a plush Bath

■ Two or three Bedrooms on the second floor share a double vanity Bath

■ This home is designed with a basement foundation.

First floor — 1,348 sq. ft.
Second floor — 528 sq. ft.
Bonus — 195 sq. ft.
Basement — 1,300 sq. ft.

Total living area 1,876 sq. ft. ■ *Price Code C* ■

New England Cottage

Photography supplied by The Meredith Corporation

■ **Total living area 1,881 sq. ft.** ■ **Price Code C** ■

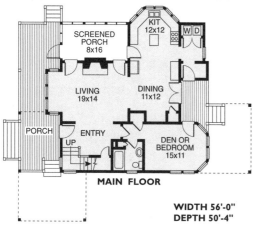

KIT
12x12

W D

SCREENED
PORCH
8x16

LIVING
19x14

DINING
11x12

PORCH

ENTRY

UP

DEN OR
BEDROOM
15x11

MAIN FLOOR

WIDTH 56'-0"
DEPTH 50'-4"

CLOS

MASTER
BEDROOM
19x12

BEDROOM
15x12

DN BATH BATH

OPEN

UPPER FLOOR

No. 32032

■ **This plan features:**

— Three bedrooms

— Three full baths

■ The Porch and the Screened Porch add options for outdoor entertaining

■ The fireplace warms the Living Room

■ The U-shaped Kitchen is open to the Dining Room

■ The full Bath is located next to the Den/Bedroom

■ The Master Bedroom has a private Bath

■ This home is designed with a crawlspace foundation.

Main level — 1,109 sq. ft.
Upper level — 772 sq. ft.

Spacious Country Charm

■ **Total living area 1,887 sq. ft.** ■ **Price Code C** ■

DIN
10'6 x 11'8

GREAT RM
15'8 x 17'

KIT
12'3 x 11'

Entry

DIN RM
11'10 x 12'

Two-Story
FOYER

Lav

Laun

GARAGE
23'4 x 23'4

Covered Entry

FIRST FLOOR

WIDTH 52'-8"
DEPTH 40'-0"

MBATH

MBR
14'8 x 17'

WI Closet

BATH 2

WI Closet

BR3
12' x 11'2

Foyer
Below

BR2
11'2 x 11'2

Balcony

PLANT SHELF

SECOND FLOOR

No. 94107

■ **This plan features:**

— Three bedrooms

— Two full and one half baths

■ The comfortable front Porch leads into the bright, two-story Foyer

■ Pillars frame the entrance to the formal Dining Room which is highlighted by a bay window

■ The expansive Great Room is accented by a hearth fireplace and a triple window opens to Kitchen/Dining Area

■ The efficient Kitchen has loads of counter and storage space the Dining Area has access to the rear yard

■ The corner Master Bedroom offers a triple window and a luxurious Master Bath

■ Two additional Bedrooms with ample closets share a full Bath

■ This home is designed with a basement foundation.

First floor — 961 sq. ft.
Second floor — 926 sq. ft.
Basement — 928 sq. ft.
Garage — 548 sq. ft.

Distinctive Detail and Design

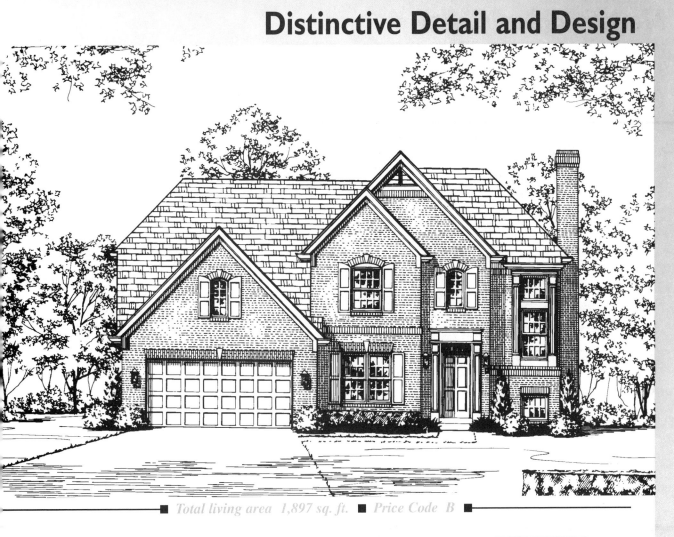

■ *Total living area 1,897 sq. ft.* ■ *Price Code B* ■

No. 92644

■ **This plan features:**

— Three bedrooms

— Two full and one half baths

■ An impressive pilaster entry opens into the Foyer with a landing staircase highlighted by decorative windows

■ The Great Room is accented by a hearth fireplace and French doors with an arched window above

■ The formal Dining Room is enhanced by a furniture alcove and a decorative window

■ This home is designed with a basement foundation.

First floor — 1,036 sq. ft.
Second floor — 861 sq. ft.
Garage — 420 sq. ft.

Distinguished Look

Total living area 1,906 sq. ft. ■ Price Code C

WIDTH 55'-4"
DEPTH 33'-0"

FIRST FLOOR

Storage · Pdr. · Breakfast · NICHE · FRENCH DOOR · Laund. · PANTRY · SERVING BAR · Family Room 19² x 13⁵ · FPL. · RANGE · DW. · STAIRS UP · Kitchen · REF. · COATS · STAIRS DN. · Garage · Dining Room 12⁰ x 11⁰ · Two Story Foyer · Living Room 12⁰ x 11⁰

© Frank Betz Associates

SECOND FLOOR

TRAPAZOID GLASS ABOVE · Vaulted M. Bath · W.i.c · LINEN · TRAY CLG. · Master Suite 17⁴ x 13⁵ · PLANT SHELF ABOVE · Bath · NICHE · STAIRS DN. · Opt. Bonus Room 16⁵ x 14⁰ · LINEN · OVERLOOK · Bedroom 2 12⁰ x 11⁰ · Foyer Below · Bedroom 3 12⁰ x 11⁰

No. 98429

■ **This plan features:**

— Three bedrooms

— Two full and one half baths

■ The Family Room, the Breakfast Room and the Kitchen are presented in an open lay-out

■ The fireplace in the Family Room provides a warm atmosphere

■ The plush Master Suite pampers the owner and features a trapezoid glass above the tub

■ Two additional Bedrooms share the use of the double vanity Bath in the hall

■ This home is designed with basement, slab and crawlspace foundation options.

First floor — 1,028 sq. ft.
Second floor — 878 sq. ft.
Bonus — 315 sq. ft.
Basement — 1,028 sq. ft.
Garage — 497 sq. ft.

Home on a Hill

Total living area 1,908 sq. ft. ■ Price Code C

No. 20501

■ **This plan features:**

— Three bedrooms

— Two full baths

■ Window walls combine with sliders to unite active areas with a huge Deck

■ Interior spaces flow together for an open feeling that is accentuated by the sloping ceilings and a towering fireplace in the Living Room

■ The Kitchen has an island counter and easy access to the Dining Room

■ The Master Suite is complete with a garden Spa, abundant closet space, and a balcony

■ This home is designed with a basement, pier/post and basement/crawlspace foundation options.

First floor — 1,316 sq. ft.
Second floor — 592 sq. ft.

FIRST FLOOR

39'-0"

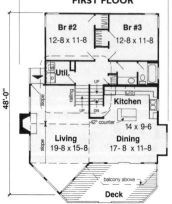

48'-0"

Br #2 12-8 x 11-8 · Br #3 12-8 x 11-8 · Util. · UP · railing · slope · Kitchen 14 x 9-6 · UP · DN · 42" counter · Living 19-8 x 15-8 · Dining 17-8 x 11-8 · slope · balcony above

Deck

SECOND FLOOR

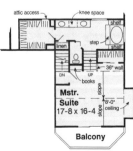

attic access · knee space · shelf · linen · step · shelf · DN · books · UP · 36" wall · Mstr. Suite 17-8 x 16-4 · 8'-0" ceiling · slope

Balcony

PIER/CRAWLSPACE OPTION

Util. · furn. · UP · w.h. · UP

Beautiful Stucco & Stone

No. 98445

This plan features:

- Three bedrooms
- Two full and one half baths
- The two-story Foyer includes a half Bath
- The vaulted Family Room is highlighted by a fireplace
- The Dining Room adjoins the Family Room
- The Master Bedroom is crowned by a tray ceiling, while the Master Bath has a vaulted ceiling
- The balcony overlooks the Family Room and Foyer
- This home is designed with crawlspace and basement foundation options.

First floor — 1,398 sq. ft.
Second floor — 515 sq. ft.
Bonus — 282 sq. ft.
Basement — 1,398 sq. ft.
Garage — 421 sq. ft.

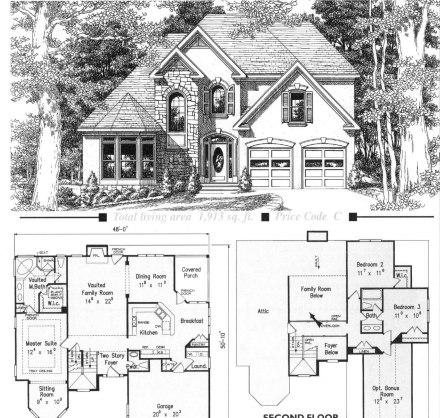

Total living area 1,913 sq. ft. ■ Price Code C

FIRST FLOOR

SECOND FLOOR

© Frank Betz Associates

Outdoor Circular Stair

No. 65012

This plan features:

- Four bedrooms
- Two full and one half baths
- The spacious kitchen offers ample cabinet space and has a built-in desk
- A turreted, two-story plant area has spiral stair access into the basement
- This home is designed with a basement foundation.

First floor — 1,293 sq. ft.
Second floor — 629 sq. ft.
Basement — 1,293 sq. ft.
Garage — 606 sq. ft.

Rear Elevation

Total living area 1,922 sq. ft. ■ Price Code C

Front Elevation

58'-0" WIDE
55'-0" DEEP

FIRST FLOOR

SECOND FLOOR

First Floor Master Suite

■ Total living area 1,926 sq. ft. ■ Price Code C ■

FIRST FLOOR

- Great Rm 14x18-6 vaulted
- Kit 11x12
- Brkfst 11x10 vaulted
- Deck
- Pantry
- Desk
- Dining 11-6x12-3
- Mas. Suite 13x16 vaulted
- Garage 20x20
- 55'-8"
- 45'-0"

SECOND FLOOR

- Br 2 11-8x11
- open to below
- Br 3 11-8x10-4

No. 98357

■ **This plan features:**

— Three bedrooms

— Two full and one half baths

■ The front Porch and dormer add to the Country appeal of this home

■ The elegant Dining Room is topped by a decorative ceiling

■ The Kitchen/Breakfast Room includes a cooktop island, a double corner sink, a walk-in Pantry, a built-in desk and a vaulted ceiling

■ The Great Room is accented by a vaulted ceiling and a fireplace

■ A double door entrance, a box window, a vaulted ceiling and a plush Bath are all features of the Master Suite

■ Two additional Bedrooms share use of the full Bath in the hall

■ This home is designed with a basement foundation.

First floor — 1,490 sq. ft.
Second floor — 436 sq. ft.
Basement — 1,490 sq. ft.
Garage — 400 sq. ft.

Front Porch Speaks of Yesteryear

No. 93290

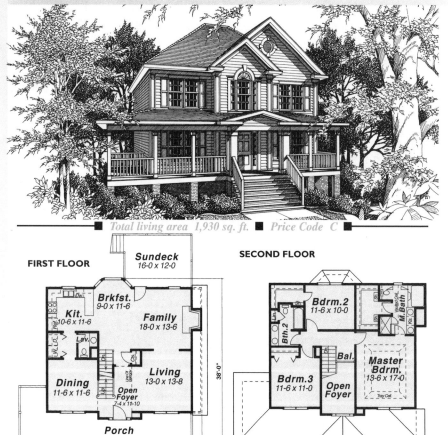

■ Total living area 1,930 sq. ft. ■ Price Code C ■

FIRST FLOOR

- Sundeck 16-0 x 12-0
- Brkfst. 9-0 x 11-6
- Kit. 10-6 x 11-6
- Family 18-0 x 13-6
- Lav.
- Dining 11-6 x 11-6
- Living 13-0 x 13-8
- Open Foyer 7-4 x 11-10
- Porch
- 38'-0"
- 42'-4"

SECOND FLOOR

- Bdrm.2 11-6 x 10-0
- Bth.2
- M.Bath
- Bal.
- Bdrm.3 11-6 x 11-0
- Open Foyer
- Master Bdrm. 13-6 x 17-0
- Tray Ceil.

■ **This plan features:**

— Three bedrooms

— Two full and one half baths

■ A couple of comfy rocking chairs and some hanging plants will compliment this charming front Porch

■ The open Foyer is flanked by the formal Living and Dining Rooms

■ The bay window Breakfast Nook overlooks the rear yard and the spacious Deck

■ Luxury in the Master Bedroom is attained with a decorative tray ceiling, an oversized walk-in closet and the well-appointed Bath

■ Secondary Bedrooms include generous closet space and share a full Bath

■ This home is designed with a basement foundation.

First floor — 981 sq. ft.
Second floor — 899 sq. ft.
Staircase — 50 sq. ft.
Basement — 425 sq. ft.
Garage — 558 sq. ft.

126

Curves and Angles Add Interest

No. 94902

This plan features:

– Four bedrooms

– Two full and one half baths

– A covered Porch shelters and welcomes visitors

– The tiled Entry provides access to all rooms on the first floor

– Transom windows, a ten-foot ceiling and a hearth fireplace are featured in the Great Room

– A snack bar and built-in Pantry are just two of the conveniences found in the Kitchen

– Topped by a decorative ceiling, the Master Suite features two walk-in closets and a Bath will all the amenities

– Three secondary bedrooms share a full Bath and linen closet

– This home is designed with a basement foundation.

– Alternate foundation options available at an additional charge. Please call 1-800-235-5700 for more information.

First floor — 944 sq. ft.
Second floor — 987 sq. ft.
Basement — 944 sq. ft.
Garage — 557 sq. ft.

Total living area 1,931 sq. ft. ■ *Price Code C*

FIRST FLOOR

SECOND FLOOR

Spectacular Sophistication

No. 94944

This plan features:

– Four bedrooms

– Two full and one half baths

■ The open Foyer with a circular window and a plant shelf leads into the Dining Room

■ The Great Room has an inviting fireplace and windows front and back

■ The open Kitchen has a work island and accesses the Breakfast Area

■ The Master Bedroom features a nine-foot boxed ceiling, a walk-in closet and a whirlpool Bath

■ Three additional Bedrooms share a full Bath with a double vanity

■ This home is designed with basement and slab foundation options

■ Alternate foundation options available at an additional charge. Please call 1-800-235-5700 for more information.

First floor — 941 sq. ft.
Second floor — 992 sq. ft.
Basement — 941 sq. ft.
Garage — 480 sq. ft.

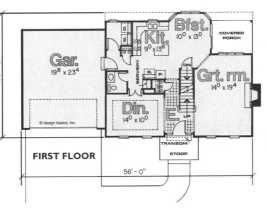

Total living area 1,933 sq. ft. ■ *Price Code C*

FIRST FLOOR

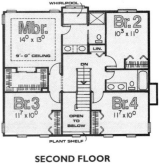

SECOND FLOOR

Standing Tall

Total living area 1,944 sq. ft. ■ Price Code A ■

No. 65024

■ This plan features:

— Four bedrooms

— Two baths

■ This open floor plan offers plenty of versatility

■ The Kitchen features a snack bar, corner sink and access to a larger Dining Area

■ The first floor includes two Bedrooms with large closets and access to a full Bath

■ Access to the outside is plentiful, with doors in the Living Room, Sunroom and Kitchen, as well as a side entrance that also includes a coat closet

First floor — 972 sq. ft.
Second floor — 972 sq. ft.

FIRST FLOOR

10,2 m
54'-0"

9,6 m
32'-0"

3,30 X 3,70
11'-0" X 12'-4"

2,70 X 2,80
9'-0" X 9'-4"

3,30 X 6,90
11'-0" X 23'-0"

3,30 X 2,80
11'-0" X 9'-4"

SECOND FLOOR

The Ultimate Kitchen

Total living area 1,950 sq. ft. ■ Price Code C ■

No. 99757

■ This plan features:

— Three bedrooms

— Two full and one half baths

■ The front Porch invites visitors and leads into the open Entry which has an angled staircase

■ The Living Room with a wall of windows and an island fireplace, opens to the Dining Room with a bright, bay window

■ The large and efficient Kitchen has a work island, a walk-in Pantry, a garden window over the sink, a skylit Nook and a nearby Deck

■ The corner Master Suite is enhanced by its Deck access, a vaulted ceiling, a large walk-in closet and a Spa Bath

■ The Guest/Utility Room has a pullman bed and a Laundry closet

■ Two second floor Bedrooms with large closets share a full Bath

■ This home is designed with a crawlspace foundation.

First floor — 1,472 sq. ft.
Second floor — 478 sq. ft.
Garage — 558 sq. ft.

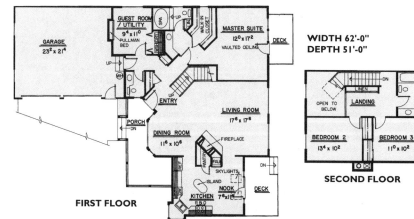

GARAGE
23² x 21⁴

GUEST ROOM / UTILITY
9⁴ x 11⁰
PULLMAN BED

SPA

WALK IN CLOSET

MASTER SUITE
12⁰ x 17²
VAULTED CEILING

DECK

ENTRY

PORCH

DINING ROOM
11⁶ x 10⁶

FIREPLACE

LIVING ROOM
17⁶ x 17⁶

PANTRY

SKYLIGHTS

ISLAND

NOOK
7⁶ x 11

KITCHEN
8⁰ x 9⁹

DECK

WIDTH 62'-0"
DEPTH 51'-0"

OPEN TO BELOW

LINEN

LANDING

BEDROOM 2
13⁴ x 10²

BEDROOM 3
11⁰ x 10²

SECOND FLOOR

FIRST FLOOR

Master-Suite Sitting Room

No. 60011

This plan features:

- Three bedrooms

- Two full and one half baths

- The upper-level balcony overlooks the vaulted Family Room and Foyer

- This home is designed with basement and crawlspace foundation options.

First floor — 1,457 sq. ft.

Second floor — 494 sq. ft.

Bonus — 275 sq. ft.

Basement — 1,457 sq. ft.

Garage — 455 sq. ft.

Total living area 1,951 sq. ft. ■ *Price Code C* ■

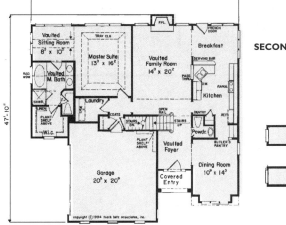

FIRST FLOOR

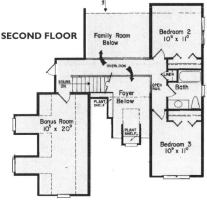

SECOND FLOOR

Room for a Large Family

No. 99129

This plan features:

- Four bedrooms

- Two full and one half baths

- The gracious Living Room archway leads into the formal Dining Room

- The Family Room has an inviting fireplace

- The L-shaped Kitchen opens into the Eating Nook, and has a built-in planning desk

- The Master Bedroom is located on the second floor and has a private Bath

- Three more Bedrooms and a full Bath complete the plan

- This home is designed with a basement foundation.

Main floor — 1,000 sq. ft.

Second floor — 960 sq. ft.

Basement — 1,000 sq. ft.

Total living area 1,960 sq. ft. ■ *Price Code C* ■

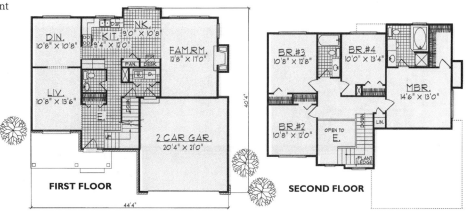

FIRST FLOOR

SECOND FLOOR

Conventional Comfort

Total living area 1,961 sq. ft. ■ **Price Code C**

WIDTH 63'-0"
DEPTH 47'-0"

FIRST FLOOR

SECOND FLOOR

No. 93349

■ **This plan features:**

— Three bedrooms

— Two full and one half baths

■ The cozy Porch accesses the two-story Foyer with a decorative window highlighting the landing staircase

■ The formal Dining Room is accented by a box window and adjoins the Kitchen

■ Crowned by a vaulted ceiling, the spacious Family Room features a hearth fireplace and is surrounded by more decorative windows

■ The efficient Kitchen has an extended counter/eating bar, a bright Dinette Area with a bay window, and access to the Deck

■ The first floor Master Bedroom has a walk-in closet and a Master Bath with a double vanity

■ This home is designed with a basement foundation.

First floor — 1,454 sq. ft.
Second floor — 507 sq. ft.
Basement — 1,454 sq. ft.
Garage — 624 sq. ft.

Exciting Elevation

Total living area 1,970 sq. ft. ■ **Price Code C**

FIRST FLOOR

SECOND FLOOR

No. 92668

■ **This plan features:**

— Three bedrooms

— Two full and one half baths

■ A combination of materials and varied rooflines make for an exciting elevation

■ The Dining Room is separated from the Foyer and the Great Room by columns

■ The U-shaped Kitchen has convenient access to the Dining Room and the Nook

■ A high ceiling and a fireplace highlight the Great Room

■ The first floor Master Suite has a decorative ceiling

■ The upstairs offers two secondary Bedroom and the Bath

■ Also upstairs are two separate Bonus Rooms for future consideration

■ This home is designed with a basement foundation.

First floor — 1,497 sq. ft.
Second floor — 473 sq. ft.
Bonus — 401 sq. ft.
Basement — 1,420 sq. ft.
Garage — 468 sq. ft.

First Floor Master Suite

No. 90624

This plan features:

- Three bedrooms
- Two full and one half baths
- The two-story Foyer is lit from above by a skylight
- The Family Room accesses the Terrace and the Garage
- The heat-circulating fireplace is located in the Living Room
- The Master Suite has vaulted ceilings and spectacular windows
- This home is designed with a basement foundation.

First floor — 1,360 sq. ft.
Second floor — 613 sq. ft.
Basement — 1,340 sq. ft.
Garage — 642 sq. ft.

■ Total living area 1,973 sq. ft. ■ Price Code C ■

FIRST FLOOR

SECOND FLOOR

National Treasure

No. 24400

This plan features:

- Three bedrooms
- Two full and one half baths
- This design has a wrap-around covered Porch
- A decorative ceiling and fireplace is located are in the Living Room
- The large Kitchen has a central island/breakfast bar
- The handy Sitting Area is found on the second floor
- This home is designed with basement, slab and crawlspace foundation options.

First floor — 1,034 sq. ft.
Second floor — 944 sq. ft.
Basement — 984 sq. ft.
Garage & storage — 675 sq. ft.

■ Total living area 1,978 sq. ft. ■ Price Code C ■

SECOND FLOOR

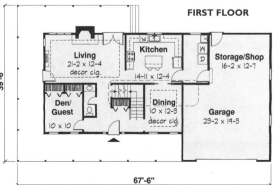

FIRST FLOOR

Victorian Touches

Total living area 1,992 sq. ft. ■ Price Code C

FIRST FLOOR

SECOND FLOOR

No. 90616

■ **This plan features:**

— Three bedrooms

— Two full and one half baths

■ The Master Suite has a high ceiling, an arched window, a private Bath, and a tower Sitting Room with an adjoining roof Deck

■ Two additional Bedrooms share a full Bath

■ The Living Room is accented by a brick fireplace and loads of windows

■ The well-equipped Kitchen has a built-in Pantry and peninsula counter

■ The sky-lit Family Room has a built-in entertainment center

■ This home is designed with a basement foundation.

First floor — 1,146 sq. ft.
Second floor — 846 sq. ft.
Basement — 967 sq. ft.
Garage — 447 sq. ft.

Glass Dining Alcove

Total living area 1,992 sq. ft. ■ Price Code C

FIRST FLOOR

SECOND FLOOR

No. 94103

■ **This plan features:**

— Four bedrooms

— Two full and one half baths

■ The covered Entry opens to a two-story Foyer accented by a medallion window

■ The formal Living and Dining Rooms are convenient for entertaining

■ The large fireplace and a wall of windows enhance Family Room

■ The efficient Kitchen has a snack bar/serving counter, a built-in Pantry and desk, a Dining Area and a nearby Laundry and Garage entry

■ The corner Master Bedroom is enhanced by a walk-in closet, Dressing Area and full Bath

■ Three additional Bedrooms with ample closets share a full Bath

■ This home is designed with a basement foundation.

First floor — 1,100 sq. ft.
Second floor — 892 sq. ft.
Basement — 1,100 sq. ft.
Garage — 474 sq. ft.

Spacious and Bright

No. 65368

This plan features:

- Three Bedrooms

- Two full and one half baths

■ Soaring ceilings in the two-story Family and Dining Rooms and a full-height stone fireplace surrounded by windows creates a spacious, sun-filled interior

■ A circular snack bar and separate Dining Area offers informal or formal dining options

■ Surrounded by angled balconies, the upper level boasts a private Computer Room and a spacious Bedroom with access to a large attic

■ This home is designed with a basement foundation.

First floor — 1,525 sq. ft.
Second floor — 470 sq. ft.
Basement — 1,525 sq. ft.
Garage — 623 sq. ft.

Total living area 1,995 sq. ft. ■ *Price Code C* ■

FIRST FLOOR

SECOND FLOOR

Terrific Open Layout

No. 92160

This plan features:

- Four Bedrooms

- Two full and one half baths

■ An impressive Porch leads in to the Entry hall that has access to the Powder Room and both the formal and informal areas

■ The corner Kitchen is open to the Eating Nook, bringing in an abundance of natural light

■ The Family Room includes a focal point fireplace visible from both the Nook and Kitchen

■ The large Master Suite has a luxurious Bath and a walk-in closet

■ Three additional Bedrooms are located in proximity to the full Bath

■ This home is designed with a crawlspace foundation.

First floor — 1,041 sq. ft.
Second floor — 954 sq. ft.

Total living area 1,995 sq. ft. ■ *Price Code C* ■

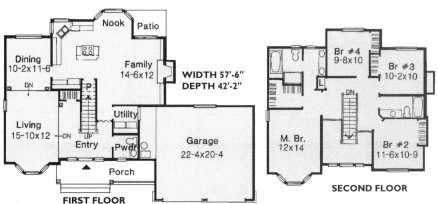

133

Backyard Oasis

■ *Total living area 1,995 sq. ft.* ■ *Price Code C* ■

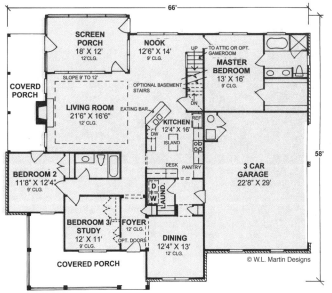

FIRST FLOOR

- SCREEN PORCH 18' X 12' 12'CLG.
- NOOK 12'6" X 14' 9' CLG.
- TO ATTIC OR OPT. GAMEROOM
- UP
- MASTER BEDROOM 13' X 16' 9' CLG.
- COVERD PORCH
- SLOPE 9' TO 12'
- OPTIONAL BASEMENT STAIRS
- LIVING ROOM 21'6" X 16'6" 12' CLG.
- EATING BAR
- DN
- REF
- KITCHEN 12'4" X 16'
- DW
- ISLAND
- BEDROOM 2 11'8" X 12'4" 9' CLG.
- DESK
- PANTRY
- 3 CAR GARAGE 22'8" X 29'
- D W LAUND.
- BEDROOM 3/ STUDY 12' X 11' 9' CLG.
- FOYER 12' CLG. OPT. DOORS
- DINING 12'4" X 13' 12' CLG.
- COVERED PORCH
- 66'
- 58'
- © W.L. Martin Designs

No. 68161

■ **This plan features:**

— Three bedrooms

— Two full baths

■ Limited windows on the sides of this home provide additional privacy from neighbors

■ Optional doors from the Foyer create a Study

■ This home is designed with slab and crawlspace foundation options.

First floor — 1,995 sq. ft.
Garage — 678 sq. ft.

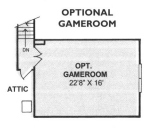

OPTIONAL GAMEROOM

- DN
- OPT. GAMEROOM 22'8" X 16'
- ATTIC

■ *Total living area 1,995 sq. ft.* ■ *Price Code C* ■

No. 20230

■ This plan features:

- Four bedrooms

- Two full and one half baths

■ The covered Porch Entry opens to the formal Dining Room and the Great Room

■ The bright Kitchen, with loads of counter space, easily serves the Eating Nook, Great Room and Dining Room

■ The Master Bedroom pampers its owners with two walk-in closets and a plush Bath

■ This home is designed with basement, slab and crawlspace foundation options.

First floor — 1,365 sq. ft.
Second floor — 630 sq. ft.
Basement — 1,419 sq. ft.
Garage — 426 sq. ft.

WIDTH 44'-0"
DEPTH 54'-0"

Bedroom #2
10-11 × 13-0

Bedroom #4
10-5 × 11-4

Bedroom #3
11-0 × 10-8

SECOND FLOOR

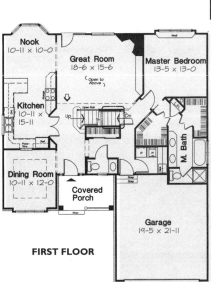

Nook
10-11 × 10-0

Great Room
18-6 × 15-6

Master Bedroom
13-5 × 13-0

Kitchen
10-11 × 15-11

M. Bath

Dining Room
10-11 × 12-0

Covered Porch

Garage
19-5 × 21-11

FIRST FLOOR

SLAB/CRAWLSPACE OPTION

Great Open Spaces

■ Total living area 1,995 sq. ft. ■ Price Code C ■

No. 98484

■ **This plan features:**

— Three bedrooms

— Two full and one half baths

■ The impressive two-story Foyer greets guests

■ The formal areas, the Living Room and the Dining Room, are located at the front of the home

■ The Master Suite includes a tray ceiling, a French door, and a vaulted ceiling in the Master Bath and walk-in closet

■ This home is designed with basement and crawlspace foundation options.

First floor — 1,071 sq. ft.
Second floor — 924 sq. ft.
Bonus — 280 sq. ft.
Basement — 1,071 sq. ft.
Garage — 480 sq. ft.

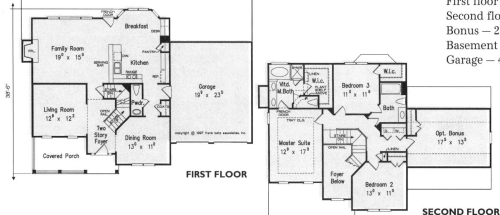

FIRST FLOOR

SECOND FLOOR

Country Living

■ Total living area 1,997 sq. ft. ■ Price Code C ■

No. 90410

■ **This plan features:**

— Three bedrooms

— Two full and one half baths

■ The eat-in Country Kitchen has an island counter and a bay window

■ The spacious Great Room has a fireplace and opens into the Dining Area

■ The first floor Master Suite includes a walk-in closet and a private Bath

■ Two additional Bedrooms share a full Bath with a double vanity

■ This home is designed with basement and crawlspace foundation options.

First floor — 1,277 sq. ft.
Second floor — 720 sq. ft.

FIRST FLOOR

SECOND FLOOR

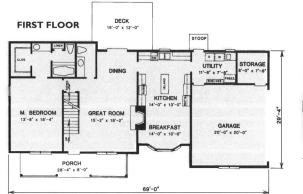

Distinctive Design

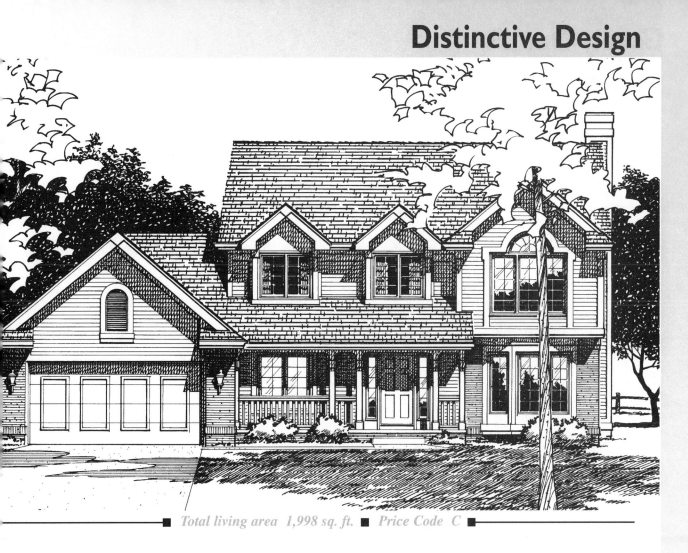

■ *Total living area 1,998 sq. ft.* ■ *Price Code C* ■

No. 94904

■ **This plan features:**

— Three bedrooms

— Two full and one half baths

■ The Living Room is distinguished by the warmth of a bay window and French doors leading to the Family Room

■ The Kitchen, with island cooktop and Breakfast Area, is designed to save steps and adjoins the Laundry and Garage entry

■ This home is designed with a basement foundation.

■ Alternate foundation options available at an additional charge. Please call 1-800-235-5700 for more information.

First floor — 1,093 sq. ft.
Second floor — 905 sq. ft.
Basement — 1,093 sq. ft.
Garage — 527 sq. ft.

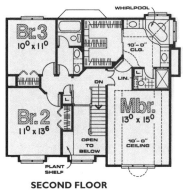

WIDTH 55'-4"
DEPTH 37'-8"

SECOND FLOOR

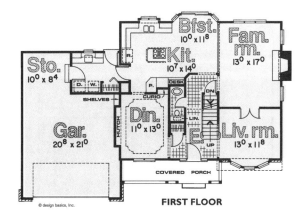

FIRST FLOOR

© design basics, inc.

137

Lovely Details

■ *Total living area 1,999 sq. ft.* ■ *Price Code C* ■

SECOND FLOOR

FIRST FLOOR

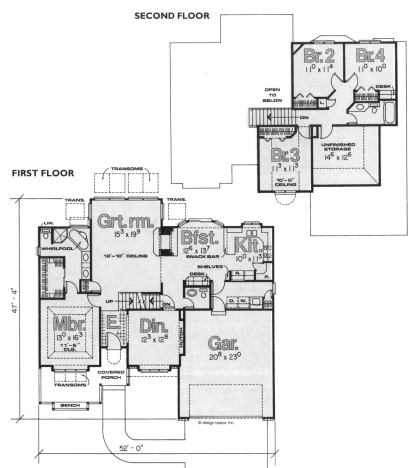

© design basics, inc.

No. 94900

■ **This plan features:**

— Four bedrooms

— Two full and one half baths

■ The covered Porch and Victorian touches create a unique elevation

■ The one and a half story Entry hall leads into the formal Dining Room

■ The Kitchen/Breakfast Area shares the fireplace and has a snack bar, a desk, a walk-in Pantry and an abundance of counter space

■ This home is designed with a basement foundation.

■ Alternate foundation options available at an additional charge. Please call 1-800-235-5700 for more information.

First floor — 1,421 sq. ft.
Second floor — 578 sq. ft.
Basement — 1,421 sq. ft.
Garage — 480 sq. ft.

Total living area 2,005 sq. ft. ■ *Price Code D*

No. 68160

■ This plan features:

— Three bedrooms

— Two full and one half baths

■ Two Bedrooms share a computer station and a BonusRoom offering expansion options

■ A large, Screen Porch off the Living Room creates a protected outdoor living area.

■ This home is designed with slab and crawlspace foundation options

■ Alternate foundation options available at an additional charge. Please call 1-800-235-5700 for more information.

First floor — 1,486 sq. ft.
Second floor — 519 sq. ft.
Bonus — 264 sq. ft.

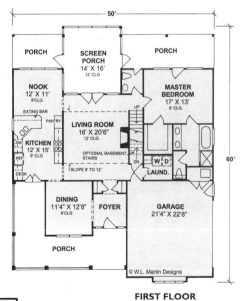

FIRST FLOOR

SECOND FLOOR

A Traditional Approach

■ *Total living area 2,013 sq. ft.* ■ *Price Code D* ■

SECOND FLOOR

- BR3 11'6 x 10'10
- BR4 11' x 8'6
- MBATH
- BATH 2
- W Closet
- Dress'g
- Balcony
- MBR 13' x 16'10
- BR2 11'2 x 10'10
- Foyer Below

FIRST FLOOR

- GARAGE 19'8 x 21'4
- KIT 11'6 x 10'4
- DIN 10'2 x 11'4
- FAM RM 13' x 15'3
- Entry
- Lav
- PANTRY
- Laun
- DIN RM 11'2 x 11'4
- LIV RM 13' x 11'3
- Two-Story FOYER
- Covered Entry
- 34'
- 56'

No. 94109

■ **This plan features:**

— Four bedrooms

— Two full and one half baths

■ The covered Entry leads into a two-story Foyer

■ The well-appointed Kitchen has direct access to the Garage

■ The bright Dinette is ideal for informal eating

■ The expansive Family Room is highlighted by a large fireplace

■ The roomy Master Suite includes a private Bath and a walk-in closet

■ Three additional Bedrooms share use of a full Bath

■ This home is designed with a basement foundation.

First floor — 1,025 sq. ft.
Second floor — 988 sq. ft.

Comfortable Vacation Living

■ *Total living area 2,017 sq. ft.* ■ *Price Code D* ■

No. 98714

■**This plan features:**

— Three bedrooms

— One full and two three-quarter baths

■ The wrap-around Deck offers views and access into the Living Room

■ The open Kitchen has a corner sink and windows, an eating bar and a walk-in Storage/Pantry

■ Two Bedroom Suites have sliding glass doors leading to the Deck, walk-in closets and plush Baths

■ The Loft Area has a walk-in closet, Attic access, a private Bath, and a Deck

■ This home is designed with a crawlspace foundation.

First floor — 1,704 sq ft
Second floor — 313 sq. ft.

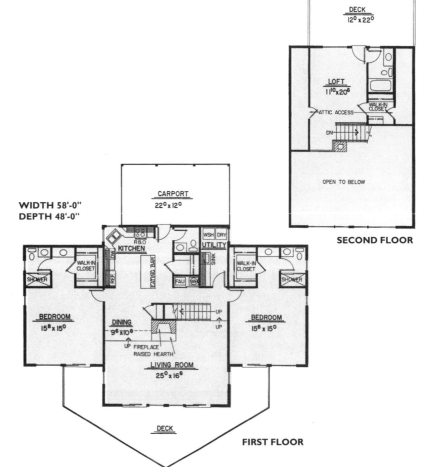

Traditionally Styled

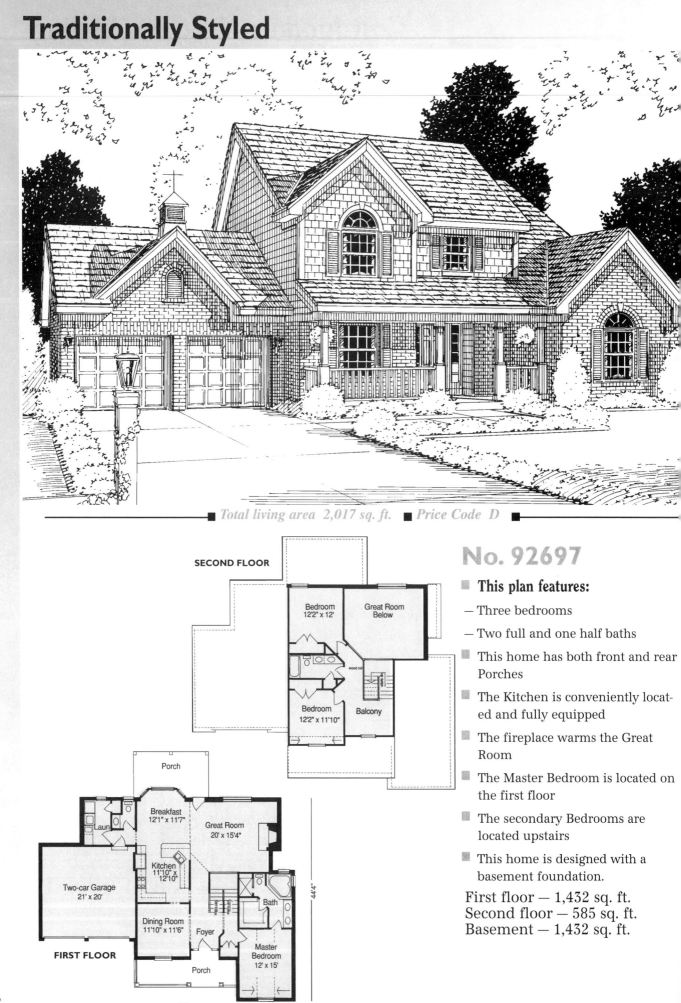

■ *Total living area 2,017 sq. ft.* ■ *Price Code D* ■

SECOND FLOOR

Bedroom 12'2" x 12'

Great Room Below

wood rail

Bedroom 12'2" x 11'10"

Balcony

Porch

Breakfast 12'1" x 11'7"

Laun

Great Room 20' x 15'4"

Kitchen 11'10" x 12'10"

Two-car Garage 21' x 20'

Bath

Dining Room 11'10" x 11'6"

Foyer

Master Bedroom 12' x 15'

FIRST FLOOR

Porch

44'4"

58'

No. 92697

■ **This plan features:**

— Three bedrooms

— Two full and one half baths

■ This home has both front and rear Porches

■ The Kitchen is conveniently located and fully equipped

■ The fireplace warms the Great Room

■ The Master Bedroom is located on the first floor

■ The secondary Bedrooms are located upstairs

■ This home is designed with a basement foundation.

First floor — 1,432 sq. ft.
Second floor — 585 sq. ft.
Basement — 1,432 sq. ft.

Modern Colonial Styling

No. 93287

This plan features:

— Three bedrooms

— Two full and one half baths

■ Brick detailing and keystones highlight this elevation

■ The two-story Foyer opens to the formal Living and Dining Rooms

■ The expansive Family Room has a hearth fireplace between built-in shelves, plus Deck access

■ The U-shaped Kitchen has a serving counter, a Breakfast Alcove, and a nearby Garage entry

■ The elegant Master Bedroom has a decorative ceiling, a large walk-in closet, and a double vanity Bath

■ The two additional Bedrooms share a full Bath, a Laundry and a Bonus Area

■ This home is designed with a basement foundation.

First floor — 987 sq. ft.

Second floor — 965 sq. ft.

Finished staircase — 72 sq. ft.

Bonus — 272 sq. ft.

Basement — 899 sq. ft.

Total living area 2,024 sq. ft. ■ *Price Code D* ■

SECOND FLOOR

WIDTH 58'-4"
DEPTH 32'-0"

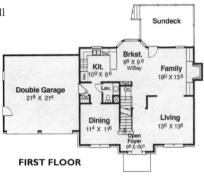

FIRST FLOOR

Exquisite Columned Porch

No. 93234

This plan features:

— Four bedrooms

— Two full and one half baths

■ An island workspace in the Kitchen easily serves the bay Breakfast Nook

■ The two-story Living Room has an oversized fireplace, access to the rear Deck, and a lovely Balcony overlook

■ The Master Bedroom has an extra large walk-in closet and a pampering Bath with Spa tub

■ This home is designed with a basement foundation.

First floor — 914 sq. ft.

Second floor — 1,032 sq. ft.

Lower staircase — 92 sq. ft.

Basement — 630 sq. ft.

Garage — 400 sq. ft.

Total living area 2,038 sq. ft. ■ *Price Code D* ■

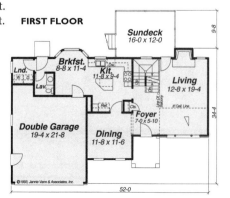

FIRST FLOOR

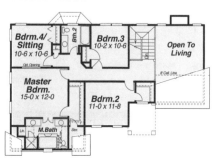

SECOND FLOOR

Attractive Covered Entry

■ *Total living area 2,044 sq. ft.* ■ *Price Code D* ■

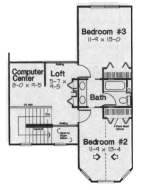

WIDTH 68'-0"
DEPTH 47'-0"

SECOND FLOOR

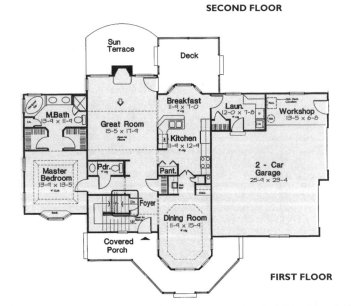

FIRST FLOOR

No. 24736

■ **This plan features:**

— Three bedrooms

— Two full and one half baths

■ The angled, covered Porch welcomes everyone to this home

■ The Great Room is accented by a vaulted ceiling and a fireplace

■ The spacious Kitchen offers a Pantry and a Breakfast Bay

■ The Master Bedroom wing has a bay window, a decorative ceiling, two walk-in closets and a plush Bathroom

■ On the second floor, two additional Bedrooms share a full Bath, a Loft and a Computer Center

■ This home is designed with basement, slab and crawlspace foundation options.

First floor — 1,403 sq. ft.
Second floor — 641 sq. ft.
Basement — 1,394 sq. ft.
Garage — 680 sq. ft.

Elegant Colonial

No. 94141

Total living area 2,050 sq. ft. ■ Price Code D ■

This plan features:

— Four bedrooms

— Two full and one half baths

■ The Master Bedroom has a walk-in closet and an attached Bath with a skylight

■ Upstairs, there are three additional Bedrooms and one full Bath

■ The Dining Room and Living Room are traditionally placed

■ The Family Room and Dinette are designed with plenty of open space and light

■ The compact Kitchen has a useful snack bar

■ This home is designed with a basement foundation.

First floor — 1,108 sq. ft.
Second floor — 942 sq. ft.
Basement — 1,108 sq. ft.
Garage — 455 sq. ft.

SECOND FLOOR

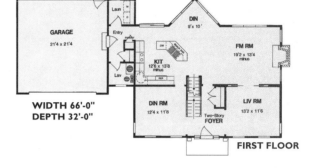

WIDTH 66'-0"
DEPTH 32'-0"

FIRST FLOOR

Contemporary Interior

No. 98407

Total living area 2,052 sq. ft. ■ Price Code D ■

This plan features:

— Four bedrooms

— Three full baths

■ The two-story Foyer is flanked by the Living Room and the Dining Room

■ The Family Room features a fireplace and a French door

■ The Breakfast Nook and Pantry are adjacent to the Kitchen

■ The Master Suite, with a tray ceiling, has an attached Bath with a vaulted ceiling and a radius window

■ This home is designed with basement, slab and crawlspace foundation options.

First floor — 1,135 sq. ft.
Second floor — 917 sq. ft.
Bonus — 216 sq. ft.
Basement — 1,135 sq. ft.
Garage — 452 sq. ft.

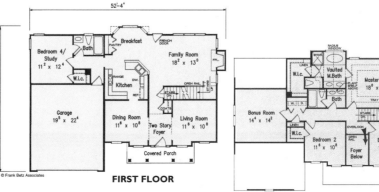

FIRST FLOOR

SECOND FLOOR

Arched Windows Add Light

■ *Total living area 2,060 sq. ft.* ■ *Price Code D* ■

SECOND FLOOR

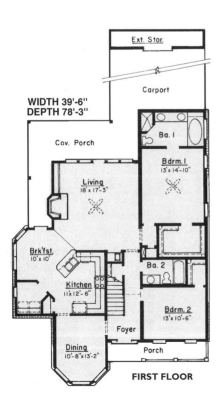

WIDTH 39'-6"
DEPTH 78'-3"

FIRST FLOOR

No. 94609

■ **This plan features:**

— Four bedrooms

— Three full baths

■ The welcoming Porch shelters entry into the Foyer

■ The spacious Living Room is enhanced by a hearth fireplace, built-in shelves and offers access to the covered Porch

■ An efficient, U-shaped Kitchen has a peninsula serving counter, a adjoining bright Breakfast Area with access to the covered Porch, and a Laundry Room

■ This home is designed with slab and crawlspace foundation options.

First floor — 1,505 sq. ft.
Second floor — 555 sq. ft.
Garage — 400 sq. ft.

Comfortable Country Ease

■ *Total living area 2,064 sq. ft.* ■ *Price Code D* ■

No. 24405

■ This plan features:

— Three or four bedrooms

— Two full and two half baths

■ The sprawling front Porch gives way to the traditional Foyer

■ The tray ceiling adds elegance to the Dining Room which directly accesses the Kitchen

■ The large Country Kitchen has a center work island, and has plenty of storage and work space

■ The Family Room is warmed by a fireplace and accented with a tray ceiling

■ A vaulted ceiling and a private bath enhance the Master Suite

■ This home is designed with basement, slab and crawlspace foundation options.

First floor — 1,104 sq. ft.
Second floor — 960 sq. ft.

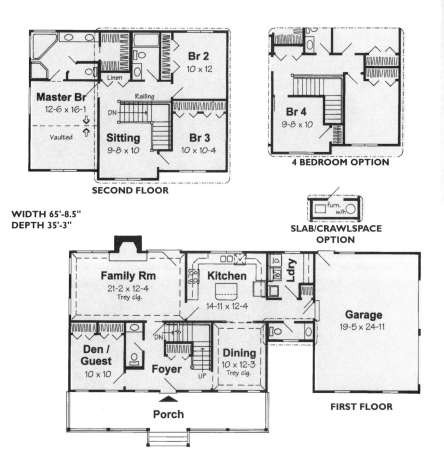

SECOND FLOOR

Master Br
12-6 x 16-1
Vaulted

Br 2
10 x 12

Linen

Sitting
9-8 x 10

Br 3
10 x 10-4

Railing

DN

4 BEDROOM OPTION

Br 4
9-8 x 10

WIDTH 65'-8.5"
DEPTH 35'-3"

SLAB/CRAWLSPACE OPTION

furn. w/h

FIRST FLOOR

Family Rm
21-2 x 12-4
Trey clg.

Kitchen
14-11 x 12-4

Ldry

Garage
19-5 x 24-11

Den / Guest
10 x 10

Foyer

Dining
10 x 12-3
Trey clg.

DN

UP

Porch

Formal Interior

■ *Total living area 2,068 sq. ft.* ■ *Price Code D* ■

DECK
20-0 x 12-0

FAMILY
19-4 x 13-4

BREAKFAST
11-4 x 10-0

KITCHEN
11-4 x 11-0

GARAGE
22-0 x 22-0

LIVING
13-4 x 11-8

FOYER

DINING
11-4 x 12-0

PORCH

PORCH

FIRST FLOOR

61'-8"

32'-0"

WALK-IN
CLOSET

BATH

BATH

BEDROOM 2
11-4 x 12-0

WALK-IN
CLOSET

WALK-IN
CLOSET

WASH DRY

LAUNDRY

OPTIONAL
BONUS ROOM
14-4 x 11-4

M. BEDROOM
13-4 x 16-0

HALL

CLOSET

CLOSET

OPEN RAIL.

BEDROOM 3
11-4 x 12-0

SECOND FLOOR

No. 90451

■ **This plan features:**

— Three bedrooms

— Two full and one half baths

■ The wrap-around Porch leads into the central Foyer from which you can access the formal Living and Dining Room

■ The large Family Room has a cozy fireplace and Deck access

■ The corner Master Bedroom has a walk-in closet and an appealing Bath

■ The additional Bedrooms plus the Bonus Room share a full Bath and the Laundry Room

■ This home is designed with basement and crawlspace foundation options.

First floor — 1,046 sq. ft.
Second floor — 1,022 sq. ft.
Bonus — 232 sq. ft.
Basement — 1,046

Beautiful Arched Windows

■ *Total living area 2,079 sq. ft.* ■ *Price Code D* ■

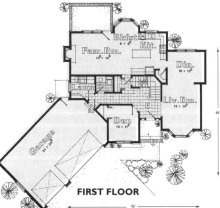

Bkfst.
8 x 8

Fam. Rm.
13 x 14

Kit.

Dim.
10 x 12

Lndry.

Liv. Rm.
13 x 14

Den
10 x 11

Garage
21 x 24

FIRST FLOOR

70

Mbr.
13 x 15

Br.
10 x 10

Mbth.

Br.
10 x 11

62

SECOND FLOOR

No. 93920

■ **This plan features:**

— Three bedrooms

— Two full and one half baths

■ The tiled Foyer leads into the Den and the formal Living Room

■ The efficient Kitchen has a work island and easily accesses the formal Dining Room

■ The Family Room with a fireplace, and the Breakfast Room are open to the Kitchen creating an expansive area

■ The Master Suite includes a walk-in closet and a pampering Bath

■ The two additional Bedrooms share a full Bathroom

■ This home is designed with a basement foundation.

First floor — 1,261 sq. ft.
Second floor — 818 sq. ft.
Basement — 1,184 sq. ft.
Garage — 752 sq. ft.

An Extraordinary Home

No. 92642

This plan features:

— Three bedrooms

— Two full and one half baths

■ An exciting roofline and a textured exterior provide a rich, solid look to this home

■ The lovely Foyer views the cozy fireplace and stylish French door in the Great Room

■ The formal Dining Room has a tray ceiling and a wide entrance to the Great Room

■ The roomy, well-equipped Kitchen includes a pass-through to the Great Room

■ Large windows in the Breakfast Area flood the room with natural light, making it a bright and cheery place to start your day

■ The private, first floor Master Bedroom has a luxurious Bath

■ This home is designed with a basement foundation.

First floor — 1,524 sq. ft.
Second floor — 558 sq. ft.
Bonus — 267 sq. ft.
Basement — 1,460 sq. ft.

Total living area 2,082 sq. ft. ■ *Price Code D* ■

SECOND FLOOR

FIRST FLOOR

Large Entertainment Room

No. 99500

This plan features:

— Three bedrooms

— Two full and one half baths

■ The charming Porch and quaint dormers enhance the curb appeal of this home

■ The Foyer has a half Bath, charming staircase and access to the elegant Dining Room

■ The Great Room, with a cozy fireplace, is open to the efficient Kitchen

■ The first floor Master Suite has a private Bath and a walk-in closet

■ The Entertainment Room on second floor keeps playful children happy

■ The two additional Bedrooms share a full Bathroom

■ This home is designed with slab and crawlspace foundation options.

First floor — 1,218 sq. ft.
Second floor — 864 sq. ft.
Garage — 472 sq. ft.

Total living area 2,082 sq. ft. ■ *Price Code D* ■

WIDTH 44'-0"
DEPTH 51'-0"

FIRST FLOOR

SECOND FLOOR

Appealing Farmhouse

■ *Total living area 2,089 sq. ft.* ■ *Price Code D* ■

FIRST FLOOR

WIDTH 56'-0"
DEPTH 38'-0"

SECOND FLOOR

No. 65135

■ **This plan features:**

— Three bedrooms

— Two full and one half baths

■ Interior doors provide privacy options in the Study and Living Rooms

■ Luxurious amenities in the Master Suite include a fireplace, large walk-in closet and Bath with separate tub and shower.

■ This home is designed with a basement foundation.

First floor — 1,146 sq. ft.
Second floor — 943 sq. ft.
Bonus — 313 sq. ft.
Basement — 483 sq. ft.

Country with Conveniences

■ *Total living area 2,091 sq. ft.* ■ *Price Code D* ■

No. 93212

■ This plan features:

— Three bedrooms

— Two full and one half baths

■ The Country-style Porch and dormers give this plan an old-fashioned feel

■ The large Living Room with a cozy fireplace opens to the Dining Room for easy entertaining

■ The formal Dining Room has a bay window and direct access to the Deck

■ The first floor Master Suite has an elegant Bath

■ This home is designed with basement, slab and crawlspace foundation options.

First floor — 1,362 sq. ft.
Second floor — 729 sq. ft.
Bonus — 384 sq. ft.
Basement — 988 sq. ft.
Garage — 559 sq. ft.

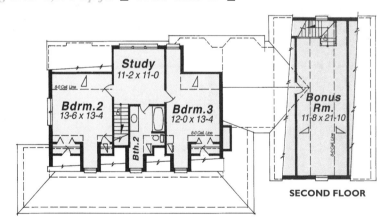

SECOND FLOOR

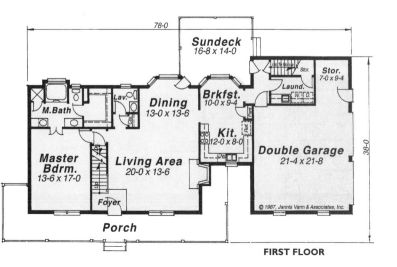

FIRST FLOOR

Accented by Quoins

■ *Total living area 2,098 sq. ft.* ■ *Price Code D* ■

No. 90471

■ **This plan features:**

— Four bedrooms

— Two full and one half baths

■ Bay windows in the front and rear of the home add to its beauty

■ The enormous Great Room spans an entire side of the home and offers a hearth fireplace and access to the Deck

■ The Kitchen is an open layout with the Breakfast Nook

■ Future expansion is provided for in the second floor Bonus Room

■ This home is designed with basement and crawlspace foundation options.

First floor — 1,048 sq. ft.
Second floor — 1,050 sq. ft.
Bonus — 284 sq. ft.
Basement — 1,034 sq. ft.
Garage — 484 sq. ft.

Updated Victorian

■ *Total living area 2,099 sq. ft.* ■ *Price Code D* ■

No. 91053

■ **This plan features:**

— Three bedrooms

— Two full and one half baths

■ The classic Victorian exterior design of this home is accented by a wonderful Turret Room and second floor covered Porch

■ The spacious formal Living Room leads into the formal Dining Room for ease in entertaining

■ The efficient, U-shaped Kitchen with loads of counter space and a peninsula snack bar, opens to an eating Nook and Family Room for informal gatherings and activities

■ The elegant Master Suite has a unique, octagon Sitting Area, a private Porch, an oversized walk-in closet, and a private Bath with a double vanity and a window tub

■ This home is designed with a crawlspace foundation.

First floor — 1,150 sq. ft.
Second floor — 949 sq. ft.
Garage — 484 sq. ft.

Comfortable Colonial

■ *Total living area 2,102 sq. ft.* ■ *Price Code D* ■

No. 93354

■ **This plan features:**

— Four bedrooms

— Two full and one half baths

■ The entry Porch leads into the central Foyer between the formal Living and Dining Rooms

■ The comfortable Family Room has a corner gas fireplace and a back yard view

■ The hub Kitchen has a work island, a Pantry, a Dinette Area with outdoor access, and nearby, a Laundry and a Garage Entry

■ This home is designed with a basement foundation.

First floor — 1,110 sq. ft.
Second floor — 992 sq. ft.
Basement — 1,110 sq. ft.
Garage — 530 sq. ft.

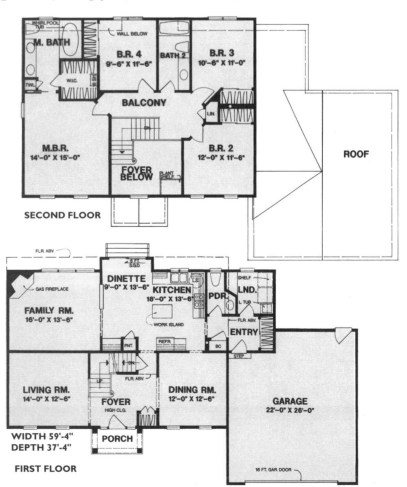

Executive Two-Story

Total living area 2,116 sq. ft. ■ Price Code D

FIRST FLOOR

SECOND FLOOR

No. 98800

■ **This plan features:**

— Three bedrooms

— Two full and one half baths

■ A gracefully curving staircase dominates the Foyer and leads to the Bedrooms

■ The Kitchen and the Breakfast Nook are separated from the Family Room by a railing and a step down

■ A built-in entertainment center and a warming fireplace highlight the sunken Family Room

■ The formal Living and Dining Rooms are adjacent to each other for comfortable entertaining

■ The lavish Master Suite boasts a Sitting Room and a deluxe Bath

■ The Bonus Room can be finished for the future needs of the family

■ This home is designed with a basement foundation.

First floor — 1,258 sq. ft.
Second floor — 858 sq. ft.
Bonus — 263 sq. ft.
Basement — 1,251 sq. ft.
Garage — 441 sq. ft.

Ready for the Future

Total living area 2,119 sq. ft. ■ Price Code D

FIRST FLOOR

SECOND FLOOR

No. 65378

■ **This plan features:**

— Three bedrooms

— Two full and one half baths

■ A wrap-around Porch provides ample space for outdoor entertaining

■ French doors off the Foyer provide privacy in the computer room

■ The media room includes the warmth of a fireplace while viewing the large screen television

■ Pampering amenities in the Master Suite include a corner fireplace and a luxurious Bath with an angled tub

■ The home is designed with a basement foundation.

First floor — 1,132 sq. ft.
Second floor — 987 sq. ft.
Basement — 1,132 sq. ft.
Garage — 556 sq. ft.

Charming Covered Porch

No. 97219

This plan features:

— Four bedrooms

— Three full and one half baths

■ The Living Room has decorative columns defining its entrance and overlooks the Porch

■ The Master Suite is crowned by a tray ceiling, and includes French doors to the lavish Master Bath

■ This home is designed with basement and crawlspace foundation options.

First floor — 1,257 sq. ft.
Second floor — 871 sq. ft.
Bonus — 444 sq. ft.
Basement — 1,275 sq. ft.
Garage — 462 sq. ft.

■ *Total living area 2,128 sq. ft.* ■ *Price Code D* ■

WIDTH 61'-0"
DEPTH 40'-6"

SECOND FLOOR

FIRST FLOOR

SECOND FLOOR W/ OPT. BONUS ROOM

Perfectly Proportioned

No. 94941

This plan features:

— Four bedrooms

— Two full and one half baths

■ The large covered Porch is framed by a wood railing

■ The Living Room is enhanced by the warmth of a bay window and has double French doors accessing the Family Room

■ The Dining Room is crowned with a decorative ceiling, and is accented by a built-in curio cabinet

■ The efficient Kitchen is located steps away from the Breakfast Area and the Dining Room

■ This home is designed with a basement foundation.

■ Alternate foundation options available at an additional charge. Please call 1-800-235-5700 for more information.

First floor — 1,093 sq. ft.
Second floor — 1,038 sq. ft.
Basement — 1,093 sq. ft.
Garage — 527 sq. ft.

■ *Total living area 2,131 sq. ft.* ■ *Price Code D* ■

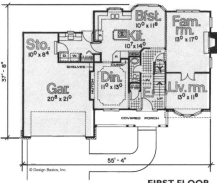

FIRST FLOOR

SECOND FLOOR

Impressive Entry

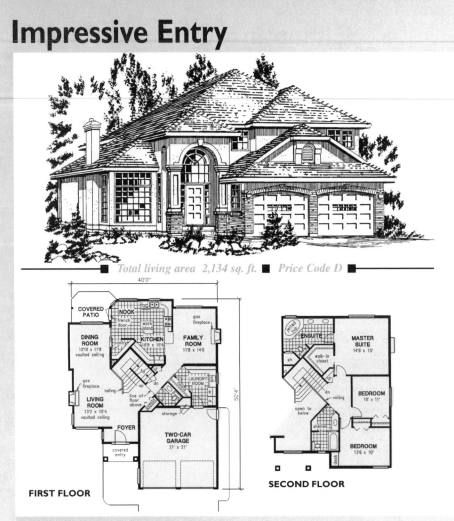

Total living area 2,134 sq. ft. ■ *Price Code D* ■

FIRST FLOOR

SECOND FLOOR

■ **This plan features:**

— Three bedrooms

— Two full and one half baths

■ The Living Room is topped by a vaulted ceiling and enhanced by a gas fireplace

■ The Dining Room is topped by a vaulted ceiling and adjoins the Living Room to create a large living space

■ Pocket doors open to the Kitchen/Nook Area from the Dining Room

■ The work island and a walk-in Pantry add to the convenience and efficiency of the Kitchen

■ The attractive French door accesses the covered Patio from the Nook Area

■ The Family Room contains another gas fireplace

■ The Master Suite includes a whirlpool Bath

■ This home is designed with a basement foundation.

First floor — 1,212 sq. ft.
Second floor — 922 sq. ft.
Basement — 1,199 sq. ft.
Garage — 464 sq. ft.

Circular Porch

Total living area 2,135 sq. ft. ■ *Price Code D* ■

■ **This plan features:**

— Four bedrooms

— Two full and one half baths

■ Pocket doors in the Solarium and an airlock Entry are energy savings features of this home

■ Built-in cabinets offers ample storage in the Laundry Room and Kitchen

■ This home is designed with a basement foundation.

First floor — 1,085 sq. ft.
Second floor — 1,050 sq. ft.
Basement — 1,050 sq. ft.
Garage — 440 sq. ft.

FIRST FLOOR

SECOND FLOOR

Master Suite with Deck

No. 91411

This plan features:

— Four bedrooms

— Two full and one half baths

■ The sunken Living Room, formal Dining Room, and Kitchen enjoy an expansive view of the Patio and backyard

■ The Living Room keeps the house toasty after the sun goes down with its fireplace

■ Skylights brighten the balcony and Master Bathroom

■ This home is designed with basement, slab and crawlspace foundation options.

First floor — 1,249 sq. ft.
Second floor — 890 sq. ft.
Garage — 462 sq. ft.

■ Total living area 2,139 sq. ft. ■ Price Code D ■

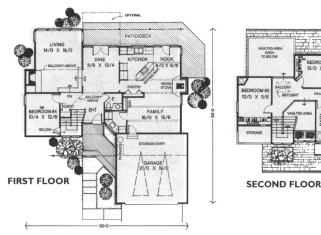

FIRST FLOOR

SECOND FLOOR

Character and Charm

No. 93442

This plan features:

— Three bedrooms

— Two full and one half baths

■ The Dining Room has direct access to the Kitchen, and can be made private by a pocket door

■ The Kitchen is made efficient by a cook-top island, an abundance of counter space, and a built-in Pantry

■ The Sun Room adjoins the Kitchen and the Family Room

■ A fireplace and a fourteen-foot ceiling highlight the Family Room.

■ The Master Suite has an inviting Bath and a walk-in closet

■ This home is designed with a basement foundation.

First floor — 1,626 sq. ft.
Second floor — 522 sq. ft.
Bonus — 336 sq. ft.
Basement — 1,626 sq. ft.
Garage — 522 sq. ft.

■ Total living area 2,148 sq. ft. ■ Price Code D ■

WIDTH 54'-7"
DEPTH 62'-8"

FIRST FLOOR

SECOND FLOOR

Details, Details, Details

Total living area 2,155 sq. ft. ■ **Price Code D**

© Frank Betz Associates

FIRST FLOOR

SECOND FLOOR

No. 98447

■**This plan features:**

– Three bedrooms

– Two full and one half baths

■This elevation is highlighted by stucco, stone and detailing around the arched windows

■The two-story Foyer allows access to the Dining Room and the Great Room

■A vaulted ceiling and a fireplace can be found in the Great Room

■The Breakfast Room has a vaulted ceiling

■The Master Suite has a tray ceiling

■This home is designed with basement and crawlspace foundation options.

First floor — 1,628 sq. ft.
Second floor — 527 sq. ft.
Bonus room — 207 sq. ft.
Basement — 1,628 sq. ft.
Garage — 440 sq. ft.

Ideal for Sloping View Site

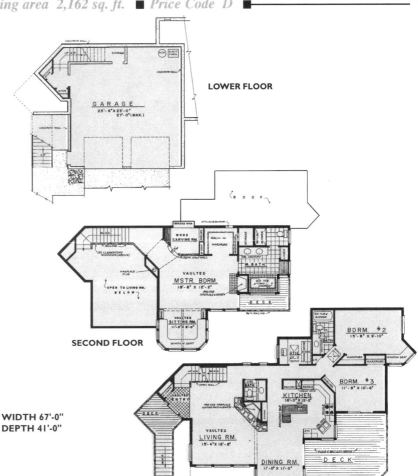

■ *Total living area 2,162 sq. ft.* ■ *Price Code D* ■

No. 91343

■ This plan features:

— Three bedrooms

— Two full and one half baths

■ A stone-faced fireplace and vaulted ceiling are located in the Living Room

■ An island food preparation center with a sink and a Breakfast bar are featured in the Kitchen

■ Sliding glass doors lead from the Dining Room to the Deck

■ This home is designed with a combo basement and crawlspace foundation option.

First floor — 1,338 sq. ft.
Second floor — 763 sq. ft.
Lower floor — 61 sq. ft.
Garage — 779 sq. ft.

LOWER FLOOR

GARAGE
25'-6" X 23'-0"
27'-0" (MAX.)

SECOND FLOOR

WOOD CARVING RM.

VAULTED MSTR. BDRM.
18'-8" X 12'-2"

M. BATH

VAULTED SITTING RM.
11'-0" X 9'-0"

WIDTH 67'-0"
DEPTH 41'-0"

BDRM. #2
13'-8" X 9'-10"

BDRM. #3
11'-8" X 10'-6"

KITCHEN
16'-0" X 13'-2"

VAULTED LIVING RM.
15'-4" X 18'-8"

DINING RM.
11'-0" X 11'-0"

DECK

FIRST FLOOR

Massive Curb Appeal

Total living area 2,175 sq. ft. ■ *Price Code D*

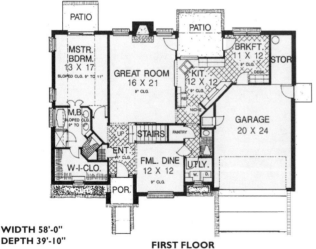

WIDTH 58'-0"
DEPTH 39'-10"

FIRST FLOOR

No. 98517

■ This plan features:

— Four bedrooms

— Two full and one half baths

■ An arched, two-story entrance starts a luxurious impression of this fine home

■ The expansive Great Room boasts a large fireplace flanked by windows

■ The angled Kitchen has a large pass-through to the Great Room

■ This home is designed with a slab foundation.

First floor — 1,472 sq. ft.
Second floor — 703 sq. ft.
Garage — 540 sq. ft.

SECOND FLOOR

A Home For All Seasons

■ *Total living area 2,176 sq. ft.* ■ *Price Code D* ■

No. 90629

■ **This plan features:**

— Three bedrooms

— One full and two three-quarter baths

■ All of the rooms have access to a Deck

■ The Living Room has a heat-circulating fireplace

■ The Kitchen has ample counter and cabinet space, and has easy access to the Dining Room and the outdoors

■ This home is designed with a basement foundation.

First floor — 1,001 sq. ft.
Second floor — 712 sq. ft.
Lower floor — 463 sq. ft.

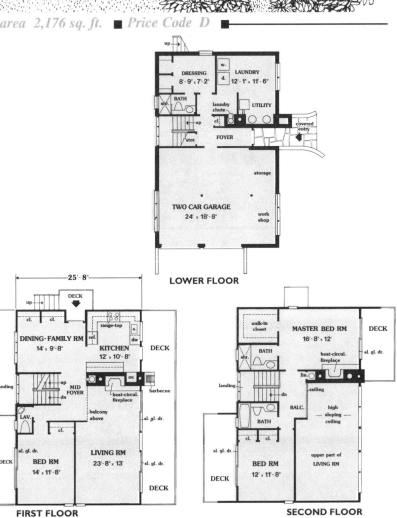

Classic Colonial Styling

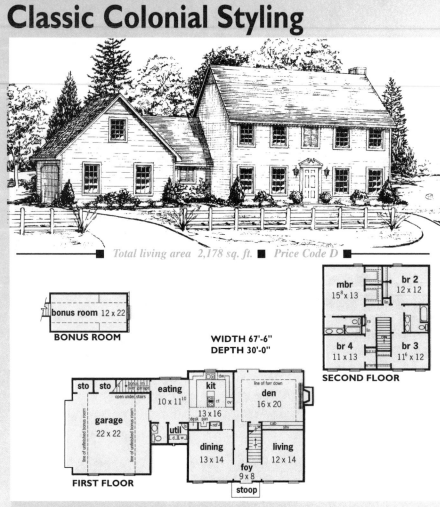

Total living area 2,178 sq. ft. ■ *Price Code D*

BONUS ROOM
bonus room 12 x 22

WIDTH 67'-6"
DEPTH 30'-0"

SECOND FLOOR
mbr 15⁸ x 13 | br 2 12 x 12
br 4 11 x 13 | br 3 11⁶ x 12

FIRST FLOOR
sto | sto
garage 22 x 22
eating 10 x 11¹⁰
kit 13 x 16
den 16 x 20
util
dining 13 x 14
living 12 x 14
foy 9 x 8
stoop

No. 92569

■ **This plan features:**

— Four bedrooms

— Two full and one half baths

■ The Formal areas are located traditionally to the front of the home, on each side of the Foyer

■ The expansive Den is enhanced by a fireplace and built-in shelves

■ The Kitchen features a work island, a built-in desk, a Pantry and a peninsula counter serving the eating area

■ Of the four Bedrooms on the second floor, the Master Suite has a private Bath and twin walk-in closets

■ This home is designed with slab and crawlspace foundation options.

First floor — 1,170 sq. ft.
Second floor — 1,008 sq. ft.
Garage — 484 sq. ft.

Modern Country Living

Total living area 2,181 sq. ft. ■ *Price Code D*

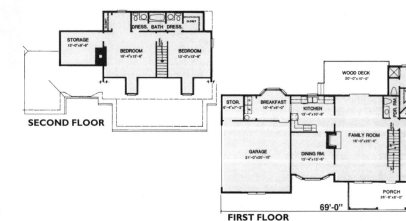

SECOND FLOOR
STORAGE 13'-0"x9'-6"
DRESS. BATH DRESS.
BEDROOM 15'-4"x13'-6"
BEDROOM 13'-0"x13'-6"

FIRST FLOOR
WOOD DECK 20'-0"x10'-0"
STOR. 6'-4"x7'-5"
BREAKFAST 10'-6"x9'-0"
KITCHEN 13'-4"x10'-6"
M. BATH
GARAGE 21'-0"x20'-10"
DINING RM. 13'-4"x13'-6"
FAMILY ROOM 16'-0"x25'-0"
M. BEDROOM 13'-4"x18'-6"
PORCH 26'-8"x6'-0"
69'-0"
42'-8"

No. 90436

■ **This plan features:**

— Three bedrooms

— Two full and two half baths

■ The expansive Family Room has a fireplace

■ The Dining Room and Breakfast Area are lit by natural light from bay windows

■ The first floor Master Suite has a deluxe Master Bath

■ This home is designed with basement, slab and crawlspace foundation options.

First floor — 1,477 sq. ft.
Second floor — 704 sq. ft.
Basement — 1,374 sq. ft.
Garage — 528 sq. ft.

Striking Arched Window

No. 97120

This plan features:

— Four bedrooms

— Two full and one half baths

— The covered corner Porch is a place to relax outdoors

— Low maintenance tiling compliments the Nook, the Kitchen, and the Utility Areas

— A focal point fireplace is located in the Great Room

— The Master Bedroom and three Secondary Bedrooms are located upstairs for privacy and quiet time

— A three-car Garage is also featured

— This home is designed with basement foundation options.

First floor — 1,113 sq. ft.
Second floor — 1,080 sq. ft.
Basement — 1,113 sq. ft.

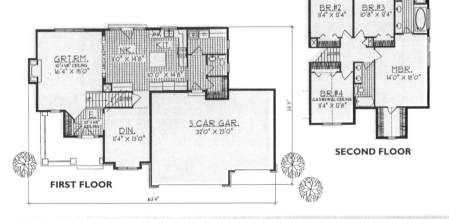

Total living area 2,193 sq. ft. ■ *Price Code D* ■

FIRST FLOOR

SECOND FLOOR

Notable Windows

No. 94950

This plan features:

— Four bedrooms

— Two full, one three-quarter and one half baths

■ Gables accenting arches enhance this brick and wood home

■ The open Entry between the formal Living and Dining Rooms provides ease in entertaining

■ The comfortable Family Room offers a fireplace, a wet bar, and a wall of windows

■ The Kitchen includes an island counter and the Breakfast Bay with the Laundry and Garage nearby

■ The luxurious Master Bedroom has a Bath with a skylight

■ This home is designed with basement and slab foundation options.

■ Alternate foundation options available at an additional charge. Please call 1-800-235-5700 for more information.

First floor — 1,179 sq. ft.
Second floor — 1,019 sq. ft.
Basement — 1,179 sq. ft.
Garage — 466 sq. ft.

Total living area 2,198 sq. ft. ■ *Price Code D* ■

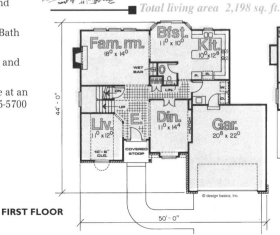

FIRST FLOOR

SECOND FLOOR

Impeccable Style

Total living area 2,198 sq. ft. ■ Price Code D

FIRST FLOOR

SECOND FLOOR

WIDTH 59'-4"
DEPTH 65'-0"

No. 97710

This plan features:

— Three bedrooms

— Two full and one half baths

■ Brick, stone, and interesting rooflines showcase the impeccable style of this home

■ Inside a deluxe staircase highlights the Foyer

■ The Dining Room has a bay window at one end and columns at the other

■ The U-shaped Kitchen has a work island in its center

■ The two-story Great Room has a warm fireplace

■ The shape of the Master Bedroom adds to its character

■ Upstairs find two Bedrooms and a full Bath

■ This home is designed with a basement foundation.

First floor — 1,706 sq. ft.
Second floor — 492 sq. ft.
Basement — 1,706 sq. ft.

Exciting Arched Accents

Total living area 2,209 sq. ft. ■ Price Code D

FIRST FLOOR

SECOND FLOOR

No. 92643

This plan features:

— Three bedrooms

— Two full and one half baths

■ A keystone arch accents the entry into the open Foyer which has a lovely angled staircase and a sloped ceiling

■ The Great Room is enhanced by an entertainment center, a hearth fireplace and a wall of windows overlooking the backyard

■ The efficient, angled Kitchen offers a work island/snackbar, the Breakfast Area and access to the backyard, the Dining Room, Laundry, and the Garage

■ The Master Bedroom wing features a lavish Bath with dual vanities, a large walk-in closet and a corner window tub

■ The two second floor Bedrooms, with walk-in closets, share a skylit Study, a double vanity Bath, and a Bonus Room

■ This home is designed with a basement foundation.

First floor — 1,542 sq. ft.
Second floor — 667 sq. ft.
Garage — 420 sq. ft.
Basement — 1,470 sq. ft.
Bonus — 236 sq. ft.

Charming and Convenient

■ *Total living area 2,209 sq. ft.* ■ *Price Code D* ■

No. 91534

■ **This plan features:**

– Three bedrooms

– Two full and one half baths

■ A central entrance opens to the formal Dining and Living Areas

■ The spacious Family Room offers an inviting fireplace and backyard views

■ The convenient Kitchen has a peninsula counter/snackbar, a Pantry, a built-in desk, an Eating Nook, and a nearby Laundry/Garage entry

■ This home is designed with a crawlspace foundation.

First floor — 1,214 sq. ft.
Second floor — 995 sq. ft.
Bonus — 261 sq. ft.

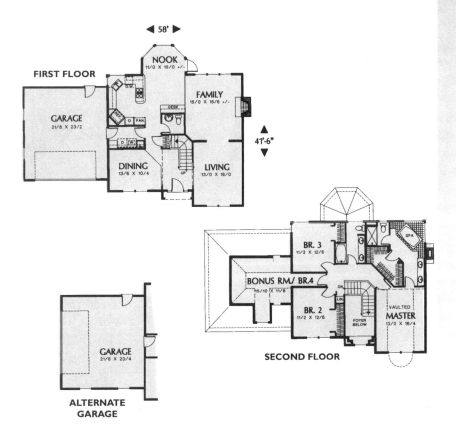

◄ 58' ►

FIRST FLOOR

NOOK
11/0 X 15/0 +/-

GARAGE
21/8 X 23/2

FAMILY
15/0 X 16/6 +/-

DESK

PAN

41'-6"

DINING
13/6 X 10/4

LIVING
13/0 X 16/0

UP

GARAGE
21/8 X 23/4

**ALTERNATE
GARAGE**

BR. 3
11/2 X 12/6

SPA

BONUS RM./ BR.4
15/10 X 11/8

DN

BR. 2
11/2 X 12/6

FOYER
BELOW

VAULTED
MASTER
13/0 X 16/4

SECOND FLOOR

Stately Stucco Living

Total living area 2,210 sq. ft. ■ Price Code D

This plan features:

— Three bedrooms

— Two full and one half baths

■ The opulent Master Suite is set apart, occupying its own private wing of the home

■ The garage includes a Storage Nook, perfect for tools and equipment

■ The secondary Bedrooms and the Bonus Room occupy the second floor and share a double vanity Bath

■ Tiling compliments the Kitchen, Breakfast Room and Sunroom

■ This home is designed with a basement foundation.

First floor — 1,670 sq. ft.
Second floor — 540 sq. ft.
Bonus — 455 sq. ft.
Basement — 1,677 sq. ft.
Garage — 594 sq. ft.

FIRST FLOOR

SECOND FLOOR

Rich Classic Lines

Total living area 2,212 sq. ft. ■ Price Code D

This plan features:

— Four bedrooms

— Three full and one half baths

■ The two-story Foyer is flooded by light through a half-round transom

■ The vaulted ceiling in the Great Room continues into the Master Suite

■ The Great Room is accented by a two-sided fireplace, and provides access to the Patio

■ A work island in the Kitchen adds to its efficiency along with a built-in desk and a Pantry

■ A tray ceiling and a recessed hutch area are located in the formal Dining Room

■ The Master Suite has a walk-in closet, a whirlpool tub, and a double sink vanity

■ This home is designed with a basement foundation.

First floor — 1,496 sq. ft.
Second floor — 716 sq. ft.
Basement — 1,420 sq. ft.
Garage — 460 sq. ft.

FIRST FLOOR

SECOND FLOOR

Kick it Up a Notch

No. 98819

This plan features:

– Four bedrooms

– Two full and one half baths

- The covered Entry leads into a formal Foyer with a great staircase

- The sunken Living Room is enhanced by a gas fireplace and decorative windows

- The Dining Room is highlighted by a built-in china cabinet and a pocket door to the Kitchen

- The spacious Kitchen/Nook and Family Room features a second fireplace, a built-in desk, and a work island

- The Master Suite includes a large walk-in closet and a whirlpool bath

- Three additional Bedrooms share a full Bath

- This home is designed with a basement foundation.

First floor — 1,090 sq. ft.
Second floor — 1,126 sq. ft.
Basement — 1,067 sq. ft.
Garage — 418 sq. ft.

■ *Total living area 2,216 sq. ft.* ■ *Price Code D* ■

FIRST FLOOR

SECOND FLOOR

Simple Elegance

No. 92622

This plan features:

– Three bedrooms

– Two full and one half baths

- The sunken Great Room, large enough for family gatherings, is enhanced by a fireplace and Deck access

- The Dining Room has direct access to the Kitchen

- The Master Bedroom has a garden Bath and a walk-in closet

- The second floor Library can double as a fourth Bedroom

- Two additional Bedrooms share a full Bath

- This home is designed with a basement foundation.

First floor — 1,134 sq. ft.
Second floor — 1,083 sq. ft.
Basement — 931 sq. ft.
Garage — 554 sq. ft.

■ *Total living area 2,217 sq. ft.* ■ *Price Code D* ■

SECOND FLOOR

FIRST FLOOR

WIDTH 57'-8"
DEPTH 37'-4"

Traditional Colonial

■ *Total living area 2,224 sq. ft.* ■ *Price Code D* ■

BASEMENT OPTION

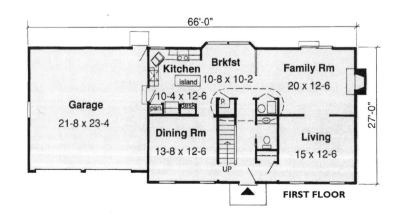

SECOND FLOOR

Br 4
11-4 x 10-8

DN

MBr 1
13-8 x 15-6

Br 2
11-8 x 16

Br 3
11-4 x 10-8

66'-0"

Kitchen
island

Brkfst
10-8 x 10-2

Family Rm
20 x 12-6

10-4 x 12-6

Garage
21-8 x 23-4

pan.

desk

p.

Dining Rm
13-8 x 12-6

Living
15 x 12-6

27'-0"

UP

FIRST FLOOR

No. 34705

■ This plan features:

— Four bedrooms

— Two full and one half baths

■ The formal Living Room and the Dining Room flank a spacious Entry

■ The family areas flow together in an open floor plan at the rear of the home

■ This ideal Kitchen has a work island, a built-in Pantry, and easy access to the Dining Room and Breakfast Area

■ This home is designed with basement, slab, and crawlspace foundation options.

First floor — 1,090 sq. ft.
Second floor — 1,134 sq. ft.
Basement — 1,090 sq. ft.
Garage — 576 sq. ft.

Fieldstone Home with Flexibility

■ *Total living area 2,234 sq. ft.* ■ *Price Code D* ■

No. 90600

■ **This plan features:**

— Four or five bedrooms

— Two full and two half baths

■ This unique design can expand from a cozy five room cottage to an eight room home

■ The Portico leads into an open Foyer with a landing staircase

■ The spacious Living/Dining Room has a hearth fireplace and a sliding glass door to backyard

■ The hub Kitchen has a peninsula snackbar, and is handy to the Dining Room, the Family Room, the Laundry/Mud Room, and the Garage Entry

■ This home is designed with a basement foundation.

First floor — 1,409 sq. ft.
Second floor — 825 sq. ft.
Basement — 1,038 sq. ft.
Garage — 511 sq. ft.

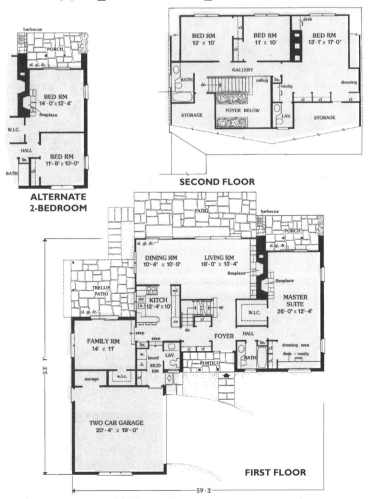

Stately Entrance

No. 24268

This plan features:

— Three or four bedrooms

— Two full and one half baths

■ A vaulted ceiling in the Living Room adds to its spaciousness

■ The formal Dining Room has easy access to both the Living Room and the Kitchen

■ The efficient Kitchen has double sinks, and ample storage and counter space

■ The informal Eating Nook has a built-in Pantry

■ The expansive Family Room has a fireplace and Patio access

■ The plush Master Suite has a vaulted ceiling and a luxurious Master Bath plus two walk-in closets

■ Two additional Bedrooms share a full Bath with a convenient Laundry chute

■ This home is designed with basement, slab, and crawlspace foundation options.

First floor — 1,115 sq. ft.
Second floor — 1,129 sq. ft.
Basement — 1,096 sq. ft.
Garage — 415 sq. ft.

Total living area 2,244 sq. ft. ■ Price Code D

FIRST FLOOR

SECOND FLOOR

Victorian Details

No. 65143

This plan features:

— Four bedrooms

— Three full and one half baths

■ Stone and clapboard siding and a gracious circular Porch create a beautiful facade

■ This home is designed with a basement foundation.

First floor — 1,358 sq. ft.
Second floor — 894 sq. ft.
Basement — 525 sq. ft.
Bonus — 312 sq. ft.

Total living area 2,252 sq. ft. ■ Price Code E

FIRST FLOOR   **SECOND FLOOR**

■ *Total living area 2,252 sq. ft.* ■ *Price Code E* ■

No. 68162

■ **This plan features:**

- Four bedrooms

- Three full baths

■ Built-in corner cabinets in the Dining Room provide places to display crystal and china

■ This home is designed with a slab foundation.

■ Alternate foundation options available at an additional charge. Please call 1-800-235-5700 for more information.

First floor — 1,505 sq. ft.
Second floor — 555 sq. ft.
Garage — 400 sq. ft.

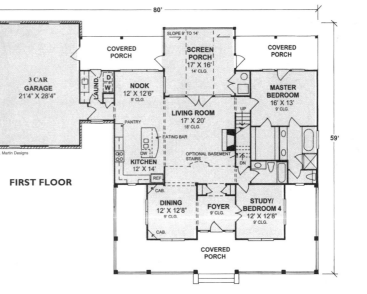

FIRST FLOOR

© W.L. Martin Designs

SECOND FLOOR

Elegant Dining Room

Total living area 2,259 sq. ft. ■ Price Code E

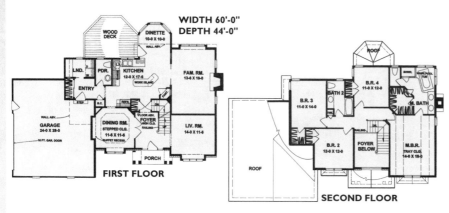

WIDTH 60'-0"
DEPTH 44'-0"

FIRST FLOOR

SECOND FLOOR

No. 93344

■ **This plan features:**

— Four Bedrooms

— Two full and one half baths

■ The grand two-story Foyer has a graceful staircase and access to the Living and Dining Rooms

■ The Dining Room has a double door Entry, boxed bay window, stepped ceiling and recessed buffet

■ A work island/snack bar, corner Pantry and a bright Dinette Area with Deck access highlights the Kitchen

■ Pocket doors lead into the expansive Family Room with a cozy fireplace

■ A tray ceiling, whirlpool tub with a separate shower, double vanity and a walk-in closet enhance the Master Suite

■ The three additional Bedrooms share a full Bath

■ This home is designed with a basement foundation.

First floor — 1,194 sq. ft.
Second floor — 1,065 sq. ft.

Nostalgic Yet Modern

Total living area 2,260 sq. ft. ■ Price Code E

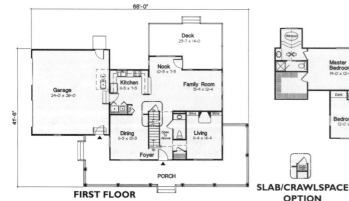

FIRST FLOOR

SLAB/CRAWLSPACE OPTION

SECOND FLOOR

No. 24732

■ **This plan features:**

— Four bedrooms

— Two full and one half baths

■ The wrap-around front Porch provides old-fashioned appeal

■ The formal Dining and Living Rooms to either side of the front Foyer provide for gracious entertaining

■ The efficient Kitchen features a Laundry closet and an extended serving counter for the eating Nook and Family Room

■ The expansive Master Bedroom has a huge walk-in closet and a plush whirlpool Bath

■ The three additional Bedrooms, with over-sized closets, share a double vanity Bath

■ This home is designed with basement, slab, and crawlspace foundation options.

First floor — 1,027 sq. ft.
Second floor — 1,233 sq. ft.
Basement — 945 sq. ft.
Garage — 632 sq. ft.

Impressive Manor

No. 98221

This plan features:

- Four bedrooms

- Two full and one half baths

- The Foyer leads to the Dining Room and Parlor both with windows overlooking the front yard

- The Family Room has a fireplace and leads into the sunny Breakfast Area

- The Master Bedroom has a plush Bath and shares a see-through fireplace with the Sitting Room

- The three additional Bedrooms share a full Bathroom

- This home is designed with a basement foundation.

First floor — 1,113 sq. ft.
Second floor — 1,148 sq. ft.
Basement — 1,113 sq. ft.
Garage — 529 sq. ft.

■ *Total living area 2,261 sq. ft.* ■ *Price Code E* ■

FIRST FLOOR

SECOND FLOOR

WIDTH 66'-0"
DEPTH 31'-0"

Elegant High Ceiling

No. 99127

This plan features:

- Three bedrooms

- Two full and one half baths

- The open Family Room features a fireplace and large windows

- The spacious Kitchen features a center island, walk-in Pantry and adjoins the Breakfast Nook

- An open U-shaped staircase leads upstairs to the Master Bedroom with large closet and private Bath

- The two additional Bedrooms, both with walk-in closets, share a full Bath on the second floor

- This home is designed with a basement foundation.

First floor — 1,271 sq. ft.
Second floor — 991 sq. ft.
Basement — 1,271 sq. ft.

■ *Total living area 2,262 sq. ft.* ■ *Price Code E* ■

SECOND FLOOR   **FIRST FLOOR**

Two-Story Farmhouse

Total living area 2,263 sq. ft. ■ Price Code E ■

FIRST FLOOR

SECOND FLOOR

No. 90458

■**This plan features:**

— Three bedrooms

— Two full and one half baths

■ The wrap-around Porch adds nostalgic appeal to this home

■ The Great Room with fireplace has direct access from the Foyer

■ The formal Dining Room has direct access to the efficient Kitchen

■ An island, double sink, plenty of counter/cabinet space and a built-in Pantry complete the Kitchen

■ The second floor Master Suite has a five-piece private Bath and a walk-in closet

■ The two other Bedrooms have walk-in closets and share a full Bath

■ This home is designed with basement and crawlspace foundation options.

First floor — 1,125 sq. ft.
Second floor — 1,138 sq. ft.
Basement — 1,125 sq. ft.

Vaulted Family Room

Total living area 2,267 sq. ft. ■ Price Code E ■

SECOND FLOOR

FIRST FLOOR

No. 98451

■**This plan features:**

— Four bedrooms

— Three full baths

■ The two-story Foyer is flanked by the Living Room which has a high ceiling

■ There is direct access to the Dining Room from the Kitchen

■ The efficient Kitchen features a peninsula counter/serving bar and is open to the Breakfast Room and the Family Room

■ A walk-in closet and private access to a full Bath can be found in the first floor Bedroom/Study

■ The Master Suite is topped by a tray ceiling in the Bedroom and a vaulted ceiling in the private Bath

■ The two additional Bedrooms on the second floor share a full Bath

■ This home is designed with basement and crawlspace foundation options.

First floor — 1,226 sq. ft.
Second floor — 1,041 sq. ft.
Basement — 1,226 sq. ft.
Garage — 440 sq. ft.

■ *Total living area 2,270 sq. ft.* ■ *Price Code E* ■

No. 97293

■ **This plan features:**

— Four bedrooms

— Two full and one half baths

■ The two-story Foyer is an outstanding first impression

■ The Living Room has elegant arched openings from the Foyer and the Dining Room

■ The sunken Family Room has a fireplace and French doors to the rear yard

■ The Breakfast Room is enhanced by decorative columns and a serving bar from the Kitchen adds convenience

■ This home is designed with basement, slab, and crawlspace foundation options.

First floor — 1,186 sq. ft.
Second floor — 1,084 sq. ft.
Garage — 440 sq. ft.

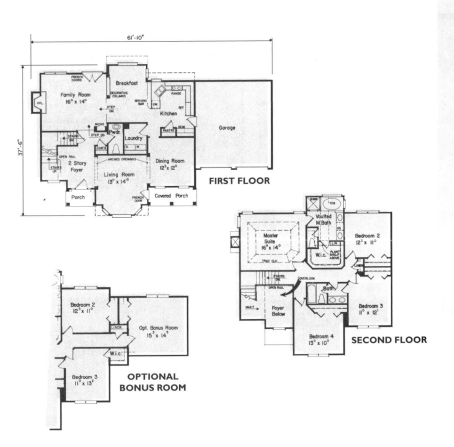

Open Floor Plan

■ *Total living area 2,287 sq. ft.* ■ *Price Code E* ■

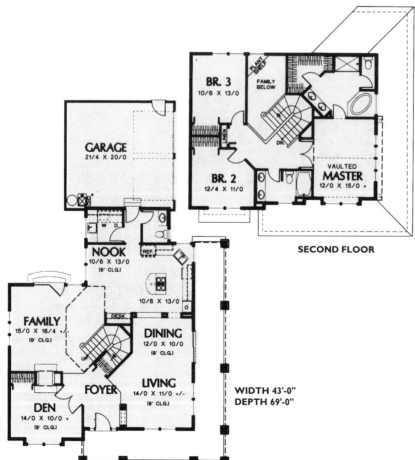

SECOND FLOOR

FIRST FLOOR

WIDTH 43'-0"
DEPTH 69'-0"

No. 91592

■**This plan features:**

— Three bedrooms

— Two full and one half baths

■The quaint wrap-around Porch shelters the Entrance

■The Foyer opens to the combined Living and Dining Rooms, the secluded Den and the Family Room

■The Den shares a terrific two-sided fireplace with the Family Room

■The second floor Master Suite has a vaulted ceiling

■This home is designed with a crawlspace foundation.

First floor — 1,371 sq. ft.
Second floor — 916 sq. ft.
Garage — 427 sq. ft.

■ *Total living area 2,292 sq. ft.* ■ *Price Code E* ■

No. 65145

This plan features:

- Three bedrooms

- Two full and one half baths

■ Extra storage throughout this design provides a place for everything

■ This home is designed with a crawlspace foundation.

■ Alternate foundation options available at an additional charge. Please call 1-800-235-5700 for more information.

First floor — 1,246 sq. ft.
Second floor — 1,046 sq. ft.
Basement — 1,246 sq. ft.
Garage — 392 sq. ft.

WIDTH 58'-0"
DEPTH 42'-2"

SECOND FLOOR

FIRST FLOOR

© Sater Design Collection

Triple Dormers Add Light

■ *Total living area 2,297 sq. ft.* ■ *Price Code E* ■

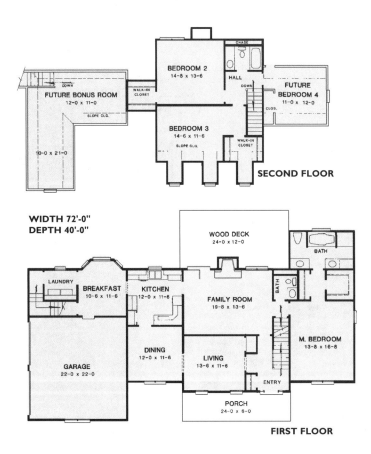

WIDTH 72'-0"
DEPTH 40'-0"

No. 90474

■ This plan features:

— Three bedrooms

— Two full and one half baths

■ The Family Room has a focal point fireplace surrounded by windows and access to the rear Deck

■ The privately located Master Bedroom features large closets and a spa Bath

■ The future Bonus Room and additional Bedrooms are on the second floor

■ This home is designed with basement and crawlspace foundation options.

First floor — 1,580 sq. ft.
Second floor — 717 sq. ft.
Bonus — 410 sq. ft.
Basement — 1,342 sq. ft.
Garage — 484 sq. ft.

Angled Front Porch

No. 65004

This plan features:

- Four bedrooms
- Two full and one half baths
- A huge, angled front Porch provides a unique, outdoor Foyer with access to the Living Room and Dining Room
- Freestanding and angled workspaces make it convenient to enjoy the Kitchen
- Luxurious appointments in the Master Suite include a fireplace, and a private Bath featuring a columned whirlpool tub
- The home is designed with a basement foundation.

First floor — 1,067 sq. ft.
Second floor — 1,233 sq. ft.
Basement — 1,067 sq. ft.

■ *Total living area 2,300 sq. ft.* ■ *Price Code E* ■

WIDTH 58'-0"
DEPTH 33'-0"

FIRST FLOOR

SECOND FLOOR

Traditional Ranch

No. 90444

This plan features:

- Three bedrooms
- Three full baths
- The Great Room has skylights, a fireplace and a vaulted ceiling
- The double L-shaped Kitchen has an eating bar open to the bayed Breakfast Room
- The Master Suite has a walk-in closet, corner garden tub, dual vanity and a linen closet
- The two additional Bedrooms, each with a walk-in closet and built-in desk, share a full Bath
- The Loft above the Great Room includes a vaulted ceiling and open-rail Balcony
- This home is designed with basement, slab and crawlspace foundation options.

Main floor — 1,996 sq. ft.
Loft — 305 sq. ft.

■ *Total living area 2,301 sq. ft.* ■ *Price Code E* ■

MAIN FLOOR

LOFT

Spacious Family Living

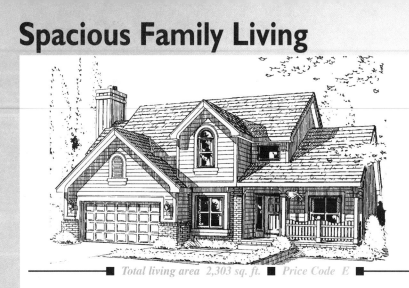

■ **Total living area** 2,303 sq. ft. ■ **Price Code E** ■

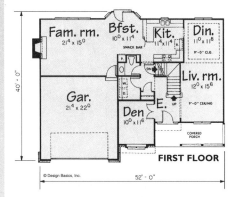

FIRST FLOOR

© Design Basics, Inc.

SECOND FLOOR

No. 94956

■ **This plan features:**

— Four bedrooms

— Two full and one half baths

■ The Entry opens to the spacious Living Room with a tiered ceiling and the Dining Room

■ The hub Kitchen is convenient to the Dining Room, the Breakfast Area and the Family Room

■ The corner Master Bedroom has a private Bath

■ The three additional Bedrooms share a double vanity Bath

■ This home is designed with basement and slab foundation options.

■ Alternate foundation options available at an additional charge. Please call 1-800-235-5700 for more information.

First floor — 1,269 sq. ft.
Second floor — 1,034 sq. ft.
Basement — 1,269 sq. ft.
Garage — 485 sq. ft.

Vaulted Ceilings

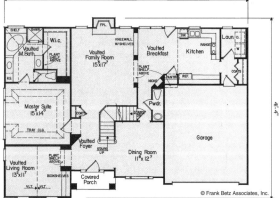

■ **Total living area** 2,308 sq. ft. ■ **Price Code E** ■

© Frank Betz Associates, Inc.

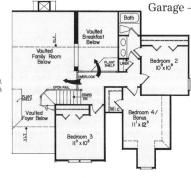

No. 98428

■ **This plan features:**

— Four bedrooms

— Two full and one half baths

■ A vaulted ceiling Foyer leads directly to the Family Room

■ A fireplace adds a warm and cozy atmosphere to the entire home

■ Knee-walls with built-in shelves and a plant shelf above separate the Family Room from the Breakfast Room

■ This home is designed with basement and crawlspace foundation options.

First floor — 1,637 sq. ft.
Second floor — 671 sq. ft.
Basement — 1,637 sq. ft.
Garage — 466 sq. ft.

Old World Charm

No. 92646

This plan features:

- Four bedrooms
- Two full and one half baths
- Balustrade railings and a front Courtyard create an impressive facade
- The Great Room has a corner fireplace, high ceiling and French doors
- The formal Dining Room is enhanced by a decorative window and furniture alcove
- The Country Kitchen with a work island and two Pantries is adjacent to the Breakfast Area, Laundry Room and Garage Entry
- The Master Bedroom features a sloped ceiling, plush Bath and a huge walk-in closet
- This home is designed with a basement foundation.

First floor — 1,595 sq. ft.
Second floor — 725 sq. ft.
Basement — 1,471 sq. ft.
Garage — 409 sq. ft.

■ *Total living area 2,320 sq. ft.* ■ *Price Code E* ■

FIRST FLOOR

SECOND FLOOR

Packed with Living Space

No. 91584

This plan features:

- Three bedrooms
- Two full and one half baths
- The staircase and hallway are the center of this home, with all living areas located like spokes off the hallway
- The formal Living Room includes a fireplace and columns to help divide the adjacent formal Dining Room
- The spacious Kitchen includes a work island, and is open to the roomy Family Room with twin windows and fireplace
- The quiet Den has French doors
- The Master Bedroom and secondary Bedrooms are on the second floor
- This home is designed with a crawlspace foundation.

First floor — 1,168 sq. ft.
Second floor — 1,157 sq. ft.
Garage — 463 sq. ft.

■ *Total living area 2,325 sq. ft.* ■ *Price Code E* ■

FIRST FLOOR   **SECOND FLOOR**

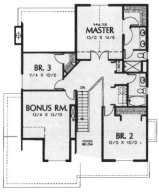

WIDTH 40'-0"
DEPTH 49'-0"

Curving Central Staircase

■ Total living area 2,333 sq. ft. ■ Price Code E ■

No. 65316

■ **This plan features:**

— Four bedrooms

— Two full and one half baths

■ A nostalgic facade with a curved Porch welcomes you into a modern and open interior.

■ Hidden behind the curving stair is a built-in computer station with convenient access to the Kitchen and Family Room.

■ The Solarium connects the front and rear Porches and can be closed off from the Dining Room on chilly winter nights.

■ Master Suite amenities include a private Bath with separate tub and shower.

■ The home is designed with a basement foundation.

First floor — 1,472 sq. ft.
Second floor — 861 sq. ft.
Basement — 1,472 sq. ft.

WIDTH 52'-8"
DEPTH 51'-0"

SECOND FLOOR

FIRST FLOOR

Storage Niche in Garage

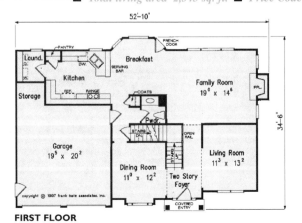

■ Total living area 2,345 sq. ft. ■ Price Code E ■

No. 60007

■ **This plan features:**

— Four bedrooms

— Two full and one half baths

■ A Sitting Area in the Master Suite provides a quiet haven after a long day.

■ The Kitchen has access to a nearby Laundry Room and Pantry.

■ The front staircase leads to a balcony.

■ This home is designed with basement and crawlspace foundation options.

First floor — 1,127 sq. ft.
Second floor — 1,218 sq. ft.
Basement — 1,127 sq. ft.
Garage — 436 sq. ft.

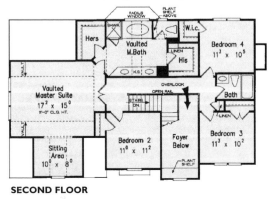

FIRST FLOOR

SECOND FLOOR

■ *Total living area 2,359 sq. ft.* ■ *Price Code E* ■

No. 68163

■ This plan features:

- Four bedrooms

- Three full baths

■ This plan can be modified for two, three, or four Bedrooms to suite your family's needs

■ Deep enough to accomodate furniture, the front Porch offers relaxing, outdoor-living space

■ This home is designed with slab, and crawlspace foundation options.

■ Alternate foundation options available at an additional charge. Please call 1-800-235-5700 for more information.

First floor — 2,036 sq. ft.
Second floor — 323 sq. ft.
Bonus — 335 sq. ft.
Garage — 484 sq. ft.

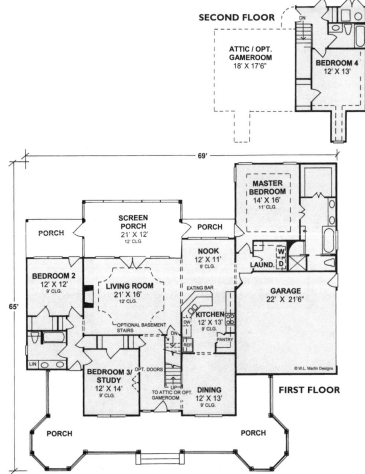

Spacious Elegance

■ *Total living area 2,349 sq. ft.* ■ *Price Code E* ■

FIRST FLOOR

© Frank Betz Associates, Inc.

SECOND FLOOR

WIDTH 56'-0"
DEPTH 47'-6"

No. 98455

■ **This plan features:**

— Four bedrooms

— Three full baths

■ This appealing home has gables, a hip roof, and keystone window accents

■ The two-story Foyer has a palladian window, a lovely staircase and opens to the Dining Room

■ The Family Room has a vaulted ceiling and an inviting fireplace

■ A vaulted ceiling and a radius window highlight the Breakfast Area and the efficient Kitchen

■ The Master Bedroom features a tray ceiling, luxurious Bath and a walk-in closet

■ This home is designed with basement and crawlspace foundation options.

First floor — 1,761 sq. ft.
Second floor — 588 sq. ft.
Basement — 1,761 sq. ft.
Bonus — 267 sq. ft.
Garage — 435 sq. ft.

Flavor of Yesteryear

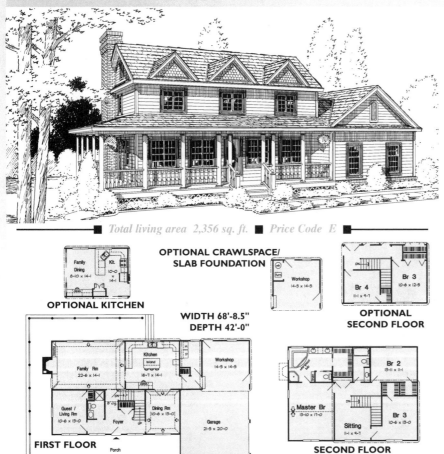

■ *Total living area 2,356 sq. ft.* ■ *Price Code E* ■

OPTIONAL KITCHEN

**OPTIONAL CRAWLSPACE/
SLAB FOUNDATION**

**OPTIONAL
SECOND FLOOR**

WIDTH 68'-8.5"
DEPTH 42'-0"

FIRST FLOOR

SECOND FLOOR

No. 24404

■ **This plan features:**

— Three or four bedrooms

— Two full and one three-quarter baths

■ The formal Living Room could double as a Guest Room

■ The huge Family Room is highlighted by a decorative ceiling, cozy fireplace, bookshelves and Porch access

■ The Country-size Kitchen has an island snack bar, built-in desk and is near the Dining Room, Laundry/Workshop and Garage

■ The Master Bedroom is enhanced by a large walk-in closet and plush Bath with a whirlpool tub

■ The two additional Bedrooms, with walk-in closets, share a full Bath and Sitting Area

■ This home is designed with basement, slab, crawlspace foundation options.

First floor — 1,236 sq. ft.
Second floor — 1,120 sq. ft.

First Floor Master Suite

No. 94613

This plan features:

– Four bedrooms

– Three full and one half baths

■ The Country Porch adds appeal and opens to the central Foyer

■ The spacious Living Room is enhanced by a fireplace

■ The efficient Kitchen has a work island

■ The Master Bedroom has a plush, private Bath

■ There are three additional Bedrooms and two full Baths on the second floor

■ This home is designed with slab and crawlspace foundation options.

First floor — 1,492 sq. ft.
Second floor — 865 sq. ft.
Bonus — 303 sq. ft.
Garage — 574 sq. ft.

Total living area 2,357 sq. ft. ■ Price Code E

FIRST FLOOR

WIDTH 66'-10"
DEPTH 49'-7"

SECOND FLOOR

Classically Detailed

No. 98409

This plan features:

– Four bedrooms

– Two full and one half baths

■ Keystones and columns accent the front triple arched Porch

■ The two-story Foyer has arched openings to the formal areas

■ The Family Room has a fireplace set between a bank of windows on the rear wall

■ The Kitchen has a convenient center island and is open to the Nook

■ The Master Suite has a tray ceiling and an optional Sitting Room

■ One of the three additional Bedrooms has a window seat

■ This home is designed with basement, slab or crawlspace foundation options.

First floor — 1,200 sq. ft.
Second floor — 1,168 sq. ft.
Basement — 1,200 sq. ft.
Garage — 527 sq. ft.

Total living area 2,368 sq. ft. ■ Price Code E

FIRST FLOOR

SECOND FLOOR

185

Coastal Delight

Total living area 2,376 sq. ft. ■ Price Code E

No. 94202

■ **This plan features:**

— Three bedrooms

— Two full baths

■ This design is perfect for coastal, water-front or low-lying terrain

■ The double-door Entry into the open Foyer leads into the Great Room

■ The Great Room has a cathedral ceiling and three sets of double doors which open to the Deck and Veranda

■ The efficient Kitchen has an island work center and adjacent Eating Nook

■ This home is designed with a pier/post foundation.

First floor — 1,736 sq. ft.
Second floor — 640 sq. ft.
Bonus — 253 sq. ft.
Garage — 840 sq. ft

Country Charm

Total living area 2,377 sq. ft. ■ Price Code E

No. 94943

■ **This plan features:**

— Four bedrooms

— Two full and one half baths

■ The charming front Porch and well-proportioned gables compliment the exterior

■ The functional T-shaped stairway adds stylish flair

■ The Family Room opens to the Media Room for versatile entertaining

■ The Breakfast Area with a bay window has direct access to the rear yard

■ The Kitchen has a work island and is open to the Breakfast Room

■ An elegant Balcony overlooks the two-story Entry and a French Door opens to the Master Suite with a whirlpool Bath and walk-in closet

■ This home is designed with a basement foundation.

■ Alternate foundation options available at an additional charge. Please call 1-800-235-5700 for more information.

First floor — 1,206 sq. ft.
Second floor — 1,171 sq. ft.
Basement — 1,206 sq. ft.
Garage — 521 sq. ft.

Easy Downsizing

No. 68176

This plan features:

- Four bedrooms
- Three full and one half baths
- ■ Once the kids are gone, a door at the top of the stairs turns this home into a single-level, making downsizing in this home possible.
- ■ The bonus room adds 258 square feet.
- ■ This home is designed with slab and crawlspace foundation options.
- ■ Alternate foundation options available at an additional charge. Please call 1-800-235-5700 for more information.

First floor — 1,558 sq. ft.
Second floor — 822 sq. ft.
Bonus — 258 sq. ft.
Garage — 486 sq. ft.

■ *Total living area 2,380 sq. ft.* ■ *Price Code E* ■

FIRST FLOOR

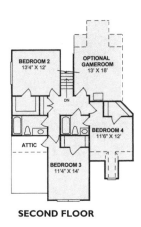

SECOND FLOOR

Curved Landing Staircase

No. 68168

This plan features:

- Three bedrooms
- Two full and one half baths
- ■ An angled Study off the Foyer creates a private area on the first floor.
- ■ The Bonus Room adds 288 square feet.
- ■ This home is designed with slab and crawlspace foundation options.
- ■ Alternate foundation options available at an additional charge. Please call 1-800-235-5700 for more information.

First floor — 1,862 sq. ft.
Second floor — 520 sq. ft.
Bonus — 288 sq. ft.
Garage — 576 sq. ft.

SECOND FLOOR

OPTIONAL GAMEROOM

■ *Total living area 2,382 sq. ft.* ■ *Price Code E* ■

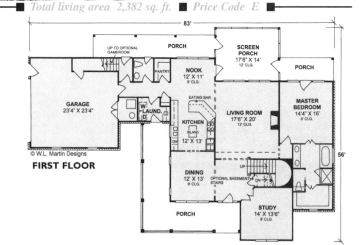

© W.L. Martin Designs

FIRST FLOOR

Sunken Family Room

Total living area 2,386 sq. ft. ■ Price Code E

FIRST FLOOR

SECOND FLOOR

No. 98486

■ This plan features:

— Four bedrooms

— Two full and one half baths

■ The grand two-story Foyer creates an impressive Entry

■ The see-through fireplace in the Family Room is shared with the Keeping Room

■ A terrific informal Living Area is created by the open floor plan between the Kitchen, Breakfast Room, and Keeping Room

■ The Master Suite has a tray ceiling above the Bedroom, an optional Sitting Room, a vaulted ceiling above the Master Bath and a walk-in closet

■ This home is designed with basement and crawl space foundation options.

First floor — 1,223 sq. ft.
Second floor — 1,163 sq. ft.
Basement — 1,223 sq. ft.
Garage — 400 sq. ft.
Bonus — 204 sq. ft.

Repeating Gables

Total living area 2,388 sq. ft. ■ Price Code E

FIRST FLOOR

SECOND FLOOR

No. 92692

■ This plan features:

— Four bedrooms

— Two full and one half baths

■ The impressive exterior features double gables and an arched window

■ The spacious Foyer separates the formal Dining Room and Living Room

■ The roomy Kitchen and Breakfast Area are adjacent to the large Family Room which has a fireplace and access to the rear Deck

■ The Master Bedroom features a private Bath with dual vanity, shower stall and whirlpool tub

■ The three additional Bedrooms share a full hall Bath

■ This home is designed with a basement foundation.

First floor — 1,207 sq. ft.
Second floor — 1,181 sq. ft.
Basement — 1,207 sq. ft.
Garage — 484 sq. ft.

A Magnificent Manor

No. 98410

This plan features:

- Four bedrooms
- Three full baths
- The efficient Kitchen opens to the formal Dining Room and Breakfast Area
- The two-story Family Room is highlighted by a fireplace framed by windows
- A tray ceiling crowns the Master Bedroom
- This home is designed with basement and crawl space foundation options

First floor — 1,428 sq. ft.
Second floor — 961 sq. ft.
Basement — 1,428 sq. ft.
Garage — 507 sq. ft.
Bonus — 472 sq. ft.

■ *Total living area 2,389 sq. ft.* ■ *Price Code E* ■

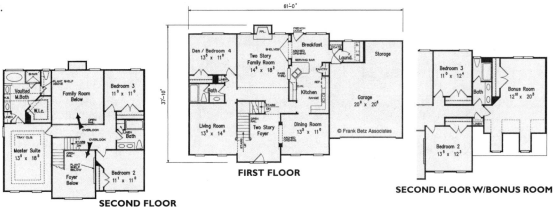

FIRST FLOOR

SECOND FLOOR

SECOND FLOOR W/BONUS ROOM

© Frank Betz Associates

Enticing Elevation

No. 97413

This plan features:

- Four bedrooms
- Two full and one half baths
- The Parlor is enhanced by bright Gazebo windows, a built-in curio and has direct access to the Porch
- The Gathering Room features a bright window wall, a cozy fireplace and elegant French doors to the Parlor
- The Kitchen has a work island and an angled Breakfast Area with access to the rear yard
- The Master Bedroom has two walk-in closets and a skylit private Bath
- This home is designed with a basement foundation.
- Alternate foundation options available at an additional charge. Please call 1-800-235-5700 for more information.

First floor — 1,183 sq. ft.
Second floor — 1,209 sq. ft.
Garage — 483 sq. ft.

■ *Total living area 2,392 sq. ft.* ■ *Price Code E* ■

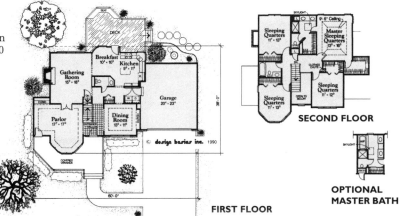

FIRST FLOOR

SECOND FLOOR

OPTIONAL MASTER BATH

© design basics inc. 1990

Distinctive Design

Total living area 2,394 sq. ft. ■ Price Code E

FIRST FLOOR

Deck 16-0 x 10-0
Lav.
M.Bath
Brkfst. 11-6 x 8-6
Family Rm. 19-8 x 13-6
Kit. 11-6 x 9-0
Master Bdrm. 15-8 x 17-6
Dining 11-6 x 13-6
Living 11-6 x 15-6
Open Foyer
50-0
47-0

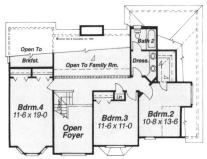

SECOND FLOOR

Open To Brkfst.
Open To Family Rm.
Bath 2
Dress.
Bdrm.4 11-6 x 19-0
Open Foyer
Bdrm.3 11-6 x 11-0
Bdrm.2 10-8 x 13-6
Lin.

No. 93210

■ **This plan features:**

— Four bedrooms

— Two full and one half baths

■ French doors open into the two-story Foyer topped by a beautiful arched window

■ Both the formal Living and Dining Rooms receive plenty of natural light through their bay windows

■ The well-appointed Kitchen includes a peninsula counter and easy access to both dining areas

■ The expansive Family Room has a fireplace and opens onto the rear Deck

■ The large Master Suite has a private Bath with double vanity and a walk-in closet

■ The three second floor Bedrooms share a full hall Bath with double vanity

■ This home is designed with a basement foundation.

First floor — 1,560 sq. ft.
Second floor — 834 sq. ft.
Basement — 772 sq. ft.
Garage — 760 sq. ft.

Additional Bath Option

Total living area 2,395 sq. ft. ■ Price Code E

No. 60005

■ **This plan features:**

— Three bedrooms

— Two full and one half baths

■ The angled Kitchen fully views the Breakfast Area and Family Room

■ A back staircase leads to a Bonus Room that adds 395 square feet

■ This home is designed with basement and crawlspace foundation options.

First floor — 1,847 sq. ft.
Second floor — 548 sq. ft.
Bonus — 395 sq. ft.
Basement — 1,803 sq. ft.
Garage — 484 sq. ft.

FIRST FLOOR

Porch
Breakfast
Kitchen
Two Story Family Room 15⁰ x 18⁴
Vaulted M.Bath
Hers
His
Master Suite 17' x 13⁶
Dining Room 12⁰ x 13
Two Story Foyer
Living/Sitting Room 12⁸ x 11³
Covered Porch
Laundry
Garage 20⁴ x 21²
60'-0"
66'-4"

SECOND FLOOR

Bedroom 2 11⁸ x 12⁴
Family Room Below
Bath
Bedroom 3 12⁰ x 12⁰
Foyer Below
Opt. Bath
Opt. Bonus Room 12⁸ x 25³

Elegant Brick Two-Story

No. 90450

This plan features:

— Four bedrooms

— Two full and one half baths

- The large two-story Great Room has a fireplace and access to a Deck

- The secluded Master Suite has two walk-in closets and a private, lavish Bath

- The Kitchen with a work island is adjacent to the Dining Room and Breakfast Nook

- The three additional Bedrooms, two with walk-in closets, share a full hall Bath

- The optional Bonus Room has a private entrance from below

- This home is designed with basement and crawlspace foundation options.

First floor — 1,637 sq. ft.
Second floor — 761 sq. ft.
Bonus — 453 sq. ft.

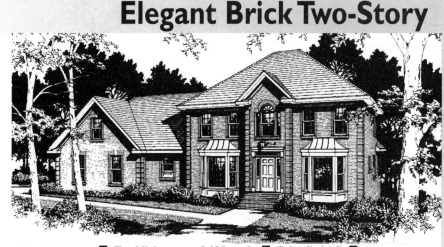

■ *Total living area 2,398 sq. ft.* ■ *Price Code E* ■

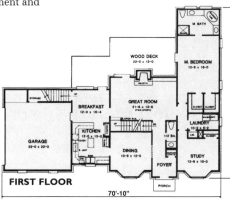

Eye-Catching Turret

No. 92651

This plan features:

— Four bedrooms

— Three full and one half baths

- The sheltered Porch leads into the open Foyer and Great Room with its high ceiling, hearth fireplace and Atrium door

- Columns frame the entrance to the Dining Room

- The efficient Kitchen with built-in Pantry, work island and bright Breakfast Area has access to the Laundry and Garage

- The Master Bedroom wing has a Sitting Area, walk-in closet and private Bath

- This home is designed with basement and slab foundation options.

First floor — 1,710 sq. ft.
Second floor — 693 sq. ft.
Basement — 1,620 sq. ft.
Garage — 467 sq. ft.

■ *Total living area 2,403 sq. ft.* ■ *Price Code E* ■

WIDTH 63'-4"
DEPTH 48'-0"

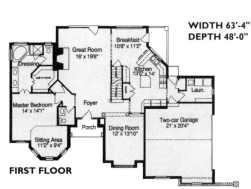

Beautiful See-Through Fireplace

■ Total living area 2,405 sq. ft. ■ Price Code E ■

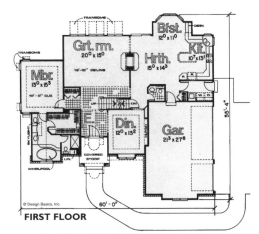

FIRST FLOOR

© Design Basics, Inc.

SECOND FLOOR

No. 99449

■ **This plan features:**

– Four bedrooms

– Two full and one half baths

■ The large transom windows at the rear of the Great Room provide natural illumination

■ The Great Room and the cozy Hearth Room share a beautiful see-through fireplace

■ The Breakfast Area has a bay window and built-in desk

■ The gourmet Kitchen includes a Pantry, work island, ample counter space and a corner sink

■ The secluded Master Suite has a skylight in the Dressing Area and a large walk-in closet

■ This home is designed with a basement foundation.

■ Alternate foundation options available at an additional charge. Please call 1-800-235-5700 for more information.

First floor — 1,733 sq. ft.
Second floor — 672 sq. ft.
Basement — 1,733 sq. ft.
Garage — 613 sq. ft.

Country Style For Today

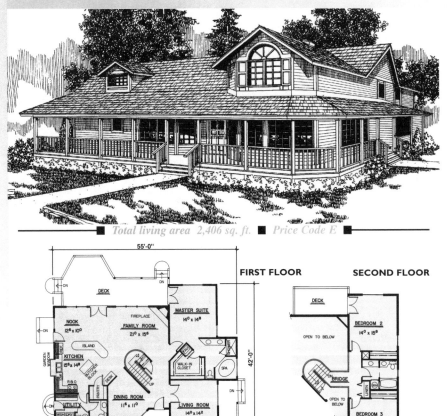

■ Total living area 2,406 sq. ft. ■ Price Code E ■

FIRST FLOOR   **SECOND FLOOR**

No. 91700

■ **This plan features:**

– Three bedrooms

– Two full and one half baths

■ The wide wrap-around Porch reflects a Farmhouse style

■ The spacious Living Room has double doors and a large front window

■ The huge, Country Kitchen has two islands and a garden window over the double sink

■ The Family Room, Eating Nook and Kitchen share an open layout

■ The Master Suite a huge walk-in closet and private Bath with a spa tub

■ This home is designed with basement and slab foundation options.

First floor — 1,785 sq. ft.
Second floor — 621 sq. ft.

Symmetrical Beauty

No. 94611

This plan features:

- Four bedrooms
- Three full and one half baths
- The spacious Family Room has a cozy fireplace
- The open Dining Room is accented by columns conveniently located
- The corner Master Bedroom has a large walk-in closet and double vanity Bath
- The second first floor Bedroom has a walk-in closet and private Bath
- This home is designed with crawl space and slab foundation options.

First floor —1,796 sq. ft.
Second floor —610 sq. ft.
Garage — 570 sq. ft.

■ *Total living area 2,406 sq. ft.* ■ *Price Code E* ■

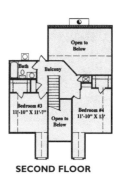

WIDTH 68'-8.5"
DEPTH 64'-8.5"

FIRST FLOOR

SECOND FLOOR

A Special Touch

No. 99133

This plan features:

- Three bedrooms
- Two full and one half baths
- The covered front Porch provides a warm welcome
- The Great Room has a fireplace with built-in cabinets to one side
- The Kitchen has a work island and is open to the large Nook Area with access to the Screened Porch
- The Master Bedroom has a tray ceiling, a walk-in closet and a private Bath
- The secondary Bedrooms are located upstairs for privacy
- This home has a three-car Garage
- This home is designed with a basement foundation.

First Floor — 1,835 sq. ft.
Second Floor — 573 sq. ft.
Basement — 1,835 sq. ft.

■ *Total living area 2,408 sq. ft.* ■ *Price Code E* ■

FIRST FLOOR

SECOND FLOOR

Thoughtfully Designed

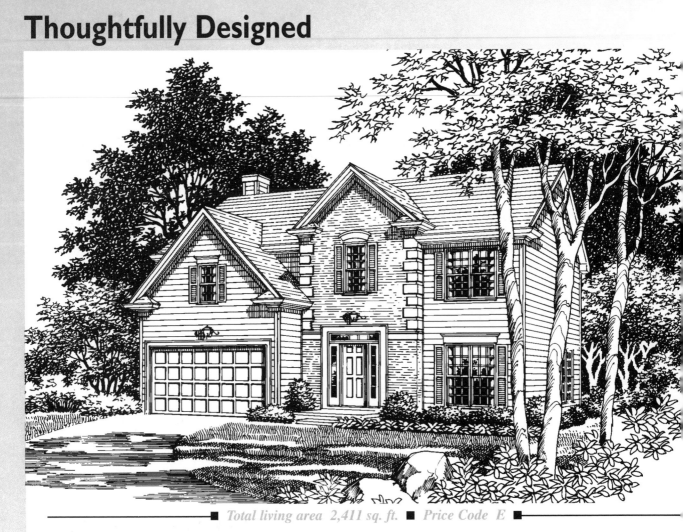

■ *Total living area 2,411 sq. ft.* ■ *Price Code E* ■

No. 93602

■ This plan features:

— Four bedrooms

— Two full and one half baths

■ The Foyer opens to the formal Living and Dining Rooms for gracious entertaining

■ The two-story Great Room has a fireplace and a wall of windows

■ The hub Kitchen has a cooktop work island, built-in Pantry and Desk, and Breakfast Alcove with backyard access

■ The Master Bedroom has a tray ceiling, window alcove, a huge walk-in closet and plush Bath

■ This home is designed with basement and slab foundation options.

First floor — 1,209 sq. ft.
Second floor — 1,202 sq. ft.
Basement — 1,209 sq. ft.
Garage — 370 sq. ft.

SECOND FLOOR

FIRST FLOOR

Two-Story Drama

No. 99116

This plan features:

– Four bedrooms

– Two full and one half baths

■ The Great Room has a rear window wall and a cozy fireplace

■ The Den has a bay window and built-in cabinets

■ The Kitchen has a Pantry, double sink and an eating bar adjacent to the Nook

■ The Master Bedroom has a private Bath as well as a huge closet

■ Three more Bedrooms share a full Bath

■ This home is designed with a basement foundation.

First floor — 1,356 sq. ft.
Second floor — 1,060 sq. ft.
Basement — 1,356 sq. ft.

■ Total living area 2,416 sq. ft. ■ Price Code E ■

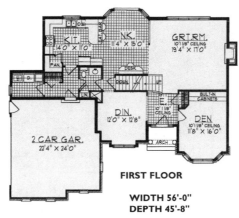

FIRST FLOOR

WIDTH 56'-0"
DEPTH 45'-8"

SECOND FLOOR

Family Room with a Fireplace

No. 93319

This plan features:

– Four bedrooms

– Two full and one half baths

■ The Kitchen has a built-in Pantry, cooktop island, double sink and a convenient Dinette Area

■ A cozy fireplace enhances the Family Room

■ This plan features a formal Living Room and Dining Room

■ The luxurious Master Suite has a plush Bath and walk-in closet

■ The three additional Bedrooms share a full hall Bath

■ This home is designed with a basement foundation.

First floor — 1,228 sq. ft.
Second floor — 1,191 sq. ft.
Basement — 1,228 sq. ft.
Garage — 528 sq. ft.

■ Total living area 2,419 sq. ft. ■ Price Code E ■

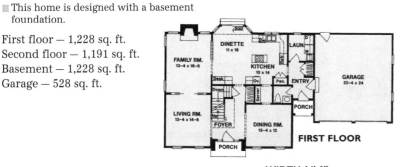

FIRST FLOOR

WIDTH 64'-0"
DEPTH 35'-0"

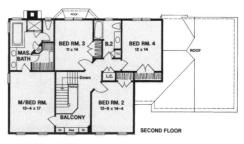

SECOND FLOOR

For The Young Family

Total living area 2,420 sq. ft. ■ **Price Code E**

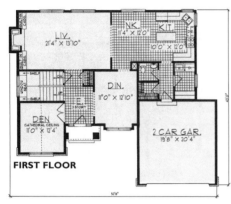

FIRST FLOOR

No. 97142

■ **This plan features:**

— Three bedrooms

— Two full and one half baths

■ Built-in cabinets surround a beautiful fire-place in the large Living Room

■ The Den has a unique window seat which provides a great retreat from the commotion of everyday life

■ The large island, centered in the Kitchen, supplies the perfect resting place for a quick snack or a convenient space to prepare special meals

■ This home is designed with a basement foundation.

First floor — 1,339 sq. ft.
Second floor 1,081 sq. ft.

SECOND FLOOR

Stucco and Stone

Total living area 2,421 sq. ft. ■ **Price Code E**

No. 93208

■ **This plan features:**

— Four bedrooms

— Two full and one half baths

■ The Laundry is located on the second floor

■ The Playroom can be used as another Bedroom

■ There is a bay window in the Living Room

■ A fireplace warms the Family Room

■ This home is designed with basement and crawlspace foundation options.

First floor — 1,090 sq. ft.
Second floor — 1,331 sq. ft.
Basement — 1,022 sq. ft.
Garage — 562 sq. ft.

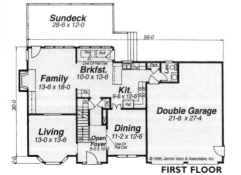

FIRST FLOOR

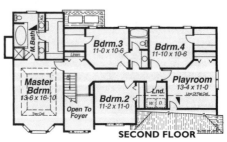

SECOND FLOOR

■ *Total living area 2,423 sq. ft.* ■ *Price Code E* ■

No. 98712

■ This plan features:

— Three bedrooms

— Three full baths

■ A gracious double-door Entry opens to the Dining and Living Rooms

■ The huge Living Room features a fireplace with wood box, wetbar and French doors to the Patio

■ The open Kitchen has a snack bar, Greenhouse Eating Nook and access to the Patio and nearby Utility/Garage Entry

■ The plush Master Suite has a cozy fireplace, huge walk-in closet and Spa tub

■ This home is designed with a slab foundation.

First floor — 1,412 sq. ft.
Second floor — 1,011 sq. ft.
Garage — 452 sq. ft.

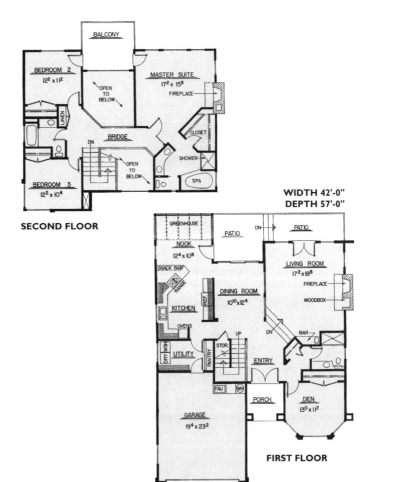

WIDTH 42'-0''
DEPTH 57'-0''

SECOND FLOOR

FIRST FLOOR

Pocket Doors in Kitchen

■ *Total living area 2,424 sq. ft.* ■ *Price Code E* ■

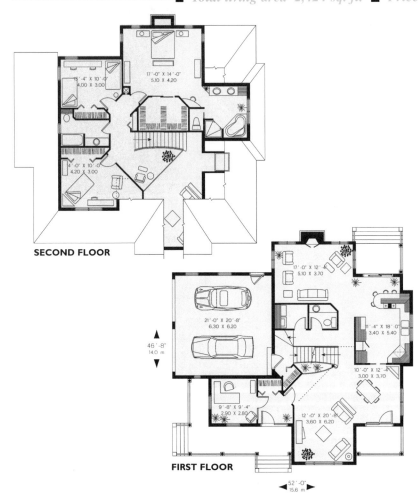

SECOND FLOOR

FIRST FLOOR

No. 65314

■ **This plan features:**

— Three bedrooms

— Two full and one half baths

■ An airlock Entry separates the Home Office from the living areas creating a secluded, work-at-home environment

■ This home is designed with a basement foundation.

First floor — 1,306 sq. ft.
Second floor — 1,118 sq. ft.
Garage — 576 sq. ft.

Stucco & Stone

No. 98419

■ This plan features:

— Three bedrooms

— Two full and one half baths

■ The Great Room features a vaulted ceiling, a fireplace and French doors to the rear yard

■ Decorative columns define the Dining Room

■ A built-in Pantry and a radius window above the double sink are featured in the Kitchen

■ The Breakfast Area is crowned by a vaulted ceiling

■ A tray ceiling is over the Master Bedroom and Sitting Area and a vaulted ceiling crowns the Master Bath

■ This home is designed with basement, slab, and crawlspace foundation options

First floor — 1,796 sq. ft.
Second floor — 629 sq. ft.
Bonus — 208 sq. ft.
Basement — 1,796 sq. ft.
Garage — 588 sq. ft.

■ Total living area 2,425 sq. ft. ■ Price Code E ■

SECOND FLOOR

FIRST FLOOR

WIDTH 54'-0"
DEPTH 53'-10"

Cascading Gable Roofs

No. 99062

■ This plan features:

— Three bedrooms

— Two full and one half baths

■ The well-designed exterior has clean lines, cascading gable roofs, covered Porch and clap board siding

■ This open floor plan features wood columns to define the Living Room and the Breakfast Room

■ The Kitchen has an angled island and abundant counter space

■ Three Bedrooms and two full Baths are on the second floor

■ This home is designed with a basement foundation.

First floor — 1,354 sq. ft.
Second floor — 1,072 sq. ft.
Basement — 1,354 sq. ft.

■ Total living area 2,426 sq. ft. ■ Price Code E ■

WIDTH 62'-6"
DEPTH 38'-6"

FIRST FLOOR

SECOND FLOOR

A Splendid Porch

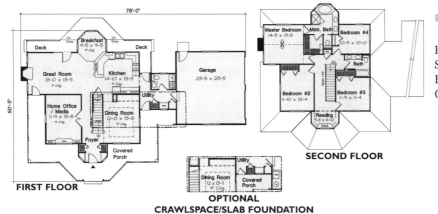

FIRST FLOOR

OPTIONAL CRAWLSPACE/SLAB FOUNDATION

SECOND FLOOR

■ *Total living area 2,426 sq. ft.* ■ *Price Code E* ■

No. 24735

■ **This plan features:**

— Four bedrooms

— Two full and one half baths

■ This attractive home has a stylish front Porch

■ The Foyer features dual closets and an attractive staircase

■ The Home Office could be used as a Media Center

■ The Great Room is open to the Kitchen and they share a serving bar

■ The Breakfast Nook overlooks the rear Deck

■ Four Bedrooms, a Reading Nook and two full Baths are on the second floor

■ This home is designed with basement, slab and crawlspace foundation options.

First Floor — 1,305 sq. ft.
Second Floor — 1,121 sq. ft.
Basement — 1,194 sq. ft.
Garage — 576 sq. ft.

Elegant Elevation

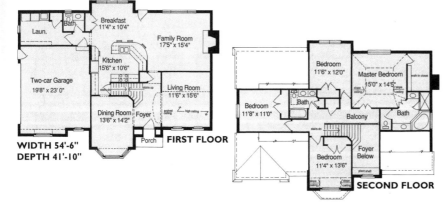

**WIDTH 54'-6"
DEPTH 41'-10"**

FIRST FLOOR

SECOND FLOOR

■ *Total living area 2,428 sq. ft.* ■ *Price Code E* ■

No. 92634

■ **This plan features:**

— Four bedrooms

— Two full and one half baths

■ A staircase and plant shelf highlight the open Foyer

■ The formal Living Room has a high ceiling and arched entry

■ A decorative bay window enhances the formal Dining Room

■ The expansive Family Room has a focal point fireplace and view of the rear yard

■ The Kitchen has a Breakfast Area, peninsula counter/snackbar and is near the Laundry and Garage Entry

■ The comfortable Master Bedroom has sloped ceiling, large walk-in closet and plush Bath

■ The three additional Bedrooms share a double vanity Bath with a skylight

■ This home is designed with a basement foundation.

First floor — 1,309 sq. ft.
Second floor — 1,119 sq. ft.
Basement — 1,277 sq. ft.
Garage — 452 sq. ft.

For A Busy Lifestyle

No. 91512

This plan features:

- Three bedrooms
- Two full and one half baths
- The Family Room has a fireplace and is open to the Kitchen and Eating Nook
- The efficient Kitchen has easy access to the Eating Nook and the Formal Dining Room
- A large multi-paned window provides a view of the front yard from the Den
- The Master Suite has a decorative ceiling, large walk-in closet and private Master Bath
- Two additional Bedrooms share a full hall Bath
- This home is designed with a crawlspace foundation.

First floor — 1,408 sq. ft.
Second floor — 1,024 sq. ft.

Total living area 2,432 sq. ft. ■ *Price Code E*

FIRST FLOOR

SECOND FLOOR

Vaulted Screen Porch

No. 68166

This plan features:

- Four bedrooms
- Three full baths
- A Juliet balcony on the second floor overlooks the Living Room
- The Bonus Room adds 302 square feet
- This home is designed with slab and crawlspace foundation options.
- Alternate foundation options available at an additional charge. Please call 1-800-235-5700 for more information.

First floor — 1,900 sq. ft.
Second floor — 538 sq. ft.
Bonus — 302 sq. ft.
Garage — 782 sq. ft.

Total living area 2,438 sq. ft. ■ *Price Code E*

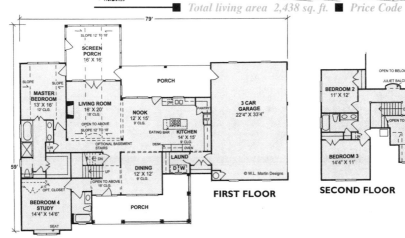

FIRST FLOOR

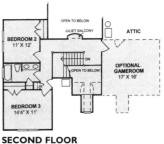

SECOND FLOOR

© W.L. Martin Designs

Eye-Catching Style

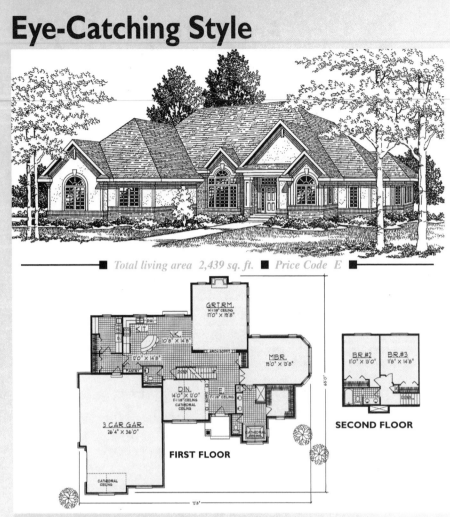

■ *Total living area 2,439 sq. ft.* ■ *Price Code E* ■

FIRST FLOOR

SECOND FLOOR

No. 99138

■ **This plan features:**

— Three bedrooms

— Two full and one half baths

■ The Dining Room has a cathedral ceiling and distinctive front windows

■ The Master Bedroom has a private Bath with a cathedral ceiling and dual vanity

■ The Great Room has an arched soffit entrance and fireplace

■ The L-shaped Kitchen has an adjacent Nook and a curved snack bar

■ The two additional Bedrooms and a full Bath are located on the second floor

■ This home is designed with a basement foundation.

First floor — 1,944 sq. ft.
Second floor — 495 sq. ft.
Basement — 1,944 sq. ft.

Traditional Cape Cod

No. 97709

■ **This plan features:**

— Three bedrooms

— Two full and one half baths

■ The Library has built-in shelves

■ The formal Dining Room has columns and a dramatic view through the Great Room

■ The Master Bedroom has a deluxe Bath and a spacious walk-in closet

■ This home is designed with a basement foundation.

First floor — 1,710 sq. ft.
Second floor — 733 sq. ft.
Bonus — 181 sq. ft.
Basement — 1,710 sq. ft.

■ *Total living area 2,443 sq. ft.* ■ *Price Code E* ■

FIRST FLOOR

SECOND FLOOR

Country Brick

No. 92653

This plan features:

- Three bedrooms
- Two full and one half baths
- The front Porch leads into a gracious open Foyer and the Great Room
- The secluded Library has built-in shelves
- The expansive Great Room is enhanced by a focal point fireplace and a sloped ceiling
- The Country-size Kitchen has an island snack bar, bright Breakfast Area, Pantry and is near the Laundry/Garage Entry
- The private Master Bedroom features a deluxe Bath and spacious walk-in closet
- The two additional Bedrooms with walk-in closets and window seats, share a double vanity Bath
- This home is designed with a basement foundation.

First floor — 1,710 sq. ft.
Second floor — 733 sq. ft.
Bonus — 181 sq. ft.
Basement — 1,697 sq. ft.
Garage — 499 sq. ft.

Total living area 2,443 sq. ft. ■ *Price Code E* ■

SECOND FLOOR

FIRST FLOOR

Two-Story Foyer

No. 60012

This plan features:

- Four bedrooms
- Three full and one half baths
- One bedroom on the first floor is privately located, making it ideal for guests
- The Bonus Room adds 314 square feet
- This home is designed with basement and crawlspace foundation options.

First floor — 1,459 sq. ft.
Second floor — 989 sq. ft.
Bonus — 314 sq. ft.
Basement — 1,459 sq. ft.
Garage — 489 sq. ft.

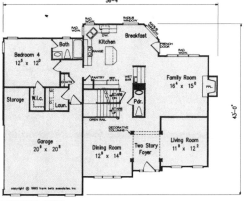

Total living area 2,448 sq. ft. ■ *Price Code E* ■

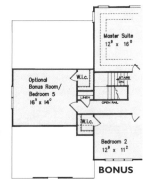

BONUS

SECOND FLOOR

FIRST FLOOR

Elegant Victorian

■ *Total living area 2,455 sq. ft.* ■ *Price Code E* ■

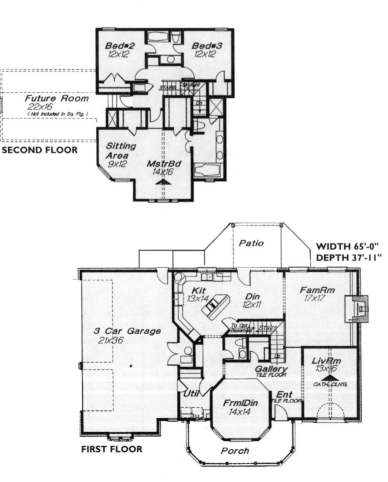

SECOND FLOOR

Bed#2 12x12
Bed#3 12x12
STAIRS
Future Room 22x16 (Not Included In Sq. Ftg.)
Sitting Area 9x12
MstrBd 14x16

FIRST FLOOR

Patio
WIDTH 65'-0"
DEPTH 37'-11"
3 Car Garage 21x36
Kit 13x14
Din 12x11
FamRm 17x17
To Opt. Basement
Stairs
Gallery TILE FLOOR
LivRm 13x16
CATH.CLNG
Util
FrmlDin 14x14
Ent TILE FLOOR
Porch

No. 98518

■ **This plan features:**

— Three bedrooms

— Two full and one half baths

■ The front Porch is a great place to sit and relax with family and friends

■ The formal Dining Room has a bay window and the Living Room features a cathedral ceiling

■ There is plenty of space for activities in the Family Room which is accented by a fireplace

■ The Master Bedroom has a Sitting Area, walk-in closet, and a private Bath

■ This home is designed with basement and slab foundation options.

First floor — 1,447 sq. ft.
Second floor — 1,008 sq. ft.
Basement — 352 sq. ft.
Garage — 756 sq. ft.

Open Living Area

No. 94124

This plan features:

- Four Bedrooms

- Two full and one half baths

■ The spacious two-story Foyer opens to the formal rooms

■ The Living Room is topped by a vaulted ceiling

■ Pocket doors separate the Family Room and the Living Room

■ The efficient Kitchen has an island, Pantry and snack bar and is open to the Dinette and Family Room

■ A bay window enhances the elegant formal Dining Room

■ The secluded Master Suite has a double door entry and plush Master Bath

■ This home is designed with a basement foundation.

First floor — 1,861 sq. ft.
Second floor — 598 sq. ft.
Basement — 1,802 sq. ft.
Garage — 523 sq. ft.

Total living area 2,459 sq. ft. ■ *Price Code E*

Family Living Area

No. 93340

This plan features:

- Four bedrooms

- Two full and one half baths

■ A vaulted ceiling tops the Foyer adding volume

■ The Living Room features a tray ceiling and is enhanced by a boxed bay window

■ The Dining Room adjoins the Living Room and has direct access to the Kitchen

■ The Kitchen features a cooktop island and is open to the Dinette

■ The Family Room has a fireplace framed by windows and adjoins the Dinette

■ Double doors add privacy to the Den

■ A tray ceiling tops the Master Bedroom which has a walk-in closet and a full Bath

■ The secondary Bedrooms share a full Bath

■ This home is designed with a basement foundation.

First floor — 1,378 sq. ft.
Second floor — 1,084 sq. ft.
Basement — 1,378 sq. ft.
Garage — 448 sq. ft.

Total living area 2,462 sq. ft. ■ *Price Code E*

Stunning First Impression

■ *Total living area 2,464 sq. ft.* ■ *Price Code E* ■

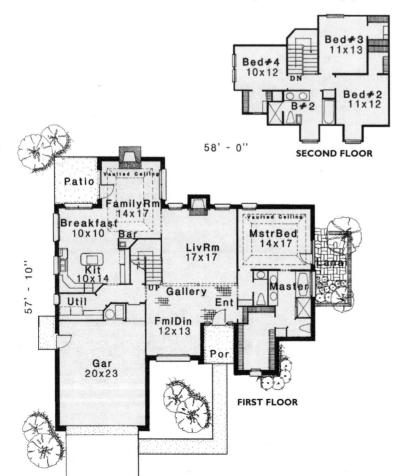

58' - 0"

SECOND FLOOR

57' - 10"

FIRST FLOOR

No. 98540

■ **This plan features:**

— Four bedrooms

— Two full and one half baths

■ This design includes dormer windows on the second floor, brick quoin corners and arched windows

■ The large Living Room has a fireplace and is open to the formal Dining Area

■ The Kitchen has a Breakfast Area, ample storage space and a work island

■ The luxurious Master Suite occupies an entire wing of the home and provides a quiet retreat

■ This home is designed with basement, slab, crawlspace foundation options.

First floor — 1,805 sq. ft.
Second floor — 659 sq. ft.
Basement — 1,800 sq. ft.
Garage — 440 sq. ft.

Country-Style Home

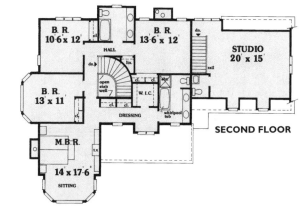

■ *Total living area 2,466 sq. ft.* ■ *Price Code E* ■

No. 99640

■ This plan features:

— Four bedrooms

— Two full and two half baths

■ The sunken formal Living Room is enhanced by a focal point fireplace, abundant windows and a stepped ceiling

■ The large fully equipped Kitchen has a central island

■ A second fireplace enhances the Family Room

■ The Master Suite features a private plush Bath and a Dressing Area

■ This home is designed with basement and slab foundation options.

First floor — 1,217 sq. ft.
Second floor — 1,249 sq. ft.
Bonus — 496 sq. ft.
Basement — 1,217 sq. ft.
Garage — 431 sq. ft.

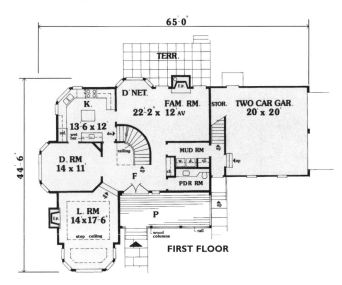

Count Your Options

Total living area 2,472 sq. ft. ■ Price Code E

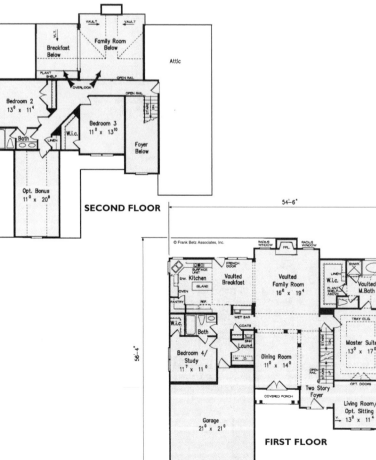

SECOND FLOOR

FIRST FLOOR

No. 97258

■ **This plan features:**

— Three bedrooms

— Three full baths

■ The impressive two-story Foyer opens to the Dining Room, the Living Room and the Family Room

■ The Master Suite features a tray ceiling in the Bedroom and a vaulted ceiling in the Master Bath

■ This home is designed with basement and crawl space foundation options

. ■ Alternate foundation options available at an additional charge. Please call 1-800-235-5700 for more information.

First floor — 1,860 sq. ft.
Second floor — 612 sq. ft.
Bonus — 244 sq. ft.
Basement — 1,860 sq. ft.
Garage — 460 sq. ft.

Isolated Master Suite

No. 90420

This plan features:

— Three bedrooms

— Two full and one half baths

■ The spacious, sunken Living Room has a cathedral ceiling

■ The isolated Master Suite has a private Bath and walk-in closet

■ The two additional Bedrooms share a unique Bath-and-a-half and ample storage space

■ The efficient U-shaped Kitchen has a double sink, ample cabinets and counter space and adjoins the Breakfast Area

■ The second floor Studio overlooks the Living Room

■ This home is designed with basement, slab and crawlspace foundation options.

First floor — 2,213 sq. ft.
Second floor — 260 sq. ft.
Basement — 2,213 sq. ft.
Garage — 422 sq. ft.

■ *Total living area 2,473 sq. ft.* ■ *Price Code E* ■

WIDTH 91'-8"
DEPTH 45'-8"

SECOND FLOOR

FIRST FLOOR

Tudor Home

No. 10673

This plan features:

— Four bedrooms

— Two and one half baths

■ The Kitchen has a Pantry and Breakfast Area that opens to the brick Patio

■ The oversized Living Room has skylights and a fireplace

■ The Master Suite contains a whirlpool tub

■ This home is designed with a basement foundation.

First floor — 1,265 sq. ft.
Second floor — 1,210 sq. ft.
Basement — 1,247 sq. ft.
Garage — 506 sq. ft.

■ *Total living area 2,475 sq. ft.* ■ *Price Code E* ■

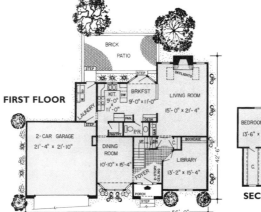

FIRST FLOOR

SECOND FLOOR

Magnificent Elevation

Total living area 2,480 sq. ft. ■ Price Code E

FIRST FLOOR

SECOND FLOOR

No. 94940

■ **This plan features:**

— Four bedrooms

— Two full and one half baths

■ The highlight of the sixteen-foot high Entry is an angled staircase

■ The formal Living and Dining Rooms have tapered columns and decorative windows and are ideal for entertaining

■ The Kitchen has a work island and adjoins the Breakfast Area

■ The Family Room has a beamed ceiling and a fireplace

■ The Master Bedroom features a tiered ceiling, walk-in closet and a plush Bath

■ This home is designed with basement and slab foundation options.

■ Alternate foundation options available at an additional charge. Please call 1-800-235-5700 for more information.

First floor — 1,369 sq. ft.
Second floor — 1,111 sq. ft.
Basement — 1,369 sq. ft.
Garage — 716 sq. ft.

Grand Styling

Total living area 2,482 sq. ft. ■ Price Code E

FIRST FLOOR

SECOND FLOOR

No. 97255

■ **This plan features:**

— Four bedrooms

— Two full and one half baths

■ The Dining Room and Living Room flank the Foyer

■ The Family Room, Breakfast Room and Kitchen share an open floor plan

■ There is a fireplace in the Family Room and a serving bar between the Kitchen and the Breakfast Room

■ The Master Suite includes a walk-in closet, a vaulted ceiling over the plush, five-piece Bath and a cozy Sitting Room

■ The three additional Bedrooms are roomy and share the full hall Bath

■ This home is designed with basement and crawlspace foundation options.

First floor — 1,205 sq. ft.
Second floor — 1,277 sq. ft.
Basement — 1,128 sq. ft.
Garage — 528 sq. ft.

French Flavor

No. 92549

This plan features:

— Four bedrooms

— Three full baths

■ The Porch opens to the Foyer with a lovely staircase

■ Elegant columns define the Dining and Den Areas

■ The efficient, U-shaped Kitchen has a serving counter, Eating Nook, and is near the Utility Area and Garage

■ The Master Bedroom features a decorative ceiling, a huge walk-in closet and plush Bath

■ The three additional Bedrooms with walk-in closets are near full Baths

■ This home is designed with slab and crawlspace foundation options.

First floor — 1,911 sq. ft.
Second floor — 579 sq. ft.
Garage — 560 sq. ft.

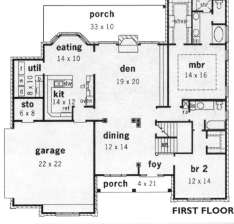

Total living area 2,490 sq. ft. ■ Price Code E

SECOND FLOOR

WIDTH 57'-10"
DEPTH 56'-10"

FIRST FLOOR

Towering Turret

No. 98236

This plan features:

— Four bedrooms

— Two full and one half baths

■ Brick and lovely decorative trim create elegant curb appeal

■ The open Kitchen arrangement includes a convenient island

■ The Bedrooms are located on the second floor for privacy

■ Three fireplaces add a special touch to the Keeping Room, the Family Room and the Living Room

■ This home is designed with basement and slab foundation options.

First floor — 1,216 sq. ft.
Second floor — 1,275 sq. ft.
Basement — 1,216 sq. ft.
Garage — 416 sq. ft.

Total living area 2,491 sq. ft. ■ Price Code E

FIRST FLOOR

SECOND FLOOR

WIDTH 54'-0"
DEPTH 44'-0"

Traditional with Modern Extras

■ *Total living area 2,492 sq. ft.* ■ *Price Code E* ■

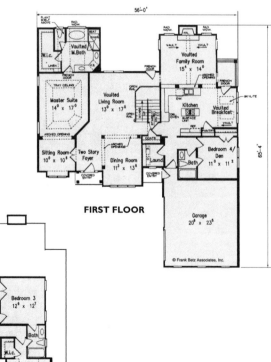

FIRST FLOOR

© Frank Betz Associates, Inc.

SECOND FLOOR

No. 97273

■ **This plan features:**

— Four bedrooms

— Four full baths

■ The side Entry Garage adds style

■ Elegant columns and arches define the formal Dining Room

■ The Kitchen has a central island and the nearby Eating Area has two large skylights

■ A decorative ceiling tops Master Bedroom

■ Alternate foundation options available at an additional charge. Please call 1-800-235-5700 for more information.

First floor — 1,948 sq. ft.
Second floor — 544 sq. ft.
Bonus — 400 sq. ft.
Basement — 1,885 sq. ft.
Garage — 511 sq. ft.

Picture of Posterity

No. 99407

This plan features:

- Four bedrooms

- Two full and one half baths

- The tiled Entry opens to the Den and Dining Room

- The Den includes French doors and would make an ideal Home Office

- The Great Room features a large fireplace framed by stunning transom windows

- The Master Bedroom is privately located and has outdoor access

- This home is designed with basement and slab foundation options.

- Alternate foundation options available at an additional charge. Please call 1-800-235-5700 for more information.

First floor — 1,777 sq. ft.
Second floor — 719 sq. ft.
Basement — 1,777 sq. ft.
Garage — 645 sq. ft.

■ *Total living area 2,496 sq. ft.* ■ *Price Code E* ■

SECOND FLOOR

© Design Basics, Inc.

FIRST FLOOR

Three-Sided Fireplace

No. 65255

This plan features:

- Three bedrooms

- Three full and one half baths

- The angled fireplace is shared by the Living Room, Dining Room, and Kitchen

- A second floor Media Room provides privacy in this open plan

- This home is designed with a basement foundation.

First floor — 1,437 sq. ft.
Second floor — 1,060 sq. ft.
Basement — 1,437 sq. ft.
Garage — 438 sq. ft.

■ *Total living area 2,497 sq. ft.* ■ *Price Code E* ■

FIRST FLOOR

SECOND FLOOR

Rewards of Success

■ Total living area 2,509 sq. ft. ■ Price Code F ■

No. 93254

■ **This plan features:**

— Three bedrooms

— Three full and one half baths

■ The formal areas located in the front of the house are each enhanced by a bay window

■ The expansive Family Room includes a fireplace flanked by windows at the rear of the house

■ An open layout is featured between the Family Room, Breakfast Area and the Kitchen

■ The lavish Master Suite is crowned by a decorative ceiling

■ This home is designed with basement, slab, and crawlspace foundation options.

First floor — 1,282 sq. ft.
Second floor — 1,227 sq. ft.
Bonus — 314 sq. ft.
Garage — 528 sq. ft.
Basement — 1,154 sq. ft.

FIRST FLOOR

SECOND FLOOR

Angled U-Shape Staircase

■ Total living area 2,519 sq. ft. ■ Price Code F ■

No. 60004

■ **This plan features:**

— Four bedrooms

— Two full and one half baths

■ Three balconies overlook the stairs, Foyer, and Family Room

■ A built-in desk in one Bedroom provides an ideal space for homework and a computer.

■ The Foyer catches a view of an arched opening between columns leading to the Family Room

■ The formal rooms are open to one another for entertaining

■ This home is designed with a basement foundation.

First floor — 1,277 sq. ft.
Second floor — 1,242 sq. ft.
Basement — 1,277 sq. ft.
Garage — 482 sq. ft.

FIRST FLOOR

SECOND FLOOR

Elegant Row House

No. 94259

This plan features:

- Three bedrooms
- Two full and one half baths
- Arched columns define the formal and casual spaces
- The Great Room has four sets of French doors to the outside
- The Master Suite features a private Bath designed for two people
- Generous Bonus Space awaits your ideas for completion
- The Guest Bedroom leads to a gallery hallway with Deck access
- This home is designed with slab and pier/post foundation options.
- Alternate foundation options available at an additional charge. Please call 1-800-235-5700 for more information.

Main Floor — 1,305 sq. ft.
Upper Floor — 1,215 sq. ft.
Bonus — 935 sq. ft.
Garage — 480 sq. ft.

■ *Total living area 2,520 sq. ft.* ■ *Price Code G* ■

FIRST FLOOR

LOWER FLOOR

SECOND FLOOR

English Countryside

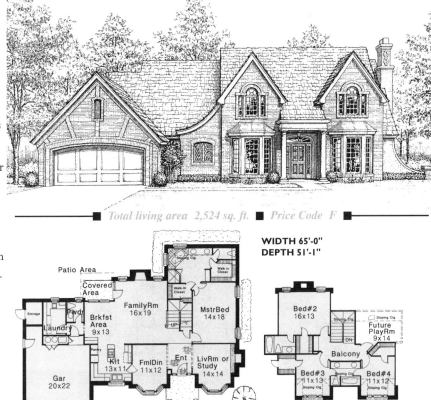

No. 98519

This plan features:

- Four bedrooms
- Three full and one half baths
- The Entry opens to the Living Room/Study, with a cozy fireplace or to the Dining Room
- The Family Room has a fireplace and accesses the covered Patio
- The Breakfast Area is adjacent to the Family Room and the Kitchen which features a center island
- The first floor Master Bedroom has two walk-in closets and a private Bath with a spa tub
- The secondary Bedrooms each have walk-in closets and the use of two full Baths
- The Bonus Room would be a perfect Playroom
- This home is designed with a slab foundation.

First floor — 1,735 sq. ft.
Second floor — 789 sq. ft.
Bonus — 132 sq. ft.
Garage — 482 sq. ft.

■ *Total living area 2,524 sq. ft.* ■ *Price Code F* ■

WIDTH 65'-0"
DEPTH 51'-1"

FIRST FLOOR

SECOND FLOOR

Cottage Influence

■ *Total living area 2,533 sq. ft.* ■ *Price Code F* ■

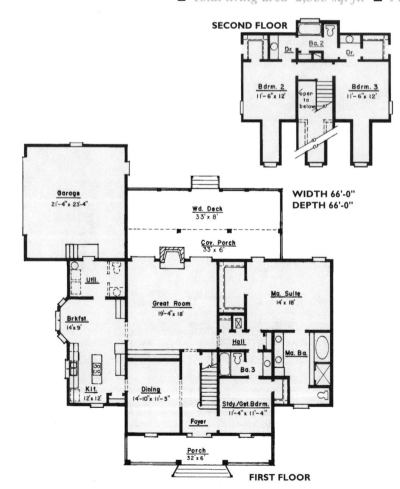

SECOND FLOOR

Ba. 2
Dr.   Dr.

Bdrm. 2   Bdrm. 3
11'-6" x 12'   open   11'-6" x 12'
                to
                below

FIRST FLOOR

WIDTH 66'-0"
DEPTH 66'-0"

Garage
21'-4" x 23'-4"

Wd. Deck
33' x 8'

Cov. Porch
33' x 6'

Util.

Great Room
19'-4" x 18'

Ma. Suite
14' x 18'

Brkfst.
14' x 9'

Hall

Ma. Ba.

Kit.
12' x 12'

Dining
14'-10" x 11'-3"

Ba. 3

Stdy./Gst.Bdrm.
11'-4" x 11'-4"

Foyer

Porch
32' x 6'

No. 94614

■ **This plan features:**

— Four bedrooms

— Three full and one half baths

■ There is a cozy Porch entry to Foyer

■ The expansive Great Room has a focal point fireplace and access to the covered Porch and Deck

■ The Kitchen has a cooktop island and is adjacent to the Breakfast Area and formal Dining Room

■ The large Master Suite has access to the Covered Porch, walk-in closet and a double vanity Bath

■ This home is designed with slab and crawlspace foundation options.

First floor — 1,916 sq. ft.
Second floor — 617 sq. ft.
Garage — 516 sq. ft.

No. 10380

Passive Solar Design

This plan features:

— Three bedrooms

— Two full and one half baths

▪ This design features exposed beams and large expanses of glass

▪ The open Great Room is a six-sided living area

▪ Spiral stairs lead to a Loft which overlooks the Great Room

▪ The sloping ceilings contain R-38 insulation

▪ The side walls contain R-24 insulation

▪ This home is designed with a basement foundation.

First floor — 2,199 sq. ft.
Loft — 336 sq. ft.
Basement — 2,199 sq. ft.
Garage — 611 sq. ft.

Total living area 2,535 sq. ft. ▪ Price Code F

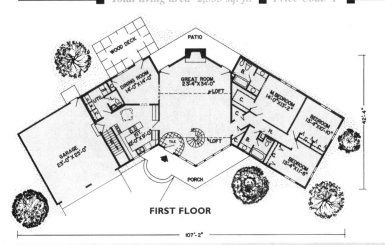

FIRST FLOOR

No. 20354

Tudor Grandeur

This plan features:

— Three bedrooms

— Two full and one half baths

▪ The two-story Foyer is impressive

▪ There are window seats in both the Living Room and the Dining Room

▪ The spacious Kitchen has a built-in Pantry and planning desk and a convenient range-top island

▪ The Master Suite has sloped ceiling and private Master Bath with Spa tub and walk-in closet

▪ The two additional Bedrooms share a full hall Bath

▪ This home is designed with a basement foundation.

First floor — 1,346 sq. ft.
Second floor — 1,196 sq. ft.
Basement — 1,346 sq. ft.
Garage — 840 sq. ft.

Total living area 2,542 sq. ft. ▪ Price Code F

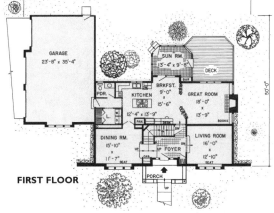

FIRST FLOOR

SECOND FLOOR

Eye-Catching Turrets

■ *Total living area 2,550 sq. ft.* ■ *Price Code F* ■

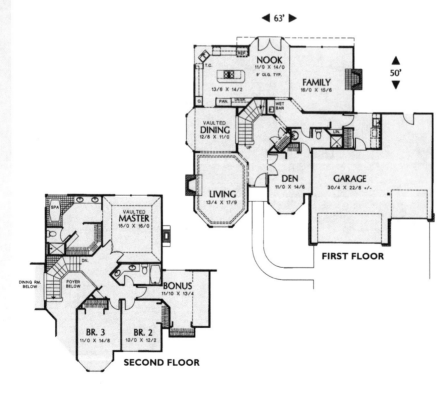

FIRST FLOOR

SECOND FLOOR

No. 91518

■ **This plan features:**

— Three bedrooms

— Three full baths

■ The two-story Foyer opens to the Living Room featuring a fireplace

■ An alcove of glass and a vaulted ceiling are located in the open Dining Area

■ The Kitchen includes a built-in Pantry and desk, cooktop island/snackbar and a Nook with double door

■ The Master Suite features a vaulted ceiling and a plush Dressing Area with walk-in closet and Spa tub

■ This home is designed with a crawlspace foundation.

First floor — 1,592 sq. ft.
Second floor — 958 sq. ft.
Bonus — 194 sq. ft.
Garage — 956 sq. ft.

Spectacular Stucco

No. 98201

This plan features:

- Four bedrooms
- Two full and one half baths
- The beautiful Porch features graduated steps, columns and French doors into the formal Dining Room
- The large Family Room has a fireplace and is open to the Breakfast Area and Kitchen
- The opulent Master Suite, with a stunning ceiling and shape, features a plush Bath and large walk-in closet
- The Kitchen has a large, angled cooktop counter with plenty of room for several stools
- The secondary Bedrooms are located on the second floor for privacy
- This home is designed with a basement foundation.

First floor — 1,803 sq. ft.
Second floor — 748 sq. ft.
Basement — 1,803 sq. ft.

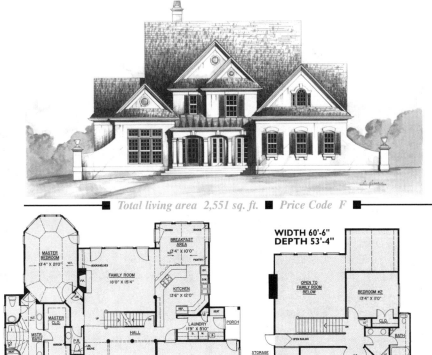

■ *Total living area 2,551 sq. ft.* ■ *Price Code F* ■

WIDTH 60'-6"
DEPTH 53'-4"

FIRST FLOOR

SECOND FLOOR

Pampering Built-ins

No. 64157

This plan features:

- Three bedrooms
- Two full and one half baths
- Well equipped and efficient, the Kitchen opens to the Leisure Room yet is visually separated from it by a built-in glass hutch on one end of the center island
- The Bonus Room adds 362 square feet
- This home is designed with a crawlspace foundation.
- Alternate foundation options available at an additional charge. Please call 1-800-235-5700 for more information.

First floor — 1,387 sq. ft.
Second floor — 1,175 sq. ft.
Bonus — 362 sq. ft.
Garage — 544 sq. ft.

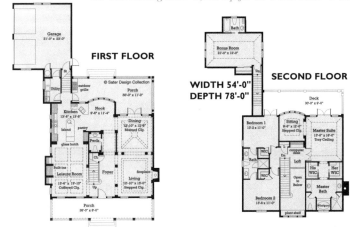

■ *Total living area 2,562 sq. ft.* ■ *Price Code I* ■

FIRST FLOOR

SECOND FLOOR

WIDTH 54'-0"
DEPTH 78'-0"

Craftsman-Style

■ Total living area 2,566 sq. ft. ■ Price Code I ■

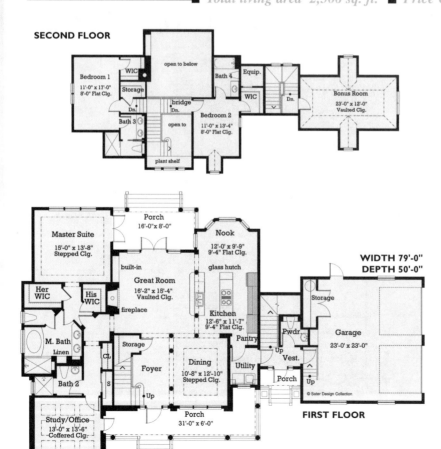

SECOND FLOOR

Bedroom 1
11'-0" x 17'-0"
8'-0" Flat Clg.

WIC

Storage

open to below

bridge

Bath 4

Equip.

WIC

Dn.

Bonus Room
23'-0" x 12'-0"
Vaulted Clg.

Dn.

Bath 3

open to

Bedroom 2
11'-0" x 13'-4"
8'-0" Flat Clg.

plant shelf

FIRST FLOOR

Porch
16'-0" x 8'-0"

Master Suite
15'-0" x 13'-8"
Stepped Clg.

built-in

Great Room
16'-2" x 15'-4"
Vaulted Clg.

fireplace

Nook
12'-0" x 9'-9"
9'-4" Flat Clg.

glass hutch

Kitchen
12'-6" x 11'-7"
9'-4" Flat Clg.

Her WIC

His WIC

M. Bath

Linen

Bath 2

CL

S

Storage

Foyer

Dining
10'-8" x 12'-10"
Stepped Clg.

Utility

Pantry

Pwdr.

Vest.

Up

Storage

Garage
23'-0" x 23'-0"

Porch

Up

© Sater Design Collection

Study/Office
13'-0" x 13'-6"
Coffered Clg.

Porch
31'-0" x 6'-0"

Up

WIDTH 79'-0"
DEPTH 50'-0"

No. 64143

■ This plan features:

— Four bedrooms

— Three full and one half baths

■ The two-story Great Room features a cozy fireplace, built-in entertainment center, and French door access to the rear Porch

■ The Bonus Room adds 379 square feet

■ This home is designed with basement and crawlspace foundation options.

■ Alternate foundation options available at an additional charge. Please call 1-800-235-5700 for more information.

First floor — 1,834 sq. ft.
Second floor — 732 sq. ft.
Bonus — 379 sq. ft.
Garage — 570 sq. ft.

In-Law Possibility

Total living area 2,566 sq. ft. ■ **Price Code I** ■

No. 64144

This plan features:

- Three bedrooms

- Four full bath

■ A vaulted-ceiling Bonus Room, with private Entry, could become an in-law apartment

■ The Bonus Room adds 379 square feet

■ This home is designed with a crawlspace foundation.

■ Alternate foundation options available at an additional charge. Please call 1-800-235-5700 for more information.

First floor — 1,834 sq. ft.
Second floor — 732 sq. ft.
Bonus — 379 sq. ft.
Garage — 570 sq. ft.

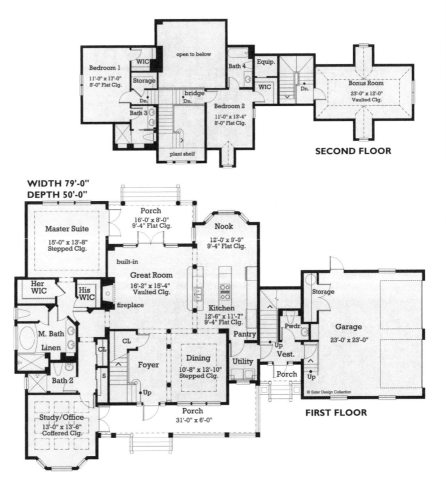

SECOND FLOOR

FIRST FLOOR

WIDTH 79'-0"
DEPTH 50'-0"

French Country Styling

■ *Total living area 2,567 sq. ft.* ■ *Price Code F* ■

SECOND FLOOR

WIDTH 55'-0"
DEPTH 48'-10"

FIRST FLOOR

No. 98533

■ **This plan features:**

— Four bedrooms

— Two full, one three-quarter, and
  one half baths

■ This design features a bay window
  with a copper roof, a large
  eyebrow dormer and an arched
  covered Entry

■ The large Great Room includes a
  brick fireplace

■ The elegant formal Dining Room
  and angled Study are located to
  each side of the Entry

■ This home is designed with basement and slab foundation options

First floor — 1,765 sq. ft.
Second floor — 802 sq. ft.
Bonus — 275 sq. ft.
Garage — 462 sq. ft.

A Traditional Home

No. 91535

This plan features:

- Three bedrooms
- Two full and one half baths
- A beautiful bay window and built-in shelves are located in the private first floor Den
- A decorative ceiling, picture window and lovely fireplace are featured in the roomy formal Living Room
- The elegant formal Dining Room is enhanced by a decorative ceiling treatment and is convenient to the Living Room and the Kitchen
- The cooktop island/eating bar, walk-in Pantry, planning desk and informal Nook area highlight the spacious Kitchen
- A relaxing atmosphere is provided by the cozy fireplace in the Family Room
- The second floor Master Suite has a private Bath and a huge walk-in closet
- The Bonus Room provides space for future expansion
- This home is designed with a crawlspace foundation.

First floor — 1,465 sq. ft.
Second floor — 1,103 sq. ft.
Bonus — 303 sq. ft.

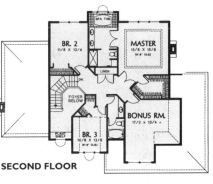

■ Total living area 2,568 sq. ft. ■ Price Code F ■

FIRST FLOOR

SECOND FLOOR

Dignified Family Home

No. 24653

This plan features:

- Three bedrooms
- Two full and one half baths
- The formal Living Room adjoins the formal Dining Room with columns between the two rooms
- The U-shaped Kitchen features a built-in Pantry
- The large Family Room is open to the Kitchen and has a focal point fireplace and a bright bay window
- The Master Suite is topped by a decorative ceiling and includes a lavish Bath
- This home is designed with basement, slab and crawlspace foundation options.

First floor — 1,245 sq. ft.
Second floor — 1,333 sq. ft.
Bonus — 192 sq. ft.
Basement — 1,245 sq. ft.
Garage — 614 sq. ft.

■ Total living area 2,578 sq. ft. ■ Price Code F ■

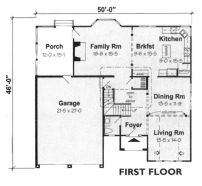

FIRST FLOOR

SECOND FLOOR

OPTIONAL CRAWLSPACE/SLAB FOUNDATION

Stunning Sunburst Transoms

Total living area 2,581 sq. ft. ■ Price Code I

No. 64142

■ **This plan features:**

— Three bedrooms

— Four full and one half baths

■ A sensible Kitchen offers a center cooktop island and a Breakfast Nook

■ The Bonus Room adds 379 square feet

■ A secluded Master Suite has access to a column-lined rear Porch

■ This home is designed with a crawlspace foundation.

■ Alternate foundation options available at an additional charge. Please call 1-800-235-5700 for more information.

First floor — 1,842 sq. ft.
Second floor — 739 sq. ft.
Bonus — 379 sq. ft.

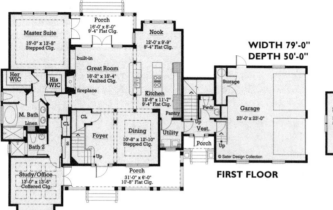

WIDTH 79'-0"
DEPTH 50'-0"

FIRST FLOOR

SECOND FLOOR

Captivating Colonial

Total living area 2,585 sq. ft. ■ Price Code F

No. 99454

■ **This plan features:**

— Four bedrooms

— Two full and one half baths

■ The Dining Room features a decorative ceiling, French doors, and hutch space

■ The Family Room has a fireplace and a bow window

■ The Breakfast Nook adjoins the efficient Kitchen

■ The Master Bedroom has a private Bath

■ This home is designed with basement or slab foundation options.

■ Alternate foundation options available at an additional charge. Please call 1-800-235-5700 for more information.

First floor — 1,362 sq. ft.
Second floor — 1,223 sq. ft.
Basement — 1,362 sq. ft.
Garage — 734 sq. ft.

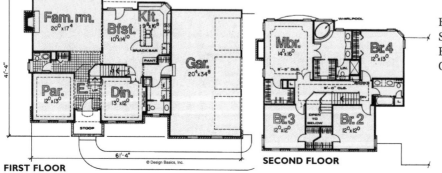

FIRST FLOOR   **SECOND FLOOR**

■ *Total living area 2,588 sq. ft.* ■ *Price Code F* ■

No. 93205

This plan features:

- Four bedrooms
- Two full and one half baths
- The wonderful wrap-around Porch adds outdoor living space
- The U-shaped Kitchen is equipped with a peninsula counter, a double sink and a Pantry
- The expansive Family Room has a large focal point fireplace
- The Master Suite is crowned by a decorative ceiling
- The Bonus Room can be used for future expansion
- This home is designed with basement, slab and crawlspace foundation options.

First floor — 1,320 sq. ft.
Second floor — 1,268 sq. ft.
Bonus — 389 sq. ft.
Basement — 1,320 sq. ft.
Garage — 482 sq. ft.

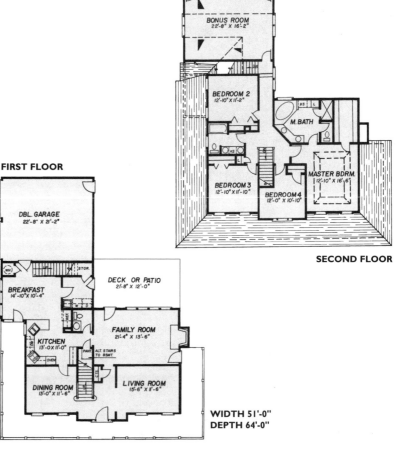

Elegant Living

Total living area 2,592 sq. ft. ■ Price Code F

No. 99142

■ **This plan features:**

— Three bedrooms

— Two full and one half baths

■ The spacious Great Room has a two-story ceiling, a fireplace and rear windows for natural light

■ The Den features built-in cabinets and is located next to the Great Room

■ The formal Dining Room, located at the front of the house, provides a quiet place for entertaining

■ The first floor Laundry is adjacent to the three-car Garage

■ The Nook is adjacent to the Kitchen and has access to the backyard through a Patio door

■ The Master Suite features generous windows, a private Bath and an extra large walk-in closet

■ This home is designed with a basement foundation.

■ Alternate foundation options available at an additional charge. Please call 1-800-235-5700 for more information.

First floor — 1,408 sq. ft.
Second floor — 1,184 sq. ft.
Basement — 1,408 sq. ft.

SECOND FLOOR

FIRST FLOOR

Upper-Level Guest Suite

Total living area 2,597 sq. ft. ■ Price Code F

No. 69003

■ **This plan features:**

— Four bedrooms

— Three full and one half baths

■ The Kitchen is flanked by the Great Room and the Hearth Room

■ One of the secondary Bedrooms has a private Bath

■ Patio doors in the Hearth Room open to a Screened Porch with a vaulted ceiling

■ This home is designed with basement, slab and crawlspace foundation options.

First floor — 1,742 sq. ft.
Second floor — 855 sq. ft.

FIRST FLOOR

SECOND FLOOR

Notable Exterior

No. 97210

This plan features:

- Four bedrooms

- Three full baths

- The two-story Foyer adds a feeling of volume and space

- The Family Room is topped by vaulted ceiling and accented by a fireplace

- The formal Living Room has an eleven-foot high ceiling

- The private Master Suite has a five-piece Bath and a large walk-in closet

- The rear Bedroom/Study is located near a full Bath

- This home is designed with basement, slab, and crawlspace foundation options.

First floor — 2,003 sq. ft.
Second floor — 598 sq. ft.
Bonus — 321 sq. ft.
Basement — 2,003 sq. ft.
Garage — 546 sq. ft.

■ *Total living area 2,601 sq. ft.* ■ *Price Code F* ■

WIDTH 60'-0"
DEPTH 61'-0"

FIRST FLOOR

SECOND FLOOR

Traditional Lines

No. 61015

This plan features:

- Four bedrooms

- Two full and one half baths

- Private grilling Porch offers quiet backyard retreat

- Family-first room complex includes Great room, Hearth Room, Kitchen and Breakfast Room

- Enclosed Patio off of Study

- This home is designed with basement, slab, and crawlspace options.

Main floor — 2,606 sq. ft.
Bonus — 751 sq. ft.
Garage — 534 sq. ft.

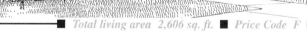

■ *Total living area 2,606 sq. ft.* ■ *Price Code F* ■

BONUS

MAIN FLOOR

Dramatic Design

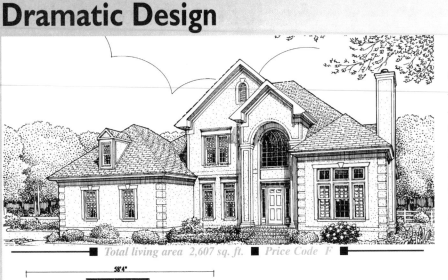

■ *Total living area 2,607 sq. ft.* ■ *Price Code F* ■

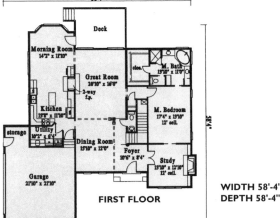

FIRST FLOOR

WIDTH 58'-4"
DEPTH 58'-4"

SECOND FLOOR

No. 93709

■ **This plan features:**

— Four bedrooms

— Two full and one half baths

■ The two-story Foyer adds a feeling of volume and space

■ The Family Room is topped by vaulted ceiling and accented by a fireplace

■ The formal Living Room has an eleven-foot high ceiling

■ The private Master Suite has a five-piece Bath and a large walk-in closet

■ The rear Bedroom/Study is located near a full Bath

■ This home is designed with a crawlspace foundation.

First floor — 1,910 sq. ft.
Second floor — 697 sq. ft.

Two-Story Family Room

■ *Total living area 2,608 sq. ft.* ■ *Price Code F* ■

FIRST FLOOR

SECOND FLOOR

WIDTH 60'-0"
DEPTH 46'-4"

No. 97216

■ **This plan features:**

— Four bedrooms

— Two full and one half baths

■ The wrap-around covered Porch enhances the exterior elevation

■ The Family Room has a fireplace and French doors to the Porch

■ The Breakfast Nook is separated from the Family Room by an open rail

■ The Kitchen features a convenient serving bar for quick meals and snacks

■ The second floor Master Suite has a tray ceiling and an optional plan for a Sitting Area

■ All of the secondary Bedrooms have an ample amount of closet space

■ The two-car Garage has storage space in the rear

■ This home is designed with a basement foundation.

First floor — 1,351 sq. ft.
Second floor — 1,257 sq. ft.
Bonus — 115 sq. ft.
Basement — 1,351 sq. ft.
Garage — 511 sq. ft.

Secluded Master Suite

No. 99499

This plan features:

- Four bedrooms
- Two full and one half baths
- The Kitchen includes an angled countertop adjoining the airy Breakfast Nook
- The Great Room has a focal point fireplace between windows overlooking the rear yard
- The Den opens from the Entry for an ideal Home Office
- The Master Bedroom is privately located and has a large Bath
- The three secondary Bedrooms make use of the upper floor, which includes an enormous Storage Area perfect for out-ofs-season gear
- This home is designed with a basement foundation.
- Alternate foundation options available at an additional charge. Please call 1-800-235-5700 for more information.

First floor — 1,847 sq. ft.
Second floor — 766 sq. ft.
Bonus — 232 sq. ft.
Garage — 719 sq. ft.

■ *Total living area 2,613 sq. ft.* ■ *Price Code F* ■

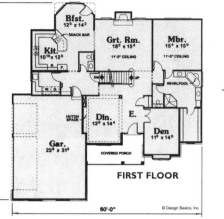

FIRST FLOOR

SECOND FLOOR

© Design Basics, Inc.

Statuesque in Appearance

No. 99489

This plan features:

- Four bedrooms
- Two full, one three-quarter, one half baths
- The formal rooms flank the Entry and provide views of the front yard
- An angled snack bar in the Kitchen adjoins the Breakfast Area
- Bedroom two is the perfect Guest Suite with its own three-quarter Bath
- The Master Suite features dual walk-in closets and a private Bath with a bay window and cathedral ceiling
- The large Bonus Room has the potential for many uses
- This home is designed with basement and crawlspace foundation options.
- Alternate foundation options available at an additional charge. Please call 1-800-235-5700 for more information.

First floor — 1,333 sq. ft.
Second floor — 1,280 sq. ft.
Basement — 1,333 sq. ft.
Garage — 687 sq. ft.

■ *Total living area 2,613 sq. ft.* ■ *Price Code F* ■

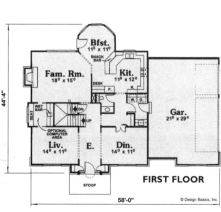

FIRST FLOOR

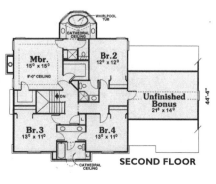

SECOND FLOOR

© Design Basics, Inc.

Colonial-Inspired Facade

■ *Total living area 2,616 sq. ft.* ■ *Price Code F* ■

WIDTH 45'-0"
DEPTH 76'-0"

SECOND FLOOR

FIRST FLOOR

No. 63030

■ **This plan features:**

— Three bedroom

— Two full and one half baths

■ With the Garage located to the
rear, this design is ideal for a
narrow lot or a site in a traditional
neighborhood development

■ The future space adds
254 square feet

■ This home is designed with a slab
foundation.

First floor — 1,447 sq. ft.
Second floor — 1,169 sq. ft.
Bonus — 254 sq. ft.
Garage — 383 sq. ft.

■ *Total living area 2,638 sq. ft.* ■ • *Price Code F* ■

No. 97409

This plan features:

- Four bedrooms

- Three full and one half baths

■ Columns define the Dining Room

■ The two-story Family Room includes a fireplace and multiple windows

■ The first floor Master Suite includes a whirlpool tub, separate shower and two vanities

■ This home is designed with a slab foundation.

■ Alternate foundation options available at an additional charge. Please call 1-800-235-5700 for more information.

First floor — 1,844 sq. ft.
Second floor — 794 sq. ft.

SECOND FLOOR

FIRST FLOOR

© Carmichael & Dame, Inc.

Colonial Styling

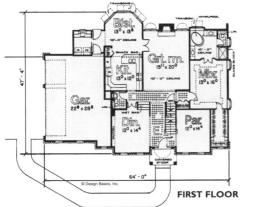
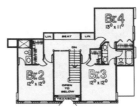

■ *Total living area 2,639 sq. ft.* ■ *Price Code F* ■

FIRST FLOOR

SECOND FLOOR

No. 97412

■ **This plan features:**

– Four bedrooms

– Two full, one three-quarter and one half baths

■ This home is Colonial on the outside and thoroughly Modern on the inside

■ The Dining Room has a built-in hutch and a wetbar

■ The Parlor may be used for formal entertaining space or as a quiet repose

■ The Great Room has a rear wall fireplace with windows to either side

■ The Kitchen has a smart arrangement and shares a snack bar with the Breakfast Area

■ The Breakfast Nook has a bay windows and transoms above

■ The Master Bedroom is located on the first floor for privacy

■ The Master Bath has a whirlpool tub, and a glass-block shower

■ This home is designed with a basement foundation.

■ Alternate foundation options available at an additional charge. Please call 1-800-235-5700 for more information.

First floor — 1,865 sq. ft.
Second floor — 774 sq. ft.

Elegant Master Suite

■ *Total living area 2,640 sq. ft.* ■ *Price Code F* ■

FIRST FLOOR

SECOND FLOOR

No. 93241

■ **This plan features:**

– Four bedrooms

– Two full and one half baths

■ The Central Foyer is highlighted by a lovely curved staircase and leads into the Formal Living and Dining Rooms

■ The Comfortable Family Room has a large fireplace and backyard views

■ The efficient Kitchen has a built-in Pantry

■ The expansive Master Bedroom has a decorative ceiling, a Sitting Room and a plush Bath

■ The three additional Bedrooms with large closets share a full Bath

■ This home is designed with basement, slab and crawlspace foundation options.

First floor — 1,307 sq. ft.
Second floor — 1,333 sq. ft.
Bonus — 308 sq. ft.
Basement — 1,307 sq. ft.
Garage — 528 sq. ft.

European Flavor

No. 97506

This plan features:

– Three bedrooms

– Two full and one half baths

■ The exterior is stucco with ornate iron railings

■ The Family Room is enhanced by a fireplace and is open to the Dining Room.

■ There are pocket doors separating the Study from the Family Room

■ The Kitchen includes a cooktop island with a snack bar, and is open to the Breakfast Area

■ The Master Bedroom is lavishly appointed and includes two walk-in closets

■ This home is designed with a slab foundation.

First floor — 2,005 sq. ft.
Second floor — 639 sq. ft.
Garage — 443 sq. ft.

■ *Total living area 2,644 sq. ft.* ■ *Price Code F* ■

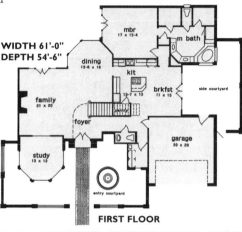

WIDTH 61'-0"
DEPTH 54'-6"

mbr 17 x 15-4
m bath
dining 13-6 18
kit 13-7 x 13
brkfst 11 x 15
side courtyard
family 21 x 20
foyer
study 13 x 13
garage 20 x 20
entry courtyard

FIRST FLOOR

br.3 13 x 15
br.2 15 x 13
open to below

SECOND FLOOR

Distinctive Brick

No. 93206

This plan features:

– Four bedrooms

– Two full and one half baths

■ The arched entrance with decorative glass leads into the two-story Foyer

■ The formal Dining Room has a tray ceiling and a decorative window

■ The efficient Kitchen with island cooktop, built-in desk and Pantry, is adjacent to the Breakfast Area and the Dining Room

■ The Master Bedroom has a tray ceiling, a French door to the Patio, and a huge private Bath with garden tub, dual vanities and walk-in closets

■ The three additional Bedrooms have ample closets and share a full Bath with a Laundry closet

■ The Second floor has future space for storage and a huge Bedroom with a full Bath

■ This home is designed with basement, slab and crawlspace foundation options.

First Floor — 2,577 sq. ft.
Future Second Floor — 619 sq. ft.
Staircase — 68 sq. ft.
Basement — 2,561 sq. ft.
Garage — 560 sq. ft.

■ *Total living area 2,645 sq. ft.* ■ *Price Code F* ■

74-0

Sundeck 17-0 x 16-0
Master Bdrm. 15-6 x 17-6
M.Bath
Family Rm. 22-4 x 13-6
Living 13-6 x 15-6
Brkfst. 13-4 x 9-6
Bath 2
Bdrm.2 11-6 x 13-4
Kit 13-4 x 12-0
Dining 13-8 x 13-5
Bdrm.4 13-6 x 11-2
Bdrm.3 11-6 x 11-6
Stoop
Double Garage 21-4 x 23-8

FIRST FLOOR

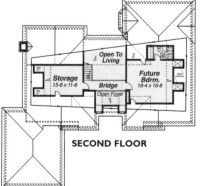

Open To Living
Storage 15-8 x 11-8
Future Bdrm. 18-4 x 16-8
Bridge
Open Foyer

SECOND FLOOR

Large Wrap-Around Porch

■ *Total living area 2,647 sq. ft.* ■ *Price Code F* ■

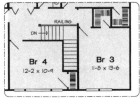

**OPTIONAL CRAWLSPACE/
SLAB FOUNDATION**

Shop
14-5 x 15-5

HW
FURN

OPTIONAL SECOND FLOOR

Br 4
12-2 x 10-9

Br 3
11-8 x 13-6

DN

RAILING

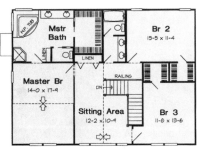

SECOND FLOOR

Mstr
Bath

Br 2
15-5 x 11-4

Master Br
14-0 x 17-9

Br 3
11-8 x 13-6

Sitting Area
12-2 x 10-9

RAILING

LINEN

DN

No. 24403

■ **This plan features:**

– Three bedrooms

– Two full and one three-quarter baths

■ The large entrance Foyer has an attractive staircase

■ The elegant Dining Room is topped by a decorative ceiling treatment

■ The expansive Family Room has a massive fireplace and built-in bookshelves

■ The efficient Kitchen features a peninsula counter/eating bar, a built-in Pantry, double sink and ample counter and cabinet space

■ This home is designed with basement, slab and crawlspace foundation options.

First floor — 1,378 sq. ft.
Second floor — 1,269 sq. ft.
Basement — 1,378 sq. ft.
Garage — 717 sq. ft.

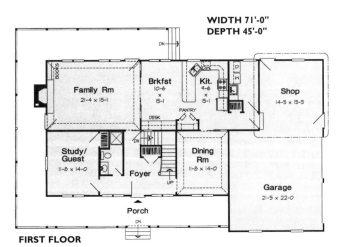

**WIDTH 71'-0"
DEPTH 45'-0"**

Family Rm
21-4 x 15-1

Brkfst
10-6 x 15-1

Kit.
9-6 x 15-1

Shop
14-5 x 15-5

Study/
Guest
11-8 x 14-0

Dining
Rm
11-8 x 14-0

Garage
21-5 x 22-0

Foyer

Porch

PANTRY

DESK

BOOKS

DN

UP

DN

FIRST FLOOR

No. 99424

This plan features:

— Four bedrooms

— Two full and one half baths

■ The open Entry is accented by a lovely landing staircase and has access to the quiet Study and the formal Dining Room

■ The central Family Room has an inviting fireplace and a cathedral ceiling that extends into Kitchen

■ The spacious Kitchen has a work island/snack bar, a built-in Pantry, a bright Breakfast Area and is near the Porch, the Utility Room and the Garage Entry

■ The secluded Master Bedroom features a large walk-in closet and lavish Bath

■ The three second floor Bedrooms share a double vanity Bath

■ This home is designed with basement and slab foundation options.

■ Alternate foundation options available at an additional charge. Please call 1-800-235-5700 for more information.

First floor — 1,906 sq. ft.
Second floor — 749 sq. ft.
Basement — 1,906 sq. ft.
Garage — 682 sq. ft.

■ *Total living area 2,655 sq. ft.* ■ *Price Code F* ■

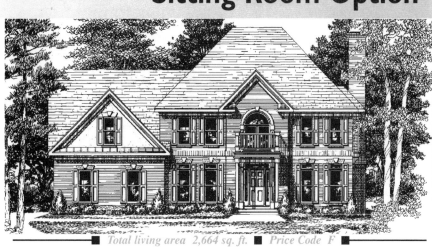

FIRST FLOOR

SECOND FLOOR

© Carmichael & Dame

No. 60008

This plan features:

— Four bedrooms

— Two full and one half baths

■ Double doors open to the Master Suite that has a tray ceiling, separate vanities, and a whirlpool tub

■ Windows fill the rear wall of the Family Room

■ This home is designed with a basement foundation.

First floor — 1,289 sq. ft.
Second floor — 1,375 sq. ft.
Basement — 1,289 sq. ft.
Bonus — 115 sq. ft.
Garage — 498 sq. ft.

■ *Total living area 2,664 sq. ft.* ■ *Price Code F* ■

OPTIONAL SITTING ROOM

FIRST FLOOR

SECOND FLOOR

Grand Country Porch

■ Total living area 2,665 sq. ft. ■ Price Code F ■

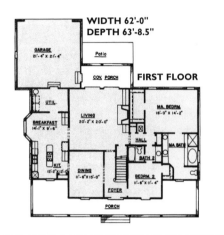

WIDTH 62'-0"
DEPTH 63'-8.5"

GARAGE 21'-4" X 21'-4"

Patio

COV. PORCH   **FIRST FLOOR**

UTIL.

BREAKFAST 14'-1" X 9'-6"

LIVING 20'-2" X 20'-0"

MA. BEDRM. 18'-0" X 14'-2"

KIT. 12'-8" X 12'-0"

HALL

MA. BATH

BATH 2

DINING 11'-8" X 15'-0"

BEDRM. 2 11'-8" X 11'-4"

FOYER

PORCH

SECOND FLOOR

BATH 3

BALCONY

BEDRM. 3 14'-8" X 12'-6"

BEDRM. 4 14'-8" X 12'-6"

No. 94615

■ **This plan features:**

— Four bedrooms

— Three full baths

■ The large front Porch provides shade and Southern-style hospitality

■ The spacious Living Room gives access to the covered Porch and Patio, and has a cozy fireplace between built-in shelves

■ The Country Kitchen has a cooktop island, a bright Breakfast Area, a Utility Room, a Garage Entry, and adjoins the Dining Room

■ The privately located Master Bedroom has a walk-in closet and a Bath

■ The first floor Bedroom has access to a full Bath

■ The two additional second floor Bedrooms with dormers, walk-in closets and vanities, share a full Bath

■ This home is designed with slab and crawlspace foundation options.

First floor — 1,916 sq. ft.
Second floor — 749 sq. ft.
Garage — 479 sq. ft.

The Right Stuff

■ Total living area 2,672 sq. ft. ■ Price Code F ■

45'- 0"

PATIO

FIREPLACE

FAMILY ROOM VAULTED CEILING 24'-3" X 14'-10"

NOOK 10'-0" X 11'-4"

KITCHEN 10'-8" X 12'-0"

PANTRY

STUDY BEDROOM 10'-0" X 13'-0"

BATH

DINING ROOM 11'-4" X 11'-8"

LNDRY.

LIVING ROOM 11'-8" CEILING 13'-4" X 13'-10"

2-CAR GARAGE OPTIONAL 3-CAR GARAGE

FOYER 10'-8" CEILING

OPTIONAL WORKBENCH

OPTIONAL DOOR

PORCH

FIRST FLOOR

52'- 4"

OPEN TO BELOW

BEDROOM 11'-8" X 12'-0"

BATH

OPTIONAL FIREPLACE

MASTER BEDROOM VAULTED CEILING 17'-0" X 16'-0"

HIS

OPEN TO BELOW

BEDROOM 11'-8" X 15'-0"

HERS

MASTER BATH

SECOND FLOOR

No. 24265

■ **This plan features:**

— Three or Four Bedrooms

— Three full baths

■ The Living Room is open to the Dining Room for easy entertaining

■ The efficient Kitchen has a double sink, built-in Pantry and peninsula counter

■ The Family Room also features a fireplace and vaulted ceiling

■ The Master Suite has a vaulted ceiling, optional fireplace, walk-in closets and a lavish Master Bath

■ This home is designed with basement, slab and crawlspace foundation options.

First floor — 1,574 sq. ft.
Second floor — 1,098 sq. ft.

Notable Master Suite

■ *Total living area 2,673 sq. ft.* ■ *Price Code F* ■

No. 99156

■ **This plan features:**

- Three bedrooms

- Two full and one half baths

■ The two-story Entry is open to the Formal Dining Room, the Den and the two-story Great Room

■ The large Kitchen has a work island, adjacent Nook which opens to the screened Porch, and is adjacent to the Laundry Room

■ The Master Suite has walk-in closets, dual sinks, a separate shower and a corner whirlpool

■ The Loft may be converted into a Sitting Area or Study

■ This home is designed with a basement foundation.

First floor — 2,018 sq. ft.
Second floor — 655 sq. ft.
Basement — 2,018 sq. ft.

SECOND FLOOR

BR.#2
12'0" X 14'4"

LOFT
8'0" X 14'4"

OPEN TO
GRT.RM.

BR.#3
12'4" X 14'4"

OPEN TO
E.

FIRST FLOOR

SCREEN PORCH
16'0" X 14'0"

GRT.RM.
2 STORY
17'0" X 19'0"

KIT.
13'0" X 14'6"

NK.
13'0" X 14'6"

MBR.
16'8" X 13'8"

3 CAR GAR.
34'4" X 23'8"

DIN.
12'4" X 12'4"

E.
2 STORY

DEN
CATHEDRAL CEILING
12'4" X 14'2"

A Grand Entrance

■ *Total living area 2,680 sq. ft.* ■ *Price Code F* ■

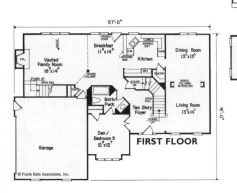

FIRST FLOOR

© Frank Betz Associates, Inc.

SECOND FLOOR

No. 98418

■ **This plan features:**

— Five bedrooms

— Three full baths

■ The arched window above the front door adds elegance to the entrance

■ The large home features two convenient staircases

■ This formal Living and Dining Rooms are divided by a set of boxed columns

■ The U-shaped Kitchen has a walk-in Pantry, a wall oven and opens to the Breakfast Area.

■ The Family Room has a fireplace and a vaulted ceiling

■ The Den or Guest Room on the first floor has a full Bath

■ The family Bedrooms and Baths are on the second floor

■ This home is designed with basement and crawlspace foundation options.

First floor — 1,424 sq. ft.
Second floor — 1,256 sq. ft.
Basement — 1,424 sq. ft.
Garage — 494 sq. ft.

Ageless Design

■ *Total living area 2,685 sq. ft.* ■ *Price Code F* ■

FIRST FLOOR   **SECOND FLOOR**

No. 97625

■ **This plan features:**

— Four bedrooms

— Two full and one half baths

■ The expansive Family Room is enhanced by a triple window and a fireplace

■ The Kitchen with a center island includes a built-in corner Desk Area perfect for a family's home computer

■ A decorative tray ceiling enhances the Master Suite, which includes a vaulted Sitting Area and a private covered Porch

■ The Master Bath enjoys a corner Spa tub and a massive walk-in closet

■ This home is designed with basement and crawlspace foundation options.

First floor — 1,249 sq. ft.
Second floor — 1,436 sq. ft.
Basement — 1,249 sq. ft.
Garage — 446 sq. ft.

■ *Total living area 2,685 sq. ft.* ■ *Price Code F* ■

No. 90838

■ This plan features:

— Three bedrooms

— Three full baths

■ There is a corner gas fireplace in the spacious Living Room

■ The Master Suite includes a private bath with a whirlpool tub, separate shower and a double vanity

■ The Kitchen is well-equipped with a work island and a Pantry and opens to the Breakfast Nook and the Utility Room

■ The two additional Bedrooms share a full Bath on the second floor

■ This home is designed with a basement foundation.

First floor — 1,837 sq. ft.
Second floor — 848 sq. ft.
Basement — 1,803 sq. ft.
Bonus — 288 sq. ft.

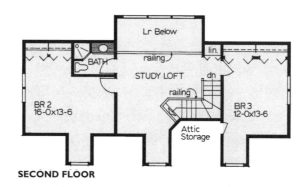

SECOND FLOOR

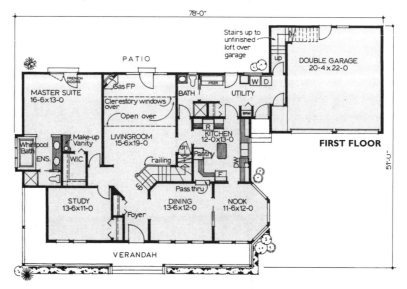

FIRST FLOOR

Modern Luxury

■ *Total living area 2,686 sq. ft.* ■ *Price Code F* ■

FIRST FLOOR

SECOND FLOOR

No. 98457

■ **This plan features:**

— Four bedrooms

— Three full and one half baths

■ The grand two-story Foyer opens to the formal Living and Dining Rooms

■ Arched openings and decorative windows enhance the Dining and Living Rooms

■ The efficient Kitchen has a work island, Pantry and a Breakfast Area open to the Family Room

■ The plush Master Suite features a tray ceiling, an alcove of windows and a whirlpool Bath

■ This home is designed with basement and crawlspace foundation options.

First floor — 1,883 sq. ft.
Second floor — 803 sq. ft.
Basement — 1,883 sq. ft.
Garage — 495 sq. ft.

240

Fashionable Country-Style

No. 99450

■ **This plan features:**

— Four bedrooms

— Two full, one three-quarter and one half baths

■ The large, covered front Porch adds old-fashioned appeal to this modern floor plan

■ The Dining Room features a decorative ceiling and a built-in hutch

■ The Kitchen has a center island and is adjacent to the gazebo-shaped Breakfast Area

■ The Great Room is accented by transom windows and a fireplace with bookcases on either side

■ The Master Bedroom has a cathedral ceiling, a door to the front Porch, and a large Bath with a whirlpool tub

■ This home is designed with basement and slab foundation options.

■ Alternate foundation options available at an additional charge. Please call 1-800-235-5700 for more information.

First floor — 1,881 sq. ft.
Second floor — 814 sq. ft.
Basement — 1,881 sq. ft.
Garage — 534 sq. ft.

■ *Total living area 2,695 sq. ft.* ■ *Price Code F* ■

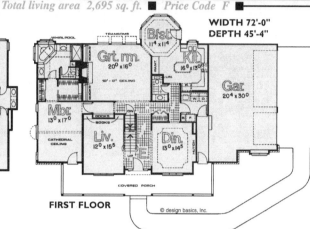

WIDTH 72'-0"
DEPTH 45'-4"

SECOND FLOOR

FIRST FLOOR

© design basics, Inc.

Tasteful Design

No. 93716

■ **This plan features:**

— Four bedrooms

— Three full and one half baths

■ The Foyer opens to the formal Dining and Living Rooms and the large Family Room

■ The Kitchen has an angled, cooktop counter open to the Breakfast Room and the Family Room

■ The private, first floor Master Bedroom features a plush Bath complete with a corner Spa tub

■ The large secondary Bedrooms are on the second floor

■ An optional summer Kitchen is included on the rear Porch

■ This home is designed with a crawlspace foundation.

First floor — 1,814 sq. ft.
Second floor — 884 sq. ft.
Garage — 552 sq. ft.

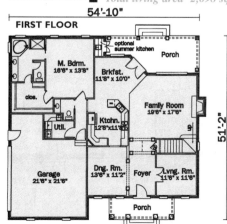

■ *Total living area 2,698 sq. ft.* ■ *Price Code F* ■

FIRST FLOOR

SECOND FLOOR

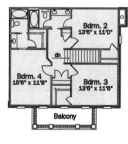

Classic Front Porch Styling

Total living area 2,701 sq. ft. ■ **Price Code F**

No. 62006

■ **This plan features:**

— Three bedrooms

— Two full, two three-quarter and one half baths

■ Southern traditional style offers gracious amenities

■ Large second floor Game Room can accommodate a variety of special interests

■ This home is designed with basement, slab and crawlspace foundation options.

First floor — 2,352 sq. ft.
Second floor — 349 sq. ft.
Garage — 697 sq. ft.

WIDTH 69'-0"
DEPTH 69'-10"

SECOND FLOOR

GAME ROOM
22'-2" x 14'-6"

FIRST FLOOR

Sprawling Two-Story

Total living area 2,702 sq. ft. ■ **Price Code F**

No. 99143

■ **This plan features:**

— Three bedrooms

— Two full and one half baths

■ The secluded Den has a cathedral ceiling

■ This spacious floor plan includes a Great Room with fireplace and a Nook opening to a Screened Porch

■ The luxurious Master Suite is privately located on the first floor

■ On the second floor is a Loft, a full Bath and two Bedrooms, one with a cathedral ceiling

■ This home is designed with a basement foundation.

First floor — 2,032 sq. ft.
Second floor — 670 sq. ft
Basement — 2,032 sq. ft.

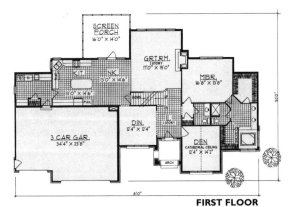

SECOND FLOOR

FIRST FLOOR

Refinement with Brilliancy

No. 97206

■ **This plan features:**

— Four bedrooms

— Three full baths

■ The two-story Foyer features a grand open rail staircase

■ The two-story Family Room is enhanced by a fireplace

■ The walk-in Pantry and ample counter space highlight the Breakfast Room

■ The secluded Study could be an additional Bedroom with a private Bath

■ The second floor Master Suite has a tray ceiling, a Sitting Area and a vaulted ceiling over the private Bath

■ This home is designed with basement, slab and crawlspace foundation options.

First floor — 1,548 sq. ft.
Second floor — 1,164 sq. ft.
Bonus — 198 sq. ft.
Basement — 1,548 sq. ft.
Garage — 542 sq. ft.

■ *Total living area 2,712 sq. ft.* ■ *Price Code F* ■

FIRST FLOOR

SECOND FLOOR

A Livable Home

No. 94965

■ **This plan features:**

— Four bedrooms

— Two full, one three-quarter and one half baths

■ The Master Bedroom is complete with a tray ceiling, two walk-in closets, and a large Bath

■ The three additional Bedrooms all have ample closet space and share two full Baths

■ The Family Room has a beamed ceiling and a fireplace

■ This home is designed with basement and slab foundation options.

■ Alternate foundation options available at an additional charge. Please call 1-800-235-5700 for more information.

First floor — 1,400 sq. ft.
Second floor — 1,315 sq. ft.
Basement — 1,400 sq. ft.
Garage — 631 sq. ft.

■ *Total living area 2,715 sq. ft.* ■ *Price Code F* ■

FIRST FLOOR

SECOND FLOOR

■ *Total living area 2,719 sq. ft.* ■ *Price Code F* ■

SECOND FLOOR

FIRST FLOOR

No. 60002

■ **This plan features:**

— Four bedrooms

— Three full and one half baths

■ The front Porch wraps around the Breakfast Area, which is open to the Kitchen

■ The Garage is located to the rear, making the design suitable for a corner lot

■ This home is designed with basement and crawlspace foundation options.

First floor — 1,906 sq. ft.
Second floor — 813 sq. ft.
Basement — 1,906 sq. ft.
Garage — 504 sq. ft.

Total living area 2,727 sq. ft. ■ Price Code F

No. 99436

■ This plan features:

— Three bedrooms

— Two full and one half baths

■ The Family Room has a wetbar and a see-through fireplace

■ The Master Suite has a tiered ceiling, a plush Bath with sky-lights and a large walk-in closet

■ The large efficient Kitchen has a cooktop island and is open to the Breakfast Area

■ This home is designed with a basement foundation.

■ Alternate foundation options available at an additional charge. Please call 1-800-235-5700 for more information.

First floor — 1,392 sq. ft.
Second floor — 1,335 sq. ft.
Bonus — 111 sq. ft.
Basement — 1,392 sq. ft.
Garage — 738 sq. ft.

Distinguished Dwelling

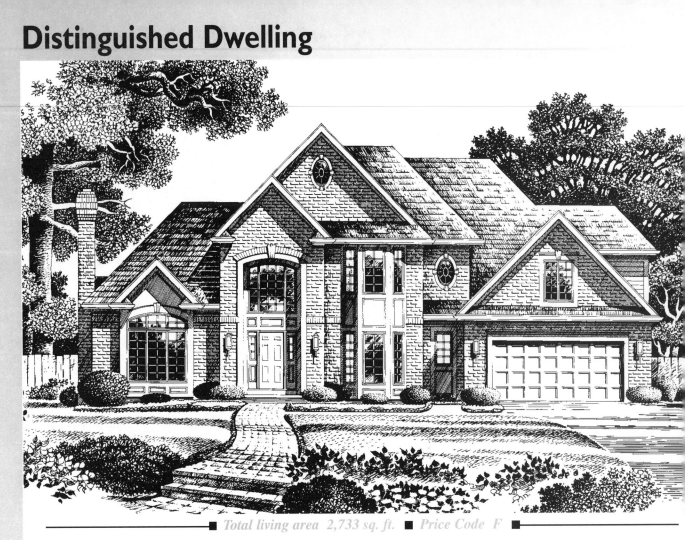

■ *Total living area 2,733 sq. ft.* ■ *Price Code F* ■

WIDTH 67'-4"
DEPTH 42'-8"

SECOND FLOOR

FIRST FLOOR

No. 94112

■ **This plan features:**

— Four bedrooms

— Two full and one half baths

■ The grand two-story Foyer has a lovely landing staircase

■ The formal Living Room has a decorative window

■ A beautiful bay window highlights the formal Dining Room

■ The convenient Kitchen has a cooktop work island

■ The luxurious Master Bedroom features a glass alcove and a plush Bath

■ This home is designed with a basement foundation.

First floor — 1,514 sq. ft.
Second floor — 1,219 sq. ft.
Basement — 1,465 sq. ft.
Garage — 596 sq. ft.

Great Room With Fireplace

No. 94988

■ This plan features:

— Four bedrooms

— Two full and one half baths

■ The Formal Dining Room has a bay window and hutch space

■ A see-through fireplace warms the Hearth Room and an expansive Great Room

■ Arched windows and French doors to the private Den enhance the Great Room

■ The Kitchen includes an island counter, a corner walk-in Pantry, a planning desk, and is open to the Breakfast Area which has a Bay window

■ The large Master Bedroom shows off the beautiful arched window arrangement and adjoins a whirlpool Bath

■ Three generous secondary Bedrooms share a double vanity Bath

■ This home is designed with a basement foundation.

■ Alternate foundation options available at an additional charge. Please call 1-800-235-5700 for more information.

First floor — 1,963 sq. ft.
Second floor — 778 sq. ft.
Basement — 1,963 sq. ft.
Garage — 658 sq. ft.

■ *Total living area 2,741 sq. ft.* ■ *Price Code F* ■

SECOND FLOOR

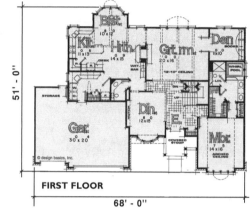

FIRST FLOOR

51' - 0"

68' - 0"

Family Matters

No. 91109

■ This plan features:

— Five Bedrooms

— Three full baths

■ A beautiful brick exterior is accentuated by arched transoms over double windows

■ The spacious Bedrooms and an oversized Great Room are desirable for a large family

■ Volume ceilings are found in the Master Suite, the Great Room, the Dining Room, the Kitchen, the Breakfast Area and Bedroom four

■ The three Bathrooms include a plush Master Bath with a double vanity and knee space

■ There is plenty of room to spread out in the Sunroom, adjacent to the Great Room, and the Rec Room above the Garage provides additional living space

■ This home is designed with a slab foundation.

First floor — 2,307 sq. ft.
Second floor — 440 sq. ft.
Garage & Storage — 517 sq. ft.

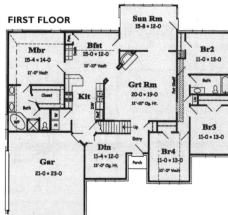

■ *Total living area 2,747 sq. ft.* ■ *Price Code F* ■

FIRST FLOOR

WIDTH 63'-1.5"
DEPTH 58'-4.75"

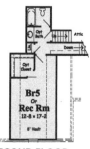

SECOND FLOOR

Gorgeous and Livable

■ *Total living area 2,750 sq. ft.* ■ *Price Code F* ■

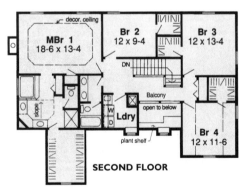

SECOND FLOOR

- MBr 1 18-6 x 13-4
- decor. ceiling
- Br 2 12 x 9-4
- Br 3 12 x 13-4
- DN
- Balcony open to below
- Ldry
- W D
- plant shelf
- Br 4 12 x 11-6

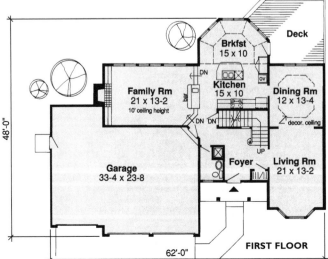

FIRST FLOOR

- Deck
- Brkfst 15 x 10
- Kitchen 15 x 10
- DN
- OV
- Dining Rm 12 x 13-4
- decor. ceiling
- Family Rm 21 x 13-2 10' ceiling height
- bar
- DN DN
- UP
- Foyer
- Living Rm 21 x 13-2
- Garage 33-4 x 23-8
- 48'-0"
- 62'-0"

No. 20196

■ This plan features:

— Four bedrooms

— Two full and one half baths

■ A bay window provides the Living Room with natural light

■ A decorative ceiling accentuates the formal Dining Room

■ The efficient Kitchen has a work island and is near the formal Dining Room and the informal Breakfast Area

■ The fantastic Master Suite has a decorative ceiling, a private Master Bath and a large walk-in closet

■ This home is designed with a basement foundation.

First floor — 1,273 sq. ft.
Second floor — 1,477 sq. ft.
Basement — 974 sq. ft.
Garage — 852 sq. ft.

Twin Gazebos

No. 68173

This plan features:

- Three bedrooms
- Two full and one half bath
- A third garage bay can become a well-placed Home Office
- The Bonus Room adds 232 square feet
- This home is designed with, slab, and crawlspace foundation options.
- Alternate foundation options available at an additional charge. Please call 1-800-235-5700 for more information.

First floor — 2,148 sq. ft.
Second floor — 610 sq. ft.
Bonus — 232 sq. ft.
Garage — 865 sq. ft.

■ *Total living area 2,758 sq. ft.* ■ *Price Code G* ■

Traditional That Has It All

No. 90443

This plan features:

- Three bedrooms
- Three full and two half baths
- The Master Suite has two closets and a private Bath with a separate shower, a corner tub and dual vanities
- The large Dining Room has a bay window and is adjacent to the Kitchen
- The formal Living Room is designed for entertaining, and the cozy Family Room has a fireplace for informal gatherings
- The two upstairs Bedrooms have walk-in closets and private Baths
- The Bonus Room is accessible for future needs
- This home is designed with basement, slab or crawlspace foundation options.

First floor — 1,927 sq. ft.
Second floor — 832 sq. ft.
Bonus — 624 sq. ft.
Basement — 1,674 sq. ft.

■ *Total living area 2,759 sq. ft.* ■ *Price Code G* ■

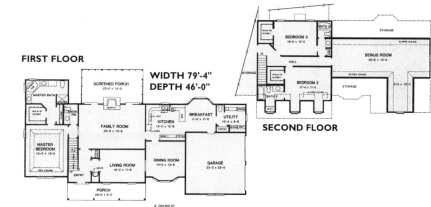

WIDTH 79'-4"
DEPTH 46'-0"

Traditional Exterior

No. 32101

■ This plan features:

— Three bedrooms

— Two full and one half baths

■ The Master Bedroom includes a private Balcony

■ The two secondary Bedrooms are identical in size

■ A see-through fireplace warms two rooms

■ The large Morning Room opens to the Terrace and the Breezeway

■ A Studio Apartment is located over the Garage

■ This home is designed with a crawlspace foundation.

First floor — 1,546 sq. ft.
Second floor — 1,218 sq. ft.
Bonus — 403 sq. ft.
Garage — 624 sq. ft.

■ Total living area 2,764 sq. ft. ■ Price Code G ■

WIDTH 89'-0"
DEPTH 63'-8"

FIRST FLOOR

SECOND FLOOR

Impressive Presence

No. 97239

■ This plan features:

— Four bedrooms

— Three full and one half baths

■ The angled Garage combines with varied rooflines to create an impressive presence

■ The Living Room has a vaulted ceiling and a decorative window

■ The Dining Room features a boxed bay window

■ The Family Room has an arched entrance

■ The Kitchen is open to the Nook and has a center island

■ The Master Suite is secluded behind the Garage on the first floor

■ The three Bedrooms with walk-in closets are on the second floor

■ The optional Bonus Room is located over the Garage

■ This home is designed with basement and crawlspace foundation options.

First floor — 1,904 sq. ft.
Second floor — 860 sq. ft.
Bonus — 388 sq. ft.
Basement — 1,904 sq. ft.
Garage — 575 sq. ft.

■ Total living area 2,764 sq. ft. ■ Price Code G ■

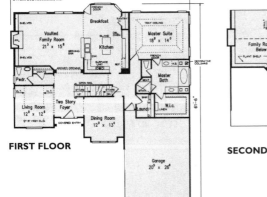

FIRST FLOOR

SECOND FLOOR

Sprawling Farmhouse

No. 91144

■ **This plan features:**

— Three bedrooms

— Two full and one half baths

■ The large covered Porch provides expanded outdoor living space

■ The Master Bedroom is situated privately and includes dual closets and vanities and a Spa tub

■ A large corner fireplace is the focus in the massive Living Room

■ Columns and arches separate the Entry from the formal Dining and Living Rooms

■ Future second floor expansion includes space for a Game Room and office

■ This home is designed with a slab foundation.

First floor — 2,289 sq. ft.
Second floor — 479 sq. ft.
Garage — 487 sq. ft.

Total living area 2,768 sq. ft. ■ *Price Code G*

SECOND FLOOR

FIRST FLOOR

Ideal Family Home

No. 93609

■ **This plan features:**

— Four bedrooms

— Two full and one half baths

■ The two-story Foyer opens to the Living Room and the Dining Room

■ Both the Grand Room and the Keeping Room have fireplaces

■ The L-shaped Kitchen has a center island and is open to the Breakfast Nook

■ The Master Bedroom has a decorative ceiling and a huge walk-in closet

■ This home is designed with basement and slab foundation options.

First floor — 1,535 sq. ft.
Second floor — 1,236 sq. ft.
Garage — 418 sq. ft.

Total living area 2,771 sq. ft. ■ *Price Code G*

FIRST FLOOR

SECOND FLOOR

Details, Details!

■ *Total living area 2,772 sq. ft.* ■ *Price Code G* ■

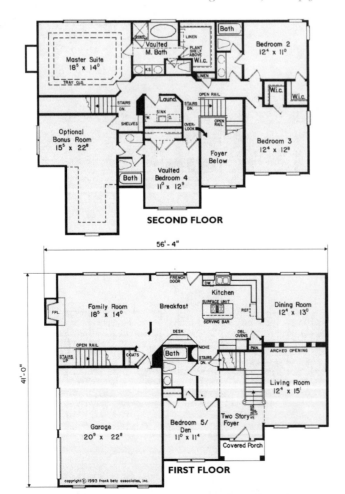

SECOND FLOOR

Master Suite 18⁵ x 14⁰ · TRAY CLG.
Vaulted M. Bath
LINEN · DRWR. · PLANT SHELF ABOVE · W.i.c. · LINEN
Bath
Bedroom 2 12⁴ x 11⁰
W.i.c. · W.i.c.
STAIRS DN. · Laund. · SINK · STAIRS DN. · OPEN RAIL · OPEN RAIL
SHELVES · OVER-LOOK
Optional Bonus Room 15⁵ x 22⁸
Foyer Below
Bedroom 3 12⁴ x 12⁸
Bath · Vaulted Bedroom 4 11⁰ x 12⁹

56'- 4"
41'- 0"

FIRST FLOOR

FRENCH DOOR · DW
Kitchen · SURFACE UNIT · SERVING BAR · REF.
Family Room 18⁵ x 14⁰ · Breakfast
Dining Room 12⁴ x 13⁰
FPL
DESK · NICHE · DBL. OVENS · PAN.
OPEN RAIL · STAIRS UP · COATS · Bath · STAIRS DN. · ARCHED OPENING
Living Room 12⁴ x 15¹
Garage 20⁹ x 22⁸
Bedroom 5/ Den 11⁴ x 11⁴
Two Story Foyer
Covered Porch

No. 98494

■ **This plan features:**

— Five bedrooms

— Four full baths

■ The exterior is appointed with keystones, arches and shutters

■ The covered Porch opens to a dramatic two-story Foyer

■ Between the Living Room and Dining Room there is an arched opening

■ The Master Suite has a tray ceiling and a vaulted Master Bath

■ This home is designed with basement and crawlspace foundation options

First floor — 1,447 sq. ft.
Second floor — 1,325 sq. ft.
Bonus — 301 sq. ft.
Basement — 1,447 sq. ft.
Garage — 393 sq. ft.

Victorian Farmhouse

No. 98581

This plan features:

— Four bedrooms

— Three full and one half baths

- The Kitchen snack bar opens to the Family Room which has a fireplace and access to the rear Deck and side Porch

- The Master Bedroom has direct access to the rear Deck

- The front Music Room has a bay window area

- This home is available with basement and slab foundation options.

First floor — 2,023 sq. ft.
Second floor — 749 sq. ft.
Bonus — 256 sq. ft.
Garage — 546 sq. ft.

Total living area 2,772 sq. ft. ■ Price Code G

MAID'S QUARTERS

SECOND FLOOR

FIRST FLOOR

WIDTH 77'-2"
DEPTH 57'-11"

Classical Details

No. 99446

This plan features:

— Four bedrooms

— Two full and one half baths

- Decorative windows and a dignified brick exterior combine to create sophisticated curb appeal

- The formal Living Room and Dining Room have elegant large bay windows

- The efficient Kitchen provides a large Pantry, two Lazy Susans and a large center work island

- The distinctive Master Suite features a built-in dresser, an extra-large walk-in closet and a luxurious Bath with an arched opening to the whirlpool and shower area

- This home is available with a basement foundation.

- Alternate foundation options available at an additional charge. Please call 1-800-235-5700 for more information.

First floor — 1,469 sq. ft.
Second floor — 1,306 sq. ft.
Basement — 1,469 sq. ft.
Garage — 814 sq. ft.

Total living area 2,775 sq. ft. ■ Price Code G

FIRST FLOOR

SECOND FLOOR

With Room for All

Total living area 2,781 sq. ft. ▪ Price Code G

FIRST FLOOR

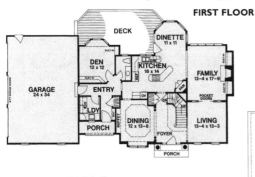

DECK

DEN
12 x 12

DINETTE
11 x 11

KITCHEN
18 x 14

FAMILY
13-4 x 17-9

GARAGE
24 x 34

ENTRY

LDY

POCKET DOORS

PORCH

BUFFET

DINING
12 x 13-8

LIVING
13-4 x 13-3

FOYER

PORCH

WIDTH 75'-0"
DEPTH 42'-6"

SECOND FLOOR

ROOF

ROOF

B 2

BR 4
10-8 x 15

M/B

LINEN

HALL

DOWN

ROOF

BR 3
13-4 x 14

BR 2
12 x 12-6

MBR
13-4 x 17

BALCONY

No. 93339

▪ **This plan features:**

— Four bedrooms

— Two full and one half baths

▪ The formal Dining and Living Room open from the Foyer

▪ An elegant ceiling treatment and a built-in buffet area are featured in the Dining Room

▪ Pocket doors separate the Family Room from the Living Room

▪ The secluded Den is equipped with built-in shelves and a sunny bay window

▪ The Master Suite has a lavish Master Bath and a walk-in closet

▪ The three additional Bedrooms share a full double vanity Bath

▪ This home is designed with a basement foundation.

First floor — 1,536 sq. ft.
Second floor — 1,245 sq. ft.

Impressive Plan

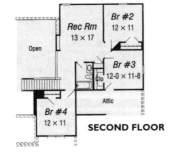

Total living area 2,786 sq. ft. ▪ Price Code G

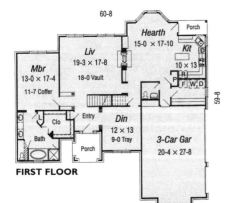

60-8

Hearth
15-0 × 17-10

Porch

Liv
19-3 × 17-8

18-0 Vault

Kit
10 × 13

Mbr
13-0 × 17-4

11-7 Coffer

Entry

Din
12 × 13
9-0 Tray

3-Car Gar
20-4 × 27-8

Clo

Bath

Porch

59-8

FIRST FLOOR

SECOND FLOOR

Rec Rm
13 × 17

Br #2
12 × 11

Open

Br #3
12-0 × 11-8

Clo

Attic

Br #4
12 × 11

No. 91133

▪ **This plan features:**

— Four bedrooms

— Two full and one half baths

▪ A see-through fireplace warms both the Living and Hearth Rooms

▪ The U-shaped Kitchen has a center island

▪ A tray ceiling graces the Dining Room

▪ The Master Suite is in its own wing

▪ Three additional Bedrooms are on the second floor

▪ This home is designed with a slab foundation.

First floor — 1,893 sq. ft.
Second floor — 893 sq. ft.
Garage — 632 sq. ft.

Ideal for Busy Lifestyles

■ *Total living area 2,788 sq. ft.* ■ *Price Code G* ■

No. 97130

■ This plan features:

— Four bedrooms

— Two full and one half baths

■ The two-story Entry opens to the spacious Family Room

■ The Family Room has built-in cabinets and a fireplace

■ The Kitchen has a walk-in Pantry, an island eating bar and a sunny Nook for family meals

■ The Master Suite has a garden Spa tub

■ The three additional Bedrooms share a full Bath which has a linen closet

■ This home is designed with a basement foundation.

First floor — 1,533 sq. ft.
Second floor — 1,255 sq. ft.
Basement — 1,533 sq. ft.

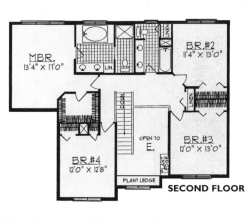

SECOND FLOOR

FIRST FLOOR

Custom Built-ins

Photography supplied by Nelson Design Group

■ *Total living area 2,789 sq. ft.* ■ *Price Code G* ■

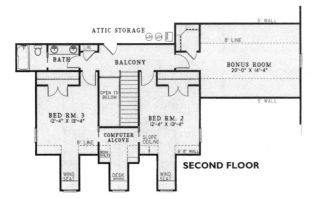

SECOND FLOOR

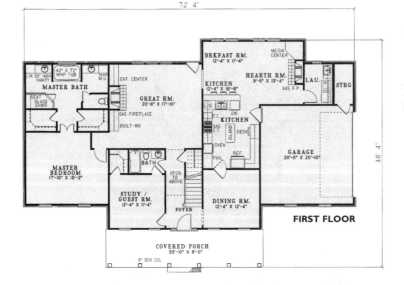

FIRST FLOOR

No. 61019

■ **This plan features:**

— Four bedrooms

— Three full baths

■ Custom built-ins surround the fireplaces in the Hearth Room and Great Room and highlight the second floor dormers

■ The Bonus Room adds 287 square feet

■ This home is designed with basement, slab, and crawlspace foundation options.

First floor — 1,977 sq. ft.
Second floor — 812 sq. ft.

Two-Story Entry

■ Total living area 2,793 sq. ft. ■ Price Code G

No. 60009

■ **This plan features:**

— Five bedrooms

— Three full baths

■ An angled hallway with built-in niche leads to the Breakfast Area and Family Room

■ Built-in bookshelves and radius windows flank the Family Room fireplace

■ This home is designed with basement and crawlspace foundation options.

First floor — 1,413 sq. ft.
Second floor — 1,380 sq. ft.
Basement — 1,413 sq. ft.
Garage — 482 sq. ft.

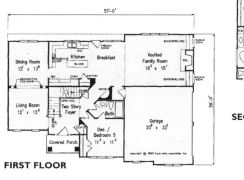

FIRST FLOOR

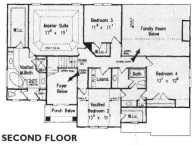

SECOND FLOOR

Three-Story Atrium View

■ Total living area 2,806 sq. ft. ■ Price Code G

No. 69005

■ **This plan features:**

— Four bedrooms

— Two full and one half baths

■ The two-story Great Room connects to a U-shape staircase that leads to the lower floor Family Room

■ This home is designed with a basement foundation.

First floor — 1,473 sq. ft.
Second floor — 785 sq. ft.
Lower floor — 548 sq. ft.

FIRST FLOOR

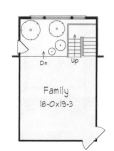

LOWER FLOOR

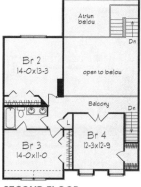

SECOND FLOOR

Elegant Design

■ *Total living area 2,824 sq. ft.* ■ *Price Code G* ■

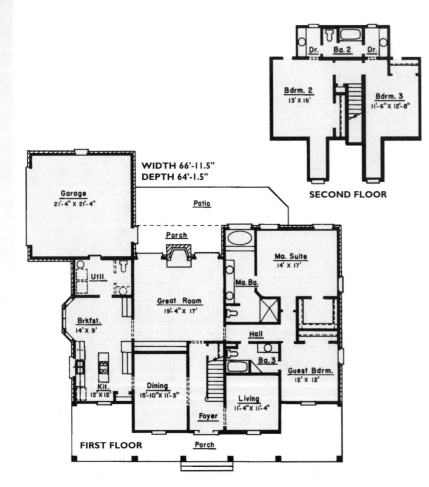

WIDTH 66'-11.5"
DEPTH 64'-1.5"

SECOND FLOOR

FIRST FLOOR

No. 94618

■ **This plan features:**

— Four bedrooms

— Three full and one half baths

■ Floor to ceiling windows and stately pillars create an impressive facade

■ The central Foyer opens to the formal Living and Dining Rooms

■ The Great Room has built-in shelving, a focal point fireplace and access to the Porch and Patio

■ The spacious Kitchen has a built-in Pantry and a Breakfast Area

■ The Master Suite has a large walk-in closet and a double vanity Bath

■ This home is designed with slab and crawlspace foundation options.

First floor — 2,120 sq. ft.
Second floor — 704 sq. ft.
Garage — 516 sq. ft.

Glorious Arches

■ *Total living area 2,840 sq. ft.* ■ *Price Code G* ■

No. 97208

■ This plan features:

— Four bedrooms

— Three full and one half baths

■ Dramatic arched openings distinguish the Family Room

■ The Kitchen with a center island is open to the Breakfast Area

■ The Master Suite has a tray ceiling and its Bath has a vaulted ceiling

■ One Bedroom has a window seat, a walk-in closet and a private Bath

■ A three-car Garage is also featured for this plan

■ This home is designed with basement and crawlspace foundation options.

First floor — 1,347 sq. ft.
Second floor — 1,493 sq. ft.
Bonus — 243 sq. ft.
Basement — 1,347 sq. ft.
Garage — 778 sq. ft.

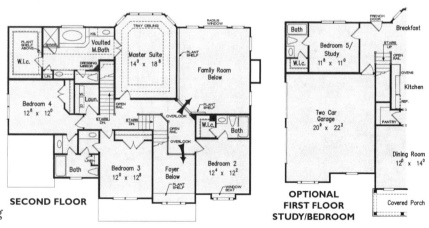

SECOND FLOOR

OPTIONAL
FIRST FLOOR
STUDY/BEDROOM

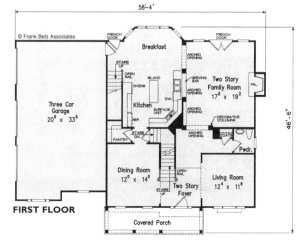

© Frank Betz Associates

FIRST FLOOR

Spacious Kitchen

■ *Total living area 2,847 sq. ft.* ■ *Price Code I* ■

WIDTH 53'-7"
DEPTH 72'-6"

© Sater Design Collection

Garage
21'-6" x 23'-0"

8'-6" x 9'-6"

Stor.

Utility

Up

Kitchen

Island

14'-0" x 15'-6"
Beamed Clg.

pantry

Pwdr.

Nook
11'-0" x 14'-6"

Porch
20'-10" x 8'-0"

Leisure Room
19'-6" x 17'-0"
Coffered Ceiling

built-in

fireplace

built-in

Up

arches

Dining
13'-0" x 15'-10"
Stepped Clg.

Foyer

Parlor
13'-0" x 15'-0"
Beamed Ceiling

Porch
28'-10" x 6'-0"

FIRST FLOOR

Bonus Room
12'-6" x 14'-0"

Bath 2   WIC

Dn.

Equip.

WIC

Bedroom 2
12'-4" x 12'-0"

Whirlpool

His WIC

Deck

Master Bath

make-up   Linen

Master Bedroom
14'-0" x 17'-6
Tray Ceiling

Bath 1

Her WIC

Dn.

Linen   Master Foyer

Loft

WIC

Core Lighting

Bedroom 1
13'-0" x 10'-0"

Open to Below

SECOND FLOOR

No. 64146

■ This plan features:

— Three bedrooms

— Two full and one half baths

■ The wide open living spaces are flooded with natural light

■ The Bonus Room adds 340 square feet

■ This home is designed with a crawlspace foundation.

■ Alternate foundation options available at an additional charge. Please call 1-800-235-5700 for more information.

First floor — 1,642 sq. ft.
Second floor — 1,205 sq. ft.
Bonus — 340 sq. ft.
Garage — 541 sq. ft.

Sophisticated Southern Styling

No. 92576

This plan features:

- Five Bedrooms
- Three full and one half baths
- The covered front and rear Porches add outdoors living space
- The Den has a large fireplace and built-in cabinets and shelves
- A cooktop island, a built-in desk, and an Eating Area complete the Kitchen
- The Master Suite has two walk-in closets and a luxurious Bath
- The four additional Bedrooms, two on the first floor and two on the second floor, share full Baths
- This home is designed with slab and crawlspace foundation options.

First floor — 2,256 sq. ft.
Second floor — 602 sq. ft.
Bonus — 264 sq. ft.
Garage — 484 sq. ft.

■ Total living area 2,858 sq. ft. ■ Price Code G ■

FIRST FLOOR

SECOND FLOOR

BONUS

Impressive Structure

No. 99461

This plan features:

- Four bedrooms
- Two full and one three-quarter and one half baths
- This design features an impressive curbside presence, and formal and informal living areas
- The private, first floor Master Suite has a tray ceiling and a graceful, bow window
- The Breakfast Room is lined with windows for relaxing outdoor views during casual meals
- The tiled, central hallways are a practical feature on the first floor
- The secondary Bedrooms share private access to a full and a three-quarter Bath
- A three-car Garage completes the plan
- This home is designed with a basement foundation.
- Alternate foundation options available at an additional charge. Please call 1-800-235-5700 for more information.

First floor — 1,972 sq. ft.
Second floor — 893 sq. ft.
Garage — 658 sq. ft.

■ Total living area 2,865 sq. ft. ■ Price Code G ■

FIRST FLOOR

SECOND FLOOR

Old World Charm

Total living area 2,867 sq. ft. ■ Price Code G

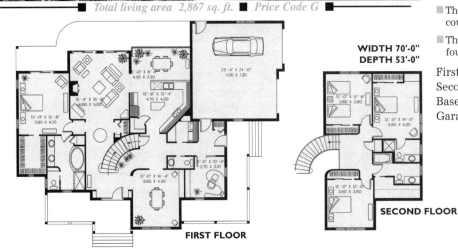

WIDTH 70'-0"
DEPTH 53'-0"

SECOND FLOOR

FIRST FLOOR

No. 65369

■ This plan features:

— Four bedrooms

— Three full and one half baths

■ Porches on three sides, keystone trim and multi-paned windows are some of the decorative details that highlight this home

■ A curving stair in the Foyer opens to a formal Dining Room

■ Conveniently located between the Kitchen and Garage, a utility corridor houses a Mudroom, Powder Room, Laundry Room and Home Office with computer port

■ The well-equipped Kitchen has ample counter and cabinet space

■ The home is designed with a basement foundation.

First floor — 1,905 sq. ft.
Second floor — 962 sq. ft.
Basement — 1,905 sq. ft.
Garage — 608 sq. ft.

Rambling Farmhouse

Total living area 2,873 sq. ft. ■ Price Code I

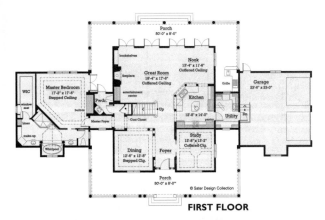

FIRST FLOOR

WIDTH 98'-0"
DEPTH 76'-0"

SECOND FLOOR

No. 64151

■ This plan features:

— Three bedrooms

— Two full and one half baths

■ Housed in its own wing, the Master Bedroom is a luxurious, private retreat.

■ The Bonus Room adds 498 square feet

■ This home is designed with a crawlspace foundation.

■ Alternate foundation options available at an additional charge. Please call 1-800-235-5700 for more information.

First floor — 2,151 sq. ft.
Second floor — 722 sq. ft.
Bonus — 498 sq. ft.

Covered Veranda Enhances

■ *Total living area 2,879 sq. ft.* ■ ● *Price Code G* ■

No. 94265

■ **This plan features:**

- Three bedrooms

- Three full baths

■ The Great Room has a corner fireplace, a wetbar and glass doors to the rear Deck

■ The Gourmet Kitchen has a center island/eating bar

■ The two Guest Bedrooms have private Baths

■ A winding staircase leads to a luxurious upper floor Master Suite that opens to a private balcony

■ This home is designed with a pier/post foundation.

■ Alternate foundation options available at an additional charge. Please call 1-800-235-5700 for more information.

First floor — 1,684 sq. ft.
Second floor — 1,195 sq. ft.
Lower floor — 1,433 sq. ft.

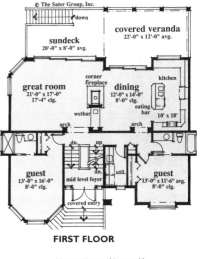

FIRST FLOOR

SECOND FLOOR

LOWER FLOOR

Impressive Elevation

Total living area 2,891 sq. ft. ■ *Price Code G*

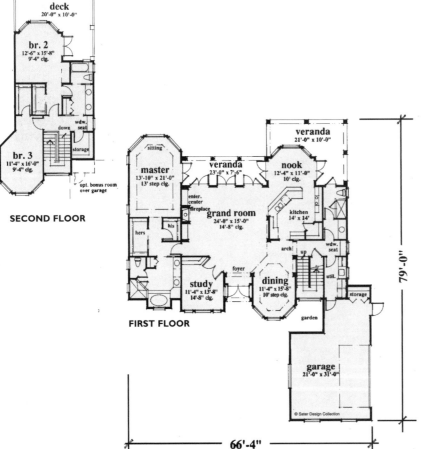

deck
20'-0" x 10'-0"

br. 2
12'-6" x 15'-8"
9'-4" clg.

br. 3
11'-4" x 16'-0"
9'-4" clg.

wdw. seat

down

storage

opt. bonus room over garage

SECOND FLOOR

veranda
21'-0" x 10'-0"

sitting

master
13'-10" x 21'-0"
13' step clg.

veranda
23'-0" x 7'-6"

nook
12'-4" x 11'-0"
10' clg.

enter. center
fireplace

his

hers

grand room
24'-0" x 15'-0"
14'-8" clg.

kitchen
14' x 14'

arch

foyer

up

wdw. seat

util.

study
11'-4" x 13'-8"
14'-8" clg.

dining
11'-4" x 15'-8"
10' step clg.

garden

storage

FIRST FLOOR

garage
21'-0" x 31'-0"

© Sater Design Collection

79'-0"

66'-4"

No. 94231

■ **This plan features:**

— Three bedrooms

— Three full baths

■ Decorative windows highlight the Study and the formal Dining Room

■ The spacious Kitchen with a walk-in pantry and a peninsula counter is convenient to the Nook and the Dining Room

■ The luxurious Master Suite has a step ceiling, a Sitting Area, two walk-in closets and a plush Bath

■ This home is designed with basement and slab foundation options.

■ Alternate foundation options available at an additional charge. Please call 1-800-235-5700 for more information.

First floor — 2,181 sq. ft.
Second floor — 710 sq. ft.
Garage —658 sq. ft.

Luxurious Master Suite

No. 24657

This plan features:

- Four bedrooms
- Three full and one half baths
- Fireplaces are located in the formal Living Room and the Family Room
- The optional Sun Room expands living space
- The Kitchen is conveniently located between the Breakfast Area and the formal Dining Room
- The plush Bath with a whirlpool tub and a vaulted ceiling, and a tray ceiling over the Bedroom highlight the Master Suite
- The three additional Bedrooms each have private access to a full Bath
- The Bonus Room is available for future expansion
- This home is designed with basement, slab and crawlspace foundation options.

First floor — 1,523 sq. ft.
Second floor — 1,370 sq. ft.
Basement — 1,722 sq. ft.
Bonus — 344 sq. ft.
Garage — 484 sq. ft.

■ *Total living area 2,893 sq. ft.* ■ *Price Code G* ■

ALTERNATE CRAWLSPACE FOUNDATION OPTION

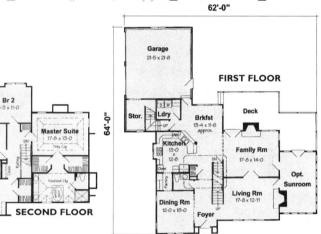

Plantation Porch

No. 94644

This plan features:

- Five bedrooms
- Three full baths
- The Family Room, accented by a fireplace, is situated at the heart of the home
- The Garage is positioned to the rear of the home to emphasize the facade
- The Future Playroom adds 225 square feet.
- This home is designed with slab and crawlspace foundation options

First floor — 2,135 sq. ft.
Second floor — 763 sq. ft.
Bonus — 538 sq. ft.
Garage — 436 sq. ft.

■ *Total living area 2,898 sq. ft.* ■ *Price Code G* ■

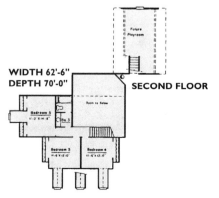

Essence of Style & Grace

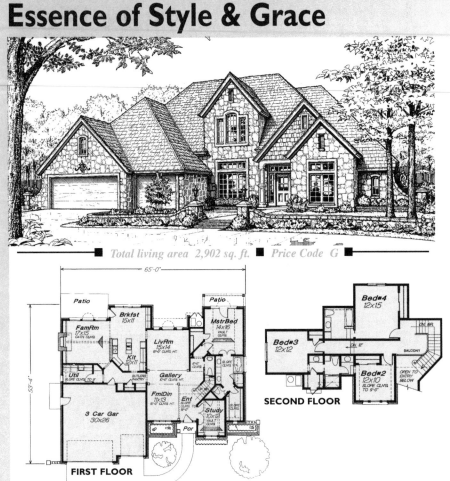

Total living area 2,902 sq. ft. ■ *Price Code G*

FIRST FLOOR

SECOND FLOOR

No. 98524

■ **This plan features:**

— Four bedrooms

— Three full and one half baths

■ French doors introduce the Study and columns define the Gallery and formal areas

■ The expansive Family Room, with an inviting fireplace and a cathedral ceiling, opens to the Kitchen

■ The Kitchen features a cooktop island, a Butler's Pantry, a Breakfast Area and Patio access

■ The first floor Master Bedroom offers a private Patio, a vaulted ceiling, twin vanities and a walk-in closet

■ Three second floor Bedrooms each have access to the full Bath

■ This home is designed with basement and slab foundation options.

First floor — 2,036 sq. ft.
Second floor — 866 sq. ft.
Garage — 720 sq. ft.

Let the Sun Shine In

Total living area 2,913 sq. ft. ■ *Price Code G*

FIRST FLOOR

SECOND FLOOR

No. 91588

■ **This plan features:**

— Four bedrooms

— Two full and one three-quarter baths

■ The two-story entrance has a lovely banister staircase

■ The Den with corner windows and French doors offers many uses

■ A Cooktop island/snack bar, a built-in desk and the Pantry highlight the efficient Kitchen

■ The Family Room is enhanced by a second fireplace

■ The lavish Master Suite has a decorative ceiling in the Bedroom and a private, plush Bath.

■ This home is designed with a crawlspace foundation.

First floor — 1,575 sq. ft.
Second floor — 1,338 sq. ft.
Garage — 864 sq. ft.

Executive Digs

No. 99463

This plan features:

- Four bedrooms

- Two full, one three-quarter and one half baths

■ The Family Room features an elegant, bowed window and shares a warm, three-sided fireplace with the Breakfast Room and Kitchen.

■ An island/snack bar, a built-in desk and a Pantry highlight the Kitchen.

■ The Master Suite features a tiered ceiling and an irresistible whirlpool tub in the luxurious Bath

■ All the secondary Bedrooms have private access to a Bath

■ Bedroom two is elegantly accented by a beautiful arched window

■ This home is designed with a basement foundation.

■ Alternate foundation options available at an additional charge. Please call 1-800-235-5700 for more information.

First floor — 1,583 sq. ft.
Second floor — 1,331 sq. ft.
Garage — 676 sq. ft.

■ *Total living area 2,914 sq. ft.* ■ *Price Code G* ■

WIDTH 58'-0"
DEPTH 59'-4"

FIRST FLOOR

SECOND FLOOR

Built-Ins Abound

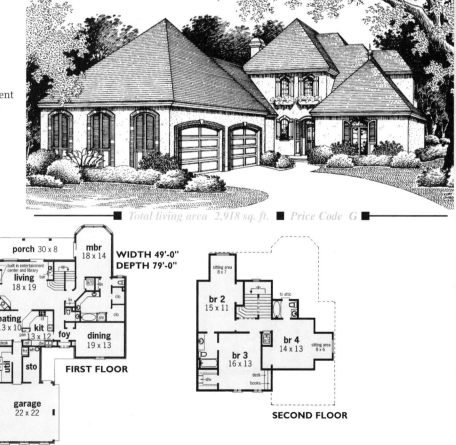

No. 65608

This plan features:

- Four bedrooms

- Two full and one half baths

■ The Living Room includes an entertainment center, bookshelves, a fireplace, a wetbar, and sliding Patio doors to the Porch

■ Sitting areas enhance upstairs Bedrooms

■ This home is designed with a slab foundation.

First floor — 1,884 sq. ft.
Second floor — 1,034 sq. ft.
Garage — 566 sq. ft.

■ *Total living area 2,918 sq. ft.* ■ *Price Code G* ■

WIDTH 49'-0"
DEPTH 79'-0"

FIRST FLOOR

SECOND FLOOR

Luxury and Style

■ *Total living area 2,927 sq. ft.* ■ *Price Code G* ■

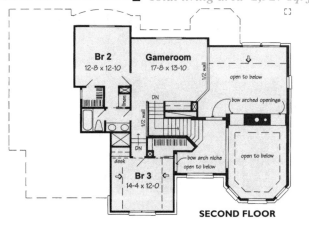

SECOND FLOOR

Br 2
12-8 x 12-10

Gameroom
17-8 x 13-10

½ wall

open to below

bow arched openings

DN

linen

½ wall

DN

desk

bow arch niche
open to below

open to below

Br 3
14-4 x 12-0

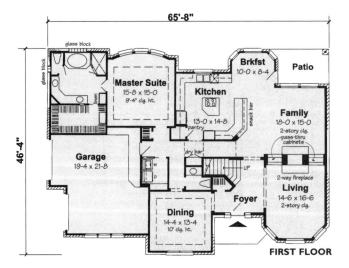

65'-8"

46'-4"

glass block

glass block

Master Suite
15-8 x 15-0
9'-4" clg. ht.

linen

Brkfst
10-0 x 8-4

Patio

Kitchen

13-0 x 14-8

pantry

snack bar

Family
18-0 x 15-0
2-story clg.
pass-thru
cabinets

dry bar

Garage
19-4 x 21-8

w
d

UP

2-way fireplace

Living
14-6 x 16-6
2-story clg.

Dining
14-4 x 13-4
10' clg. ht.

Foyer

FIRST FLOOR

No. 20507

■ **This plan features:**

– Three bedrooms

– Two full and one half baths

■ A two-story ceiling and a two-way fireplace are featured in the formal Living Room and the Family Room

■ A cooktop island, a built-in Pantry and a peninsula counter/eating bar are located in the Kitchen

■ The first floor Master Suite is crowned by a tray ceiling and has a lavish Bath

■ Two additional Bedrooms, one with a sloped ceiling and built-in desk, are found on the second floor

■ This home is designed with crawlspace and slab foundation options.

First floor — 1,979 sq. ft.
Second floor — 948 sq. ft.

No. 99400

This plan features:

- Four bedrooms

- Three full and one half baths

■ The majestic Entry opens to the Den and the Dining Room highlighted by boxed windows and decorative ceilings

■ The expansive Great Room shares a see-through fireplace with Hearth Room, and has French doors to a covered Veranda

■ The lovely Hearth Room is enhanced by three skylights above triple arched windows and an entertainment center

■ The Hub Kitchen has a work island/snack bar, pantry, a bright Breakfast Area and the nearby Laundry/Garage Entry

■ The sumptuous Master Bedroom has corner windows, two closets and vanities, and a garden whirlpool tub

■ This home is designed with basement and slab foundation options.

■ Alternate foundation options available at an additional charge. Please call 1-800-235-5700 for more information.

First floor — 2,084 sq. ft.

Second floor — 848 sq. ft.

Basement — 2,084 sq. ft.

Garage — 682 sq. ft.

■ Total living area 2,932 sq. ft. ■ Price Code G ■

SECOND FLOOR

FIRST FLOOR

No. 97735

This plan features:

- Four bedrooms

- Three full and one half baths

■ This floor plan is designed to offer the comfort of informal living with the amenities of an artful showplace

■ Split stairs from the Breakfast Area lead to a lower level that can be accessed for additional living space

■ Three Bedrooms on the second floor easily access the full Bath and the Computer Loft

■ This plan is designed with a basement foundation.

First floor — 1,978 sq. ft.

Second floor — 958 sq. ft.

Garage — 651 sq. ft.

■ Total living area 2,936 sq. ft. ■ Price Code G ■

FIRST FLOOR

SECOND FLOOR

269

Lasting Impression

■ *Total living area 2,940 sq. ft.* ■ *Price Code G* ■

FIRST FLOOR

© Frank Betz Associates, Inc.

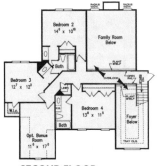

SECOND FLOOR

No. 98458

■ **This plan features:**

—Four bedrooms

—Three full and one half baths

■ The two-story Foyer is enhanced by a cascading staircase with an open rail

■ The Living Room is topped by a 12- foot tray ceiling

■ Double doors lead from the Dining Room to the covered Porch

■ The Master Suite includes a Sitting Area and a pampering Bath

■ Three additional Bedrooms have private access to the full Bath and Bonus Room

■ This home is designed with basement, slab and crawlspace foundation options.

First floor — 2,044 sq. ft.
Second floor — 896 sq. ft.
Bonus — 197 sq. ft.
Basement — 2,044 sq. ft.
Garage — 544 sq. ft.

WIDTH 63'-0"
DEPTH 54'-0"

Bay Master Suite

■ *Total living area 2,941 sq. ft.* ■ *Price Code G* ■

FIRST FLOOR

SECOND FLOOR

No. 60010

■ **This plan features:**

— Four bedrooms

— Three full and one half baths

■ The front stairway rises to a bridge spanning the Great Room and Foyer

■ An optional fourth Bedroom can add 281 square feet to the home

■ This home is designed with basement and crawlspace foundation options.

First floor — 2,165 sq. ft.
Second floor — 776 sq. ft.
Bonus — 281 sq. ft.
Basement — 2,165 sq. ft.
Garage — 517 sq. ft.

Two-Story Columns

Total living area 2,954 sq. ft. ■ Price Code K

No. 64201

This plan features:

- Four bedrooms

- Two full and one half baths

- The Loft extends the columns of the Living Room to the two-story, coffered ceiling

- An island cooktop, corner Pantry, built-in refrigerator and a bay window nook highlight the Kitchen

- This home is designed with a crawlspace foundation.

- Alternate foundation options available at an additional charge. Please call 1-800-235-5700 for more information.

First floor — 1,373 sq. ft.
Second floor — 1,581 sq. ft.

WIDTH 64'-6"
DEPTH 52'-2"

FIRST FLOOR

© Sater Design Collection

Porch
30'-0" x 10'-0"

Nook
9'-0" x 13'-10"
Stepped Clg.

Kitchen
Island
11'-10" x 10'-10"

Leisure Room
18'-6" x 14'-0"
Stepped Ceiling
fireplace
built-in
built-in

Dining
13'-0" x 13'-0"
Beamed Clg.

Utility

Foyer

Living
12'-6" x 16'-4"
Coffered Ceiling

Garage
23'-0" x 26'-4"

Porch
34'-0" x 8'-0"

SECOND FLOOR

Whirlpool
Master Bath
make-up

Master Deck

Bedroom 3
12'-0" x 10'-4"
WIC   WIC

Master Suite
14'-0" x 14'-8"
Tray Ceiling

Bedroom 1
11'-4" x 16'-0"

Bedroom 2
11'-4" x 12'-2"

Bath

Study
11'-6" x 13'-2"
Coffered Clg.
computer desk

Loft

Open to Foyer Below

Open to Below

Impressive Two-Story

Total living area 2,957 sq. ft. ■ Price Code G

ALTERNATE FOUNDATION OPTION

No. 24594

This plan features:

- Four bedrooms

- Two full and one half baths

- The two-story Foyer is highlighted by a lovely, angled staircase and a decorative window

- The Kitchen has a work island and an open Breakfast Area

- The spacious, yet cozy Family Room offers a fireplace and Future Sunroom access

- The private Master Suite offers a walk-in closet and a pampering Bath

- This home is designed with basement, slab and crawlspace foundation options.

First floor — 1,497 sq. ft.
Second floor — 1,460 sq. ft.
Future Sunroom — 210 sq. ft.
Basement — 1,456 sq. ft.
Garage — 680 sq. ft.

ALTERNATE FOUNDATION OPTION

crawl access

Master Suite
14-0 x 17-4

Br 2
11-0 x 12-2

Br 3
11-8 x 12-0

Br 4
11-8 x 11-10

Study
19-8 x 9-4

laundry chute

open to foyer

SECOND FLOOR

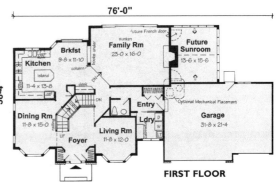

76'-0"

38'-4"

Future French door
sunken
Family Rm
23-0 x 16-0

Brkfst
9-8 x 11-10

Kitchen
11-4 x 13-8
island

Future Sunroom
13-6 x 15-6

Optional Mechanical Placement

Dining Rm
11-8 x 15-0

Entry

Garage
31-8 x 21-4

Living Rm
11-8 x 12-0

Ldry

Foyer

FIRST FLOOR

Timeless Beauty

■ *Total living area 2,957 sq. ft.* ■ *Price Code G* ■

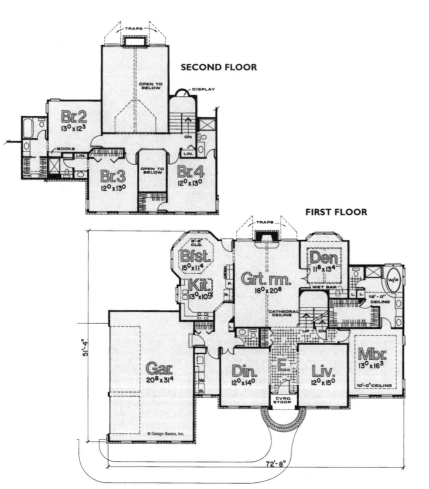

SECOND FLOOR

Br 2
13⁰x12³

Br.3
12⁰x13⁰

Br.4
12⁰x13⁰

FIRST FLOOR

Bfst.
15⁰x11⁴

Kit.
13⁰x10⁹

Grt. rm.
16⁰x20⁸

Den
11⁸x13⁴

Mbr.
13⁰x16³

Gar.
20⁸x31⁴

Din.
12⁰x14⁰

Liv.
12⁰x15⁰

© Design Basics, Inc.

51'-4"

72'-8"

No. 94994

■ This plan features:

– Four bedrooms

– Two full, two three-quarter and one half baths

■ The two-story Entry hall accesses formal Dining and Living Rooms

■ The spacious Great Room has a cathedral ceiling and a fireplace

■ The Kitchen has a pantry, a work island and a glass Breakfast Area

■ The Master Bedroom wing offers a luxurious dressing/Bath Area

■ This home is designed with a basement foundation.

■ Alternate foundation options available at an additional charge. Please call 1-800-235-5700 for more information.

First floor — 2,063 sq. ft.
Second floor — 894 sq. ft.
Basement — 2,063 sq. ft.
Garage — 666 sq. ft.

Celebrating the Sea and the Sun

■ *Total living area* *2,957 sq. ft.* ■ *Price Code G* ■

No. 94261

This plan features:

Three bedrooms

Three full and one half baths

With its many windows and Porches this home is perfect for waterfront living

This home is made for entertaining, with Guest Rooms each having its own Bath

Reminiscent of old widow's walks, this home has an observation balcony

The lower floor includes Garage space and Storage

This home is designed with a pier/post foundation.

First floor — 1,642 sq. ft.
Second floor — 1,165 sq. ft.
Lower floor — 150 sq. ft.

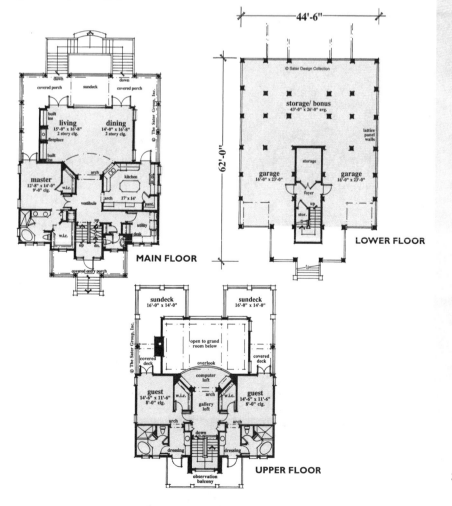

Stately Colonial Home

Total living area 2,959 sq. ft. ■ Price Code G

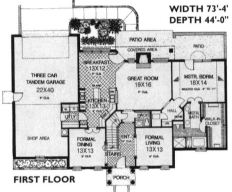

WIDTH 73'-4'
DEPTH 44'-0"

FIRST FLOOR

SECOND FLOOR

No. 98534

■ This plan features:

—Four bedrooms

—Three full and one half baths

■ Stately columns and arched windows project luxury and quality that is evident throughout this home

■ The Entry is highlighted by a palladian window, a plant shelf and an angled staircase

■ The formal Living and Dining Rooms are located off the Entry for ease in entertaining

■ The comfortable Great Room has an inviting fireplace and opens Kitchen/Breakfast Area and the Patio

■ The Master Bedroom wing offers Patio access, a luxurious Bath and a walk-in closet

■ This home is designed with a basement, crawlspace and combination basement/crawlspace foundation options.

First floor — 1,848 sq. ft.
Second floor — 1,111 sq. ft.
Garage & shop — 722 sq. ft.

Rewards of Success

Total living area 2,965 sq. ft. ■ Price Code G

FIRST FLOOR

SECOND FLOOR

No. 92535

■ This plan features:

— Four bedrooms

— Three full and one half baths

■ The open Foyer is flanked by the formal Dining and Living Rooms

■ An expansive Den has a large fireplace nestled between sliding glass doors to the back yard

■ Built-in cabinets and shelves provide an added convenience in the Den

■ A well-appointed Kitchen serves the formal Dining Room and the informal Kitchen with equal ease

■ The Master Bedroom has the lavish Bath and a walk-in closet

■ Three additional Bedrooms and two full Baths occupy the second floor

■ This home is designed with slab and crawl space foundation options.

First floor — 2,019 sq. ft.
Second floor — 946 sq. ft.
Garage — 577 sq. ft.

Total living area 2,979 sq. ft. ■ Price Code G

No. 99452

■ This plan features:

-Four bedrooms

-Two full and one half baths

■ The Dining Room has a built-in hutch and a bay window

■ The cozy Den and the Great Room have high ceilings and transom windows

■ The cozy Gathering Room features a fireplace and a cathedral ceiling

■ The secluded Master Bedroom is a world away from the busy areas of the home

■ Upstairs are three Bedrooms and two full Baths

■ This home is designed with a basement foundation.

■ Alternate foundation options available at an addition charge. Please call 1-800-235-5700 for more information.

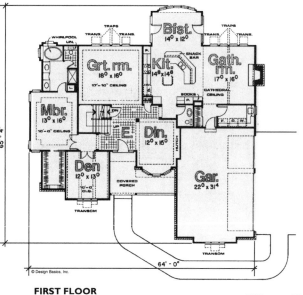

FIRST FLOOR

First floor — 2,158 sq. ft.
Second floor — 821 sq. ft.
Basement — 2,158 sq. ft.
Garage — 692 sq. ft.

SECOND FLOOR

275

English Tudor Styling

■ *Total living area 2,986 sq. ft.* ■ *Price Code G* ■

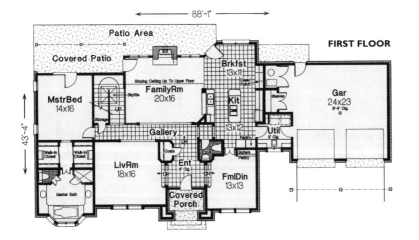

SECOND FLOOR

FIRST FLOOR

No. 98546

■ **This plan features:**

—Four bedrooms

—Three full and one half baths

■ This Tudor-styled gem has a unique mix of exterior materials

■ In the tiled Entry, turn left into the Living Room or right into the Dining Room

■ At the end of the Gallery is the Master Bedroom, which has dual walk-in closets

■ Upstairs, access the future Bonus Room that is located over the Garage

■ This home is designed with basement, slab, and crawlspace foundation options.

First floor — 2,082 sq. ft.
Second floor — 904 sq. ft.
Bonus — 408 sq. ft.
Garage — 605 sq. ft.

Bookshelves in Great Room

No. 66005

This plan features:

- Four bedrooms

- Three full and one half baths

- Each Bedroom has a large closet and an adjacent Bathroom

- Access from the Garage is through a hall, which houses the Utility Room and a Pantry

- This home is designed with a slab foundation.

First floor — 2,169 sq. ft.
Second floor — 833 sq. ft.
Bonus — 272 sq. ft.
Garage — 675 sq. ft.

■ *Total living area 3,002 sq. ft.* ■ *Price Code H* ■

FIRST FLOOR

WIDTH 65'-0"
DEPTH 67'-7"

SECOND FLOOR

Optional Fourth Bedroom

No. 99149

This plan features:

- Four bedrooms

- Two full and one half baths

- Built-in shelves flank the Great Room fireplace

- The Breakfast Nook provides access to the three-season porch

- This home is designed with a basement foundation.

First floor — 2,039 sq. ft.
Second floor — 970 sq. ft.

■ *Total living area 3,009 sq. ft.* ■ *Price Code H* ■

WIDTH 69'-8"
DEPTH 72'-0"

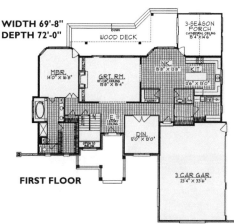

FIRST FLOOR

SECOND FLOOR

Friendly Front Porch

■ *Total living area 3,011 sq. ft.* ■ *Price Code H* ■

DETACHED CARPORT

FIRST FLOOR

First floor — 2,361 sq. ft.
Second floor — 650 sq. ft.
Carport — 864 sq. ft.

SECOND FLOOR

No. 96500

■ **This plan features:**

—Three bedrooms

—Two full and one half baths

■ The wrap-around front Porch and double French doors are an inviting sight

■ The Central Foyer, with a lovely landing staircase, opens to the Dining and Great Rooms

■ The fireplace is framed by a built-in credenza in the Great Room

■ The Kitchen boasts a buffet counter, a Pantry and a practical Peninsula counter/snack bar

■ The Master Bedroom offers direct access to the Sun Room, a walk-in closet and a luxurious Bath

■ This home is designed with crawl-space and slab foundation options.

Total living area 3,017 sq. ft. ■ **Price Code H** ■

No. 99453

This plan features:

- Four bedrooms

- Three full and one half baths

- The formal Dining Room is high-lighted by a recessed hutch space and transom windows

- The spacious Living Room has a fourteen-foot, five-inch ceiling and large transom windows

- The Kitchen/Breakfast Area boasts a work island, a Pantry and a planning desk

- The Master Suite includes dual wardrobes and is topped by a vaulted ceiling

- This home is designed with a basement foundation.

- Alternate foundation options available at an additional charge. Please call 1-800-235-5700.

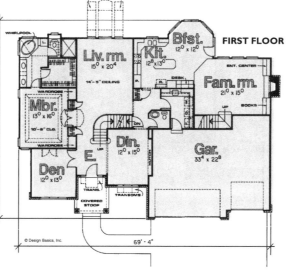

FIRST FLOOR

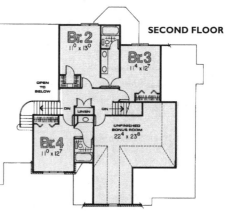

SECOND FLOOR

First floor — 2,179 sq. ft.
Second floor — 838 sq. ft.
Basement — 2,179 sq. ft.
Garage — 813 sq. ft.

Striking Arched Transoms

■ *Total living area 3,019 sq. ft.* ■ *Price Code H* ■

First floor — 1,561 sq. ft.
Second floor — 1,458 sq. ft.
Bonus — 160 sq. ft.
Basement — 1,561 sq. ft.
Garage — 748 sq. ft.

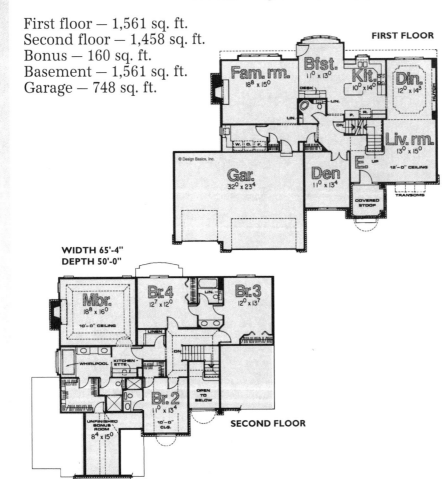

WIDTH 65'-4"
DEPTH 50'-0"

No. 97403

■ **This plan features:**

—Four bedrooms

—Two full, one three-quarter and one half baths

■ The formal Living Room has oak flooring and a twelve-foot-high ceiling

■ There is a decorative ceiling and hutch space in the formal Dining Room

■ The gourmet Kitchen includes a central island, a roomy Pantry and a lazy Susan

■ The comfortable Family Room is enhanced by a brick fireplace

■ This home is designed with a basement foundation.

■ Alternate foundation options available at an additional charge. Please call 1-800-235-5700 for more information.

Home of Distinction

■ *Total living area 3,022 sq. ft.* ■ *Price Code H* ■

No. 24656

■ This plan features:

- Three bedrooms

- Three full and one half baths

- The two-story Foyer has a graceful, angled staircase

- Columns frame the entrance to the Living Room

- The L-shaped Kitchen has a walk-in Pantry, a cooktop island, a built-in desk and a bright Breakfast Alcove

- The spacious Family Room has an inviting fireplace and Porch access

- The plush Master Suite has a tray ceiling, two walk-in closets and a huge Bath with a window seat

- This home is designed with basement, slab, and crawlspace foundation options.

First floor — 1,623 sq. ft.
Second floor — 1,399 sq. ft.
Bonus — 264 sq. ft.
Basement — 1,584 sq. ft.
Garage — 492 sq. ft.

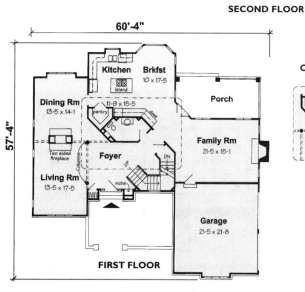

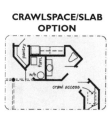

CRAWLSPACE/SLAB OPTION

Splendor and Distinction

■ *Total living area 3,025 sq. ft.* ■ *Price Code H* ■

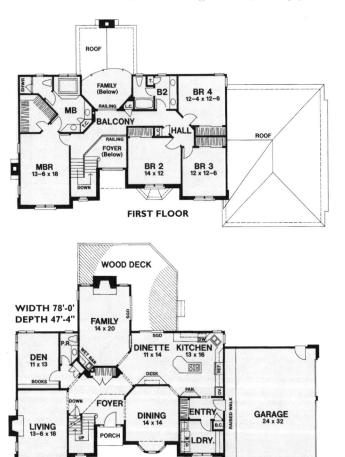

FIRST FLOOR

WIDTH 78'-0"
DEPTH 47'-4"

SECOND FLOOR

No. 93322

■ **This plan features:**

— Four bedrooms

— Two full and one half baths

■ An expansive Kitchen has a cook-top island/eating bar and a corner double sink

■ The spacious Family Room is equipped with a built-in wetbar and a cozy fireplace

■ The formal Living Room with a second fireplace

■ A bay window adds elegance to the formal Dining Room

■ The Master Suite offers a privacy amd luxurious Master Bath

■ This home is designed with a basement foundation.

First floor — 1,720 sq. ft.
Second floor — 1,305 sq. ft.
Basement — 1,720 sq. ft.
Garage — 768 sq. ft.

Stately Stone and Stucco

■ *Total living area 3,027 sq. ft.* ■ *Price Code H* ■

No. 98402

■ This plan features:

—Four bedrooms

—Three full and one half baths

■ The expansive two-story Great Room is enhanced by a fireplace, wetbar and French doors to the rear yard

■ The convenient Kitchen has a cooktop island, a Pantry, a Breakfast Alcove, and a nearby Laundry and Garage Entry

■ The open Keeping Room is accented by a wall of windows

■ The Master Suite wing offers tray ceiling, a plush Bath and access to the Study/Sitting Room

■ This home is designed with basement, slab and crawlspace foundation options.

First floor — 2,130 sq. ft.
Second floor — 897 sq. ft.
Basement — 2,130 sq. ft.
Garage — 494 sq. ft.

SECOND FLOOR

FIRST FLOOR

Five Bedrooms Provide Privacy for All

■ *Total living area 3,027 sq. ft.* ■ *Price Code H* ■

FIRST FLOOR

SECOND FLOOR

No. 60000

■ This plan features:

—Five bedrooms

—Four full and one half baths

■ Triple arches and a dramatic roofline comprise this home's facade

■ Bay windows illuminate Master Suite Sitting Room

■ An older child or live-in relative will appreciate the privacy of the lone first floor Bedroom

■ French doors in the Living Room open onto the covered front Porch

■ This home is designed with a basement foundation.

First floor — 1,645 sq. ft.
Second floor — 1,382 sq. ft.
Basement — 1,645 sq. ft.
Garage — 473 sq. ft.

With Attention to Detail

■ *Total living area 3,029 sq. ft.* ■ *Price Code H* ■

No. 93604

■ This plan features:

- Four bedrooms

- Three full and one half baths

■ The formal Living Room and Dining Room are perfect for entertaining

■ The two-story Grand Room has a focal point fireplace

■ The gourmet Kitchen has a work island and a bright Breakfast Area

■ This home is designed with basement, and slab foundation options.

■ This plan is not to be built within a 50 mile radius of Atlanta, GA.

First floor — 2,115 sq. ft.
Second floor — 914 sq. ft.
Basement — 2,115 sq. ft.
Garage — 448 sq. ft.

Columns and Keystones

■ *Total living area 3,029 sq. ft.* ■ *Price Code H* ■

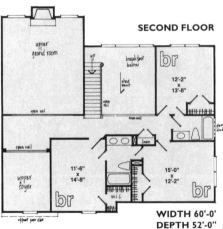

SECOND FLOOR

upper grand room

up

breakfast below

shed vault

br
12'-2"
x
13'-8"

open rail

open rail

linen

upper foyer

11'-6"
x
14'-8"

br

15'-0"
x
12'-2"

br

w.i.c.

WIDTH 60'-0'
DEPTH 52'-0''

FIRST FLOOR

tub

2 story grand room
17'-0"
x
20'-0"

brk
23'-9"
x
16'-0"

k

island

laundry

mbr
14'-4" x 15'-6"

2 story foyer

pantry

din
12'-6" x 14'-9"

liv
14'-4"
x
11'-5"

gar

52'-0"

60'-0"

No. 93603

■ **This plan features:**

— Four bedrooms

— Three full and one half baths

■ The gracious two-story Foyer opens to the vaulted Living Room and the spacious Dining Room

■ The two-story Grand Room has a fireplace between outdoor views

■ The spacious and efficient Kitchen has a work island and a Breakfast Area with backyard access

■ The Master Bedroom offers a decorative ceiling, two walk-in closets and a garden window tub

■ Three second floor Bedrooms with great closets share two full Baths

■ This home is designed with basement and slab foundation options.

First floor — 2,115 sq. ft.
Second floor — 914 sq. ft.
Basement — 2,115 sq. ft.
Garage — 448 sq. ft.

Graceful Two-Story Entry

■ *Total living area 3,034 sq. ft.* ■ *Price Code H* ■

No. 93041

■ **This plan features:**

— Five bedrooms

— Two full and one half baths

■ A stucco and brick exterior is accented by an arched, two-story Entry

■ All major living areas are located with views to the rear grounds

■ The Kitchen, the Breakfast Area, and the Family Room are open to one another for comfort and convenience

■ An island cooktop and a double sink, along with an abundance of storage space make the Kitchen even more convenient

■ The Master Suite has an angled whirlpool tub, a separate shower and dual vanities

■ This home is designed with crawl-space and slab foundation options.

WIDTH 64'-4'
DEPTH 53'-4"

First floor — 1,974 sq. ft
Second floor — 1,060 sq. ft
Garage — 531 sq. ft.

FIRST FLOOR

SECOND FLOOR

287

Regal Residence

■ *Total living area 3,039 sq. ft.* ■ *Price Code H* ■

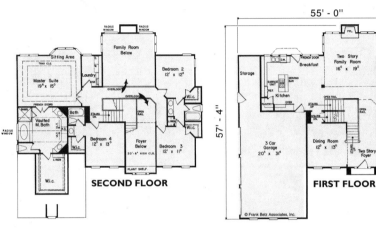

SECOND FLOOR

FIRST FLOOR

© Frank Betz Associates, Inc.

No. 98405

■ **This plan features:**

— Five bedrooms

— Four full baths

■ The spacious two-story Family Room is enhanced by a fireplace and lots of windows

■ The Kitchen has a cooktop island/serving bar, a walk-in Pantry and a Breakfast Area

■ The first floor Guest Room/Study has easy access to a full Bath

■ The luxurious Master Suite offers a tray ceiling, a Sitting Area and a huge walk-in closet

■ This home is designed with basement and crawlspace foundation options.

First floor — 1,488 sq. ft.
Second floor — 1,551 sq. ft.
Basement — 1,488 sq. ft.
Garage — 667 sq. ft.

Opulent Interiors

■ *Total living area 3,040 sq. ft.* ■ *Price Code H* ■

WIDTH 72'-6"
DEPTH 35'-0"

SECOND FLOOR

FIRST FLOOR

No. 98207

■ **This plan features:**

— Four bedrooms

— Three full and one half baths

■ Stately columns lead guests through the Foyer, into the Library, and Formal Dining Room

■ The open Kitchen connects to the massive morning Keeping Room, which has a special ceiling and a two-sided fireplace

■ The Bedrooms are located on the second floor, including the pampering Master Suite

■ This home is designed with basement and slab foundation options.

First floor — 1,478 sq. ft.
Second floor — 1,562 sq. ft.
Basement — 1,478 sq. ft.
Garage — 545 sq. ft.

Classic Brick Exterior

■ *Total living area 3,054 sq. ft.* ■ *Price Code* **H** ■

No. 66003

■ **This plan features:**

— Four bedrooms

— Three full and one half baths

■ The Family Room is enclosed by a patio. An entertainment center nestles beneath the stairs

■ Upstairs Bedroom ceilings slope to create a sheltering environment for children

■ This home is designed with basement and slab foundation options.

First floor — 2,187 sq. ft.
Second floor — 867 sq. ft.
Garage — 673 sq. ft.

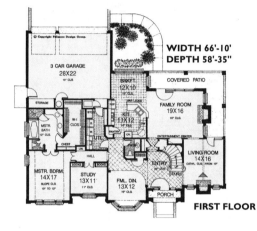

WIDTH 66'-10'
DEPTH 58'-35"

FIRST FLOOR

SECOND FLOOR

Stucco Accents

No. 99456

■ **This plan features:**

— Four bedrooms

— Two full, one three-quarter and one half baths

■ Stucco accents and graceful window treatments enhance the front of this home

■ The open combination of the Kitchen, the Breakfast Area and the Family Room creates comfort and convenience

■ The open Living Room and handsome curved staircase add drama to the Entry

■ The elegant Master Bedroom has a ten-foot vaulted ceiling

■ The home is designed with a basement foundation.

■ Alternate foundation options available at an additional charge. Please call 1-800-235-5700 for more information.

First floor — 1,631 sq. ft.
Second floor — 1,426 sq. ft.
Basement — 1,631 sq. ft.
Garage — 681 sq. ft.

■ *Total living area 3,057 sq. ft.* ■ *Price Code H* ■

FIRST FLOOR

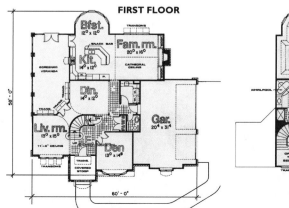

SECOND FLOOR

Stately Presence

■ *Total living area 3,062 sq. ft.* ■ *Price Code H* ■

SECOND FLOOR

FIRST FLOOR

No. 98596

■ **This plan features:**

— Four bedrooms

— Three full and one half baths

■ The Patio and the covered Patio expand outdoor living spaces

■ A Cathedral ceiling in the Living Room provides added volume

■ The future Playroom on the second floor has a perfect location for keeping peace and quite on the first floor

■ This home is designed with basement, slab, and crawlspace foundation options.

First floor — 2,115 sq. ft.
Second floor — 947 sq. ft.
Bonus — 195 sq. ft.
Garage — 635 sq. ft.

No. 98211

This plan features:

– Four bedrooms

– Three full and one half baths

High volume ceilings top all of the rooms in this home

An extended staircase is located in the Foyer as columns define the spaces

A massive three sided glass wall is featured in the Master Suite

The huge Kitchen, Keeping Room and Breakfast Room create an open living space

This home is designed with basement and crawlspace foundation options.

First floor – 2,035 sq. ft.
Second floor – 1,028 sq. ft.
Basement – 2,035 sq. ft.
Garage – 530 sq. ft.

Total living area 3,063 sq. ft. ■ Price Code H

FIRST FLOOR

SECOND FLOOR

WIDTH 56'-0"
DEPTH 62'-6"

Windows Illuminate Living Areas

No. 65008

This plan features:

– Three bedrooms

– Two full and one half baths

A bay-shaped front deck adds living space to this home

An angled, three-sided fireplace is open to the Living Area, Dining Room, and Kitchen

The secondary Bedrooms share the second floor Sitting Room

This home is designed with a slab foundation.

First floor – 1,437 sq. ft.
Second floor – 1,635 sq. ft.
Garage – 474 sq. ft.

Total living area 3,072 sq. ft. ■ Price Code H

WIDTH 36'-0'
DEPTH 62'-0"

FIRST FLOOR

SECOND FLOOR

Executive Retreat

■ *Total living area 3,079 sq. ft.* ■ *Price Code F* ■

■ **This plan features:**

— Five bedrooms

— Two full and one half baths

■ This executive-style brick home offers an updated design

■ Bring your work home to this study that features a vaulted ceiling

■ The large Master Bedroom includes a Master Bath and large walk-in closet

■ The kids will spend a lot of time on the second floor, where there are four Bedrooms and the Rec Room

■ This home is designed with a slab foundation.

First floor — 1,823 sq. ft.
Second floor — 1,256 sq. ft.
Garage — 479 sq. ft.

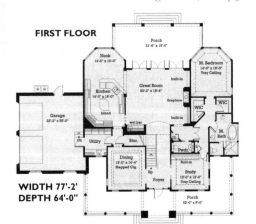

FIRST FLOOR

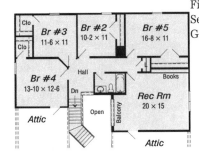

SECOND FLOOR

Volume Ceilings

■ *Total living area 3,082 sq. ft.* ■ *Price Code K* ■

■ **This plan features:**

— Three bedrooms

— Three full and one half baths

■ Triple French doors open the Great Room to the rear Porch.

■ A curved balcony connects two Bedroom suites featuring three-quarter Baths and walk-in closets

■ This home is designed with basement and crawlspace foundation options.

■ Alternate foundation options available at an additional charge. Please call 1-800-235-5700.

First floor — 2,138 sq. ft.
Second floor — 944 sq. ft.
Bonus — 427 sq. ft.

European-Style Elegance

■ *Total living area 3,084 sq. ft.* ■ *Price Code H* ■

No. 92500

First floor — 1,981 sq. ft.
Second floor — 1,103 sq. ft.
Garage — 544 sq. ft.

■ **This plan features:**

— Four bedrooms

— Three full and two half baths

■ The central Great Room has a decorative ceiling, an inviting fireplace, a wetbar, and an expansive view

■ The country-size Kitchen has a peninsula counter serving the bright Breakfast Area, and nearby Utility/Garage access

■ The Master Bedroom wing is enhanced by a decorative ceiling, an arched window, and a double Master Bath

■ Three additional Bedrooms have walk-in closets and access to two full Baths

■ This home is designed with crawl-space and slab founation options.

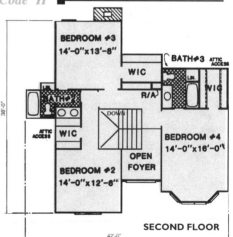

SECOND FLOOR

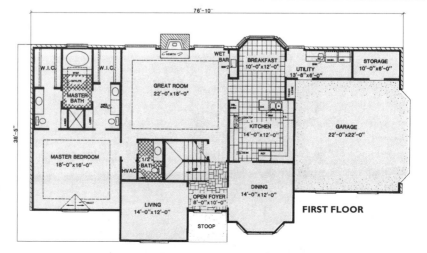

FIRST FLOOR

French Doors To Veranda

Total living area 3,098 sq. ft. ■ Price Code J

This plan features:

— Three bedrooms

— Three full and one half baths

■ Great Room appointments include built-in cabinetry, fireplace, wetbar, two-story ceiling and French doors to the covered Veranda

■ Double-doors lead into the Master Bedroom which features a 5-piece Bath, his and her closets and private access to the Study

■ This home is designed with a crawlspace foundation.

■ Alternate foundation options available at an additional charge. Please call 1-800-235-5700 for more information.

First floor — 2,146 sq. ft.
Second floor — 952 sq. ft.
Basement — 929 sq. ft.
Garage — 1,004 sq. ft.

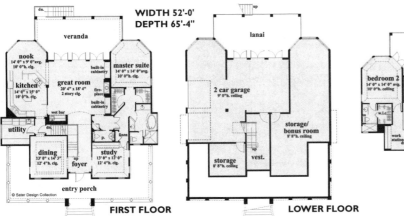

WIDTH 52'-0'
DEPTH 65'-4"

FIRST FLOOR   LOWER FLOOR   SECOND FLOOR

Impressive Fieldstone Facade

Total living area 3,110 sq. ft. ■ Price Code H

This plan features:

— Four bedrooms

— Three full and one half baths

■ A double door leads into the two-story Entry which has curved staircase

■ The Formal Living Room features a marble hearth fireplace, a triple window, and built-in bookshelves

■ The Formal Dining Room is defined by columns and had a lovely bay window

■ The Great Room has an entertainment center, a fieldstone fireplace, and a cathedral ceiling

■ A vaulted ceiling crowns the Master Bedroom which offers a plush Bath and two walk-in closets

■ This home comes with basement and slab foundation options.

First floor — 2,190 sq. ft.
Second floor — 920 sq. ft.
Garage — 624 sq. ft.

FIRST FLOOR

WIDTH 69'-0"
DEPTH 53'-10"

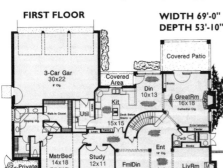

SECOND FLOOR

Old World Style

■ *Total living area 3,112 sq. ft.* ■ *Price Code H* ■

No. 98532

■ **This plan features:**

— Four bedrooms

— Three full and one half baths

■ A curved staircase is featured in the Gallery

■ Columns and an arched window enhance the Dining Room

■ The angled Kitchen with a large Pantry is open to the informal Dining Area and the Family Room

■ This home is designed with slab and crawlspace founation options.

First floor — 2,263 sq. ft.
Second floor — 849 sq. ft.
Bonus — 430 sq. ft.
Garage — 630 sq. ft.

SECOND FLOOR

FIRST FLOOR

On A Grand Scale

Total living area 3,113 sq. ft. ■ Price Code H

No. 97288

■This plan features:

— Four bedrooms

— Four full baths

■The Dining Room's entrance is defined by columns

■The Family Room has a two-story ceiling and a cozy fireplace

■The Study is tucked into the right rear corner of the home

■The Kitchen includes a cooktop island, the built-in Pantry, and plenty of counter space

■This home is designed with basement and crawlspace foundation options.

First floor — 1,595 sq. ft.
Second floor — 1,518 sq. ft.
Basement — 1,595 sq. ft.
Garage — 475 sq. ft.

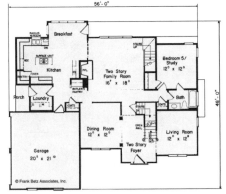

FIRST FLOOR

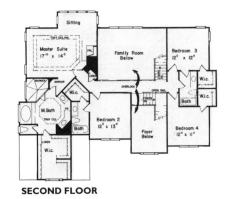

SECOND FLOOR

Morning Kitchen In Master Suite

Total living area 3,127 sq. ft. ■ Price Code K

No. 64148

■This plan features:

— Three bedrooms

— Two full and one half baths

■Angled windows in the Leisure Room and nook maximize natural light

■The Powder Room is set off from the traffic flow allowing guests thoughtful privacy

■This home is designed with slab and crawlspace foundation options.

■Alternate foundation options available at an additional charge. Please call 1-800-235-5700 for more information.

First floor — 1,664 sq. ft.
Second floor — 1,463 sq. ft.
Garage — 599 sq. ft.

FIRST FLOOR

WIDTH 59'-10'
DEPTH 62'-0''

SECOND FLOOR

Triple Stairway

No. 60001

This plan features:

- Four bedrooms
- Three full and one half baths
- A medley of stucco, stone and roof lines creates a stunning first impression.
- Triple-wide stair landing rises to a bridge spanning the foyer and Family Room.
- This home is designed with crawlspace and basement foundation options.

First floor — 1,681 sq. ft.
Second floor — 1,452 sq. ft.
Basement — 1,681 sq. ft.
Garage — 760 sq. ft.

■ *Total living area 3,133 sq. ft.* ■ *Price Code H* ■

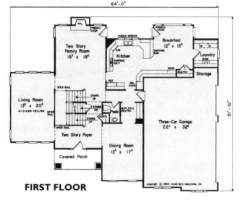

FIRST FLOOR

SECOND FLOOR

Rustic Elegance

No. 93512

This plan features:

- Four bedrooms
- Two full and one half baths
- The Foyer offers easy access to all parts of this home
- With a vaulted ceiling and a wall of windows, the Great Room brings the outside in
- The Master Bathroom has every amenity you need to pamper yourself
- Cooks will appreciate that the kitchen is conveniently located between the Breakfast Area and the Dining Room
- This home is designed with basement, slab, and crawlspace foundation options.

First floor — 1,782 sq. ft.
Second floor — 1,355 sq. ft.

■ *Total living area 3,137 sq. ft.* ■ *Price Code H* ■

FIRST FLOOR

SECOND FLOOR

Commanding Curved Stairway

■ Total living area 3,144 sq. ft. ■ Price Code H ■

No. 69002

■**This plan features:**

— Four bedrooms

— Four full and one half baths

■ Families will enjoy the ample storage in this home with walk-in closets, Pantry, two guest closets, and Utility Room storage

■ The garage has thoughtful direct access to both the Utility Room and the back yard

■ This home is designed with a basement foundation.

First floor — 1,724 sq. ft.
Second floor — 1,420 sq. ft.

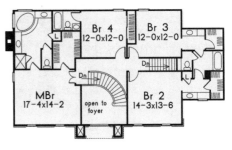

FIRST FLOOR

Patio

Family 24-4x15-6
Bar
Brk 12-0x14-0
Kitchen
11-0x12-0
Garage 21-1x31-5
Living 17-4x13-6
Foyer
Up
Dining 14-3x13-3
W D

30'-0"
77'-6"

SECOND FLOOR

Br 4 12-0x12-0
Br 3 12-0x12-0
MBr 17-4x14-2
open to foyer
Br 2 14-3x13-6
Dn

Three Front Porches

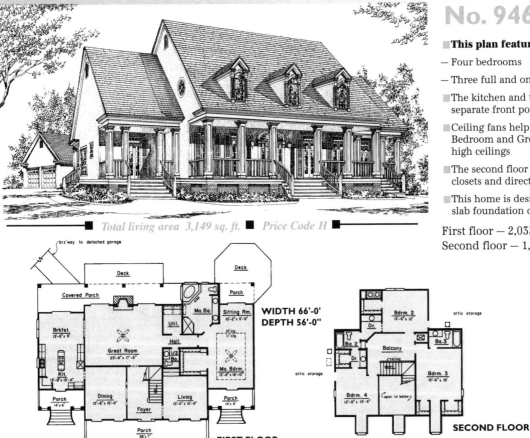

■ Total living area 3,149 sq. ft. ■ Price Code H ■

No. 94622

■**This plan features:**

— Four bedrooms

— Three full and one half baths

■ The kitchen and the Master Bedroom access separate front porches

■ Ceiling fans help circulate air in the Master Bedroom and Great Room, which feature high ceilings

■ The second floor Bedrooms have walk-in closets and direct access to a Bath

■ This home is designed with crawlspace and slab foundation options.

First floor — 2,033 sq. ft.
Second floor — 1,116 sq. ft.

brz'way to detached garage

Deck
Covered Porch
Deck
Porch
Ma. Ba.
Sitting Rm. 10'-2" x 5'-9"
Brkfst. 13'-8" x 9'
Util.
Hall
Great Room 23'-6" x 17'-8"
1/2 Ba.
Ma. Bdrm. 15'-8" x 18'-10"
Kit. 13'-8" x 9'
Porch 14'-6"
Dining 12'-8" x 15'-6"
Foyer
Living 13'-6" x 12'-6"
Porch 14'-6"
Porch 58'-7"

WIDTH 66'-0'
DEPTH 56'-0"

FIRST FLOOR

Bdrm. 2 13'-6" x 12'
attic storage
Ba. 2
Balcony ceiling
Ba. 3
attic storage
Bdrm. 3 13'-6" x 15'
Bdrm. 4 12'-6" x 13'-6"
open to below

SECOND FLOOR

Traditional Energy Saver

■ *Total living area 3,169 sq. ft.* ■ *Price Code H* ■

No. 20071

■ This plan features:

- Four bedrooms

- Two full, one three-quarter, and one half baths

■ A heat storing floor in the Sunroom adjoins the Living Room and Breakfast Room

■ The Living Room has French doors and a massive fireplace

■ The balcony overlooks the soaring two-story Foyer and Living Room

■ The ideal Kitchen is centrally located between the formal and informal Dining Rooms

■ This home is designed with a basement foundation.

First floor — 2,186 sq. ft.
Second floor — 983 sq. ft.
Basement — 2,186 sq. ft.
Garage — 704 sq. ft.

Curving Stairway

Total living area 3,172 sq. ft. ■ *Price Code H* ■

FIRST FLOOR

SECOND FLOOR

No. 94995

■ **This plan features**

– Four bedrooms

– Two full, one three-quarter, and one half baths

■ The spacious formal Entry with an arched transom is enhanced by acurved staircase

■ The Great Room is inviting with a cozy fireplace and triple arched transoms

■ The open Kitchen, the Breakfast Nook and the Hearth Area combine efficiency and comfort for all

■ The Master Bedroom retreat offers a private back door, a double walk-in closet and a whirlpool Bath

■ Generous closets and Baths enhance the three second floor Bedrooms

■ This home is designed with a basement foundation.

■ Alternate foundation options available at an additional charge. Please call 1-800-235-5700 for more information.

First floor — 2,252 sq. ft.
Second floor — 920 sq. ft.
Basement — 2,252 sq. ft.
Garage — 646 sq. ft.

All Seasons

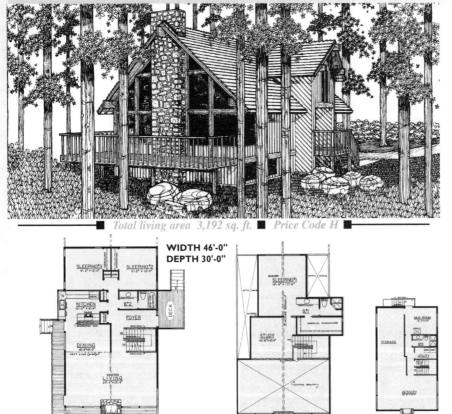

Total living area 3,192 sq. ft. ■ *Price Code H* ■

WIDTH 46'-0"
DEPTH 30'-0"

FIRST FLOOR

SECOND FLOOR

BASEMENT

No. 91319

■ **This plan features:**

– Three bedrooms

– One full and two three-quarter baths

■ A wall of windows takes full advantage of the view

■ An open stairway leads to the upstairs Study and the Master Bedroom

■ The Master Bedroom has the private Master Bath and a walk-in wardrobe

■ The efficient Kitchen includes a Breakfast Bar that serves the Dining Area

■ The formal Living Room has a vaulted ceiling and a stone fireplace

■ This home is designed with a basement foundation.

First floor — 1,306 sq. ft.
Second floor — 598 sq. ft.
Basement — 1,288 sq. ft.

A Whisper of Victorian Styling

■ *Total living area 3,198 sq. ft.* ■ *Price Code H* ■

No. 93333

■ This plan features:

- Four bedrooms

- Two full and one half baths

- The formal Living Room features wrap-around windows and direct access to the front Porch, and the cozy Den which has built-in book-shelves and a window seat

- The elegant, formal Dining Room is accented by a stepped ceiling

- The bright, all-purpose Sunroom can be used year round

- The Family Room has a tray ceiling topping a circle-head window, and a massive, hearth fireplace

- This home is designed with a basement foundation.

First floor — 1,743 sq. ft.
Second floor — 1,455 sq. ft.

Cottage Appeal

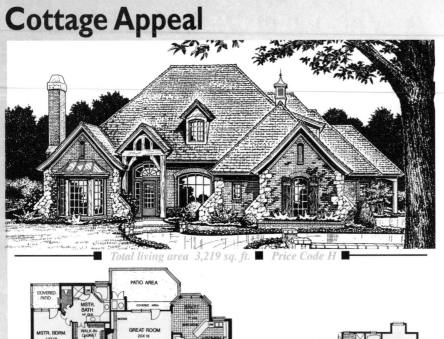

Total living area 3,219 sq. ft. ■ Price Code H

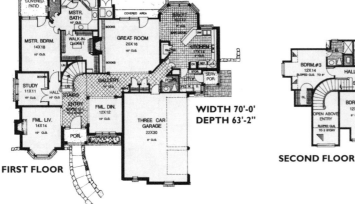

FIRST FLOOR

WIDTH 70'-0'
DEPTH 63'-2"

SECOND FLOOR

No. 98588

■ **This plan features:**

— Four bedrooms

— Three full and one half baths

■ A curving staircase accents the formal Entry with gracious elegance

■ Enhanced by a fireplace and a bay window the Living Room is a welcoming spot

■ The Great Room has a fireplace and access to the rear Patio

■ The three-car Garage offers additional storage space and an easy Entry into the home

■ This home is designed with basement and slab foundation options.

First floor — 2,337 sq. ft.
Second floor — 882 sq. ft.
Bonus — 357 sq. ft.
Garage — 640 sq. ft.

Stately Structure

Total living area 3,219 sq. ft. ■ Price Code H

No. 98401

■ **This plan features:**

— Five bedrooms

— Four full baths

■ The two-story Foyer is highlighted by a banister staircase

■ The two-story Family Room has a fireplace framed by radius windows

■ The expansive and efficient Kitchen has a cooktop island/serving bar

■ The elegant Master Bedroom offers a see-thru fireplace shared with the Master Bath

■ This home is designed with basement and crawlspace foundation options.

First floor — 1,665 sq. ft.
Second floor — 1,554 sq. ft.
Basement — 1,665 sq. ft.
Garage — 462 sq. ft.

FIRST FLOOR

SECOND FLOOR

Luxury Living

No. 93505

This plan features:

- Four bedrooms

- Two full and one three-quarter baths

- The Living Room has a vaulted ceiling and an elegant fireplace

- The formal Dining Room adjoins the Living Room and has a built-in buffet

- The Kitchen has an island cooktop, a walk-in Pantry, and an open layout with the Family Room

- The vaulted Family Room has a corner fireplace and Deck access

- A huge walk-in closet, a built-in entertainment center, and a full Bath with every amenity are featured in the Master Suite

- This home is designed with basement, slab and crawlspace foundation options.

First floor — 2,125 sq. ft.
Second floor — 1,095 sq. ft.
Basement — 2,125 sq. ft.

■ *Total living area 3,220 sq. ft.* ■ *Price Code H* ■

WIDTH 89'-9"
DEPTH 57'-0"

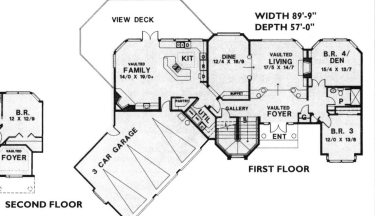

FIRST FLOOR

SECOND FLOOR

Master Suite Reading Room

No. 69001

This plan features:

- Four bedrooms

- Three full and one half baths

- The Master Suite has a separate Reading Room complete with a fireplace and bookshelves

- A banquette in the Breakfast Area features a bay window

- This home is designed with basement, slab, and crawlspace foundation options.

First floor — 2,273 sq. ft.
Second floor — 961 sq. ft.

■ *Total living area 3,234 sq. ft.* ■ *Price Code H* ■

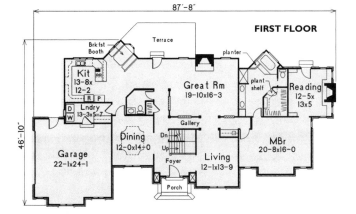

FIRST FLOOR

SECOND FLOOR

Stately Appeal

■ *Total living area 3,235 sq. ft.* ■ *Price Code H* ■

SECOND FLOOR

FIRST FLOOR

No. 99437

■ **This plan features:**

— Four bedrooms

— Two full and one three-quarter, and one half baths

■ The grand entrance is created through the two-story, columned Portico

■ A stunning, central staircase highlights the Entry

■ The Family Room is massive and includes a fireplace surrounded by built-in shelving and a cathedral ceiling

■ The opulent Master Bedroom offers a tray ceiling and a lovely Sitting Area viewing the rear yard

■ This home is designed with a basement foundation.

First floor — 1,717 sq. ft.
Second floor — 1,518 sq. ft.
Basement — 1,717 sq. ft.
Garage — 633 sq. ft.

Plenty of Attention to Detail

No. 92582

This plan features:

- Four bedrooms
- Three full and one half baths
- The Dining Room has three windows with segmented keystone arches above them
- The centrally located Den has a fireplace with built-in cabinets and shelves to either side
- The Master Bedroom is located in its own wing and has a huge walk-in closet
- The Garage has two Storage Areas
- This home is designed with slab and crawlspace foundation options.

First floor — 2,545 sq. ft.
Second floor — 711 sq. ft.
Garage — 484 sq. ft.

■ *Total living area 3,256 sq. ft.* ■ *Price Code I* ■

WIDTH 59'-10'
DEPTH 72'-10"

FIRST FLOOR

SECOND FLOOR

Foyer Offers Great First Impression

No. 98400

This plan features:

- Four bedrooms
- Three full and one half baths
- The two-story Foyer between the formal Living and Dining Rooms provides a grand first impression
- Radius windows and a huge fireplace are located in the Family Room
- The Kitchen has a Pantry, a cooktop/serving bar, a two-story Breakfast Area, and a Butler's Pantry
- The expansive Master Bedroom offers a tray ceiling, the cozy Sitting Room and the luxurious Bath
- This home is designed with basement and crawlspace foundation options.

First floor — 1,418 sq. ft.
Second floor — 1,844 sq. ft.
Basement — 1,418 sq. ft.
Garage — 840 sq. ft.

■ *Total living area 3,262 sq. ft.* ■ *Price Code I* ■

SECOND FLOOR

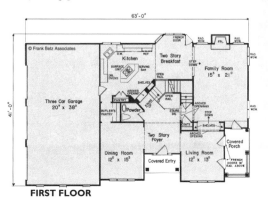

FIRST FLOOR

305

Southern Mansion

■ *Total living area 3,273 sq. ft.* ■ *Price Code I* ■

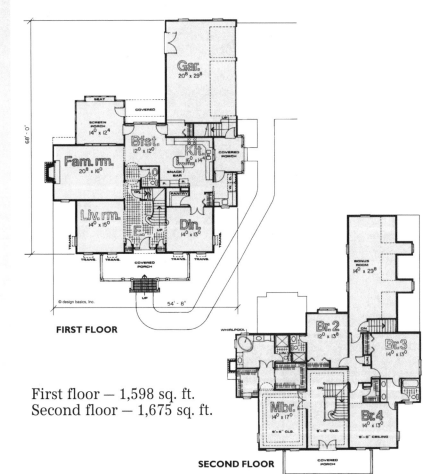

First floor — 1,598 sq. ft.
Second floor — 1,675 sq. ft.

No. 99485

■ **This plan features:**

— Four bedrooms

— Two full and one half baths

■ The prominent Entry opens to the formal Dining and Living Rooms

■ The Grand Family Room is warmed by a fireplace and views the Screened Porch

■ French doors open to the Master Suite, which is topped by a decorative ceiling and includes two walk-in closets, two vanities and oval whirlpool Bath

■ The secondary Bedrooms have private access to the full Bath

■ This home is designed with a basement foundation.

■ Alternate foundation options available at an additional cost. Please call 1-800-235-5700 for more information.

Glorious Gables

No. 94933

This plan features:

- Four bedrooms

- Two full, one three-quarter and one half bath

- The arched windows and the arched Stoop graciously greet one and all into the tiled Entry with a cascading staircase

- An arched ceiling topping decorative windows highlights the Living and Dining Rooms

- A double door leads into the quiet Library which has built-in book shelves

- The hub Kitchen has an angled work island/snack bar, a built-in Pantry, a Breakfast Area with outdoor access, and a nearby Laundry Room

- This home is designed with basement and slab foundation options.

- Alternate foundation options available at an additional charge. Pleasec call 1-800-235-5700 for more information.

First floor — 1,709 sq. ft.
Second floor — 1,597 sq. ft.
Basement — 1,709 sq. ft.
Garage — 721 sq. ft.

Total living area 3,306 sq. ft. ■ Price Code 1

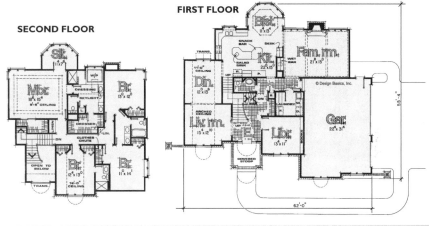

Eye-Catching Tower

No. 99438

This plan features:

- Four bedrooms

- Three full and one half baths

- The Dining Room is illuminated by a bay of windows for pleasant meals

- The Study with built-ins offers many options

- The Family Room, with a fireplace, is open to the Breakfast Area and the gourmet Kitchen

- The first floor Master Bedroom spans the depth of the home and contains every luxury imaginable

- This home is designed with basement and slab foundation options.

- Alternate foundation options available at an additional charge. Pleasec call 1-800-235-5700 for more information.

First floor — 2,117 sq. ft.
Second floor — 1,206 sq. ft.
Garage — 685 sq. ft.

Total living area 3,323 sq. ft. ■ Price Code 1

OPTIONAL BASEMENT STAIR LOCATION

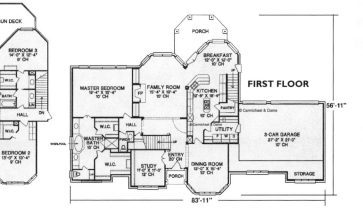

Three Fireplaces

Total living area 3,335 sq. ft. ■ **Price Code I**

FIRST FLOOR

SECOND FLOOR

No. 92219

■ **This plan features:**

— Four bedrooms

— Two full, one three-quarter, and one half baths

■ Fireplaces warm the formal Dining Room, Living Room, and Family Room

■ The Master Bedroom has access to a private covered patio

■ This home is designed with basement, slab, and crawlspace foudnation options.

First floor — 2,432 sq. ft.
Second floor — 903 sq. ft.
Basement — 2,432 sq. ft.
Garage — 742 sq. ft.

WIDTH 90'-0"
DEPTH 45'-4"

Stunning Entry

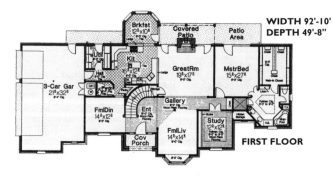

Total living area 3,339 sq. ft. ■ **Price Code I**

FIRST FLOOR

SECOND FLOOR

No. 66029

■ **This plan features:**

— Four bedrooms

— Three full and one half baths

■ A curving staircase and views through the house highlight the Entry

■ The focal-point fireplace in the Great Room is surrounded by glass, filling the room with natural light

■ This home is designed with a slab foundation.

First floor — 2,326 sq. ft.
Second floor — 1,013 sq. ft.
Bonus — 256 sq. ft.
Garage — 704 sq. ft.

WIDTH 92'-10'
DEPTH 49'-8"

Storage Solutions

No. 61023

This plan features:

- Five bedrooms
- Five full and one half baths
- A coffered ceiling, gas fireplace and built-ins highlight the Great Room
- All upper level Bedrooms have private Baths, ample closets and share a large Laundry Room
- This home is designed with basement, slab, and crawlspace foundation options.

First floor — 1,974 sq. ft.
Second floor — 1,396 sq. ft.
Garage — 572 sq. ft.

■ *Total living area 3,370 sq. ft.* ■ *Price Code I* ■

FIRST FLOOR

SECOND FLOOR

Fabulous Foyer

No. 65613

This plan features:

- Four bedrooms
- Four full baths
- The Living Room and the Study have fireplaces with built-in shelves
- All Bedrooms have their own full Baths and walk-in closets
- Perfect for entertaining, the Living Room, Dining Room, and Sunroom are separated by a angled wetbar
- This home is designed with a crawlspace foundation.

First floor — 2,743 sq. ft.
Second floor — 629 sq. ft.

■ *Total living area 3,372 sq. ft.* ■ *Price Code I* ■

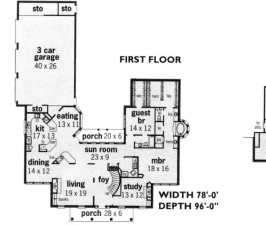

FIRST FLOOR

SECOND FLOOR

WIDTH 78'-0'
DEPTH 96'-0''

Arches Enhance Style

■ *Total living area* 3,393 *sq. ft.* ■ *Price Code I* ■

SECOND FLOOR

OPTIONAL BASEMENT STAIR LOCATION

First floor — 1,786 sq. ft.
Second floor — 1,607 sq. ft
Garage — 682 sq. ft.

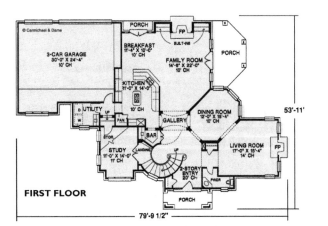

FIRST FLOOR

No. 99442

■ **This plan features:**

— Four bedrooms

— Three full and one half baths

■ The open layout of the active areas is defined by arched openings and a peninsula serving counter

■ The Living Room is graced by a fireplace and adjoins the Dining Room

■ The mid-level Study is brightened by a large front window

■ This plan has four huge Bedrooms, including the Master Bedroom and three full Baths upstairs

■ This home is designed with a basement and slab founation.

■ Alternate foundation options are available at an additional charge. Please call 1-800-235-5700 for more information.

Luxurious Yet Cozy

■ *Total living area 3,395 sq. ft.* ■ *Price Code I* ■

No. 98403

■ **This plan features:**

- Four bedrooms

- Three full and one half baths

■ The Living Room is enhanced by a fieldstone fireplace and a vaulted ceiling

■ The open Kitchen has a work island, a serving bar, a bright Breakfast Area, a walk-in Pantry, and nearby a Laundry and a Garage Entry

■ The corner Master Suite includes a cozy fireplace and a vaulted Sitting Room

■ This home is designed with basement, slab and crawlspace foundation options.

First floor — 2,467 sq. ft.
Second floor — 928 sq. ft.
Bonus — 296 sq. ft.
Basement — 2,467 sq. ft.
Garage — 566 sq. ft.

SECOND FLOOR

WIDTH 64'-6"
DEPTH 62'-10"

FIRST FLOOR

311

Country Cottage Charm

Total living area 3,512 sq. ft. ■ **Price Code 1** ■

No. 98536

■**This plan features:**

— Four bedrooms

— Two full and one half baths

■The vaulted Master Bedroom has a private skylighted Bath and a large walk-in closet with built-in chests

■The Family Room has built-in book shelves, a fireplace, and overlooks the covered Veranda

■The huge three-car Garage has a separate Shop Area

■This home is designed with slab and crawlspace foundation options.

First floor — 2,787 sq. ft.
Second floor — 636 sq. ft.
Garage — 832 sq. ft.

FIRST FLOOR

WIDTH 101'-0'
DEPTH 58'-8"

SECOND FLOOR W/ OPTIONAL BONUS ROOM & LOFT

Game Room with Vaulted Ceiling

Total living area 3,435 sq. ft. ■ **Price Code 1** ■

No. 62015

■**This plan features:**

— Three bedrooms

— Three full and one half baths

■A wraparound Porch shades the main living areas and extends entertaining space

■The Breakfast Area leads into the Sunroom, which features a corner fireplace

■This home is designed with basement, slab, and crawlspace foundation options.

First floor — 2,343 sq. ft.
Second floor — 1,092 sq. ft.
Garage — 845 sq. ft.

FIRST FLOOR   **SECOND FLOOR**

Beautiful Balconies

■ *Total living area 3,443 sq. ft.* ■ *Price Code I* ■

No. 91562

This plan features:

- Three bedrooms
- Two full and one half baths
- Cascading steps lead up to a gracious entrance
- An elegant ceiling tops a decorative window in the Dining Room
- The Kitchen has a cooktop island/ snack bar, a corner Pantry, and an eating Nook with outdoor access
- The corner Master Bedroom offers a private Balcony, a decorative ceiling and a deluxe Dressing Area with a roomy walk-in closet
- This home is designed with a crawl-space foundation.

First floor — 1,989 sq. ft.
Second floor — 1,349 sq. ft.
Lower level — 105 sq. ft.
Bonus — 487 sq. ft.

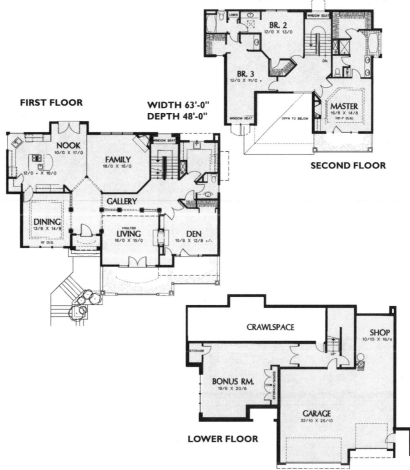

Spotlight on Lines, Textures

Total living area 3,444 sq. ft. ■ Price Code 1

FIRST FLOOR

- Breakfast 10'10" x 17'2"
- Deck
- Kitchen 13'6" x 16'7"
- Laun.
- Bath
- Hall
- Sunken Great Room 15'2" x 21'1"
- Hall
- Three-car Garage 22' x 38'
- Dining Room 14'3" x 14'11"
- Foyer
- Porch
- Library 11'10" x 12'9"
- 72'6"
- 55'8"

SECOND FLOOR

- Bath
- Bedroom 12'4" x 13'3"
- Bath
- Dressing
- walk-in closet
- Bedroom 12'1" x 12'7"
- Balcony
- Master Bedroom 14'2" x 17'6"
- walk-in closet
- Bath
- Bedroom 14'3" x 16'5"
- Foyer Below

■ **This plan features:**

— Four bedrooms

— Three full and one half baths

■ With stone, stucco, and wood included in the facade, this home packs plenty of visual interest

■ The stairway can be accessed from three rooms: the Foyer, the Kitchen, and the Sunken Great Room

■ The Sunken Great Room features a fireplace and access to the Deck

■ On the second floor, the Master Bedroom includes a Bath, Dressing Area and walk-in closet

■ This home is designed with a basement foundation.

First floor — 1,678 sq. ft.
Second floor — 1,766 sq. ft.
Bonus — 1,639 sq. ft.
Garage — 761 sq. ft.

Two-Story Brick Colonial

Total living area 3,445 sq. ft. ■ Price Code 1

FIRST FLOOR

- Gazebo
- Deck
- Screened-in Porch
- Breakfast 21'8" x 13'10"
- Hearth Room 14'10" x 17'2"
- Laun.
- Kitchen 21'8" x 13'10"
- Three-car Garage 22'2" x 32'6"
- Bath
- Hall
- Dining Room 14'10" x 14'6"
- Foyer
- Living Room 15'0" x 13'4"
- Porch
- 71'8"
- 38'-10"

SECOND FLOOR

- Bedroom 13'7" x 17'1"
- Dressing
- Dressing
- Master Bedroom 16'11" x 20'8"
- Hall
- Bedroom 16'10" x 12'9"
- Bath
- Bedroom 15'10" x 12'0"
- Balcony

■ **This plan features:**

— Four bedrooms

— Three full and one half baths

■ The Kitchen features a center island and a large Breakfast Area

■ Your family will like spending evenings by the fire in the Hearth Room

■ The Master Bedroom features a luxurious Bath with Dressing Room and walk-in closet

■ Two of the Secondary Bedrooms include full Baths

■ This home is designed with a basement foundation.

First floor — 1,666 sq. ft.
Second floor — 1,036 sq. ft.
Basement — 1,612 sq. ft.
Garage — 740 sq. ft.

Grandeur Personified

No. 94990

This plan features:

- Four bedrooms

- Two full, one three-quarter, and one half baths

- The Master Bedroom is enhanced by a decorative ceiling and a luxurious Bath

- Upstairs, three additional Bedrooms have ample closet space, two full and and one three-quarter baths

- French doors and an arched window accent the Den

- The Dining Room has a built-in hutch and an adjacent Butler's Pantry

- The Great Room, with an eleven-foot ceiling has curved wall of transom windows and a cozy fireplace

- This house is designed with a basement foundation.

- Altenate foundation options available at an addiional charge. Please call 1-800-235-5700 for more information.

First floor — 2,375 sq. ft.
Second floor — 1,073 sq. ft.
Basement — 2,375 sq. ft.
Garage — 672 sq. ft.

Total living area 3,448 sq. ft. ■ Price Code I

SECOND FLOOR

FIRST FLOOR

Master Suite Fireplace

No. 63040

This plan features:

- Four bedrooms

- Two full and one half baths

- The Living Room has views to the front and side and opens onto a rear Patio

- The Kitchen, featuring an island and a Pantry, is open to the Breakfast Nook and Family Room

- This home is designed with a slab foundation.

First floor — 1,971 sq. ft.
Second floor — 1,482 sq. ft.
Garage — 610 sq. ft.

Total living area 3,453 sq. ft. ■ Price Code I

WIDTH 73'-0"
DEPTH 62'-0"

FIRST FLOOR

SECOND FLOOR

Country Estate Home

Total living area 3,480 sq. ft. ▪ **Price Code I**

FIRST FLOOR

WIDTH 73'-0"
DEPTH 56'-6.5"

SECOND FLOOR

No. 98508

▪ **This plan features:**

— Four bedrooms

— Three full and one half baths

▪ The two-story Entry has a lovely curved staircase

▪ The Formal Living and Dining Rooms are gracefully defined with columns and decorative windows

▪ A hardwood floor and a massive fireplace accent the Great Room

▪ The hub Kitchen has a cooktop island, a bright Breakfast Area, and a nearby Utility/Garage Entry

▪ The Master Bedroom has the private Lanai and a Dressing Area

▪ This home is designed with a slab foundation.

First floor — 2,441 sq. ft.
Second floor — 1,039 sq. ft.
Garage — 660 sq. ft.
Future Playroom — 271 sq. ft.

■ *Total living area 3,485 sq. ft.* ■ *Price Code I* ■

No. 24599

■ **This plan features:**

- Four bedrooms

- Three full baths

- The open Foyer has an angled staircase and a vaulted ceiling

- Columns define entrance to the Living and Dining Rooms

- The open Kitchen has a cooktop island/snack bar, a walk-in Pantry and a bright Breakfast Area

- The sunken Family Room has a fireplace and loads of windows

- The pampering Master Suite has a vaulted ceiling, two walk-in closets and a whirlpool Bath

- This home is designed with basement, slab, and crawlspace foundation options.

First floor — 2,012 sq. ft.
Second floor — 1,473 sq. ft.
Basement — 2,012 sq. ft.
Garage — 750 sq. ft.

OPTIONAL CRAWLSPACE

SECOND FLOOR

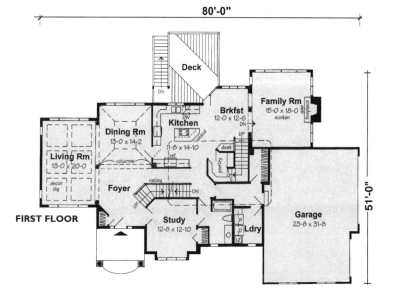

FIRST FLOOR

Tasteful Sprawling Home

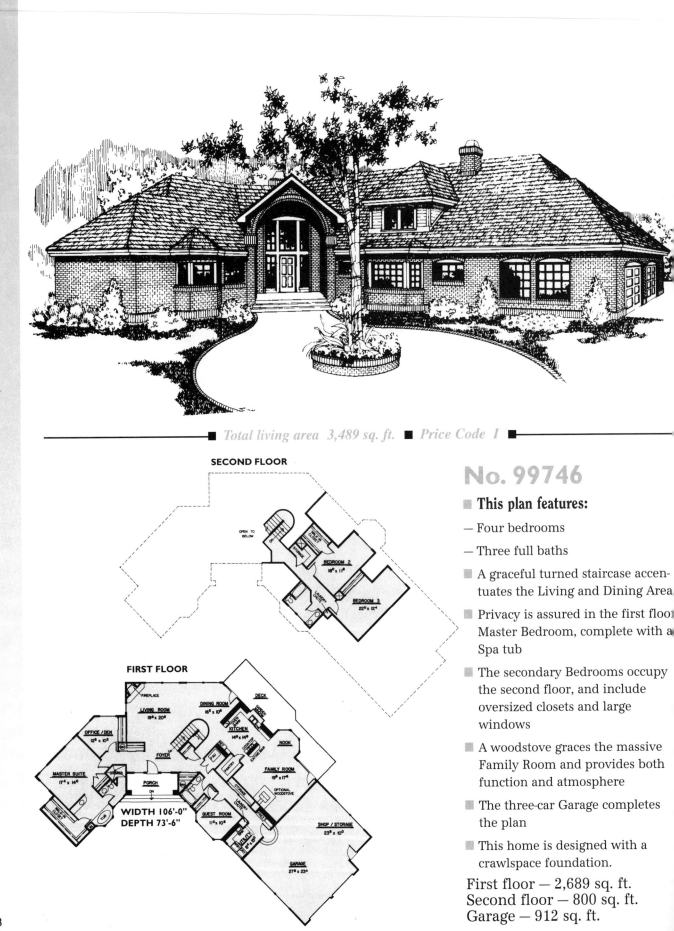

Total living area 3,489 sq. ft. ■ **Price Code I** ■

SECOND FLOOR

FIRST FLOOR

WIDTH 106'-0"
DEPTH 73'-6"

No. 99746

■ **This plan features:**

— Four bedrooms

— Three full baths

■ A graceful turned staircase accentuates the Living and Dining Area

■ Privacy is assured in the first floor Master Bedroom, complete with a Spa tub

■ The secondary Bedrooms occupy the second floor, and include oversized closets and large windows

■ A woodstove graces the massive Family Room and provides both function and atmosphere

■ The three-car Garage completes the plan

■ This home is designed with a crawlspace foundation.

First floor — 2,689 sq. ft.
Second floor — 800 sq. ft.
Garage — 912 sq. ft.

Unusual and Dramatic

■ *Total living area 3,500 sq. ft.* ■ *Price Code I* ■

No. 92048

First floor — 2,646 sq. ft.
Second floor — 854 sq. ft.
Basement — 2,656 sq. ft.

This plan features:

- Four bedrooms

- Three full and one half baths

- The elegant Entry has decorative windows, arched openings, and a double curved staircase

- The Family Room has a vaulted ceiling and a large fireplace between sliders to the Deck

- The hub Kitchen has a work island/serving counter, a Breakfast Alcove and nearby, a Deck, a Dining Area, a Laundry, and a Garage Entry

- The secluded Master Suite has a lovely bay window, two walk-in closets and a plush Bath

- Three second floor Bedrooms, one with a private Bath, offer ample closet space

- This home is designed with a basement foundation.

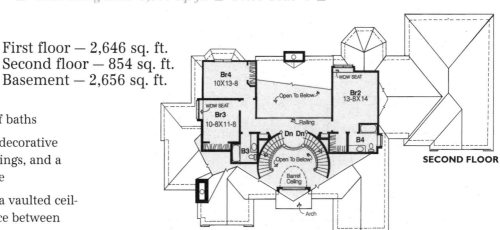

SECOND FLOOR

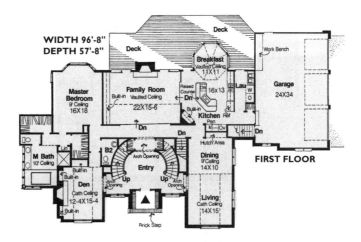

WIDTH 96'-8"
DEPTH 57'-8"

FIRST FLOOR

Duplex Delight

■ *Total living area 3,502 sq. ft.* ■ *Price Code G* ■

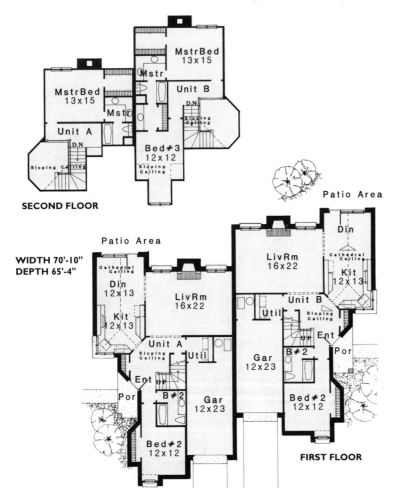

SECOND FLOOR

WIDTH 70'-10"
DEPTH 65'-4"

Patio Area

FIRST FLOOR

No. 92294

■ This plan features:

— Five bedrooms

— Four full baths

■ This duplex has two units, one with two Bedrooms and one with three Bedrooms

■ Both units have cathedral ceilings in the Kitchen and the Dining Room

■ The large Living Rooms both feature cozy fireplaces

■ The Master Bedrooms have a walk-in closets and private Bath access

■ Convenient access to the single-car Garages is through the Utility Rooms

■ This home is designed with a slab foundation

Main floor — 2,400 sq. ft.
Upper floor —1,102 sq. ft.
Garage — 552 sq. ft.

■ *Total living area 3,512 sq. ft.* ■ *Price Code J* ■

No. 98535

■ **This plan features:**

— Four bedrooms

— Three full and one half baths

■ A circular stairway highlights the Entry

■ The formal Dining Room has a lovely bay window

■ The angled Kitchen contains all the conveniences that any cook would need

■ The large, informal Dining Area is adjacent to the Kitchen

■ The Master Suite occupies one wing of the house, with a plush Bath and a huge walk-in closet

■ This home is designed with a slab foundation.

First floor — 2,658 sq. ft.
Second floor — 854 sq. ft.
Bonus — 168 sq. ft.
Garage — 660 sq. ft.

SECOND FLOOR

WIDTH 86'-0"
DEPTH 58'-1"

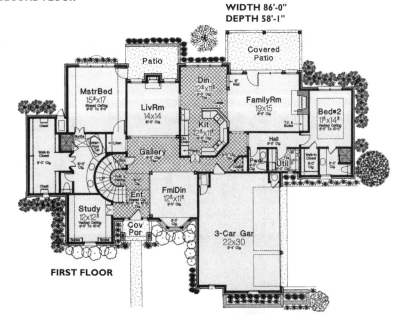

FIRST FLOOR

Windows Distinguish Design

■ *Total living area 3,525 sq. ft.* ■ *Price Code J* ■

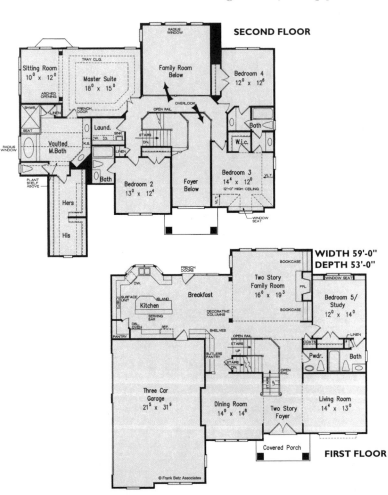

SECOND FLOOR

FIRST FLOOR

WIDTH 59'-0"
DEPTH 53'-0"

No. 98438

■ **This plan features:**

— Five bedrooms

— Four full and one half baths

■ A hall through the Butler's Pantry connects the Kitchen/Breakfast Area with the Dining Room

■ The two-story Family Room has a fireplace with built-in bookcases on either side

■ The upstairs Master Suite has a Sitting Room, a double-size closet, and a vaulted Master Bath

■ Three additional Bedrooms are located upstairs with private access to a Bath

■ This home is designed with basement and crawlspace foundation options.

First floor — 1,786 sq. ft.
Second floor — 1,739 sq. ft.
Basement — 1,786 sq. ft.
Garage — 704 sq. ft.

■ *Total living area 3,537 sq. ft.* ■ *Price Code J* ■

No. 66030

■ **This plan features:**

– Three bedrooms

– Two full, one-three quarter, and one half baths

■ The formal Dining Room enjoys magnificent views of the circular staircase in the foyer

■ In the Study, a built-in desk is hidden behind double-doors

■ This home is designed with a slab foundation.

First floor — 2,862 sq. ft.
Second floor — 675 sq. ft.
Bonus — 416 sq. ft.
Garage — 702 sq. ft.

WIDTH 78'-9"
DEPTH 72'-3"

Dramatic Impact

■ *Total living area 3,542 sq. ft.* ■ *Price Code J* ■

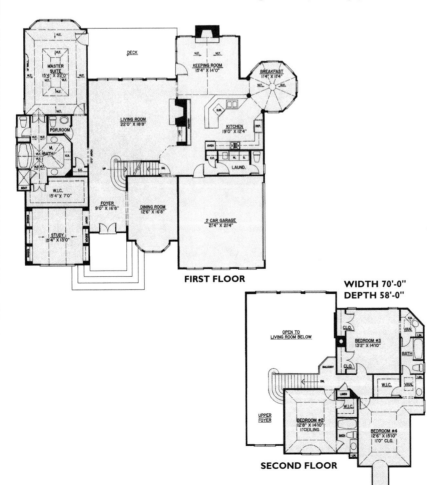

FIRST FLOOR

WIDTH 70'-0"
DEPTH 58'-0"

SECOND FLOOR

No. 98237

■ **This plan features:**

— Four bedrooms

— Three full and one half baths

■ A bay window highlights the elegant formal Dining Room

■ The efficient Kitchen opens into a glass octagonal shaped Breakfast Area

■ A vaulted ceiling crowns the Keeping Room

■ Three additional Bedrooms on the second floor each have private access to the full Bath

■ This home is designed with basement, slab, and crawlspace foundation options.

First floor — 2,552 sq. ft.
Second floor — 990 sq. ft.
Basement — 2,552 sq. ft.
Garage — 458 sq. ft.

Stability and Style

Photography supplied by the Meredith Corporation

■ *Total living area 3,614 sq. ft.* ■ *Price Code J* ■

No. 32076

■ This plan features:

— Four bedrooms

— Three full and one half baths

■ The Kitchen features an angled island cooktop counter with room enough informal dining

■ The spacious, well-lit Family Room has a large fireplace and is flanked by French doors

■ The Keeping Room off the Kitchen, is ideal for a variety of informal activities including meals, and features a fireplace and French doors leading to the Screened Porch

■ The first floor Master Bedroom enjoys an opulent Bath, dual walk-in closets and plenty of privacy

■ This home is designed with a basement foundation.

First floor — 2,391 sq. ft.
Second floor — 1,223 sq. ft.
Basement — 2,391 sq. ft.
Garage — 484 sq. ft.

WIDTH 61'-0"
DEPTH 68'-0"

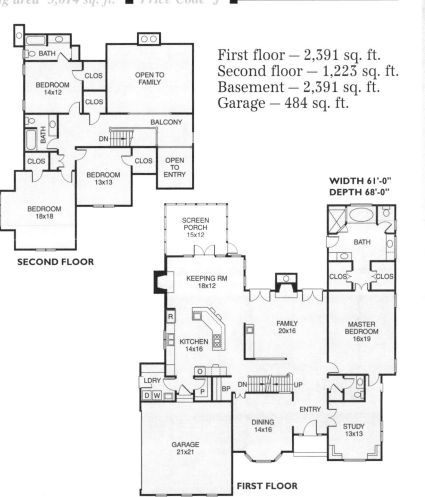

325

Stately Stone

■ *Total living area 3,615 sq. ft.* ■ *Price Code J* ■

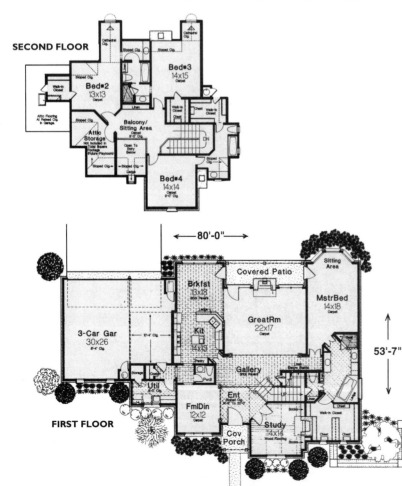

SECOND FLOOR

FIRST FLOOR

No. 92287

■ This plan features:

— Four bedrooms

— Three full baths

■ Easy-care tiling is found throughout the Entry Hall, the Gallery Hall, the Kitchen, and the adjoining Breakfast Room

■ The first floor Master Bedroom ensures privacy from guests and children sleeping upstairs

■ French doors open to the Study which includes a fireplace and built-in bookshelves

■ The Formal Dining Room has easy access off the entrance

■ This home is designed with a slab foundation.

First floor — 2,373 sq. ft.
Second floor — 1,242 sq. ft.
Bonus — 200 sq. ft.
Garage — 780 sq. ft.

Stone, Stucco, and Brick Siding

■ *Total living area 3,619 sq. ft.* ■ *Price Code J* ■

No. 66034

■ **This plan features:**

— Three bedrooms

— Three full and one half baths

■ Beautiful and practical, the exterior of this home is almost maintenance-free

■ The cozy study, with fireplace and built-in book shelves, opens to the Entry through double doors

■ A curving balcony overlooks the Entry and Great Room

■ This home is designed with a slab foundation.

First floor — 2,317 sq. ft.
Second floor — 1,302 sq. ft.
Garage — 672 sq. ft.

WIDTH 74'-0"
DEPTH 56'-0"

FIRST FLOOR

SECOND FLOOR

A Grand Presence

■ *Total living area 3,620 sq. ft.* ■ *Price Code J* ■

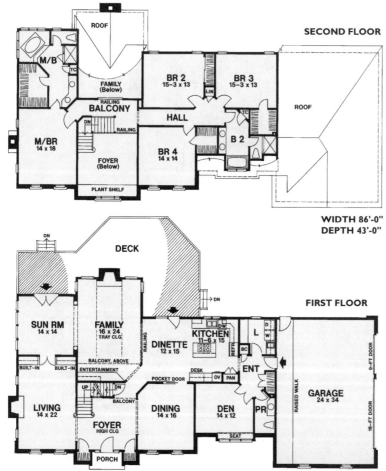

ROOF

SECOND FLOOR

M/B
TC

FAMILY
(Below)

BR 2
15-3 x 13

BR 3
15-3 x 13

LIN

ROOF

RAILING
BALCONY

HALL

TC

B 2

M/BR
14 x 18

DN   RAILING

FOYER
(Below)

BR 4
14 x 14

PLANT SHELF

WIDTH 86'-0"
DEPTH 43'-0"

DN

DECK

DN

FIRST FLOOR

SUN RM
14 x 14

FAMILY
16 x 24
TRAY CLG.

KITCHEN
11-6 x 15

DW

RAILING

DINETTE
12 x 15

D
W

BUILT-IN   BUILT-IN

BALCONY, ABOVE
ENTERTAINMENT

REFR   BC

ENT

DESK

PAN

OV

RAISED WALK

GARAGE
24 x 34

9-FT DOOR

LIVING
14 x 22

UP   DN
BALCONY

POCKET DOOR

DINING
14 x 16

DEN
14 x 12

PR

FOYER
HIGH CLG.

SEAT

16-FT DOOR

PORCH

No. 93330

■ This plan features:

— Four bedrooms

— Two full and one half baths

■ The gourmet Kitchen has a cook-top island, a built-in Pantry and desk

■ The formal Living Room has a focal point fireplace and double-door access to the Sunroom

■ A pocket door separates the formal Dining Room from the informal Dinette Area

■ The expansive Family Room has a fireplace and a built-in entertainment center

■ The luxurious Master Bath highlights the Master Suite

■ This home is designed with a basement foundation.

First floor — 2,093 sq. ft.
Second floor — 1,527 sq. ft.
Basement — 2,093 sq. ft.
Garage — 816 sq. ft.

■ *Total living area 3,623 sq. ft.* ■ *Price Code J* ■

No. 94999

■ **This plan features:**

— Four bedrooms

— Two full, two three-quarter and
one half baths

■ The ideal Kitchen has a work
island/snack bar, a bright
Breakfast Area, and is handy to
the Hearth Room, the Laundry
Area and the Garage

■ The Great Room features a fireplace wall with an entertainment
center, bookcases and a wetbar

■ The exquisite first floor Master
Suite includes the Sitting Room
with a built-in bookcase and a fireplace

■ This home is designed with a
basement foundation.

■ Alternate foundation options
available at an additional charge.
Please call 1-800-235-5700 for more
information.

First floor — 2,603 sq. ft.
Second floor — 1,020 sq. ft.
Basement — 2,603 sq. ft.
Garage — 801 sq. ft.

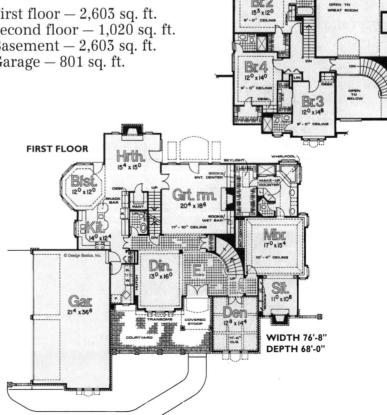

Past Luxuries Revisited

■ *Total living area 3,658 sq. ft.* ■ *Price Code J* ■

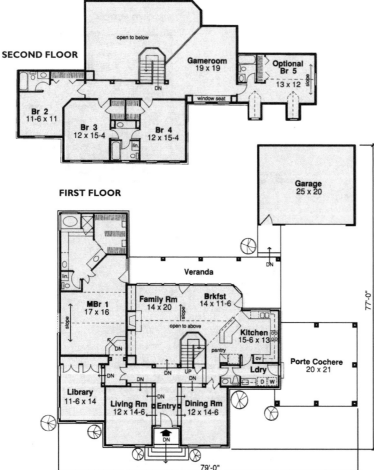

SECOND FLOOR

open to below

Gameroom
19 x 19

Optional
Br 5
13 x 12

window seat

Br 2
11-6 x 11

Br 3
12 x 15-4

Br 4
12 x 15-4

FIRST FLOOR

Garage
25 x 20

Veranda

MBr 1
17 x 16

Family Rm
14 x 20

Brkfst
14 x 11-6

open to above

Kitchen
15-6 x 13

pantry

Porte Cochere
20 x 21

Ldry

Library
11-6 x 14

Living Rm
12 x 14-6

Entry

Dining Rm
12 x 14-6

77'-0"

79'-0"

No. 20405

■ **This plan features:**

— Four bedrooms (with optional fifth bedroom)

— Four full and one half baths

■ Arched openings into the formal Living and Dining Rooms are enhanced by columns

■ A short hall leads past the Library to the private Master Suite which has a luxurious garden Spa and private access to the Veranda

■ The open arrangement of the Kitchen, the Breakfast Area, and the Family Room creates an easy traffic pattern

■ A Game Room on the second floor provides sharing activities

■ This home is designed with a crawlspace foundation.

First floor — 2,423 sq. ft.
Second floor — 1,235 sq. ft.
Garage — 507 sq. ft.

Traditional Splendor

■ *Total living area 3,688 sq. ft.* ■ *Price Code J* ■

No. 91339

■ **This plan features:**

— Six bedrooms

— Four full and one half baths

■ The two-story Entry, illuminated by a palladian window, opens to the gracious Living Room

■ The bright and efficient Kitchen with an angled counter/eating bar and a walk-in Pantry, opens to the Family Room and the Deck

■ The luxurious Master Suite shares a two-way fireplace with Den

■ Four second floor Bedrooms share two full Baths

■ This home is designed with basement and crawlspace foundation options.

First floor — 2,498 sq. ft.
Second floor — 1,190 sq. ft.
Bonus — 130 sq. ft.
Basement — 1,464 sq. ft.

SECOND FLOOR

FIRST FLOOR

WIDTH 112'-0"
DEPTH 49'-0"

Spectacular Voluminous Entry

■ *Total living area 3,689 sq. ft.* ■ *Price Code J* ■

First floor — 2,617 sq. ft.
Second floor — 1,072 sq. ft.
Basement — 2,617 sq. ft.
Garage — 1,035 sq. ft.

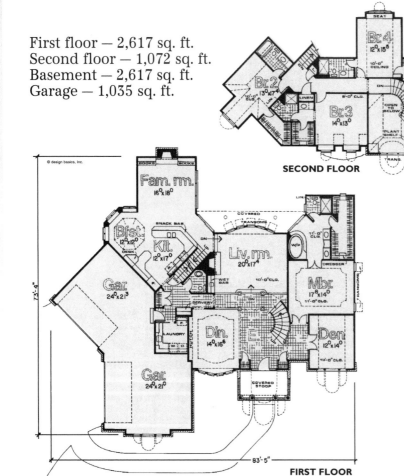

SECOND FLOOR

FIRST FLOOR

No. 99464

■ **This plan features:**

— Four bedrooms

— Two full, two three-quarter, and one half baths

■ The spectacular Entry of this home has a curving staircase and defining columns leading into the sunken Living Room

■ Double doors introduce the Master Suite which has access to the private back Patio, a whirlpool tub and large walk-in closet

■ A beautiful arched window in each secondary Bedroom adds natural light and elegance

■ This home is designed with a basement foundation.

■ Alternate foundation options available at an additional charge. Please call 1-800-235-5700 for more information.

Light-Filled Breakfast Room

■ Total living area 3,693 sq. ft. ■ Price Code J ■

No. 60006

This plan features:

– Five bedrooms

– Three full and one half baths

■ The radius Breakfast Nook is designed to start every morning with natural light

■ The luxurious Master Suite and Bath are crowned with vaulted tray ceilings

■ This home is designed with basement and crawlspace foundation options.

First floor — 1,873 sq. ft.
Second floor — 1,820 sq. ft.
Basement — 1,873 sq. ft.
Garage — 552 sq. ft.

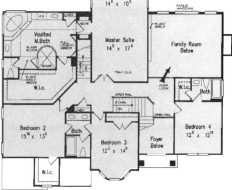

Executive Estate

■ *Total living area 3,745 sq. ft.* ■ *Price Code J* ■

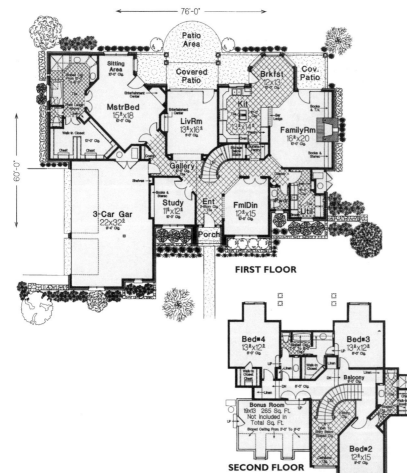

FIRST FLOOR

SECOND FLOOR

No. 98527

■ **This plan features:**

— Four bedrooms

— Three full and one half baths

■ The two-story Foyer is highlighted by a curved staircase

■ The hub kitchen easily services the Breakfast Area, the Patio, and formal Dinning Room

■ The Study features built-in shelves for books and electronic equipment

■ The sumptuous Master Suite features a large closet, Sitting Area, and entertainment center

■ This home is designed with a slab foundation.

First floor — 2,655 sq. ft.
Second floor — 1,090 sq. ft.
Bonus — 265 sq. ft.
Garage — 704 sq. ft.

Touch of French Styling

■ *Total living area 3,750 sq. ft.* ■ *Price Code J* ■

No. 99439

First floor — 2,274 sq. ft.
Second floor — 1,476 sq. ft.
Garage — 744 sq. ft.

This plan features:

— Four bedrooms

— Three full and one half baths

A grand staircase dominates the Entry and provides an elegant first impression

A fireplace and an abundance of windows accent the Great Room

The first floor Master Suite includes the whirlpool Bath and a large walk-in closet

Three secondary Bedrooms, two Baths and the Game Room make the second floor a comfortable retreat

This home is designed with basement and slab foundation options.

Alternate foundation options available at an additional charge. Please call 1-800-235-5700 for more information.

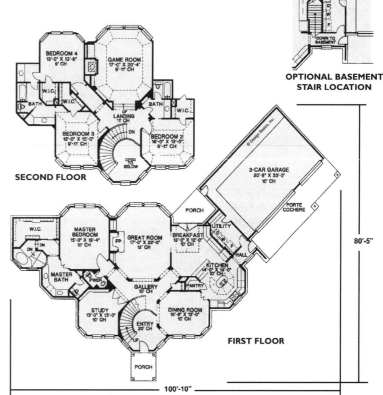

OPTIONAL BASEMENT STAIR LOCATION

SECOND FLOOR

FIRST FLOOR

Grandeur Within

■ *Total living area 3,775 sq. ft.* ■ *Price Code K* ■

First floor — 1,923 sq. ft.
Second floor — 1,852 sq. ft.
Basement — 1,923 sq. ft.
Garage — 726 sq. ft.

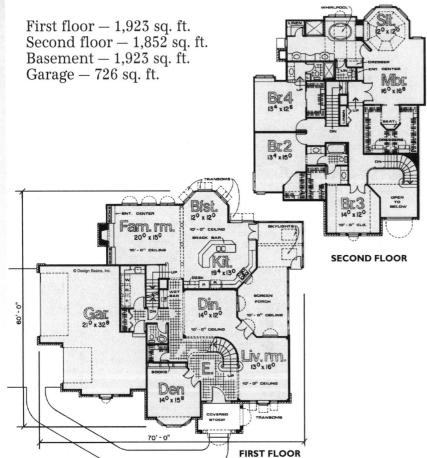

SECOND FLOOR

FIRST FLOOR

No. 99443

■ This plan features:

— Four bedrooms

— Two full, one three-quarter and
 one half baths

■ A cascading staircase dominates
 the tiled front Entry hall

■ The Den has a bay window and
 built-in bookcases

■ The Living and Dining Rooms
 have ten-foot ceilings and access
 the Screened Porch

■ The upstairs Master Suite has
 built-ins, a Sitting Area and the
 wonderful, whirlpool Bath

■ Three secondary Bedrooms all
 have walk-in closets and share two
 Baths

■ This home is designed with a
 basement foundation.

■ Alternate foundation options are
 available at an additional charge.
 Please call 1-800-235-5700 for more
 information.

Opulent Luxury

■ *Total living area 3,783 sq. ft.* ■ *Price Code K* ■

No. 92237

This plan features:

Four bedrooms

Three full and one half baths

Magnificent columns frame the elegant two-story Entry which has a graceful banister staircase

A stone hearth fireplace and built-ins are featured in the formal Living Room

The comfortable Family Room has a huge fireplace, a cathedral ceiling and access to the Covered Veranda

The Master Bedroom wing has a pullman ceiling, a Sitting Area, a private covered Patio and a huge Master Bath

Three additional Bedrooms on second floor have walk-in closets

This home is designed with basement and slab foundation options.

First floor — 2,804 sq. ft.
Second floor — 979 sq. ft.
Basement — 2,804 sq. ft.
Garage — 802 sq. ft.

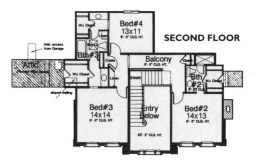

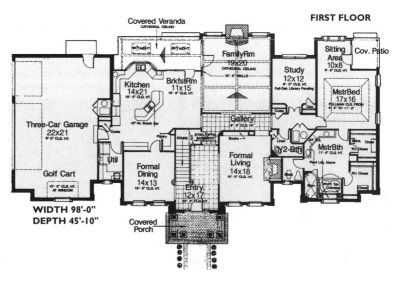

Traditional Elegance

■ *Total living area 3,813 sq. ft.* ■ *Price Code K* ■

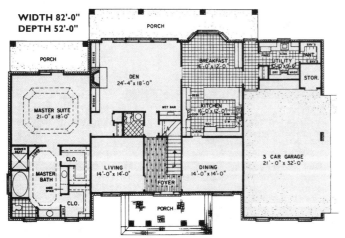

SECOND FLOOR

WIDTH 82'-0"
DEPTH 52'-0"

FIRST FLOOR

No. 92504

■ **This plan features:**

— Four bedrooms

— Three full and one half baths

■ The elegant entrance leads into the two-story Foyer

■ Floor-to-ceiling windows are featured in the formal Living and Dining Rooms

■ The spacious Den has a hearth fireplace and Porch access

■ The Kitchen is equipped with lots of counter and storage space

■ The three additional Bedrooms, on the second floor, have walk-in closets

■ This home is designed with slab and crawlspace foundation options.

First floor — 2,553 sq. ft.
Second floor — 1,260 sq. ft.
Garage — 714 sq. ft.

Full Length Covered Porch

■ *Total living area 3,833 sq. ft.* ■ *Price Code K* ■

No. 99087

This plan features:

- Five bedrooms

- Three full and one half baths

- Natural light floods the entrance Foyer through the dramatic palladium-style window

- The grand Family Room has a fireplace framed by sliders to a covered Porch

- The first floor Master Suite features a large walk-in closet and the Bath, with a separate bathtub and stall shower

- Three additional Bedrooms, a Guest Room, and two Bathrooms are on the second floor

- This home is designed with basement foundation.

First floor — 2,538 sq. ft.
Second floor — 1,295 sq. ft.
Basement — 2,538 sq. ft.
Garage — 900 sq. ft.

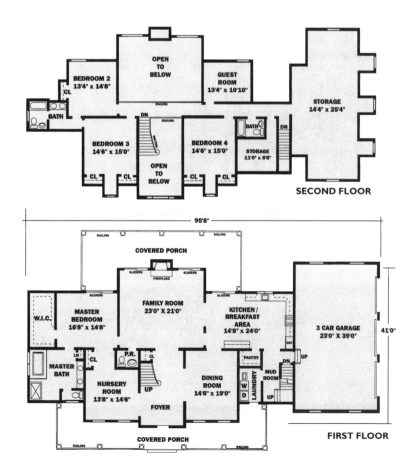

Stunning Stucco

■ *Total living area 3,837 sq. ft.* ■ *Price Code K* ■▶

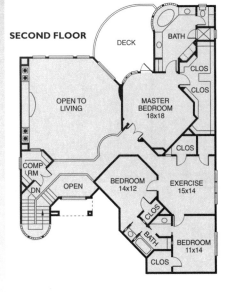

SECOND FLOOR

DECK

BATH

CLOS

CLOS

OPEN TO LIVING

MASTER BEDROOM 18x18

CLOS

COMP RM

DN

OPEN

BEDROOM 14x12

EXERCISE 15x14

CLOS

BATH

BEDROOM 11x14

CLOS

First floor — 2,091 sq. ft.
Second floor — 1,746 sq. ft.
Garage — 641 sq. ft.

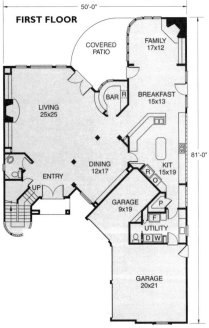

FIRST FLOOR

50'-0"

COVERED PATIO

FAMILY 17x12

BAR R

BREAKFAST 15x13

LIVING 25x25

81'-0"

DINING 12x17

KIT 15x19

ENTRY

UP

GARAGE 9x19

P

F

UTILITY

D W

GARAGE 20x21

No. 32113

■ **This plan features:**

— Three bedrooms

— Two full and two half baths

■ The Garage with a separate bay is ideal for storing a boat or antique car

■ The two-story Living Room has a full wall of windows and a fireplace nestled between built-in shelving

■ A unique wetbar has a curved countertop and services the covered Patio

■ The Family Room includes a second fireplace, more built-in shelves and adjoins the Breakfast Nook

■ The Master Bedroom has access to the private Deck

■ This home is designed with a slab foundation.

Total living area 3,869 sq. ft. ■ **Price Code K** ■

Photography supplied by The Meredith Corporation

No. 32042

This plan features:

- Three bedrooms

- Two full, two three-quarter and one half baths

- Special features of this home include the Office, Den, and Sunroom all on the first floor

- On the lower floor find the Game Room with a bar

- The Screened Porch and a multi-level Deck add to the living space outdoors

- The Master Bedroom, with a spacious private Bath, is located next to the secondary Bedroom on the first floor

- This home is designed with a basement foundation.

First floor — 2,072 sq. ft.
Second floor — 522 sq. ft.
Lower floor — 1,275 sq. ft.

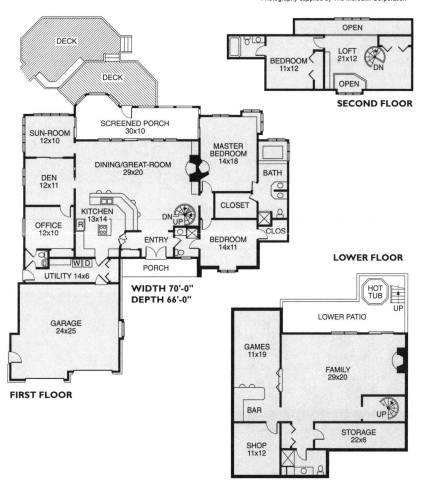

Mansion Mystique

Photography supplied by The Meredith Corporation

■ *Total living area 3,895 sq. ft.* ■ *Price Code H* ■

SECOND FLOOR

OPEN TO FAMILY

OFFICE 10x13

OPEN TO GREAT-ROOM

BRIDGE

DN

DN

BEDROOM 12x12

BEDROOM 12x18

CLOS

BEDROOM 12x14

OPEN TO ENTRY

BONUS ROOM 10x19

FIRST FLOOR

PATIO

FAMILY 15x19

DECK

WIDTH 73'-8"
DEPTH 72'-2"

BRKFST 12x10

PORCH

UP

MASTER BEDROOM 15x18

CLOS

KIT 18x14

GREAT-ROOM 18x16

O R

BATH

CLOS

W D

DN

LDRY

DINING 12x17

ENTRY

GUEST/ STUDY 14x11

GARAGE 20x14

UP

PORCH

No. 32146

■ **This plan features:**

— Four bedrooms

— Four full and one half baths

■ The Entry includes a lovely, curved staircase

■ Multi-purpose rooms include the Guest Room/Study and an upstairs Office

■ Both the Family Room and the Great Room have fireplaces

■ The L-shaped Kitchen opens to the Breakfast Area

■ Upstairs, find three more Bedrooms, two Baths, and the Bonus Room

■ This home is designed with a basement foundation.

First floor — 2,727 sq. ft.
Second floor — 1,168 sq. ft.
Bonus — 213 sq. ft.
Basement — 2,250 sq. ft.
Garage — 984 sq. ft.

342

"English Manor" Home

Total living area 3,904 sq. ft. ■ Price Code K

No. 99402

This plan features:

- Four bedrooms

- Two full, one three quarter and one half baths

- The Entry has columns and a curved staircase

- The formal Dining Room is accented by a decorative ceiling

- A spectacular bow window and a raised, hearth fireplace highlight the Living Room

- The private Master Bedroom includes the charming Sitting Area, a decorative ceiling, two walk-in closets and the luxurious Bath

- The second floor Bedrooms have walk-in closets and private Bath access

- This home is designed with a basement foundation.

First floor — 2,813 sq. ft.
Second floor — 1,091 sq. ft.
Basement — 2,813 sq. ft.
Garage — 1,028 sq. ft.

Brick Opulence and Grandeur

■ *Total living area 3,921 sq. ft.* ■ *Price Code K* ■

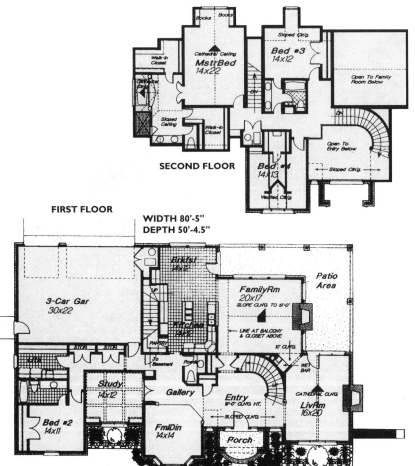

SECOND FLOOR

FIRST FLOOR

WIDTH 80'-5"
DEPTH 50'-4.5"

No. 92248

■ **This plan features:**

— Four bedrooms

— Three full and one half baths

■ Both the Living and Family Rooms offer high ceilings, decorative windows and large fireplaces

■ The Kitchen has a cooktop serving island, a walk-in Pantry, a bright Breakfast Area and Patio access

■ The lavish Master Bedroom has a cathedral ceiling, two walk-in closets, and a plush Bath

■ Two additional Bedrooms on the second floor have ample closets and share the double-vanity Bath

■ This home is designed with a basement and slab foundation option.

First floor — 2,506 sq. ft.
Second floor — 1,415 sq. ft.
Basement — 2,400 sq. ft.
Garage — 660 sq. ft.

■ *Total living area 3,923 sq. ft.* ■ *Price Code K* ■

No. 63041

This plan features:

- Three bedrooms

- Two full and two half baths

- A pair of turrets house two secondary Bedrooms on the second floor

- Windows and doors flood the Family Room with light

- This home is designed with a slab foundation.

First floor — 2,553 sq. ft.
Second floor — 1,370 sq. ft.
Bonus — 760 sq. ft.
Garage — 1,153 sq. ft.

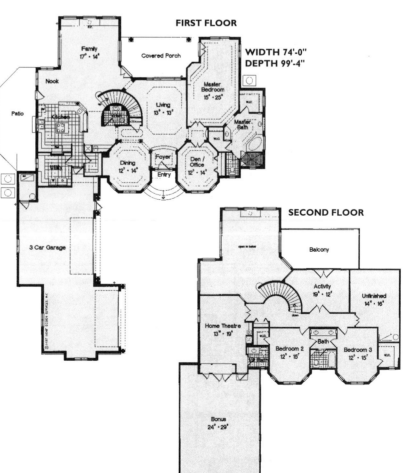

WIDTH 74'-0"
DEPTH 99'-4"

An Estate of Epic Proportion

■ *Total living area 3,936 sq. ft.* ■ *Price Code K* ■

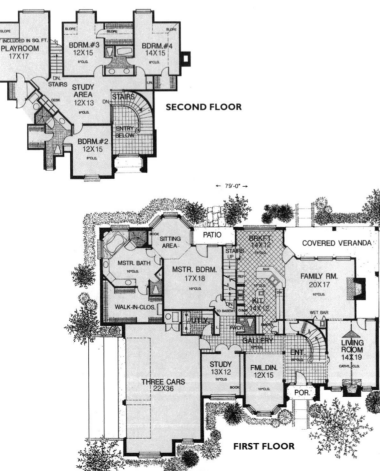

SECOND FLOOR

FIRST FLOOR

No. 98539

■ **This plan features:**

— Four bedrooms

— Three full and one half baths

■ The Living Room has a cathedral ceiling and an inviting fireplace that is nestled between decorative windows

■ The enormous Master Bedroom has a walk-in closet, a sumptuous Bath and a bright Sitting Area

■ The Family Room has a wetbar, a fireplace, and access to the covered Veranda

■ This home is designed with basement and slab foundation options.

First floor — 2,751 sq. ft.
Second floor — 1,185 sq. ft.
Bonus — 343 sq. ft.
Garage — 790 sq. ft.

346

Outstanding Appeal

■ *Total living area 3,949 sq. ft.* ■ *Price Code K* ■

No. 98437

■ This plan features:

- Five bedrooms

- Four full and one half baths

■ The Formal Dining and Living Rooms are off the two-story Foyer

■ The Kitchen has a walk-in Pantry and a work island

■ The Breakfast Room accesses the rear yard through a French door

■ The second floor Master Suite is topped by a tray ceiling

■ Four additional Bedrooms have ample closets and private access to a full Bath

■ This home is designed with basement and crawlspace foundation options.

First floor — 2,002 sq. ft.
Second floor — 1,947 sq. ft.
Basement — 2,002 sq. ft.
Garage — 737 sq. ft.

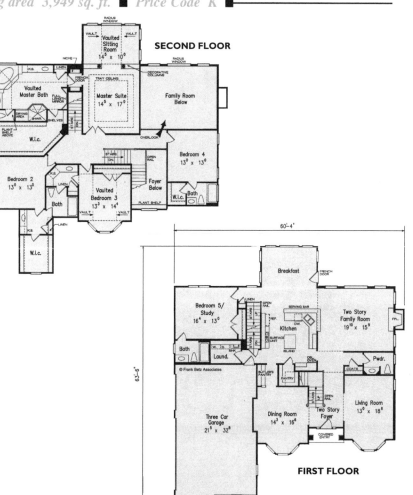

Stunning Two Story Entry

■ *Total living area 3,950 sq. ft.* ■ *Price Code K* ■

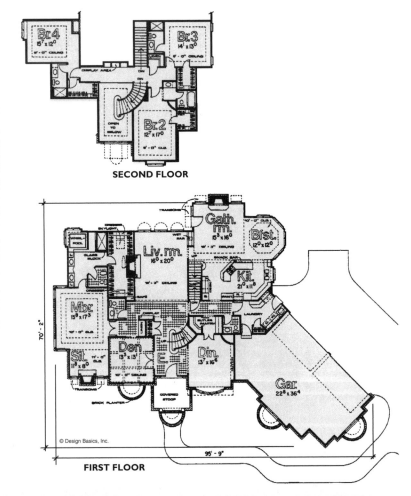

SECOND FLOOR

FIRST FLOOR

© Design Basics, Inc.

No. 99462

■ **This plan features:**

— Four bedrooms

— Two full, two three-quarter and two half baths

■ The spectacular two-story Entry showcases a floating, curved staircase

■ The spacious Kitchen easily serves all areas with an island cooktop/serving bar

■ Triple arched windows highlight the Living Room

■ The Gathering Room shares a two way wetbar with the Living Room

■ The luxurious Master Suite has a tiered ceiling and a cozy Sitting Room

■ This home is designed with a basement foundation.

First floor — 2,839 sq. ft.
Second floor — 1,111 sq. ft.
Garage — 885 sq. ft.

Luxurious Styling

■ *Total living area 4,000 sq. ft.* ■ *Price Code K* ■

No. 98586

■ This plan features:

- Four bedrooms

- Three full and one half baths

■ The Master Bedroom has access door to the covered Patio and shares a two-sided fireplace with the Study

■ The Living Room has a cathedral ceiling, a fireplace and a wetbar

■ The Kitchen includes the Pantry, a snack bar, and a work island

■ This home is designed with basement, slab and crawlspace foundation options.

First floor — 2,860 sq. ft.
Second floor — 1,140 sq. ft.
Garage — 720 sq. ft.

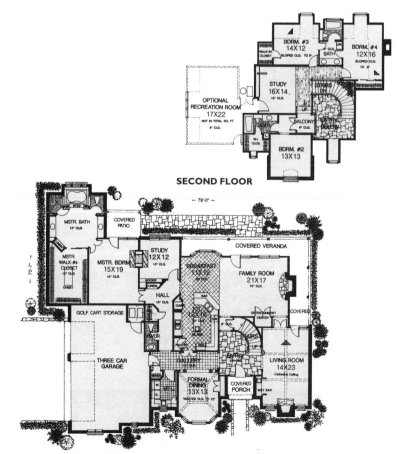

Western Farmhouse

■ *Total living area* **4,116 sq. ft.** ■ *Price Code* **L** ■

SECOND FLOOR

FIRST FLOOR

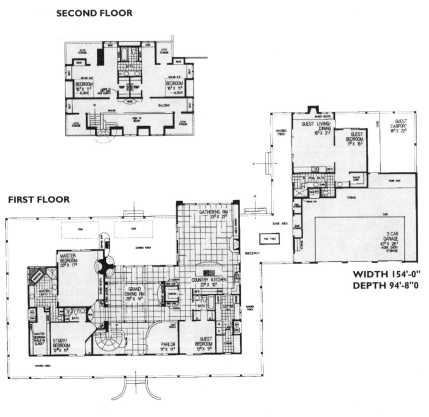

WIDTH 154'-0"
DEPTH 94'-8"0

No. 99278

■ This plan features:

— Six bedrooms

— Five full baths

■ The central entrance boasts a circular stairway and a dramatic curved Parlor

■ The grand Dining Room offers a built-in china alcove, a service counter and circular fireplace

■ The Country Kitchen, with a cook top island, overlooks the expansive Gathering Room

■ The Master Bedroom is highlighted by a raised hearth fireplace, Porch access and the plush Bath

■ This home is designed with a slab foundation.

First floor — 3,166 sq. ft.
Second floor — 950 sq. ft.
Guest House/Carport — 680 sq. ft.

■ *Total living area 4,119 sq. ft.* ■ *Price Code L* ■

No. 63042

■ **This plan features:**

- Four bedrooms

- Three full and one half baths

■ The Home Office provides secluded space to work at home

■ The three-car Garage includes extra room for a work space

■ This home is designed with a slab foundation.

First floor — 3,460 sq. ft.
Second floor — 659 sq. ft.
Garage — 985 sq. ft.

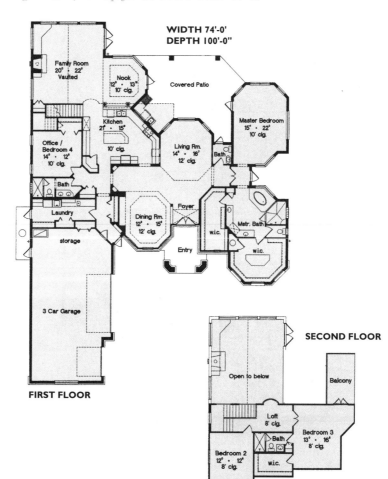

WIDTH 74'-0'
DEPTH 100'-0"

Family Room
20' · 22'
Vaulted

Nook
12' · 13'
10' clg.

Covered Patio

Kitchen
21' · 15'

Office /
Bedroom 4
14' · 12'
10' clg.

10' clg.

Living Rm.
14' · 16'
12' clg.

Master Bedroom
15' · 22'
10' clg.

Bath

Bath

Laundry

Dining Rm.
12' · 15'
12' clg.

Foyer

Mstr. Bath

w.i.c.

storage

Entry

w.i.c.

3 Car Garage

FIRST FLOOR

SECOND FLOOR

Open to below

Balcony

Loft
8' clg.

Bedroom 3
13' · 16'
8' clg.

Bath

Bedroom 2
12' · 12'
8' clg.

w.i.c.

Magnificent Stature

■ *Total living area 4,166 sq. ft.* ■ *Price Code L* ■

SECOND FLOOR

OPEN ABOVE LIVING ROOM
CATHEDRAL CLG.

MEDIA AREA
10X16
9' CLG.

STAIRS

BALCONY
9' CLG.

DN

OPTIONAL BDRM.#5
HOBBY ROOM W/ BATH
13X16
NOT INCLUDED IN SQ. FT.

BDRM.#4
13X18
9' CLG.

BDRM.#3
14X14
9' CLG.

SITTING AREA

SITTING AREA

FIRST FLOOR

COVERED PATIO

WIDTH 90'-0"
DEPTH 63'-5"

STUDY
14X14
10' CLG. VAULTED TO 11'

COVERED PATIO

BRKFT.
14X13
10' CLG. VAULTED TO 11'

FAMILY ROOM
23X18
10' CLG.

STOR.

MSTR. BDRM.
16X19
10' CLG.

LIVING RM.
15X17
CATHEDRAL CLG.
FROM 2 STORY HT.

14' BAR LEDGE

KIT.
13X14

SHOP AREA

MSTR. BATH
10' CLG.

STAIRS

HALL

GALLERY ENTRY

FORMAL DINING
12X14
10' CLG.

THREE CAR GARAGE

WALK-IN CLOSET

NURSERY
GUEST BDRM.
12X14
10' CLG.

COVERED PORCH

No. 98590

■ This plan features:

— Four bedrooms

— Three full and one half baths

■ A two-story cathedral ceiling crowns the Living Room of this Manor-style home

■ The first floor Master Suite features the private, octagonal Study with a wetbar

■ The second floor includes the Media Area and the Bonus Space

■ The expansive Family Room opens to the covered Patio

■ This home is designed with basement, slab, and crawlspace foundation options.

First floor — 3,168 sq. ft.
Second floor — 998 sq. ft.
Bonus — 320 sq. ft.
Garage — 810 sq. ft.

Traditional Treasure

■ *Total living area 4,196 sq. ft.* ■ *Price Code L* ■

No. 90481

■ This plan features:

- Four bedrooms

- Three full and one half baths

■ Porches and Decks compliment the exterior of the home

■ The Dining and Living rooms are traditionally placed on either side of the Foyer

■ The Sunroom is a perfect relaxing place to unwind

■ The secondary Bedrooms are tucked away on the opposite side of the house from the Master Bedroom

■ A three-car Garage is also featured in this plan

■ This home is designed with basement and crawlspace foundation options.

First floor — 3,118 sq. ft.
Second floor — 1,078 sq. ft.
Basement — 3,118 sq. ft
Garage — 704 sq. ft.

SECOND FLOOR

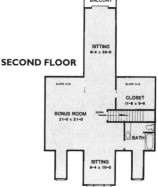

FIRST FLOOR

■ *Total living area 4,204 sq. ft.* ■ *Price Code L* ■

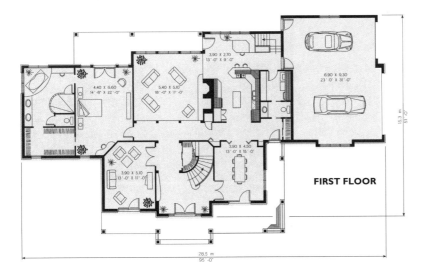

FIRST FLOOR

No. 65240

■ **This plan features:**

— Five bedrooms

— Three full and one half baths

■ A curved staircase in the Foyer greets visitors

■ There are built-in desks in the Kitchen and Master Bedroom

■ This home is designed with a basement foundation.

First floor — 2,482 sq. ft.
Second floor — 1,722 sq. ft.
Garage — 792 sq. ft.

SECOND FLOOR

Traditional Stucco and Stone

■ *Total living area 4,209 sq. ft.* ■ *Price Code L* ■

No. 97141

■ This plan features:

- Four bedrooms

- Three full and one half baths

- There is the Study, complete with a fireplace and a cathedral ceiling

- The terrific Bonus Room could become the fifth Bedroom

- The Master Suite has an expansive walk-in closet

- Convenience is unsurpassed in the open Kitchen/Nook Area

- The Great Room is complimented by soffits, columns, and a central fireplace flanked by built-in cabinets

- This home is designed with a basement foundation.

First floor — 2,639 sq. ft.
Second floor — 1,570 sq. ft.

SECOND FLOOR

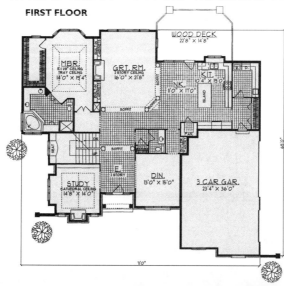

FIRST FLOOR

Classic Home

■ *Total living area 4,228 sq. ft.* ■ *Price Code L* ■

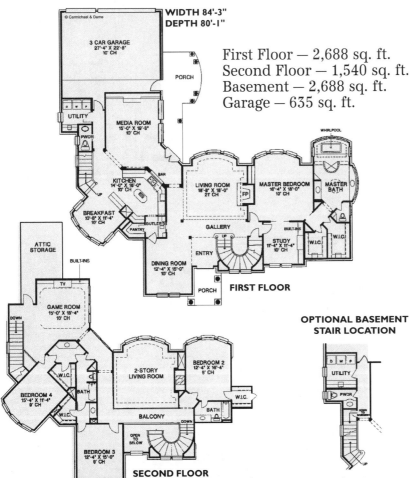

WIDTH 84'-3"
DEPTH 80'-1"

First Floor — 2,688 sq. ft.
Second Floor — 1,540 sq. ft.
Basement — 2,688 sq. ft.
Garage — 635 sq. ft.

**OPTIONAL BASEMENT
STAIR LOCATION**

No. 99440

■ **This plan features:**

– Four bedrooms

– Three full and one half baths

■ The Butler's Pantry connects the Kitchen to the Dining Room

■ The Master Suite is highlighted by a bow window, a pampering Bath and two walk-in closets

■ Up the curved staircase find three Bedrooms, all with walk in closets

■ Also upstairs is the Game Room with built-in cabinets

■ This home is designed with basement and slab foundation options.

■ Alternate foundation options available at an additional charge. Please call 1-800-235-5700 for more information.

Photography supplied by The Meredith Corporation

■ *Total living area 4,283 sq. ft.* ■ *Price Code L* ■

No. 32063

■ This plan features:

— Four Bedrooms

— Four full and one half baths

■ The bow-shaped front Deck mirrors the home's eyebrow dormer and large arched window

■ The Kitchen has a double sink, work island and a built-in Pantry

■ The Great Room is highlighted by a fireplace and screened Porch access

■ The second floor Bedrooms all have private Bath access

■ The lower floor contains the Media Room, the Play Room, and the Guest Suite

■ This home is designed with a basement foundation.

First floor — 1,642 sq. ft.
Second floor — 1411 sq. ft.
Lower floor — 1,230 sq. ft.
Basement — 412 sq. ft.

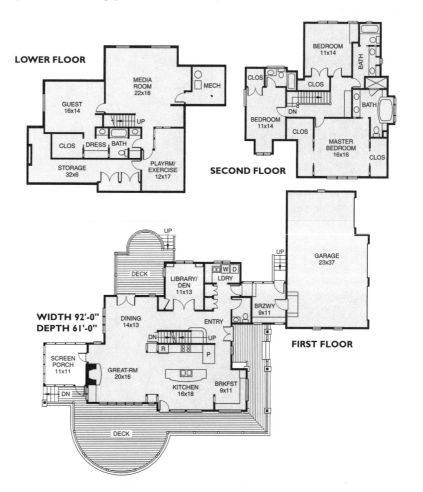

Luxurious Country

Photography supplied by The Meredith Corporation

■ *Total living area 4,292 sq. ft.* ■ *Price Code L* ■

MASTER BEDROOM 16x21
DRESSING
BATH
CLOS CLOS
BEDROOM 12x12
BATH
DN
HALL
DN
LDRY
W D
BEDROOM 14x13
BEDROOM 14x13
BEDROOM 12x12
BATH
SECOND FLOOR

WIDTH 64'-0"
DEPTH 65'-0"

PORCH
BRKFST 9x9
PORCH
PLAYROOM 14x12
UP
MUDRM
FAMILY 21x15
KITCHEN 14x11
R
MECH
GARAGE 21x26
P
UP
LIVING 14x15
ENTRY
DINING 14x16
FIRST FLOOR
PORCH

No. 32046

■ This plan features:

— Five bedrooms

— Four full and one half baths

■ A welcoming front Porch adds style to this luxurious Country home

■ The Living Room and the Dining Room are located in the front of the home

■ The Family Room in the rear has a fireplace and doors to the rear Porch

■ The Kitchen is designed in a convenient U-shape with a serving bar

■ Upstairs the spacious the Master Bedroom is enhanced by a Dressing Area and a plush Bath

■ This home is designed with a crawlspace foundatin.

First floor — 1,928 sq. ft.
Second floor — 2,364 sq. ft.
Garage — 578 sq. ft.

Lavish Appointments

■ *Total living area 4,326 sq. ft.* ■ *Price Code L* ■

No. 98563

■ This plan features:

– Four bedrooms

– Four full and one half baths

■ The circular staircase to the second floor accents the marble Entry Hall

■ A sloped ceiling and a fireplace enhance the Living Room

■ The Dining Room has a rear wall of windows

■ The Kitchen has a center island with a cooktop

■ The Study has a fireplace and a lovely arched window

■ The lavish Master Bedroom includes Sitting and Exercise Areas and a lavish Bath

■ This home is designed with slab foundation.

First Floor — 3,145 sq. ft.
Upper Floor — 1,181 sq. ft.
Garage — 792 sq. ft.

Sensational Entry

■ *Total living area 4,362 sq. ft.* ■ *Price Code L* ■

First floor — 2,764 sq. ft.
Second floor — 1,598 sq. ft.
Basement — 2,764 sq. ft.
Garage — 743 sq. ft.

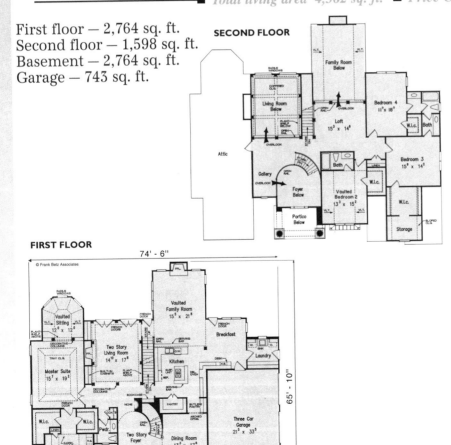

SECOND FLOOR

Family Room Below

Living Room Below

Attic

Loft
15³ x 14⁴

Bedroom 4
11⁹ x 18⁰

W.i.c.

Bath

Gallery

Foyer Below

Bath

Bedroom 3
15³ x 14²

W.i.c.

Vaulted Bedroom 2
13³ x 15²

W.i.c.

Portico Below

Storage

FIRST FLOOR

© Frank Betz Associates

74' - 6"

65' - 10"

Vaulted Sitting
12⁰ x 12⁰

Two Story Living Room
14¹⁰ x 17⁸

Vaulted Family Room
15³ x 21⁸

Breakfast

Kitchen

Laundry

Master Suite
15⁷ x 19²

Bookcase

Pantry

Three Car Garage
21³ x 33⁸

W.i.c.   W.i.c.

Pwdr.

Two Story Foyer

Dining Room
13³ x 17⁶

Vaulted M.Bath

Portico

No. 98404

■ **This plan features:**

— Four bedrooms

— Three full and one half baths

■ The two-story Living Room is accented by columns, a massive fireplace and French doors to the rear yard

■ The ideal Kitchen has a cooktop island/serving bar, a walk-in Pantry, and a Breakfast Area

■ The secluded Master Suite offers the vaulted Sitting Area with radius windows and decorative columns, walk-in closets and the lavish Bath

■ Three second floor Bedrooms have walk-in closets and private access to full Baths

■ This homes is designed with basement and crawlspace foundation options.

Desks and Shelves in Upstairs Bedrooms

■ *Total living area 4,440 sq. ft.* ■ *Price Code L* ■

No. 65610

■ **This plan features:**

— Four bedrooms

— Five full and one half baths

■ The Garage includes workbenches, a bay for a golf cart, and extra Storage Space

■ There are three fireplaces

■ This home is designed with a crawlspace foundation.

First floor — 3,465 sq. ft.
Second floor — 975 sq. ft.
Bonus — 440 sq. ft.
Garage — 808 sq. ft.

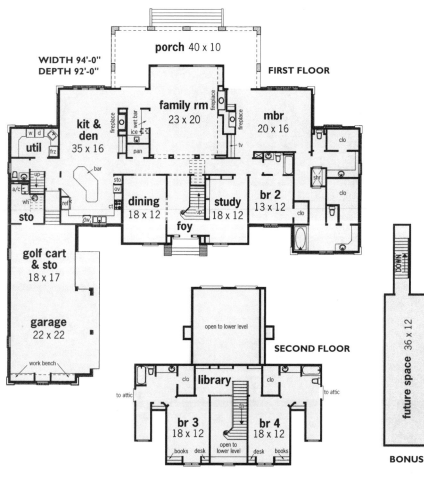

Magnificent Presence

■ *Total living area 4,500 sq. ft.* ■ *Price Code L* ■

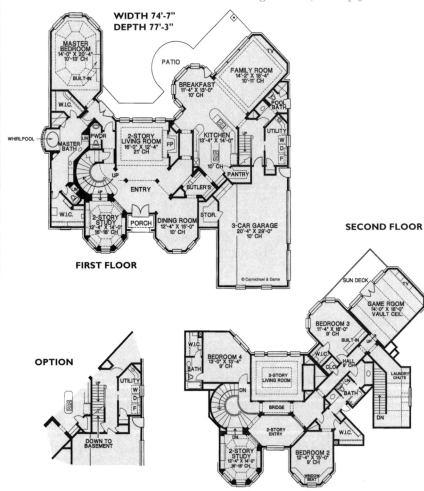

WIDTH 74'-7"
DEPTH 77'-3"

FIRST FLOOR

OPTION

SECOND FLOOR

No. 99410

■ This plan features:

— Four bedrooms

— Three full, one three-quarter, and one half baths

■ A curved staircase leads to the elevated two-story Study and the Master Suite

■ The Dining Room is connected to the Kitchen by the Butler's Pantry

■ The two-story Living Room has a fireplace and distinctive windows

■ The Breakfast Bay adjoins the Family Room with a built-in entertainment center

■ The three-car Garage has an adjoining Storage Room

■ This home is designed with basement and slab foundation options.

First floor — 2,897 sq. ft.
Second floor — 1,603 sq. ft.
Basement — 2,897 sq. ft.
Garage — 793 sq. ft.

High Impact Two-Story

■ *Total living area 4,532 sq. ft.* ■ *Price Code L* ■

No. 99373

■ **This plan features:**

- — Four bedrooms

- — Three full and one half baths

- ■ The two-story Family Room is enhanced by three walls of windows and a cozy fireplace

- ■ The spacious Master Suite has a see-through fireplace in the Sitting Area

- ■ The gourmet Kitchen and Breakfast Area open to a Lanai

- ■ The Guest Suite has private Deck and walk-in closet

- ■ This home is designed with a slab foundation.

First floor — 3,158 sq. ft.
Second floor — 1,374 sq. ft.
Garage — 758 sq. ft.

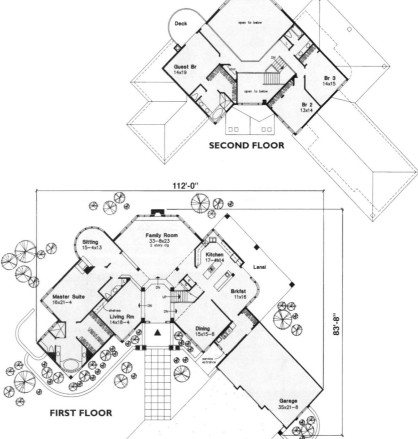

SECOND FLOOR

FIRST FLOOR

European Richness

■ *Total living area 4,589 sq. ft.* ■ *Price Code L* ■

FIRST FLOOR

SECOND FLOOR

No. 97716

■ This plan features:

— Four bedrooms

— Three full and two half baths

■ The grand Foyer leading to the Gallery greets your guests elegantly

■ The Great Room is located at the center of the home and has a fireplace and Terrace access

■ The Kitchen easily serves the warm Hearth Room, the Breakfast Area and the Terrace

■ The rear Terrace is perfect for entertaining in warm weather

■ The three-car Garage completes this luxurious home

■ This home is designed with a basement foundation.

First floor — 3,392 sq. ft.
Second floor — 1,197 sq. ft.
Basement — 3,392 sq. ft.

WIDTH 87'-0''
DEPTH 82'-0''

Taste of Tudor

■ *Total living area 4,614 sq. ft.* ■ *Price Code L* ■

No. 98587

■ **This plan features:**

— Five bedrooms

— Five full and two half baths

■ The graceful, turned staircase balances the formal Dining Room

■ The first floor Master Bedroom has the bright Sitting Area, the private Bath and an enormous walk-in closet

■ French doors lead to the Study, lined with built-in bookshelves

■ The second floor Playroom provides many useful options in this home

■ The large covered Patio spans the rear of the home

■ This home is designed with a slab foundation.

First floor — 3,188 sq. ft.
Second floor — 1,426 sq. ft.
Garage — 740 sq. ft.

Turrets Highlight Design

■ Total living area 4,759 sq. ft. ■ Price Code L ■

First floor — 3,546 sq. ft.
Second floor — 1,213 sq. ft.
Garage — 822 sq. ft.

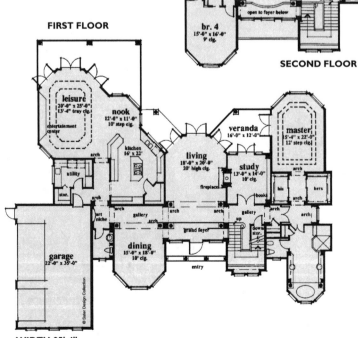

FIRST FLOOR

SECOND FLOOR

WIDTH 95'-4"
DEPTH 83'-0"

No. 94230

■ **This plan features:**

— Four bedrooms

— Two full, one three-quarter, and one half baths

■ Triple arches protect Entry into the Grand Foyer and Gallery which have arched entries

■ The spacious Kitchen has the large walk-in Pantry and a cook-top/work island

■ The Master Suite wing offers Veranda access, two walk-in closets and two vanities, and a garden window tub

■ Three second floor Bedrooms have walk-in closets, a balcony and full Bath access

■ This home is designed with a slab foundation.

■ Alternate foundation options available at an additional charge. Please call 1-800-235-5700 for more information.

A Country Manor

Photography supplied by the Meredith Corporation

■ *Total living area 5,288 sq. ft.* ■ *Price Code L* ■

No. 32006

■ **This plan features:**

— Four bedrooms

— Four full and one half baths

■ The grand Master Suite, located on the first floor, shares a fireplace with the Master Bath

■ The three-car Garage and Laundry Room are located off the Kitchen

■ Three Bedrooms, an Au Pair Suite, three Baths and Playroom complete the second floor

■ The second floor Balcony connects the Bedroom wings and overlooks Living Room above Foyer

■ This home is designed with a basement foundation.

First floor — 3,322 sq. ft.
Second floor — 1,966 sq. ft.
Basement — 3,275 sq. ft.
Garage — 774 sq. ft.

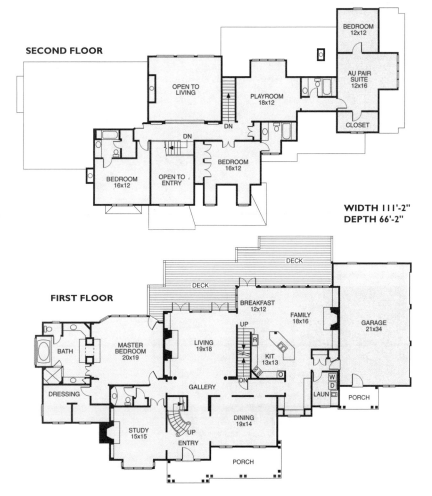

SECOND FLOOR

BEDROOM
12x12

AU PAIR
SUITE
12x16

OPEN TO
LIVING

PLAYROOM
18x12

CLOSET

DN

DN

DN

BEDROOM
16x12

BEDROOM
16x12

OPEN TO
ENTRY

WIDTH 111'-2"
DEPTH 66'-2"

DECK

DECK

FIRST FLOOR

BREAKFAST
12x12

FAMILY
18x16

GARAGE
21x34

BATH

MASTER
BEDROOM
20x19

LIVING
19x18

UP
R

KIT
13x13

LAUN

W
D

PORCH

DRESSING

GALLERY

DN

STUDY
15x15

UP

DINING
19x14

ENTRY

PORCH

French Chateau

■ *Total living area 5,354 sq. ft.* ■ *Price Code L* ■

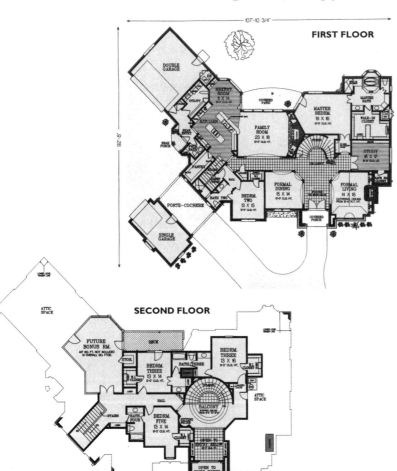

FIRST FLOOR

SECOND FLOOR

No. 66015

■ This plan features:

— Five bedrooms

— Four full and one half baths

■ A two-story Foyer with dramatic circular staircase defines the elegant style of this home

■ Fireplaces flanked by built-ins are featured in the formal Living Room and Family Room

■ The gourmet Kitchen has a wetbar with wine cooler and huge, walk-in Pantry

■ This home is designed with basement and slab foundation options.

First floor — 3,920 sq. ft.
Second floor — 1,434 sq. ft.
Bonus — 427 sq. ft.
Garage — 740 sq. ft.

Magnificent Manor

■ *Total living area 5,389 sq. ft.* ■ *Price Code L* ■

No. 66026

■ This plan features:

- Five bedrooms

- Four full and two half baths

■ The high ceilings on the first and second floors give this home palatial proportions

■ A spectacular Master Bedroom includes an octagonal Library with French door access to the Living Room and wet bar

■ This home is designed with a slab foundation.

First floor — 3,746 sq. ft.
Second floor — 1,643 sq. ft.
Garage — 920 sq. ft.

■ *Total living area 5,474 sq. ft.* ■ *Price Code L* ■

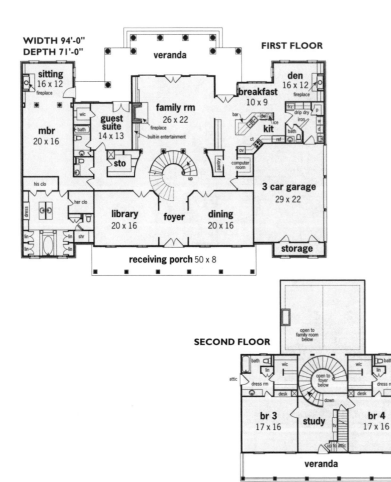

WIDTH 94'-0"
DEPTH 71'-0"

FIRST FLOOR

veranda

sitting
16 x 12
fireplace

den
16 x 12
fireplace

breakfast
10 x 9

family rm
26 x 22
fireplace

guest
suite
14 x 13

wic
bath

kit

mbr
20 x 16

built-in entertainment

sto

computer
room

his clo

library
20 x 16

foyer

dining
20 x 16

3 car garage
29 x 22

her clo

dress

receiving porch 50 x 8

storage

SECOND FLOOR

open to
family room
below

bath
lin
wic

dress rm
desk

open to
foyer
below

bath
lin
shr

dress rm
desk

down

br 3
17 x 16

study

br 4
17 x 16

attic

attic

veranda

No. 65615

■ **This plan features:**

— Four bedrooms

— Four full and two half baths

■ The central, circular staircase is open to the Foyer and Family Room

■ A fireplace flanked by built-in entertainment shelves enhances the Family Room

■ Luxurious amenities in the Master Bedroom include a Sitting Area with fireplace and a Dressing Room/Bath

■ This home is designed with a slab foundation.

First floor — 4,193 sq. ft.
Second floor — 1,281 sq. ft.

A Country Estate

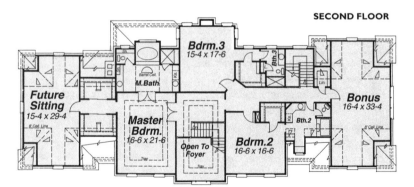

Total living area 5,730 sq. ft. ■ **Price Code L**

No. 93200

This plan features:

— Four bedrooms

— Four full and one half baths

■ The gorgeous two-story Foyer is illuminated by a lovely arched window

■ The Guest Room is located on the first floor

■ The Library is tucked into a corner of the house for quiet study

■ The sunken Family Room has a fireplace and built-in shelves

■ The gourmet Kitchen has two built-in Pantries and a work island/serving bar

■ This home is designed with a basement foundation.

First floor — 3,199 sq. ft.
Second floor — 2,531 sq. ft.
Basement — 3,199 sq. ft.
Bonus— 440 sq. ft.
Garage — 748 sq. ft.

SECOND FLOOR

Future Sitting 15-4 x 29-4

M.Bath

Bdrm.3 15-4 x 17-6

Bth.3

Bonus 16-4 x 33-4

Master Bdrm. 16-6 x 21-6

Open To Foyer

Bth.2

Bdrm.2 16-6 x 16-6

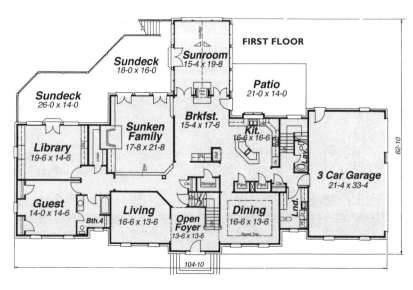

FIRST FLOOR

Sundeck 18-0 x 16-0

Sunroom 15-4 x 19-8

Patio 21-0 x 14-0

Sundeck 26-0 x 14-0

Brkfst. 15-4 x 17-6

Kit. 16-6 x 16-6

Library 19-6 x 14-6

Sunken Family 17-8 x 21-8

3 Car Garage 21-4 x 33-4

Guest 14-0 x 14-6

Bth.4

Living 16-6 x 13-6

Open Foyer 13-6 x 13-6

Dining 16-6 x 13-6

104-10

62-10

Everything You Need...
...to Make Your Dream Come True!

You pay only a fraction of the original cost for home designs by respected professionals.

You've Picked Your Dream Home!

You can imagine your new home situated on your lot in the morning sunlight. You can visualize living there, enjoying your family, entertaining friends and celebrating holidays. All that remains are the details. That's where we can help. Whether you plan to build it yourself, act as your own general contractor or hire a professional builder, your Garlinghouse Co. home plans will provide the perfect design and specifications to help make your dream home a reality.

We can offer you an array of additional products and services to help you with your planning needs. We can supply materials lists, construction cost estimates based on your local material and labor costs and modifications to your selected plan if you would like.

For over 90 years, homeowners and builders have relied on us for accurate, complete, professional blueprints. Our plans help you get results fast... and save money, too! These pages will give you all the information you need to order. So get started now... We know you'll love your new Garlinghouse home!

Sincerely,

James D. McNair III

Chief Executive Officer

EXTERIOR ELEVATIONS

Elevations are scaled drawings of the front, rear, left, and right sides of a home. All of the necessary information pertaining to the exterior finish materials, roof pitches, and exterior height dimensions of your home are defined.

CABINET PLANS

These plans, or in some cases elevations, will detail the layout of the kitchen and bathroom cabinets at a larger scale. This gives you an accurate layout for your cabinets or an ideal starting point for a modified custom cabinet design. Available for most plans. You may also show the floor plan without a cabinet layout. This will allow you to start from scratch and design your own dream kitchen.

TYPICAL WALL SECTION

This section is provided to help your builder understand the structural components and materials used to construct the exterior walls of your home. This section will address insulation, roof components, and interior and exterior wall finishes. Your plans will be designed with either 2x4 or 2x6 exterior walls, but most professional contractors can easily adapt the plans to the wall thickness you require.

FIREPLACE DETAILS

If the home you have chosen includes a fireplace, the fireplace detail will show typical methods to construct the firebox, hearth and flue chase for masonry units, or a wood frame chase for a zero-clearance unit. Available for most plans.

FOUNDATION PLAN

These plans will accurately dimension the footprint of your home including load bearing points and beam placement if applicable. The foundation style will vary from plan to plan. Your local climatic conditions will dictate whether a basement, slab or crawlspace is best suited for your area. In most cases, if your plan comes with one foundation style, a professional contractor can easily adapt the foundation plan to an alternate style.

ROOF PLAN

The information necessary to construct the roof will be included with your home plans. Some plans will reference roof trusses, while many others contain schematic framing plans. These framing plans will indicate the lumber sizes necessary for the rafters and ridgeboards based on the designated roof loads.

TYPICAL CROSS SECTION

A cut-away cross-section through the entire home shows your building contractor the exact correlation of construction components at all levels of the house. It will help to clarify the load bearing points from the roof all the way down to the basement. Available for most plans.

DETAILED FLOOR PLANS

The floor plans of your home accurately dimension the positioning of all walls, doors, windows, stairs and permanent fixtures. They will show you the relationship and dimensions of rooms, closets and traffic patterns. The schematic of the electrical layout may be included in the plan. This layout is clearly represented and does not hinder the clarity of other pertinent information shown. All these details will help your builder properly construct your new home.

STAIR DETAILS

If stairs are an element of the design you have chosen, the plans will show the necessary information to build these, either through a stair cross section, or on the floor plans. Either way, the information provides your builders the essential reference points that they need to build the stairs.

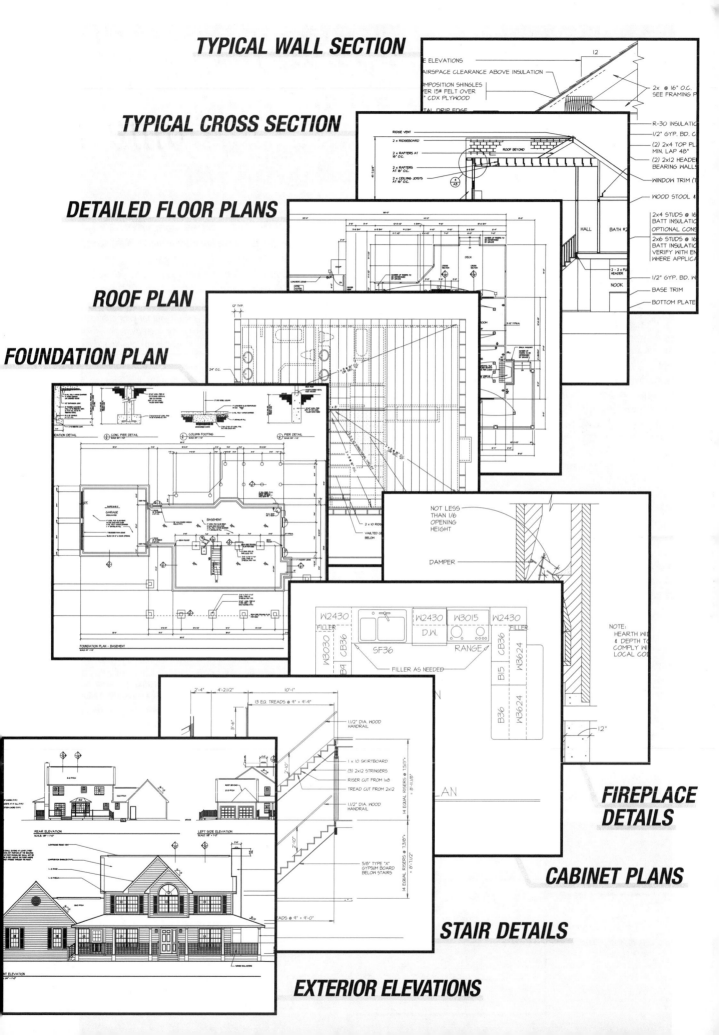

TYPICAL WALL SECTION

TYPICAL CROSS SECTION

DETAILED FLOOR PLANS

ROOF PLAN

FOUNDATION PLAN

FIREPLACE DETAILS

CABINET PLANS

STAIR DETAILS

EXTERIOR ELEVATIONS

Garlinghouse Options & Extras
...Make Your Dream A Home

Reversed Plans Can Make Your Dream Home Just Right!

"That's our dream home...if only the garage were on the other side!"

You could have exactly the home you want by flipping it end-for-end. Check it out by holding your dream home page of this book up to a mirror. Then simply order your plans "reversed." We'll send you one full set of mirror-image plans (with the writing backwards) as a master guide for you and your builder.

The remaining sets of your order will come as shown in this book so the dimensions and specifications are easily read on the job site...but most plans in our collection come stamped "REVERSED" so there is no construction confusion.

As Shown   Reversed

We can only send reversed plans with multiple-set orders. There is a $50 charge for this service.

Some plans in our collection are available in Right Reading Reverse. Right Reading Reverse plans will show your home in reverse, with the writing on the plan being readable. This easy-to-read format will save you valuable time and money. Please contact our Customer Service Department at (860) 659-5667 to check for Right Reading Reverse availability. (There is a $135 charge for this service.)

Specifications & Contract Form

We send this form to you free of charge with your home plan order. The form is designed to be filled in by you or your contractor with the exact materials to use in the construction of your new home. Once signed by you and your contractor it will provide you with peace of mind throughout the construction process.

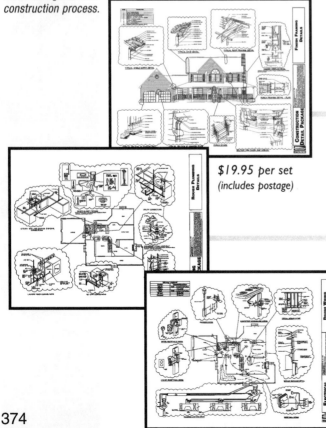

$19.95 per set
(includes postage)

Remember To Order Your Materials List

It'll help you save money. Available at a modest additional charge, the Materials List gives the quantity, dimensions, and specifications for the major materials needed to build your home. You will get faster, more accurate bids from your contractors and building suppliers — and avoid paying for unused materials and waste. Materials Lists are available for all home plans except as otherwise indicated, but can only be ordered with a set of home plans. Due to differences in regional requirements and homeowner or builder preferences... electrical, plumbing and heating/air conditioning equipment specifications are not designed specifically for each plan. However, non-plan specific detailed typical prints of residential electrical, plumbing and construction guidelines can be provided. Please see below for additional information.

Detail Plans Provide Valuable Information About Construction Techniques

Because local codes and requirements vary greatly, we recommend that you obtain drawings and bids from licensed contractors to do your mechanical plans. However, if you want to know more about techniques — and deal more confidently with subcontractors — we offer these remarkably useful detail sheets. These detail sheets will aid in your understanding of these technical subjects. **The detail sheets are not specific to any one home plan and should be used only as a general reference guide.**

RESIDENTIAL CONSTRUCTION DETAILS

Ten sheets that cover the essentials of stick-built residential home construction. Details foundation options — poured concrete basement, concrete block, or monolithic concrete slab. Shows all aspects of floor, wall and roof framing. Provides details for roof dormers, overhangs, chimneys and skylights. Conforms to requirements of Uniform Building code or BOCA code. Includes a quick index and a glossary of terms.

RESIDENTIAL PLUMBING DETAILS

Eight sheets packed with information detailing pipe installation methods, fittings, and sized. Details plumbing hook-ups for toilets, sinks, washers, sump pumps, and septic system construction. Conforms to requirements of National Plumbing code. Color coded with a glossary of terms and quick index.

RESIDENTIAL ELECTRICAL DETAILS

Eight sheets that cover all aspects of residential wiring, from simple switch wiring to service entrance connections. Details distribution panel layout with outlet and switch schematics, circuit breaker and wiring installation methods, and ground fault interrupter specifications. Conforms to requirements of National Electrical Code. Color coded with a glossary of terms.

Modifying Your Favorite Design, Made *EASY!*

CATEGORIES	ESTIMATED COST
KITCHEN LAYOUT — PLAN AND ELEVATION	$175.00
BATHROOM LAYOUT — PLAN AND ELEVATION	$175.00
FIREPLACE PLAN AND DETAILS	$200.00
INTERIOR ELEVATION	$125.00
EXTERIOR ELEVATION — MATERIAL CHANGE	$140.00
EXTERIOR ELEVATION — ADD BRICK OR STONE	$400.00
EXTERIOR ELEVATION — STYLE CHANGE	$450.00
NON BEARING WALLS (INTERIOR)	$200.00
BEARING AND/OR EXTERIOR WALLS	$325.00
WALL FRAMING CHANGE — 2X4 TO 2X6 OR 2X6 TO 2X4	$240.00
ADD/REDUCE LIVING SPACE — SQUARE FOOTAGE	QUOTE REQUIRED
NEW MATERIALS LIST	QUOTE REQUIRED
CHANGE TRUSSES TO RAFTERS OR CHANGE ROOF PITCH	$300.00
FRAMING PLAN CHANGES	$325.00
GARAGE CHANGES	$325.00
ADD A FOUNDATION OPTION	$300.00
FOUNDATION CHANGES	$250.00
RIGHT READING PLAN REVERSE	$575.00
ARCHITECTS SEAL (Available for most states.)	$300.00
ENERGY CERTIFICATE	$150.00
LIGHT AND VENTILATION SCHEDULE	$150.00

OPTION #1

Modifying Your Garlinghouse Home Plan

Simple modifications to your dream home, including minor non-structural changes and material substitutions, can be made between you and your builder by marking the changes directly on your blueprints. However, if you are considering making significant changes to your chosen design, we recommend that you use the services of The Garlinghouse Design Staff. We will help take your ideas and turn them into a reality, just the way you want. Here's our procedure!

When you place your Vellum order, you may also request a free Garlinghouse Modification Kit. In this kit, you will receive a red marking pencil, furniture cut-out sheet, ruler, a self addressed mailing label and a form for specifying any additional notes or drawings that will help us understand your design ideas. Mark your desired changes directly on the Vellum drawings. NOTE: Please use only a **red pencil** to mark your desired changes on the Vellum. Then, return the redlined Vellum set in the original box to us. **IMPORTANT**: Please **roll** the Vellums for shipping, **do not fold** the Vellums for shipping.

We also offer modification estimates. We will provide you with an estimate to draft your changes based on your specific modifications before you purchase the vellums, for a $50 fee. After you receive your estimate, if you decide to have us do the changes, the $50 estimate fee will be deducted from the cost of your modifications. If, however, you choose to use a different service, the $50 estimate fee is non-refundable. (Note: Personal checks cannot be accepted for the estimate.)

Within 5 days of receipt of your plans, you will be contacted by the Design Staff with an estimate for the design services to draw those changes. A 50% deposit is required before we begin making the actual modifications to your plans.

Once the design changes have been completed to your vellum plan, a representative will call to inform you that your modified Vellum plan is complete and will be shipped as soon as the final payment has been made. For additional information call us at 1-860-659-5667. Please refer to the Modification Pricing Guide for estimated modification costs.

OPTION #2

Reproducible Vellums for Local Modification Ease

If you decide not to use Garlinghouse for your modifications, we recommend that you follow our same procedure of purchasing our Vellums. You then have the option of using the services of the original designer of the plan, a local professional designer, or architect to make the modifications to your plan.

With a Vellum copy of our plans, a design professional can alter the drawings just the way you want, then you can print as many copies of the modified plans as you need to build your house. And, since you have already started with our complete detailed plans, the cost of those expensive professional services will be significantly less than starting from scratch. Refer to the price schedule for Vellum costs.

IMPORTANT RETURN POLICY: Upon receipt of your Vellums, if for some reason you decide you do not want a modified plan, then simply return the Kit and the unopened Vellums. Reproducible Vellum copies of our home plans are copyright protected and only sold under the terms of a license agreement that you will receive with your order. Should you not agree to the terms, then the Vellums may be exchanged, less the shipping and handling charges, and a 20% exchange fee. For any additional information, please call us at 1-860-659-5667.

Questions?

Call our customer service department at **1-860-659 5667**

"How to obtain a construction cost calculation based on labor rates and building material costs in <u>your</u> Zip Code area!"

ZIP-QUOTE!
HOME COST CALCULATOR

ZIP QUOTE
HOME COST CALCULATOR

WHY?

Do you wish you could quickly find out the building cost for your new home without waiting for a contractor to compile hundreds of bids? Would you like to have a benchmark to compare your contractor(s) bids against? *Well, Now You Can!!,* with **Zip-Quote** Home Cost Calculator. Zip-Quote is only available for zip code areas within the United States.

HOW?

Our new **Zip-Quote** Home Cost Calculator will enable you to obtain the calculated building cost to construct your new home, based on labor rates and building material costs within your zip code area, without the normal delays or hassles usually associated with the bidding process. Zip-Quote can be purchased in two separate formats, an itemized or a bottom line format.

"How does **Zip-Quote** actually work?" When you call to order, you must choose from the options available, for your specific home, in order for us to process your order. Once we receive your **Zip-Quote** order, we process your specific home plan building materials list through our Home Cost Calculator which contains up-to-date rates for all residential labor trades and building material costs in your zip code area. "The result?" A calculated cost to build your dream home in your zip code area. This calculation will help you (as a consumer or a builder) evaluate your building budget. This is a valuable tool for anyone considering building a new home.

All database information for our calculations is furnished by Marshall & Swift, L.P. For over 60 years, Marshall & Swift L.P. has been a leading provider of cost data to professionals in all aspects of the construction and remodeling industries.

OPTION 1

The **Itemized Zip-Quote** is a detailed building material list. Each building material list line item will separately state the labor cost, material cost and equipment cost (if applicable) for the use of that building material in the construction process. Each category within the building material list will be subtotaled and the entire Itemized cost calculation totaled at the end. This building materials list will be summarized by the individual building categories and will have additional columns where you can enter data from your contractor's estimates for a cost comparison between the different suppliers and contractors who will actually quote you their products and services.

OPTION 2

The **Bottom Line Zip-Quote** is a one line summarized total cost for the home plan of your choice. This cost calculation is also based on the labor cost, material cost and equipment cost (if applicable) within your local zip code area.

COST

The price of your **Itemized Zip-Quote** is based upon the pricing schedule of the plan you have selected, in addition to the price of the materials list. Please refer to the pricing schedule on our order form. The price of your initial **Bottom Line Zip-Quote** is $29.95. Each additional **Bottom Line Zip-Quote** ordered in conjunction with the initial order is only $14.95. **Bottom Line Zip-Quote** may be purchased separately and does NOT have to be purchased in conjunction with a home plan order.

FYI

An **Itemized Zip-Quote** Home Cost Calculation can ONLY be purchased in conjunction with a Home Plan order. The **Itemized Zip-Quote** can not be purchased separately. The **Bottom Line Zip-Quote** can be purchased separately and doesn't have to be purchased in conjunction with a home plan order. Please consult with a sales representative for current availability. If you find within 60 days of your order date that you will be unable to build this home, then you may exchange the plans and the materials list towards the price of a new set of plans (see order info pages for plan exchange policy). The **Itemized Zip-Quote** and the **Bottom Line Zip-Quote** are NOT returnable. The price of the initial **Bottom Line Zip-Quote** order can be credited towards the purchase of an **Itemized Zip-Quote** order only. Additional **Bottom Line Zip-Quote** orders, within the same order can not be credited. Please call our Customer Service Department for more information.

Itemized Zip-Quote is available for plans where you see this symbol. **ZIP**

Bottom Line Zip-Quote is available for all plans under 4,000 square feet. **BL**

SOME MORE INFORMATION

Itemized and Bottom Line Zip-Quotes give you approximated costs for constructing the particular house in your area. These costs are not exact and are only intended to be used as a preliminary estimate to help determine the affordability of a new home and/or as a guide to evaluate the general competitiveness of actual price quotes obtained through local suppliers and contractors. However, Zip-Quote cost figures should never be relied upon as the only source of information in either case. Land, sewer systems, site work, landscaping and other expenses are not included in our building cost figures. Garlinghouse and Marshall & Swift L.P. can not guarantee any level of data accuracy or correctness in a Zip-Quote and disclaim all liability for loss with respect to the same, in excess of the original purchase price of the Zip-Quote product. All Zip-Quote calculations are based upon the actual blueprints and do not reflect any differences or options that may be shown on the published house renderings, floor plans, or photographs.

Ignoring Copyright Laws Can Be
A $100,000 Mistake

Recent changes in the US copyright laws allow for statutory penalties of up to **$100,000** per incident for copyright infringement involving any of the copyrighted plans found in this publication. The law can be confusing. So, for your own protection, take the time to understand what you can and cannot do when it comes to home plans.

••• WHAT YOU CANNOT DO •••

You Cannot Duplicate Home Plans

Purchasing a set of blueprints and making additional sets by reproducing the original is **illegal**. If you need multiple sets of a particular home plan, then you must purchase them.

You Cannot Copy Any Part of a Home Plan to Create Another

Creating your own plan by copying even part of a home design found in this publication is called "creating a derivative work" and is **illegal** unless you have permission to do so.

You Cannot Build a Home Without a License

You must have specific permission or license to build a home from a copyrighted design, even if the finished home has been changed from the original plan. It is **illegal** to build one of the homes found in this publication without a license.

What Garlinghouse Offers

Home Plan Blueprint Package

By purchasing a multiple set package of blueprints or a vellum from Garlinghouse, you not only receive the physical blueprint documents necessary for construction, but you are also granted a license to build one, and only one, home. You can also make simple modifications, including minor non-structural changes and material substitutions, to our design, as long as these changes are made directly on the blueprints purchased from Garlinghouse and no additional copies are made.

Home Plan Vellums

By purchasing vellums for one of our home plans, you receive the same construction drawings found in the blueprints, but printed on vellum paper. Vellums can be erased and are perfect for making design changes. They are also semi-transparent making them easy to duplicate. But most importantly, the purchase of home plan vellums comes with a broader license that allows you to make changes to the design (ie, create a hand drawn or CAD derivative work), to make an unlimited number of copies of the plan, and to build one home from the plan.

License To Build Additional Homes

With the purchase of a blueprint package or vellums you automatically receive a license to build one home and only one home, respectively. If you want to build more homes than you are licensed to build through your purchase of a plan, then additional licenses may be purchased at reasonable costs from Garlinghouse. Inquire for more information.

IMPORTANT INFORMATION TO READ BEFORE YOU PLACE YOUR ORDER

How Many Sets Of Plans Will You Need?

The Standard 8-Set Construction Package

Our experience shows that you'll speed every step of construction and avoid costly building errors by ordering enough sets to go around. Each tradesperson wants a set — the general contractor and all subcontractors; foundation, electrical, plumbing, heating/air conditioning and framers. Don't forget your lending institution, building department and, of course, a set for yourself. * Recommended For Construction *

The Minimum 4-Set Construction Package

If you're comfortable with arduous follow-up, this package can save you a few dollars by giving you the option of passing down plan sets as work progresses. You might have enough copies to go around if work goes exactly as scheduled and no plans are lost or damaged by subcontractors. But for only $60 more, the 8-set package eliminates these worries. * Recommended For Bidding *

The Single Study Set

We offer this set so you can study the blueprints to plan your dream home in detail. They are stamped "study set only-not for construction", and you cannot build a home from them. In pursuant to copyright laws, it is illegal to reproduce any blueprint.

An Important Note About Building Code Requirements:

All plans are drawn to conform to one or more of the industry's major national building standards. However, due to the variety of local building regulations, your plan may need to be modified to comply with local requirements — snow loads, energy loads, seismic zones, etc. Do check them fully and consult your local building officials.

A few states require that all building plans used be drawn by an architect registered in that state. While having your plans reviewed and stamped by such an architect may be prudent, laws requiring non-conforming plans like ours to be completely redrawn forces you to unnecessarily pay very large fees. If your state has such a law, we strongly recommend you contact your state representative to protest.

The rendering, floor plans, and technical information contained within this publication are not guaranteed to be totally accurate. Consequently, no information from this publication should be used either as a guide to constructing a home or for estimating the cost of building a home. Complete blueprints must be purchased for such purposes.

the Garlinghouse company

Order Form

Plan prices guaranteed until 3/15/04— After this date call for updated pricing

Order Code No. **CHP27**

____ set(s) of blueprints for plan #_____ $_____

____ Vellum & Modification kit for plan #_____ $_____

____ Additional set(s) @ $30 each for plan #_____ $_____

____ Mirror Image Reverse @ $50 each $_____

____ Right Reading Reverse @ $135 each $_____

____ Materials list for plan #_____ $_____

____ Detail Plans @ $19.95 each
     ❏ Construction ❏ Plumbing ❏ Electrical $_____

____ Bottom line ZIP Quote @ $29.95 for plan #_____ $_____

____ Additional Bottom Line Zip Quote
     @ $14.95 for plan(s) #_____

_____ $_____

____ Itemized ZIP Quote for plan(s) #_____ $_____

Shipping (see charts on opposite page) $_____

Subtotal $_____

Sales Tax (CT residents add 6% sales tax) $_____

TOTAL AMOUNT ENCLOSED $_____

Send your check, money order or credit card information to:
(No C.O.D.'s Please)

Please submit all United States & Other Nations orders to:

Garlinghouse Company
174 Oakwood Drive
Glastonbury, CT. 06033

ADDRESS INFORMATION:

NAME:_____   EMAIL ADDRESS:_____

STREET:_____

CITY:_____   STATE:_____ ZIP:_____

DAYTIME PHONE:_____

Credit Card Information

Charge To: ❏ Visa   ❏ Mastercard

Card # | | | | | | | | | | | | | | | | |

Signature _____ Exp. ____/____

ORDER TOLL FREE — 1-800-235-5700
Monday-Friday 8:00 a.m. to 8:00 p.m. Eastern Time
or FAX your Credit Card order to 1-860-659-5692
All foreign residents call 1-800-659-5667

Please have ready: 1. Your credit card number 2. The plan number 3. The order code number ⇨ **CHP27**

Garlinghouse 2002 Blueprint Price Code Schedule

Additional sets with original order $50

BEST PLAN VALUE IN THE INDUSTRY!

	1 Set	4 Sets	8 Sets	Vellums	ML	Itemized ZIP Quote
A	$345	$385	$435	$525	$60	$50
B	$375	$415	$465	$555	$60	$50
C	$410	$450	$500	$590	$60	$50
D	$450	$490	$540	$630	$60	$50
E	$495	$535	$585	$675	$70	$60
F	$545	$585	$635	$725	$70	$60
G	$595	$635	$685	$775	$70	$60
H	$640	$680	$730	$820	$70	$60
I	$685	$725	$775	$865	$80	$70
J	$725	$765	$815	$905	$80	$70
K	$765	$805	$855	$945	$80	$70
L	$800	$840	$890	$980	$80	$70

Shipping — (Plans 1-59999)

	1-3 Sets	4-6 Sets	7+ & Vellums
Standard Delivery (UPS 2-Day)	$25.00	$30.00	$35.00
Overnight Delivery	$35.00	$40.00	$45.00

Shipping — (Plans 60000-99999)

	1-3 Sets	4-6 Sets	7+ & Vellums
Ground Delivery (7-10 Days)	$15.00	$20.00	$25.00
Express Delivery (3-5 Days)	$20.00	$25.00	$30.00

International Shipping & Handling

	1-3 Sets	4-6 Sets	7+ & Vellums
Regular Delivery Canada (7-10 Days)	$25.00	$30.00	$35.00
Express Delivery Canada (5-6 Days)	$40.00	$45.00	$50.00
Overseas Delivery Airmail (2-3 Weeks)	$50.00	$60.00	$65.00

Our Reorder and Exchange Policies

If you find after your initial purchase that you require additional sets of plans you may purchase them from us at special reorder prices (please call for pricing details) provided that you reorder within 6 months of your original order date. There is a $28 reorder processing fee that is charged on all reorders. For more information on reordering plans please contact our Customer Service Department.

Your plans are custom printed especially for you once you place your order. For that reason we cannot accept any returns.

If for some reason you find that the plan you have purchased from us does not meet your needs, then you may exchange that plan for any other plan in our collection. We allow you sixty days from your original invoice date to make an exchange. At the time of the exchange you will be charged a processing fee of 20% of the total amount of your original order plus the difference in price between the plans (if applicable) plus the cost to ship the new plans to you. Call our Customer Service Department for more information. Please Note: Reproducible vellums can only be exchanged if they are unopened.

Important Shipping Information

Please refer to the shipping charts on the order form for service availability for your specific plan number. Our delivery service must have a street address or Rural Route Box number — never a post office box. (PLEASE NOTE: Supplying a P.O. Box number <u>only</u> will delay the shipping of your order.) Use a work address if no one is home during the day.

Orders being shipped to APO or FPO must go via First Class Mail.

For our International Customers, only Certified bank checks and money orders are accepted and must be payable in U.S. currency. For speed, we ship international orders Air Parcel Post. Please refer to the chart for the correct shipping cost.

Index

Option Key

BL Bottom-line Zip Quote	**ML** Materials List Available	**ZIP** Itemized Zip Quote	**RRR** Right Reading Reverse	**DUP** Duplex Plan	

Index

Option Key

BL Bottom-line Zip Quote   **ML** Materials List Available   **ZIP** Itemized Zip Quote   **RRR** Right Reading Reverse   **DUP** Duplex Plan

CRE▲TIVE HOMEOWNER®

How-To Books for...

REMODELING BASEMENTS, ATTICS & GARAGES

Cramped for space? This book shows you how to find space you may not know you had and convert it into useful living areas. 40 colorful photographs and 530 full-color drawings.

BOOK #: 277680   192pp.   8½"x10⅞"

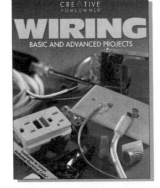

WIRING: Basic and Advanced Projects
(Conforms to latest National Electrical Code)

Included are over 700 full-color photos and illustrations and no-nonsense step-by-step instructions. Shows how to replace receptacles and switches; repair a lamp; install ceiling and attic fans; and more.

BOOK #: 277049   256pp.   8½"x10⅞"

BATHROOMS: Design, Remodel, Build

Shows how to plan, construct, and finish a bathroom. Remodel floors; rebuild walls and ceilings; and install windows, skylights, and plumbing fixtures. Specific tools and materials are given for each project. Includes 600 photos and color illustrations.

BOOK #: 277055   224pp.   8½"x10⅞"

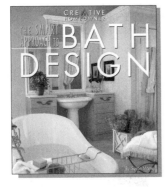

The Smart Approach to BATH DESIGN

Everything you need to know about designing a bathroom like a professional is explained in *this book*. Creative solutions and practical advice about space, the latest in fixtures and fittings, and safety features accompany over 150 photographs.

BOOK #: 287225   176pp.   9"x10"

BUILD A KIDS' PLAY YARD

Here are detailed plans and step-by-step instructions for building the play structures that kids love most: swing set, monkey bars, balance beam, playhouse, teeter-totter, sandboxes, kid-sized picnic table, and a play tower that supports a slide. 200 color photographs and illustrations.

BOOK #: 277662   144 pp.   8½"x10⅞"

CABINETS & BUILT-INS

26 custom cabinetry projects are included for every room in the house, from kitchen cabinets to a bedroom wall unit, a bunk bed, computer workstation, and more. Also included are chapters on tools, techniques, finishing, and materials.

BOOK #: 277079   160 pp.   8½"x10⅞"

DECKS: Planning, Designing, Building

With this book, even the novice builder can build a deck that perfectly fits his yard. The step-by-step instructions lead the reader from laying out footings to adding railings. Includes three deck projects, 500 color drawings, and photographs.

BOOK #: 277162   192pp.   8½"x10⅞"

FURNITURE REPAIR & REFINISHING

From structural repairs to restoring older finishes or entirely refinishing furniture: a hands-on step-by-step approach to furniture repair and restoration. More than 430 color photographs and 60 full-color drawings.

BOOK #: 277335   240pp.   8½"x10⅞"

HOUSE FRAMING

Written for those with beginning to intermediate building skills, this book is designed to walk you through the framing basics, from assembling simple partitions to cutting compound angles on dormer rafters. More than 400 full-color drawings.

BOOK #: 277655   240pp.   8½"x10⅞"